Jerusalem

JERUSALEM

EDITED BY
Msgr. John M. Oesterreicher
and Anne Sinai

PREPARED UNDER THE AUSPICES OF THE
American Academic Association for Peace
in the Middle East

The John Day Company
AN Intext PUBLISHER
NEW YORK

Library of Congress Cataloging in Publication Data

Main entry under title:

Jerusalem.

   Includes bibliographical references.
   1.   Jerusalem—Addresses, essays, lectures.
I.   Oesterreicher, John M., 1904–   ed.   II.   Sinai, Anne, ed.
DS109.J43   915.694'4'03   73-18538
ISBN 0-381-98266-1

The John Day Company, 257 Park Avenue South, New York, N.Y. 10010.

Published on the same day in Canada by Longman Canada Limited.

Printed in the United States of America.

ACKNOWLEDGMENTS

"The Jewish Presence in Jerusalem Throughout the Ages," by Menashe Harel, is reprinted by permission of *Christian News From Israel*, Jerusalem quarterly, Vol. XXI, No. 1, Spring 1970.

"Christians in Jerusalem: 1948–1971," by Ori Stendel, is reprinted by permission of *Christian News From Israel*, Jerusalem quarterly, Vol. XXII, No. 2(6), 1971.

"The Biblical Concept of Jerusalem," by Shemaryahu Talmon, is reprinted by permission of *Journal of Ecumenical Studies*, Vol. VIII, No. 2 (Spring, 1971).

The excerpts from *Israel: An Echo of Eternity*, by Abraham Joshua Heschel, in "Jerusalem in Jewish Consciousness," by Mordecai S. Chertoff, are reprinted by permission of Farrar, Straus and Giroux, 1971.

"The Sanctity of Jerusalem in Islam," by Hava Lazarus-Yafeh, is reprinted by permission of *Molad*, Jerusalem quarterly, Aug.-Sept., 1971.

"The Christian Churches in Present-Day Israel," by Gabriel Grossman, O.P., is reprinted by permission of the *Freiburger Rundbrief—Contributions to the Furthering of Friendship between the Old and the New People of God*, XXIII (1971), Nos. 85–88, pp. 38–42.

Reprinted with the permission of Farrar, Straus & Giroux, Inc. from *Israel: an Echo of Eternity* by Abraham Joshua Heschel, copyright © 1967, 1968, 1969 by Abraham Joshua Heschel.

Excerpt from *The Fathers According to Rabbi Nathan*, translated by Judah Goldin, reprinted by permission of Yale University Press. Copyright © 1955 by Yale University Press.

CONTENTS

II
THE COMMUNITIES

III
THE HOLY CITY

IV
APPENDICES

PREFACE

American Academic Association for Peace in the Middle East

The American Academic Association for Peace in the Middle East is a non-profit non-sectarian association of American academicians who are concerned with the issues of the Arab-Israel conflict in all their ramifications. The Association attempts to utilize the best talents in the American academic community to stimulate, through analysis and research, new ideas and approaches to an Arab-Israeli rapprochement towards the attainment of a just and lasting peace in the Middle East.

The Association publishes a quarterly journal, *Middle East Information Series*, and periodic area studies, such as this book.

AAAPME publications are read and used by academicians, Middle East specialists and students as text, source, background, and research material.

Michael Curtis, *Chairman*
Board of Directors

INTRODUCTION

"Be warned, my son, of the making of many books there is no end" (Eccles. 12:12). This warning by the Hebrew critic of all human endeavors, who hides behind the designation Koheleth, is certainly much more justified today than when first uttered, over two thousand years ago. Still, there are cogent reasons for disregarding this word of caution and writing of Jerusalem: The City of David is different from all other cities; it has no peer.

A famous sixteenth century map depicts the earth as a trifoliate herb, a clover, its leaves representing three continents: Europe, Asia, and Africa. The stylized leaves grow out of, and are held together by, a stem that in this old woodcut appears as a circle, with Jerusalem's skyline and name sketched in. It is, no doubt, unusual to turn the earth into a three-leafed clover; still, the transformation is easily explained. Hannover, the hometown of Heinrich Buenting, the cartographer who cut the map, carried a clover in its coat of arms. In using a clover to symbolize the earth, Buenting did what we all are wont to do: he saw the wide, unfamiliar world in the likeness of the small space he knew intimately.

Uncommon. though the herbal symbolism may be, the concept of Jerusalem as the stem from which other parts of the plant grow, in fact, as the midpoint of the universe, is stranger still. Yet, it has a long tradition. St. Augustine, for instance, commenting on Psalm 31:22—which may be rendered: "Blessed be the Lord! He shows me His steadfast love in a fortified [or fenced] city"—speaks of God's people and its Holy City as encircled by the nations of the world and placed, as it were, in the center of the world(CSL 38, 219).

Centuries earlier, the Book of Enoch (XXVI, 1) calls Jerusalem "the middle of the earth," while the Book of Jubilees (VIII,19) refers to the City as "the earth's navel," a term that occurs in the rabbinical literature of later times as *tabbur ha-arets*. I very much doubt that all the ancient writers who refer to Jerusalem in what to a prosaic mind must seem extravagant language meant their statements to be taken literally. They often qualify them—"the earth's middle" or "the center of the land," for instance—by "as it were" or "is not inaptly called."

Though there can be no question that the ancient authors spoke of the Jerusalem of mortar and stone, they did not approach it with the mind of a surveyor measuring distances or that of a cartographer determining longitude and latitude. Even the cartographer Buenting knew that he could not fit the whole inhabited world into his trifolium. England, a part of Scandinavia, and a portion of the "New World" are all floating in the sea, to the north and southwest of the clover design. All this goes to show that Buenting, like the rabbis and the fathers of the Church, was not interested in an exact geographical location. His and their concern was the moral centrality of Jerusalem, its place in the realm of the spirit. In the words of the prophet:

> From Zion issues revelation
> and the word of the Lord from Jerusalem. (Isaiah 2:3)

In quoting this prophetic oracle, I do not wish to imply that only a believer in the God of Abraham, Isaac, and Jacob can see the singularity of the Holy City; that he speak of its uniqueness is a purely subjective stance depending on faith alone. Jerusalem is the Mother City, not only of believers in the Living God, but also of all men and women who share, actively or passively, in the culture of the West. To be sure, there have been other influences, Greek and Roman for instance, and there may be others in years to come; still, were it not for Jerusalem, "West" would denote no more than a point of the horizon where the sun is seen to set.

It is from Mt. Zion, not from Olympus or one of Rome's seven hills, that *torah*, God's instruction to Israel on how to walk in His sight, went out into the world and, with it, certain seminal ideas. There is first "the gospel of creation," the tenet that the world is not a product of chance, much less mischance; that all created things—nature, if you wish—are blessed and thus a potential source of blessing; that what we call "matter" is not an enemy but a companion of the spirit and thus worthwhile— good. It is this message that stimulates and justifies our search for knowledge and its application, our scientific advances and technological development without, however, being responsible for their abuse.

Among the other values that entered the world of man with God's *torah*, His revelation to Israel, are a reverence for life, an affirmation that persists through denials and violations galore; a passion for social justice, even though what ought to be a flame has through the centuries rarely been more than a flicker; an awakening and, for all the powerful forces of retardation, an advance of conscience; a regard for time as a creative force, and not a mere race toward death; a sense of history that can, despite its horrors and nightmares, despite evil and suffering, see meaning and forward movement in human events.

This, then, is the centrality and singular role of Jerusalem: to be the teacher of true humanism, of man's concern for man. For Scripture, to be sure, this human concern but reflects a divine concern; it is *imitatio Dei*. Yet, even when withdrawn from their wellspring, these values remain values, though they never cease to be biblical, Jewish values, indeed, values descending from Mt. Zion. This, alas, is often an occasion for resentment; hence, men, in their hard-to-understand contrariness, wish to divorce the City from the people to which it belongs by divine grace and human right, by origin and destiny, tradition and significance.

As I began this introduction, a news report from Beirut appeared in the press, implying that President Gafaar Mohamed Nimeri of the Sudan and Emperor Haile Selassie of Ethiopia were planning to visit, together with other Arab and African leaders, Pope Paul and seek from him a commitment "to work for the return of East Jerusalem to Arab control" (*New York Times*, Dec. 5, 1973). Elsewhere in this book, I explain why I think very little of Jordan's claim to be the rightful master of the Old City. I need not restate my opinion here, nor do I wish to dwell on the strange fact that the Arabs dare lay claim to Jerusalem, over which they have never ruled except through conquest, and that, at the same time, they invoke against Israel "the principle of inadmissibility of acquiring territory by war."

This is not the place for taking issue with four African statesmen who, though beset with problems at home—in the Sudan, for instance, the Muslim Arabs of the North have, till recently, sought to bring their black "fellow-citizens," Christian as well as pagan, into subjection by the bloodiest measures—find it necessary to meddle in problems that are not their own, nor do I wish to spend much time in castigating the unparalleled impertinence of leaders who wish to entrap the Pope in a scheme of bringing Old Jerusalem under Muslim control. Even if it did not materialize, the planned Roman visit of four African rulers proves, however negatively, the singularity of Jerusalem. For no other city would men go to such extremes.

Even if my discussion of ancient Jewish and Christian lore, yesterday's cartography and today's politics should have convinced a reader of Jerusalem's role, he may still wonder whether this book does not bear out Koheleth's verdict. There is indeed an abundance of books on the Holy City. Yet, this one is different. It is not a tale, woven by a poet, of the wonder of the City; nor a record by a historian of the events that led up to its present life. It is neither a journalist's enthusiastic report on the achievements of its builders, heroes, and singers; nor a reformer's lament over dreams unfulfilled or problems still unresolved. Nor is it one of those marvelous collections of pictures—photographs, sketches, or paintings—that is meant to be enjoyed and grace a coffee table.

"Jerusalem" avoids one-sidedness; it looks at David's city, capital of

Israel and "center" of the world, from as many angles as possible. Though we hope it will be enjoyed as well, its chief purpose is to inform. It is a book for students and teachers, for all who wish to know more and are ready to listen to experts in their fields. Each contributor has given his best and bears sole responsibility for his findings and views.

My own part in the composition of the book is minimal. The main editorial work has been done by Mrs. Anne Sinai; to her must go all credit and recognition. But I am glad to join my name to hers, because I see it as an opportunity to identify myself once again with the destiny of a city dear to me, because dear to the Holy Ones, Blessed be He.

We would like to express appreciation to Mrs. Rivka Hadary of Jerusalem for her untiring efforts, particularly in establishing contact with Israeli authors. We extend our gratitude and thanks to Dr. Judith A. Diesendruck, National Director of AAAPME for her valued assistance. A special thanks is due to Mrs. Myrna Hamada, for her devoted and excellent secretarial work.

John M. Oesterreicher

I

THE
DOCUMENTED
PAST

I

Jerusalem in Archaeology and History

MICHAEL AVI-YONAH

i. *The Archaeological History of Jerusalem*

The foundation of Jerusalem was determined by geographical consideration of two kinds: general and specific. In general the nucleus of the city,
dating to the era of urban consolidation at the beginning of the Early
Bronze Age (about 4000 B.C.), was set up as one of the many settlements
along the main watershed of the Holy Land, the mountain chain running
north to south through Samaria and Judaea. In this respect Jerusalem had
much in common with the other sites from Dothan, Sichem, Bethel,
Gibeon, Hebron, down to Beersheba, which were strung along the watershed line and were connected by what one may call the "Road of the
Patriarchs" (Abraham, Isaac, and Jacob). In fact Jerusalem was rather less
favored than the others, which had more water and fertile land at their
disposal. The specific selection of the actual site was determined by the
configuration of the ground and the one available water source. A ridge
running southeast from the watershed splits in two, a flat and higher hill
on the west and a narrow and lower hill on the east. In the eastern slope
of the latter was, however, the only spring in the region, the Gihon. The
eastern hill or rather its southern part, was selected as the site of the city.
It was defensible by contemporary standards, inasmuch as there were
valleys on the east (the Kidron), the south (the Ben Hinnom Valley), and
the west (The Tyropoeon, called "the Valley" [*ha-Gey*]) in biblical times.
Only on the north did the ridge of the city continue uninterrupted and
it was there that the main fortifications were erected. The city, which is
already mentioned in the Egyptian texts of the late twentieth century

3

B.C., was dedicated to the god Shalem (from the root meaning "whole," "peaceful") and was called "Foundation of Salem" (Jeru-Shalem). The earliest evidence of habitation is a city wall which continued into the Iron Age and a number of tombs in the vicinity, with the characteristic pottery of the Early and Middle Bronze Age. The name of Jebus which was given to the city in Late Canaanite times refers to some of its upper class, possibly Indo-Aryan, invaders. This small settlement was captured about 1005 B.C. by David and his men and became the capital of the United Israelite monarchy. It was David who by settling in Jerusalem and bringing the Ark of the Convenant to the city made it into the national and religious capital of Israel; the effects of this decision are felt to this day. The city itself did not grow in David's time; but he did erect an altar on a flat rock north of it on the future site of the Temple. It was David's son Solomon who enlarged the city northwards; he filled up a gap in the ridge (the *Millo* or "fill") and built a sumptuous palace and a rather modest sanctuary north of it. The new buildings necessitated a longer wall, so as to include them within the fortified area. In particular the saddle by which the Temple mount was joined to the hills further north was strengthened by two towers, Meah and Hahananiel. From the time of Solomon to that of Hezekiah the fortified area of the city did not change much, although later kings made some additions on the west. The necropolis of Jerusalem, consisting of rock-cut tomb-caves, extended into the Kidron Valley east, and the Central Valley west of the city. Only the kings of the Davidic dynasty were allowed to be buried inside the city; the remains of their tombs, much spoiled by Roman quarries, probably have been discovered in the southern part of the City of David.

Already during the time of the monarchy the city spread westward, over the second hill, in an unfortified suburb called the *Mishneh* (or the "Second" Jerusalem). Evidence of this settlement has been found over the whole area of the Armenian and Jewish quarters of the present Old City, the remains of the houses resting directly upon the rock. Hezekiah decided to make the city secure before the impending Assyrian attack at the end of the eighth century B.C. He had a tunnel cut leading from the Gihon spring to a pool in the Central Valley (an earlier tunnel from the city to the spring has been assigned to the Canaanites, but recent research suggests a Solomonic date for it). The Gihon itself was stopped up from the outside and in the course of time was quite forgotten. To make the pool secure Hezekiah built a new wall ("the other wall" as the Bible has it) across the western hill; its remains were found only in 1972. It was this wall which withstood the onslaught of Sennacherib and succumbed to Nebuchadnezzar in 586 B.C. The remains of the Israelite city excavated on the eastern hill show that the available area was enlarged by terracing, and that the local population kept in its houses many pottery idols (most of them fertility goddesses) thus explaining the strictures of the prophets against the prevailing idolatry. Valuable epigraphic evidence has been found from the times of the Judaean monarchy, in particular the inscription of Hezekiah commemorating the cutting of his tunnel (the so-called "Siloam inscription") and the epitaph of a "royal steward" (perhaps one Shebna, who lived in the time of Isaiah).

The exiles returning from Babylon found the city desolate; the systematic destruction of the terraces with their houses on the east slope of the City of David shows the ferocity of the Babylonian conquerors. Nehemiah, who obtained permission to "repair" the wall, gave up the walls of Hezekiah and that of David and Solomon as hopeless, and constructed a new line on the upper ridge of the City of David. The Temple had been already reconstructed in a poor fashion and dedicated, after many difficulties, in 519 B.C. The long period of Persian rule was one of reconvalescence for Jerusalem; the evidence of its autonomy has been found in the many jar handles stamped with a pentagram and the words "Jerusalem" or "the city" *(ha-'ir)*. Nehemiah strengthened the defenses of the Temple on the north side, setting up a citadel called *ha-birah* (or Baris in Persian).

The Hellenistic period (332–63 B.C.) witnessed a great increase in the material wealth in the city. Already the high priest Simeon the Just (*ca.* 200 B.C.) was able to raise the wall, and improve the water supply, as we are told by Ben Sira. When the wave of Hellenization reached Jerusalem under the Seleucids, a gymnasium in the Greek fashion was established near the Temple; the opposition to the new fashions led to the religious persecution of Antiochus IV Epiphanes and to the Maccabaean revolt. In order to secure the planned new city of "Antioch-by-Jerusalem" on the western hill, the king ordered there the erection of a fortress, the notorious Acra, which remained a stronghold of the Hellenizers till its fall in 142 B.C. As a result first of the desecration of the Temple by the Seleucids and then of its rededication by Judas Maccabaeus in 164 B.C., Jerusalem was divided between the Jewish eastern part (the Temple Mount and the City of David) and the Syrian-Hellenistic part on the western hill. Both parties fortified their positions; fragments of a wall directed against the western hill were found in the central valley, while a Hasmonaean tower and wall are still standing above the eastern slope towards the Kidron.

When the town was reunited, the Hasmonaeans included "Antioch" on the western hill in their city. They built a wall round the western hill, remains of which are still visible in the Citadel courtyard; its extension southward and eastward had been excavated at the end of the last century. Hellenistic or Hasmonaean remains (the two cannot be clearly separated, because of the widespread adoption of the material Greek culture by the Jews in that period) have been uncovered in the Jewish quarter of the Old city, including columns, capitals, finely painted stucco and a relief representing horns of plenty with a pomegranate. Two of the

splendid tombs near Jerusalem, the tomb of the priestly family Bene
Hezir (the so-called "Tomb of St. James" with its *nefesh* "monument," the
so-called "Tomb of Zecharaiah") in the Kidron Valley, and the tomb of
one Jason, a sea-captain under Jannaeus, west of the city, are both assigned to that period.

When Herod captured Jerusalem in 37 B.C. and put an end to Hasmonaean domination, a new building period began in the city, which
transformed its external aspect. He built for himself a palace in the
northwestern section of the Old City (remains of the foundation platform
of this palace were recently found for a length of 400 meters). The palace
was protected by three huge towers; the base of one, the Phasael, still
stands and is called popularly "David's Tower." On the eastern hill the
Temple esplanade was doubled in size and given its present trapezoidal
shape by very high enclosure walls, one of which became consecrated as
the Western or "Wailing" wall. The whole was surrounded by a broad
street, recently excavated. It was crossed in the west by two arches, a
northern one (the so-called "Wilson's Arch") leading by a viaduct to the
western hill (the Upper City) while the other ended in a staircase descending into the Tyropoeon Valley. The gates in the enclosure were
approached by broad staircases, now excavated. On the top of the esplanade Herod rebuilt the Temple with great splendor, raising the height
of the Sanctuary to 50 meters and surrounding it with porches around
three courts, an Inner Court, the Court of the Women, and a vast outer
court. In the southern part of the latter a royal basilica served as a market
and money exchange. To secure the Temple Herod transformed the old
Baris into a powerful fortress called Antonia in honor of Mark Antony.
Herod also added a second wall on the north, enclosing the markets in
the Upper Tyropoeon. The Upper City, the aristocratic quarter, was
filled with palaces of the rich; there stood the Hasmonaean royal palace,
the palaces of the high priests Ananias and Caiaphas and many other. In
fact Herod's city was the one which Jesus saw.

After Herod there were few changes in Jerusalem; King Agrippa I
(A.D. 41–44) added a third wall on the north; the procurator Pontius
Pilatus made an aqueduct from the vicinity of Hebron (recently it has
been suggested that the aqueduct was the work of the Hasmonaeans and
that Pilate only repaired it). More tombs (including the "Herodian tomb"
west of the city, the "Tombs of the Judges" and the "Tombs of the Kings"
of Adiabene, today the region of Mosul—the royal family of this country
had adopted Judaism and settled in Jerusalem) were added in the north,
the "Tomb of Absalom" in the east. Excavations in the Jewish quarter
and near the traditional site of the House of Caiaphas, have uncovered
many Herodian houses, one of them, that of the Bar Kathros family,
untouched since it perished in the flames in A.D. 70.

The siege of Titus ended in the destruction of the Temple and of the

Herodian city. Only the three towers of Herod were left standing. Jerusalem was refounded by the emperor Hadrian as Aelia Capitolina, a Roman colony. The Old city bears to this day the mark of the Roman colonial plan, a square intersected by two streets at right angles; although in this particular case the geometric purity of the plan was marred by some necessary topographical adjustments. The city was equipped with the usual adjuncts of a Roman colony: a capitol, forum, baths, temple of Venus, and at least two triumphal arches (one of them the traditional Ecce Homo arch). Under its pseudonym of Aelia, Jerusalem led the quiet and undistinguished life of a small provincial town.

Its status was completely changed with the accession of Constantine and the adoption of Christianity as the official religion of the Roman empire. Jerusalem now became a Christian holy city, a status expressed on the material plane in a vast building activity: including the first Church of the Resurrection (Anastasis, commonly called Church of the Holy Sepulchre). Recent work has established the place of the apse of its basilica and the stylobate of the Golgotha court. Byzantine Jerusalem as illustrated on the Medaba Mosaic map was a vast conglomerate of churches, monasteries, hospices, hospitals, homes for the aged and other charitable foundations. Among the churches built during this period that of St. John the Baptist is still surviving; the remains of other famous churches, that of the Eleona on the Mount of Olives, that of St. Stephen outside the north gate and quite recently that of the Theotokos (the "nea" of Justinian) have been excavated and identified. Byzantine Jerusalem was extended by a wall built by the empress Eudocia round "Mt. Zion" on the foundations of the Hasmonaean wall.

The Arab conquest of 638 led to the establishment of the first al-Aqsa Mosque at the south side of the Temple esplanade; the building was reshaped many times, the last one being Fatimid. In 691 the Umayyad caliph Abd al-Malik erected the Dome of the Rock on the site of the Temple. Excavations have now revealed a complex of Umayyad palaces, khans or caravanserais and other buildings south of the Temple enclosure, built to a large extent with the stones fallen from the Temple walls.

In 1099 Jerusalem was taken by the men of the First Crusade. There followed a period of feverish building activity in the then fashionable Romanesque style. The Church of the Holy Sepulchre and that of St. Anne are the most prominent examples of Crusader work still standing. The Latin kings of Jerusalem set up a palace on the ruins of that of Herod; their vaults, marked with the cross of Lorraine had been uncovered last in 1971. Other communities of Oriental Christians, such as the Armenians and the Georgians, also built churches at that time; even the Teutons had their own church, recently excavated in the Jewish quarter of the Old City.

Although the Mamelukes who succeeded the Crusaders were a most unruly society, yet they adorned Jerusalem with a large number of Muslim devotional buildings, madrasas, zawiyes, turbes, etc. Their characteristic masonry of alternating layers of red and white stone and their stalactite semi-domes are a feature of old Jerusalem, which still bears the imprint of a medieval city. The Mamelukes tried to ring the Haram esh Sharif (the "Noble Sanctuary" of the Temple Mount) with a belt of Muslim architecture, and largely succeeded.

Under Ottoman rule (1517–1917) Jerusalem received its present walls (although some Mameluke work was incorporated in them at the Damascus and Lions gates); but on the whole this was a period of decay. The archaeological history of Jerusalem might be said to have ended in 1864 when the first houses were built outside the walls (in the Jewish quarter, Neve Shaananim, still standing) and the first excavation (that of the "Tombs of the Kings" by F. de Saulcy) inaugurated a new era of settlement and of research.

ii. The Eternal City: From the Iron Age to the Ottomans

The wayfarer, forty centuries ago, traveling from Ur or Haran, seeking to avoid the thronged "Way of the Sea" and the equally bustling "King's Highway," would prefer the less-frequented road traversing the central watershed of Canaan, passing through numerous city-states, most of which had been established in the great wave of urbanization at the beginning of the third millennium B.C. There was Shechem, set in its lush fields, Bethel, dominating the highlands south of Baal Hazor, Gibeon, in the middle of a fertile plain. Trudging up and down the ridges he would espy a city of no great dimensions crowning a spur of the watershed. This was the town founded by (the god) Shalem—Canaanite Jerusalem. The reason for this location for the city was obvious: the proximity of the spring of Gihon, the only source of living water within a radius of three miles.Shalem's area, now established as about 15 acres—and even this extent was achieved only by dint of much terracing—admits a population of about 15,000. It possessed the usual water installations, including a tunnel giving access to the spring from within the walls. The kings, who, according to the usual Semitic concept, ruled as priests and representatives on earth of the local deity (the *el elyon*—"most high god"), bear titles combined with the word zedek ("just"), e.g., Melchizedek (Gen. 14:18), Adonizedek (Josh. 10:1); but from the el-Amarna letters and II Samuel 24:16, respectively, we know of one called after a Horrian goddess and another who had an Indo-Aryan name. The population, apparently, had become mixed at an early date, with the non-Semitic elements predominating, as was the case elsewhere in Canaan. In the late Bronze Age, the period preceding Joshua's conquest, the kings of Jerusalem seem to have enjoyed some sort of precedence in the southern hill-country, though the rulers of Hebron and the far more powerful lords of Shechem disputed this. There was nothing to indicate the city's destiny as a national and religious focus.

THE CITY OF GOD

Jebusite Jerusalem successfully withstood the onslaught of Joshua and his warriors, and it remained a thorn in the flesh of Israel, separating the House of Joseph and Benjamin from Judah and the southern tribes. Nor were the rulers of the city, an enclave in the midst of the Israelites, averse from enlisting Philistine support. Indeed, when the hour of national unity had struck, and David was crowned king over all Israel, one of his first acts was to launch an attack on the Jebusite stronghold. Recent excavations indicate that the capture of the city was effected through its water tunnel, the sinnor of the Bible (II Sam. 5:8). As Joab and his warriors were the kings' men, David was not beholden to any tribe for the city and it became royal domain. Thither he moved his court and administration and it became known as the City of David. He fortified the citadel of Zion, and it was during his reign that, for the first time in its history, Jerusalem became the capital of an empire extending from the Euphrates to the Brook of Egypt. But the king concerned himself not only with mundane affairs. By bringing up the Ark of the Convenant from Kiryat Ye'arim, he transferred the amphictyonic shrine of Shiloh to Jerusalem, and by selecting the threshing floor of Aravnah, the last Jebusite ruler, for the site of an altar, he endowed the city with the status of chief sanctuary of Israel, "the place which the Lord thy God shall choose to put His name there" (Deut. 12:21). The notion of Jerusalem the Holy as distinct from its physical existence dates from this time and is the result of the acts of David; he, more than any other individual associated with it, is the father of the city as it has evolved in history. Fittingly he was buried within its walls.

David gave Jerusalem its soul; Solomon's main concern was its body. He erected the Temple and the royal palace. Although in design and ornamentation the sanctuary was the fruit of Canaanite and Phoenician traditions, the spirit in which it was dedicated, as I Kings 8:60 affirms: "The Lord is God and there is none else," bespeaks its importance in the history of monotheism. Under Solomon, the city became an intrepot of international commerce—"and the king made silver to be in Jerusalem as stones" (I Kings 10:27). The reek of corruption attendant upon riches and luxury rose in Solomon's declining years, and Israel's spiritual mission was forgotten with the importation of foreign wives, the resurgence of idolatry, and the enfeeblement of the national fibre.

When, during the reign of Rehoboam, the kingdom was divided, Jerusalem remained the capital of the smaller Judaean monarchy, over-shadowed materially by its more powerful, dissident sister-state, Israel. While some of the servants of the Lord in Israel remained true to the Temple, the new shrines in Dan and Bethel drew away the fickle multitudes. Yet, politically diminished though it was, Jerusalem remained steadfast in its loyalty to the Davidic dynasty. The interval of two centuries intervening between the break-up of the United Kingdom and the destruction of Israel in the north was a period of fluctuation for Jerusalem, but under the surface its spiritual physiognomy was being formed. There were good kings and bad, some more, others less, fortunate, and fortune did not always favor the virtuous. Uzziah and Manasseh saw to the city's defenses but neglected its spiritual life; Hezekiah did much in both the material and religious spheres. For a short time Athaliah reduced Jerusalem almost to the status of a dependency of Samaria and Tyre. On one occasion Jehoash of Israel breached the walls of the city, and plundered its treasures. In the eighth century, as the Assyrian menace banked up like a storm cloud, prophecy, which had been frequent in all Israel, became more and more concentrated in Jerusalem. The dominating figure of Isaiah stood stalwart by the king's side in an hour of dire peril, when the Assyrian hosts encamped beneath the ramparts. Jerusalem was delivered from the cruel hand of the Ninevites, and, although in the end it succumbed to another enemy, the reprieve, which lasted five generations, was of decisive import for Jerusalem and Judaism.

In these fateful years the ambivalent prophetic attitude toward the Holy City crystallized. Without mercy the envoys of God castigated its sins, its hypocrisies, the superficiality of its worship, its social injustices, while in the same breath almost they painted a vivid picture of a city cleansed of iniquity, the teacher of true religion to all peoples, the chosen seat of the Almighty. Some of this prophetic vision was realized even before the Babylonian captivity. Religious reform during the reigns of Hezekiah and Josiah put an end to idolatry, and service at places of worship like that recently uncovered at Arad, which had flourished since the days of Solomon, was abolished. Partial reform, however, was not enough to save the city. No sooner had Jerusalem and its Temple gone down in the dust of Nebuchadnezzar's conquest than a purer image became enshrined in the fantasy of the exiles in Mesopotamia. The praise of Zion rose loud and clear by the waters of Babylon and found its immortal formulation in Psalm 137: "If I forget thee, O Jerusalem, let my right hand forget her cunning." The sanctuary and the city as it was to be restored were planned in meticulous detail in the later visions of Ezekiel.

When the hour of return came after 50 years in captivity, reality scarcely corresponded to the rosy visions of the prophets. Throughout its history there is this dichotomy of the living, mundane city, and the ideal city of the dreamers. Yet the specifically Jewish conception, as distinct from that of other religions, was that body and soul should go together in God's service, that the real city should correspond as much as possible to the ideal, and that the ideal should make the real viable. The revival of Jerusalem after the Return to Zion perhaps furnishes the best example of this correlation. The tardiness of the Return, and the hardships and difficulties encountered by the repatriates, delayed the reconstruction and resettlement of the city. The Second Temple, much poorer than the First, was only dedicated 17 years after the Return. And even then it was left unfortified and at the mercy of its many enemies for half a century. When Nehemiah finally succeeded in rebuilding its walls, he was compelled to confine himself to a smaller area than the city's previous precincts and exercise his authority as Persian governor to oblige every tenth family to take up residence within it. Once this was accomplished and the reforms of Ezra were put into effect there was no epoch in its long history in which Jerusalem approached more closely to the prophetic ideal of living according to the Law. For the rest of the Persian period Judaea and the capital were governed by high priests as a nomocracy; for the first time in its history the city wielded a spiritual hegemony over the Babylonian Diaspora.

But this state of quietude, "the day of small deeds," could not last. New forms had appeared in the international arena and they soon challenged the seclusion of the Holy City. The conquests of Alexander and the establishment of the Hellenistic monarchies rudely shattered its restful life. Under the Ptolemies Egyptian troops were quartered in the Temple citadel, and the large number of Judaean captives deported were destined to become the nucleus of the flourishing community of Alexandria. Agents of the royal fisc demonstrated an increasing interest in Jerusalem's economic possibilities, in terms of expanding trade and industry. For a time the conservative element succeeded in combining godliness with material prosperity. The resources, newly acquired, enabled the High Priest, Simon the Just, to carry out much-needed improvements in the Temple and the city, but soon the innovating Hellenists clashed with the establishment. Actually the younger priests, the hope of the conservative classes, were first to adopt the new way of life, centering around physical exercises in the gymnasium. On the slippery path of assimilation, these seemingly harmless essays in Greek athletics soon led to participation in games in honor of pagan gods. By degrees Jerusalem became engulfed in the morass of Late Hellenism. Internecine bickering broke out when the authority of the high priesthood was undermined and positions and honors were sold to the highest bidder.

When the struggle between the two leading families of the era, the Oniads and the Tobiads, became more violent, the king Antiochus IV intervened—intent upon achieving three objectives in a single stroke; to hellenize both city and Temple, to channel the Temple treasures into the bottomless pit of the Seleucid exchequer, and to secure his rear in the struggle for the Egyptian crown. Typically, the momentum of revolution carried the most extreme party to power. It was the High Priest Menelaus and the more radical Hellenizers of his party who finally persuaded the king that the time was ripe for the establishment of "Antioch in Jerusalem," and for the thorough paganization of the Temple. When the king complied, incidentally assuring himself of a fortress, the Acra, inside the walls and dominating the Temple, he initiated the first religious persecution in history and raised a hornet's nest of resistance.

The Maccabaean revolt centered round Jerusalem, although there was little fighting in the city itself, until Judas Maccabaeus, by a series of brilliant strategic and tactical victories, beat off all Syrian attempts to raise the siege of the garrison in the Acra, and finally secured the Temple area. The sanctuary was reconsecrated, but in a neat historical parallel the city remained divided between the Jews and their adversaries for nineteen years. The Temple and the Lower City were in the hands of the Hasmonaeans for most of this time, while the Upper City ("Antioch") and the Acra were held by the Hellenizers and Syrian troops. This state of affairs came to an end when Simon the Hasmonaean took the Acra in 143 B.C. Jerusalem became the capital of an expanding Hasmonaean state. New walls, a new palace, the first of the bridges connecting the Upper City and Temple, and some monumental tombs in the vicinity attest the prosperity then enjoyed. Yet not even the victory of the party faithful to the Law could clear the atmosphere in which the city now lived. However hard the Hasmonaean kings tried to follow the Law they were constrained to adopt at least the technical achievements of Hellenistic civilization. Once again, even under a Jewish dynasty loyal to the Torah, there was conflict between the mundane and the ideal Jerusalem. The quarrel of the Sadducees and the Pharisees which ended in fratricidal war and foreign intervention was but one aspect of this tragedy. In vain did the last Hasmonaean ruler appeal to popular sentiment by representing the Temple utensils, the seven-branched candelabrum and the table of shewbread, on his coins. He could not prevail against Herod the Idumaean and the Roman legions.

Yet even under the rule of this Roman vassal the sacred character of the city asserted itself. Although Herod did all he could to strengthen his hold on it by building himself a palace in the western part of the Upper City, strengthening it with great towers, and building another fortress, the Antonia, overlooking the Temple, this was only one aspect of his activity in Jerusalem. Parallel to the creation of the new political-military focus in the west, and the construction of a theater and hippodrome in the Graeco-Roman style, he undertook a vast rebuilding of the Temple. The enclosure around the sacred edifice was enlarged to double its former size, the walls constructed for this purpose changing the course of two valleys. To this day the huge masonry of that part of the Herodian enclosure venerated as the Western Wall is an object of admiration. Almost nothing, however, has remained of the architectural splendors of the Temple courts, their double porticos, the royal basilica and the multicolored paving. The sanctuary itself was doubled in height—the measurements on the ground were strictly adhered to—to dominate the city. In the reconstruction all religious prescriptions were strictly observed, while the services continued without interruption. The new edifice was of three varieties of marble and richly gilded—in the words of Josephus it resembled "a snowy mountain glittering in the sun." Even the rabbis who were not partial to Herod were forced to admit that "he who has not seen the sanctuary built has not seen a magnificent building." It is Herod's Temple which has lived in the memory of the generations as the prototype of the sanctuary-to-be. Its dimensions were carefully recorded in the Mishna in the undying hope that one day it would rise again from its ashes.

The majesty of Herodian Jerusalem, later enhanced by his grandson Agrippa I, who constructed the Third Wall, greatly enlarging the metropolitan area, was no more than the facade of a far more momentous evolution within. Jerusalem was now the heart of a Diaspora extending from Persia to Italy. On the occasion of the Three Feasts—Passover, Pentecost, and Tabernacles—on which pilgrimage to the Holy City was enjoined by the Torah, it was thronged with strangers from all parts of the world. The Temple treasury waxed rich on the gifts showered upon it by the devout.

But physical well-being was not, and never has been, the main purpose of life in Jerusalem. The century between the siege of the city by Herod and its destruction by Titus in A.D. 70 was marked by some of the most significant developments in its history, destined to leave their mark throughout the ages. Beneath the Hellenized court and the worldly high-priestly aristocracy the Pharisees assiduously expounded the Law. The flowering of Jewish nomocracy, which was to provide the nation with its protective armor throughout the Middle Ages and to save Judaism from extinction, began in the schools of Jerusalem, under the leadership of successive "pairs" of scholars, the last of whom were Hillel and Shamai. Their work was continued by the descendants of Hillel and such outstanding figures as Rabbi Yohanan Ben Zakai right down to the days of the great siege.

Not all, however, were prepared to follow the path of the Law. The miraculous rise and the grievous decline of the Hasmonaean commonwealth had left the people in a state of traumatic shock. Feeling themselves innocent of the crime of idolatry, for which they had once suffered the penalty of exile, they tried to comprehend the cause of their distress. Psychologically, it was on this soil that the messianic fervor, characteristic of the last days of Jerusalem before the siege, burgeoned and flourished. Some of the Jews joined the Zealots and made ready for the war of "the Sons of Light against the Sons of Darkness." Others left the city, already doomed in their eyes, and, remaining true to their ideal conception of Jerusalem, prayed for its realization with the advent of the messianic era, which they were convinced was at hand. The voice of many prophets rose again in the streets and market places. One of them was that of Jesus of Nazareth, which has reverberated down the centuries. The evolution of Christianity, the Last Supper, the trial and crucifixion of Jesus, although barely noticed at the time in the whirl of events, were pregnant with momentous historical development, later to change the character of the city in the eyes of millions.

This ferment was to shape the story of the Holy City no less decisively. Its liberation from Roman domination marked the beginning of the great struggle of the Jews against the Empire. Once the fortresses were taken one by one, and sacrifices for the welfare of the emperor were no longer offered up in the Temple, Jerusalem became the insurrectionary capital of Israel. The new silver coinage, struck in defiance of the Roman Government, bore on one side the inscription "Jerusalem the Holy," and a myrtle branch, possibly the arms of the city. In the first three years of the revolt no enemy threatened its defenses, which in the meantime had hastily been repaired. But internal faction gravely sapped its capacity for resistance. When the supreme hour of trial came in the year A.D. 70, Jerusalem with 25,000 warriors valiantly withstood an army four times as big for five months. And even after the capture and the ravishing of the Temple the surviving Zealots fought on for a month in the Upper City. The memory of the calamity has been enshrined in many legends; the Arch of Titus in Rome is its abiding monument.

DAYS OF AFFLICTION

Titus quartered the Tenth Legion among the ruins of Jerusalem, leaving only the three towers of Herod as testimony to the strength of the city and the magnitude of his victory. Yet life went on. A small community gathered among the shards of past glories, including many Jews. Seven synagogues were still in use on "Mt. Zion." But even now Jerusalem's cup of sorrows was not yet full. In 130 the emperor Hadrian visited it and resolved to erect a Roman colony on the site. The perimeter of the new city, Aelia Capitolina, was ploughed by the governor Tineius Rufus, according to the Roman custom; to the Jews this seemed the ultimate outrage. A vast conspiracy was formed, and when the hour struck the people rallied round their spiritual leader, Rabbi Akiva, and their prince and general, Simon Bar Kosiba, better known as Bar Kochba, "Son of a Star." Within a short time the Romans had been compelled to evacuate the city and for two more years Jewish rule was restored. Sacrifices were probably offered on the restored altar, the Sanhedrin, the Jewish senate, resumed its sessions, and coins were struck again. Finds in the Judaean desert caves throw light on the orderly process of administration under Bar Kochba. But in the third year of the war the Jewish forces were compelled to withdraw from the Holy City. Coins, undated, inscribed "Jerusalem," indicate their aim of once again liberating it, an aspiration that was long to be denied.

The tragic conclusion of Bar Kochba's War marks a turning point in Jerusalem's history. Hadrian undid the work of David and attempted to obliterate its very name. Aelia Capitolina, the surrogate city of Roman imperialism, did indeed vegetate for two centuries as an utterly insignificant provincial town. Jews were forbidden to set foot even within its limits, while the Christian community was purged of its Judaeo-Christian elements. The erection of the colony on the ruins, however, had two lasting effects: the work of construction wrought havoc with whatever remained of the City of David, which was used as a quarry, while the squarish shape of the Roman camp, adopted as the plan of Aelia, is still recognizable in the layout of the Old City of Jerusalem today.

With the passage of the second century the Jewish community in the Land of Israel regained its legal status, and the restrictions on the pilgrimage of Jews were set aside, at least "de facto." In the second half of the third century a leading sage, Rabbi Yohanan of Tiberias, could say: "Anyone who wishes to go up to the earthly Jerusalem, goes up."

In the fourth century the status of Jerusalem was again completely transformed. Adoption of Christianity as the State religion converted it from a forgotten backwater into the Holy City of the dominant faith. Helena the empress and her son Constantine wrought mightily to make it a Christian center. The Church of the Anastasis (Resurrection), forerunner of the Church of the Holy Sepulchre, became its focal point and was gradually surrounded by other churches, monasteries, hospices, and infirmaries for pilgrims. The Madaba Mosaic map offers a vivid glimpse of the internal aspect of Byzantine Jerusalem in the sixth century, when the emperor Justinian gave it its Christian form. One of the greatest benefactors of the city was the empress Eudocia, who resided there in the middle of the fifth century. It was due to her, apparently, that Jews were again permitted to reside in it.

Byzantine Jerusalem was a splendid city, materially as well as reli-

giously. It did, indeed, experience two crises: the first in the middle of
the fourth century, when the emperor Julian made his abortive attempt
to restore the Temple, and the second in 614 when the Persian conquest
shook the city to its foundations. But even though the "True Cross" taken
by the Persians was restored by Heraclius in a triumphal procession,
which marked the last great day of Byzantine Jerusalem, the strength had
gone out of the regime. Less than ten years later the patriarch Sophronius
surrendered the Holy City to the Caliph Omar, and the long rule of the
Muslims began.

Koranic tradition, as interpreted in later days, identified "the furthest
Mosque" (al-Aqsa) with the house of prayer erected on the southern flank
of the Temple Mount. In 691 the Caliph Abd al-Malik built the Dome of
the Rock to compete with the shrine in Mecca; nevertheless Jerusalem
enjoyed only the third place in the hierarchy of sanctity, coming after
Mecca and Medina, the holy cities par excellence. Arab rule was tolerant;
the Christian community and that reconstructed by the Jews lived peace-
ably under the rule of the caliphs. But, when the power of the central
authority of Islam began to disintegrate in the eighth and ninth centuries,
the lot of the "unbelievers" was aggravated. The oppression of the Seljuks, the real rulers of the decaying Abbasid Caliphate, the interference
with the pilgrimages and the attempts of Caliph Hakim to destroy the
Church of the Holy Sepulchre finally provoked the counterblast of the
Crusades.

Medieval Europe, having passed the nadir of the Dark Ages, was
ready for the enterprise of recovering the Tomb of Christ. The First
Crusade was victorious in 1099, but at the cost of incredible suffering.
After the massacre of the Muslim and Jewish inhabitants, the feudal
kingdom of Jerusalem was set up in the Holy Land. The city was divided
up among the several claimants and all the energy of European crafts-
manship was invested in its architectural transformation. The Church of
the Holy Sepulchre was reconstructed and enlarged, the Citadel was
converted into a royal palace, the great complex of the Hospital (the
demesne of the Knights of St. John) was erected, while the Templars set
themselves up in the Dome of the Rock, fondly believed to have been
Solomon's Temple. The Teutonic knights occupied what is now the
Jewish quarter, and some Jewish craftsmen were permitted to shelter in
the shadow of the royal palace. For a century Jerusalem was an outpost
of medieval Europe, with its Latin churches, its art and architecture, its
feudal chivalry and its mixed population. But there was one thing which
this enclave of Europe in Asia lacked: a settled agricultural population
upon which its cities could rest secure. The Crusaders did not strike root
in the Holy Land, and once the European presence was drastically reduced their kingdom collapsed like a house of cards. Jerusalem was lost
in 1187, and though temporarily reoccupied for 15 years (1229–1244), it

remained under Muslim domination till 1917. While the political capital of the country was at Gaza or at Safed, the rulers earnestly tried to endow Jerusalem with the character of a Muslim sanctuary. The Dome of the Rock was cleared of all traces of Christian worship, al-Aqsa Mosque was rebuilt, the Temple square surrounded by arched porticos, which adjoined a series of "madrases" and "zawiyas" (houses of study and Islamic monasteries), and the vicinity of the Temple itself crowded with pious foundations and monumental tombs. The remains of this splendid architecture are still visible in the Old City and, though sadly neglected, constitute one of its main charms. Throughout the turbulent Mameluke period, Jerusalem was regarded as an honorable city of refuge or place of banishment for court grandees out of favor; as such it enjoyed a certain prominence also from the worldly point of view. The Sultan Qalawoun repaired the old aqueduct from the south, and the walls, in particular the Citadel and the Damascus Gate, were restored and embellished. During this period the present-day image of the city was formed. The Jewish and Christian communities persisted, though with some difficulty, the Jews strengthened by successive waves of settlement, following each of the great medieval expulsions, the last of which was that from Spain. The Franciscan Custodia di Terra Sancta maintained its status in the Holy Sepulchre and on Mt. Zion.

In 1517 Jerusalem fell to the Turks, whose dominion was to last for exactly four centuries. In the beginning Ottoman rule was energetic and beneficent (the Sultan Suleiman gave the walls their present aspect and made some improvements to the water supply), but the internal decay which set in in the empire almost immediately after his death caused the Holy City to sink to its lowest ebb in the seventeenth and eighteenth centuries. With the decline of the pilgrimages, partly as a result of the wars of religion in Europe and partly because of the spread of nationalism, the Greek Orthodox community, whose members were Ottoman subjects, gained a strong position in the Holy Places. The corrupt and oppressive rule of the pashas vitiated all economic and spiritual life.

At the end of the eighteenth century appeared the first signs of change. The harbinger of the European intrusion, Napoleon Bonaparte, never reached Jerusalem, yet his appearance in the Holy Land was symptomatic. European influence, mostly in religious guise, grew apace. The French protected the Roman Catholic institutions, the Russians the Greek Orthodox, the British and the Prussians the Protestant. Schools, hospices and hospitals for the pilgrims multiplied. Religious groups, like the German Templars and the Swedish founders of the American Colony, settled in Jerusalem, which, beginning in 1864 with the creation of Sir Moses Montefiore's quarter of Mishkenot Sha'ananim, began to spread beyond the city walls. This Jewish suburb ushered in an enlargement of the Jewish community which went on without interruption until, by the end of the nineteenth century Jerusalem had a Jewish majority. Now, with the spread of European culture, communications, transport and the general amenities of living were much improved.

The meeting between Theodor Herzl, founder of the World Zionist Organization, and Kaiser Wilhelm II of Germany in 1898, in the gates of Jerusalem, may be taken as inaugurating a new era of the gradual restoration of the Holy City's true character, the highlights of which were the withdrawal of the Turks in 1917, the establishment of the Hebrew University on Mt. Scopus in 1925, and finally its reunification in 1967.

Jerusalem's status as the capital of the Holy Land is inextricably bound up with its Biblical past: only when it was Jewish or, at least governed by nations inspired by the Bible, was it this country's chief city. This may appear ancillary rather than essential, but its stormy chronicles prove that failing a material substratum, the link between the heavenly and the worldly city becomes more and more tenuous. The view of the Jewish Sages that the Holy City must be a place of human habitation and not merely a sacred ruin has been vindicated throughout the ages.

II

Jerusalem in the Modern Era: 1860–1967

ZE'EV VILNAY
(Translated from the Hebrew by Claire Remba)

THE ORIGINS OF THE NEW CITY: 1860–1917

At the turn of the nineteenth century, during the period of Ottoman rule in Palestine, the entire population of Jerusalem—Jews, Muslims and Christians—was concentrated, as in the past, within the walls of the old city. The Ottoman soldiers who guarded its gates would open them at sunrise and close them at sunset to guard the inhabitants against the many dangers in the surrounding area.

The various religious communities lived in their respective quarters, in impoverished houses crowded together along narrow, serpentine alleys. The Jews, who constituted the largest ethnic element (they were Sephardim, of Middle East and North African background, of long standing and Ashkenazim, of European background, of recent arrival), lived simple and modest lives side by side in an extremely crowded quarter. The Armenians were their neighbors to the west and the Muslims their neighbors to the east. Many of these Jews subsisted on the funds of the Halukkah, charitable funds which were collected overseas for distribution among needy Jews in Palestine, mainly from the Jewish communities of Europe. Local sources of income were few and inadequate—there were some opportunities but only for laborers, shopkeepers and small businessmen. Despite the impoverished conditions and the restrictions imposed by the Ottoman rulers however, Jews continued to immigrate to the Holy City, inspired by the great and ancient longing for the privilege of living in the City of God, the Eternal City of Israel.

Because of the tremendous congestion in the Jewish Quarter many

19

were forced to live outside in rented Arab houses, but even this measure did not solve the problem, for even when houses were available in the Muslim Quarter they were dilapidated, and commanded high rentals.

A visitor who spent some time in Jerusalem in 1859 relates:

> As one walked in a part of the city where the Jews lived, near Mt. Zion to the east, one's heart ached and one's spirit was moved to great pity, as one observed the sorry conditions in which throngs of Jewish families lived, after having come here with mythical memories of the sanctity and magnificence of this city in ancient times. Any observer would be particularly shocked at the appearance of their living accommodations, which were like holes in the ground which Europeans would not have converted into living quarters even for their cattle. The dampness of the winter and lack of air in the summer brought upon the miserable people who resided in them all kinds of aches and maladies which all the doctors' and pharmacists' potions in the area could not cure. If generous people wish to help these miserable persons, the greatest necessity would be clean and healthy housing facilities.[1]

Another visitor, in 1860, reported:

> The price of living accommodations in Jerusalem is beyond belief, and impoverished Jewish families are paying very high rental fees for horrid homes, the kind which Jews in London would not have rented out for cattle or sheep.[2]

CHRISTIAN INSTITUTIONS

The Christian population also began to acquire parcels of land outside the walls in this period.[3] The Russian community purchased a large plot in 1860 and began the construction of a magnificent church and other large buildings which were intended as inns for Russian pilgrims. These buildings are now in the heart of the New City. The plot of land was about to be purchased by Jews but they were forestalled by the Russians, who quickly expedited a large payment to its Arab owners. The State of Israel acquired most of the Russian buildings several years ago and converted them into government offices.

In 1874, the "Fathers of Zion," an order of Catholic monks, obtained an area of land upon which they erected a large edifice known as the Ratisbonne Monastery, in honor of their founder. Today, the majority of the inhabitants of this particular area is Jewish. The Germans acquired a parcel of land in the western sector of the Old City, on the border of the historic Valley of Refaim and in 1878 founded a proud settlement which they called Refaim. It is known as the German Colony today and all its inhabitants are Jewish. In the north of Jerusalem, Kerem Avraham (The Vineyard of Abraham) was established as a special project by Mrs. James Finn, the wife of the British Consul. She built a house there—one of the first outside the walls—and employed Jews to work the land, her secret purpose being to convert them to Christianity. Kerem Avraham is today a section inhabited completely by Orthodox Jews, and Mrs. Finn's house is the Gadna (para-military youth organization) center in Jerusalem. Near Kerem Avraham the Germans acquired an area of land on which they built educational and vocational institutions for Arabs and which they named after their founder, Schneller. Today the spot is an Israeli Army base. A group of Christians, the majority of whom were of Swedish descent, but who had come from the United States, built themselves a small settlement on a crossroads leading northward to Nablus, which they called "The American Colony." Today a tourists' inn stands in its place, serving mostly Christian visitors. In 1870 a group of Arab workers appeared in the New City to begin construction of a large building on the slope of the mountain to the west of the Mamilla Pool. The initiative and financing of this project came from a rather eccentric Dutch countess named Jeanne Marks. Her objective was to build a hospice for those "one hundred and forty-four thousand" who would appear in the Holy City at the onset of eternal redemption, as predicted in the New Testament. The building was never completed and became an abandoned ruin which was subsequently acquired by Jews. The large Super Sol (supermarket) building now rises in this area and the new Plaza Hotel is nearby. Both are at the edge of Independence Park.

THE JEWISH QUARTERS

The isolated Jewish quarters, with their small crowded houses roofed in red tile, lay spread out over a large area among rocks and thorny brush. Narrow twisted paths connected the neighborhoods and the only means of transportation was by foot. The most important road emanated from the Jaffa Gate to the city of Jaffa itself, Jerusalem's ancient port. The very first house outside of the Jaffa Gate had been used as an Ottoman customs house where officials inspected the belongings of those who entered the Old City.

Through the years, tiny little shops were built all along the road near the Jaffa Gate. From these meager beginnings grew Jaffa Road, which became a main artery and the traffic and business center of the New City. Initially, traffic was mainly by foot or on the backs of donkeys. Occasionally a caravan of pilgrims would pass through the street, or even a caravan of mules or camels laden with sundry items needed by the residents. In the middle of the nineteenth century wagons began to be built. The first wagoneers, in 1875, were German Ashkenazim, residents of Refaim. Gradually, Jews learned this trade and acquired wagons with which to transport both residents and tourists.

DEMOGRAPHY

According to one estimate, the population of Jerusalem had doubled by 1896, 36 years since settlement had begun in the New City. Of the city's 45,120 residents, 28,112 were Jews, 8,748 were Christians, and 8,560 were Muslims. The ethnic and national groupings among the Jews included Ashkenazim (15,074); Sephardim (7,900); North Africans (2,420); Yemenites (1,288); Georgians (670); Bucharans (530); Persians (230). The exact breakdown of population in the New City and the Old City at this period is not known.

According to still another census, there were 5,645 Jewish families in Jerusalem in 1898. Of these, 4,492 families lived by the fruit of their own physical labor or by small trades. About 300 families lived off money which they had brought with them upon immigration or which they had left in their countries of origin. About 200 families were supported by their parents and about 651 families subsisted either from funds from the Halukkah or from financial support which they received from children or other relatives abroad.

THE EARLY TWENTIETH CENTURY

At the onset of the twentieth century the New City continued to expand both in numbers and in area. Arabs too, began to leave the Old City and to build homes outside the northern wall in the direction of Mt. Scopus. As the years sped by, these homes developed into a quarter known in Arabic as *Wadi El Joz*. On the slopes of Mt. Scopus, the Sheikh Jarrah quarter arose, named after a holy Muslim tomb which stood nearby. Muslims also lived along the roads toward Nablus to the north and toward Jericho to the east. In order to facilitate mobility between the Old City and the outside Arab sections Herod's Gate (which had been sealed until the end of the nineteenth century) was opened. It was called *Bab a Jarrah* in Arabic, as was the Arab quarter near it. A large high school, called Rashadiya, the most important for Jerusalem's Muslim population, was constructed there.

According to one estimate made in 1900 there were 45,536 residents in

Jerusalem. Of this total, 28,288 (the majority) were Jewish (15,180 were Ashkenazim and 13,048 were Sephardim); 8,748 were Christians and 8,560 were Muslims.

THE NEW QUARTERS AND INSTITUTIONS

The neighborhood of Zikhron Moshe was added in 1905. It was considered, in its time, to be the most modern in the city and the elite of Jewish Jerusalem were among its inhabitants. The Jews' communal, cultural, and Zionist activities were concentrated there, as was Lemel, the first and most progressive school in the New City. In addition, a Teachers' College, then the epitome of Hebrew education in the country, was founded in Zikhron Moshe.

Within three years, in 1908, still more new quarters were established. Some were built near already existing sections and two were indeed pioneering ventures: Shaarei Chesed in the western sector, founded by Orthodox Ashkenazim, and Givat Shaul at the very edge of the northwestern sector, founded by indigent Ashkenazim and Sephardim. These were the most distant quarters in Jerusalem.

With the enlargement of the New City, hospitals also came into being. The old Rothschild and Bikur Holim hospitals were transferred from the Old City and a new hospital, founded by a physician named Wallach, was constructed and named Shaarei Zedek.

An old age home was built at the very entrance to the New City near the Egged (Israel's largest transportation cooperative) Bus Terminal (which was on the other side of the street) and a psychiatric hospital was built directly opposite the home.

By 1912, according to one estimate, there were approximately 70,000 residents in Jerusalem. About 45,000 of these were Jews, 15,000 were Christians and 10,000 were Muslims. The majority of the residents of the Old City were non-Jews and the majority in the New City were Jews.

On the eve of the outbreak of World War I, Jerusalem was in the process of rapid expansion. Many immigrants came, new quarters were added, and opportunities for gaining a livelihood increased through the opening of more stores and offices, particularly along Jaffa Street, which became the hub of the New City.

The onset of World War I, in 1914, brought catastrophe for the country as a whole and for Jerusalem in particular. Immigration ceased, opportunities for self support diminished, the flow of funds from abroad stopped, and Ottoman rule increased the burdens upon the city and its inhabitants. Young people were forced to join the Turkish Army. Food supplies for the citizenry became scarce, and everything was oriented toward the large military force which was encamped in the country. The Jews suffered grievously, many dying of starvation.

The city itself became a military center for the Turks and their German allies. The Command Headquarters were based in the Augusta-Victoria building, high on Mt. Scopus. From Jerusalem, army battalions marched toward the military front in the south, the Sinai Desert, and the Suez Canal. The government actually forced many residents into the battlefields to work under extraordinarily difficult conditions, paving roads and constructing army encampments.

THE BRITISH CONQUEST OF PALESTINE

The British Army in Sinai succeeded in defeating the Turkish and German armies and began marching toward central Palestine, much to the secret delight of its inhabitants. The conquest of Jerusalem followed British victories in the south of the country. The British Army spread out from the south and the coast to the hills of Jerusalem and, after heavy battles in its immediate vicinity, marched victoriously into the Holy City, to the jubilation of its Jewish residents. A new era began in the history of Jerusalem.

Upon the arrival of the British Army in 1917, the city had about 53,410 residents, of which 31,147 were Jews, 11,663 were Christians, and 10,000 were Muslims. Some 20,000 residents had perished as a result of starvation and war.

The Jews saw liberation in the coming of the British. A tremendous impression was made on the entire population by the festive arrival of Lord Edmund Allenby, Commander in Chief of the Army, his staff, and the French and Italian commanders.

Lord Allenby issued a pronouncement to the inhabitants of Jerusalem in which he indicated that even though Jerusalem was still in a state of war he wished all people to continue in their various occupations without fear. He also included a statement which indicated that the Holy Places of all the religions would be protected in accordance with the wishes of the various religious groups to whom they belonged.

The following 30 years[4] were fraught with severe problems for the Jewish people as a result of periodic Arab riots, the restrictive immigration policies of the British Mandatory Government, World War II, and the Holocaust. The year 1948 brought with it the War of Liberation, the establishment of the State, and the opening of its gates to mass immigration.

THE NEW JERUSALEM AS THE CAPITAL OF ISRAEL

In December, 1949, following the War of Independence, the State of Israel pronounced the New City of Jerusalem as its capital. The city had some 84,000 inhabitants at that time, mostly Jewish.

The Knesset (Parliament) moved into a privately owned building in the heart of Jerusalem. This building is today a tourist office, since the Knesset moved into its own new building several years later. Government offices were moved into a compound known as Hakirya (now near the new Knesset building).

The first Mayor of Israeli Jerusalem was Daniel Auster. The object of the city government was to reconstruct and rehabilitate the city, to cure it of its wounds, to absorb new immigrants, build houses for them, and to develop economic projects as their sources of income.

Many of these immigrants were settled to the south of the city in the old British camp of El-Alamein which was converted into a rather primitive absorption center *(Ma'abara)* and renamed Talpiot. The majority of the thousands of immigrants settled in this manner came from the Muslim countries of the Middle East and North Africa.

Immigrants also settled in Refaim, the German Quarter, which the British Army had, of course, abandoned, and in other quarters from which the earlier (Arab) inhabitants had fled (during 1947–48) such as Katamon, Talbieh, Bakaa, Abu-Tor, and others. Abandoned Arab villages became Jewish settlements and these quarters became suburbs of Jerusalem.

In 1950 there were about 123,000 residents in the Israeli sector of Jerusalem, almost all of them Jewish. Additional residential areas were built with government aid and in cooperation with various institutions. They expanded in all directions—Kiryat Hayovel and Kiryat Menahem in the west, others in the vicinity of Gonen and Talpiot in the south and still others in the north, near the Jordanian border. The city spread itself over the magnificent mountains roundabout, its size far larger than in the days of the British Mandatory period. An Israeli enclave, surrounded by a sector still under Jordanian rule, remained on the heights of Mt. Scopus. The buildings of the Hebrew University and Hadassah Hospital, guarded by Israeli police, were located within this enclave. Only once in every two weeks did a convoy, under the supervision of the United Nations go up there carrying a change of guards and supplies for their maintenance.

Later, a new large suburb housing the new Hebrew University and Hadassah Hospital was erected within the city on a rocky crest overlooking Ein Kerem. Hakirya, the government office buildings, were constructed near the University, the Hospital, and the Knesset. Nearby, the

Israel Museum was opened. It became the largest and most important museum in Israel.

In the years that followed, the city continued to grow, its residential areas multiplied and its economic enterprises, particularly in the industrial areas of Romema and Givat Shaul increased. A generation of immigrants was absorbed through a network of educational institutions and army service and participated in Hebrew cultural and civic activities.

The most sacred and revered sites in Jewish tradition were located in the Old City, which was under Jordanian rule. These were: the site of the Temple Mount, the Western or Wailing Wall, the Jewish Quarter, and the remnants of the synagogues where Jews had worshipped. Outside the wall were Yad Avshalom, the Grave of Zachariah, and the tombs of the prophets. The ancient Jewish cemetery, the holiest and largest in the Jewish world, was located at the foot of the Mount of Olives.

In the armistice agreement between Jordan and Israel on April 3, 1949, under the supervision and responsibility of representatives of the U.N. Security Council, a paragraph (8) had been included which guaranteed Israel "freedom of movement in essential roads . . . a resumption of orderly work on the cultural and humanitarian institutions on Mt. Scopus and free access to them." It also assured Israel "free access to Jewish Holy Places and cultural institutions, and use of the cemetery on the Mount of Olives." However, in actuality, the United Nations supervisors did nothing to implement this paragraph, much to the distress of the Jews. This situation continued until the Six Day War of 1967.

Israel Jerusalem had some 195,000 residents at the time of the outbreak of the Six Day War. The Mayors of Israeli Jerusalem 1948–1967 were: Daniel Auster, 1949–1950; Shlomo Zalman Shragai, 1950–1952; Yitzchak Kariv, 1952–1955; Gershon Agron, 1955–1959; Mordechai Ish-Shalom, 1959–1964; Teddy Kollek,[5] 1965–19

JERUSALEM UNDER JORDANIAN RULE

For nearly 20 years, from the end of the War of Independence in 1948 to the Six Day War of 1967, East Jerusalem, including the Old City with its surrounding walls and a section of the New City which spread from the wall northward to the top of Mt. Scopus was under Jordanian rule.

Under Jordan, the city grew and its inhabitants increased, bolstered by Arab refugees who had fled from the New City and the surrounding villages which had been occupied by the Israeli Army during the war. The Jewish Quarter in the Old City became a Muslim refugee quarter. The Arab sections outside the wall also spread to areas such as Wadi El Joz and Sheikh Jarrah on the heights of Mt. Scopus. King Hussein began to build a palace on its northern peak, high on Tel Alful, (historically Givat Shaul). The Arab settlement of Abu-Tor or A-Tori grew up in the south, on the border of Israel's Givat Hananiah. The village of Silwan arose on the slopes of the Mount of Olives and Ras Al Emod grew up on its peak, on the side of the road leading to Jericho.

King Hussein of Jordan did much to improve the condition of the mosques in the courtyard of the Temple. He added a golden dome and ceramic facing to the Mosque of Omar (The Dome of the Rock), moved the iron fence that surrounded the Foundation Stone and also restored the al-Aqsa Mosque. Arabic inscriptions in both mosques now attest to his accomplishments. (King Abdullah, his grandfather, was assassinated at the entrance to the al-Aqsa Mosque in 1951). Hussein also converted part of the courtyard of the Temple into a Muslim Pantheon where his great-grandfather and many other Muslim and Arab leaders were buried.

Several hotels were built during the Jordanian rule, the largest being the Intercontinental, constructed at the top of the Mount of Olives and providing a magnificent view of the city. From the hotel the Jordanians built a road which joined with the road to Jericho, going directly over the monuments of the nearby Jewish cemetery.

Tourism was an extremely important facet of the economic life of the city, and to encourage it further many tourist stores were opened along the streets leading to the Holy Places. The government trained Muslim and Christian guides and also special police, whose main concern was the tourist and his comfort.

The year 1964 marked a special year for Jerusalem. Pope Paul VI was the most honored guest ever to arrive in the city, and the first Pontiff who had ever actually made a pilgrimage to the Holy Land. He first arrived in Jordanian Jerusalem, where he was received at the home of the Papal Representative on the heights of the Mount of Olives. From there he toured the Holy Places. On January 5, he passed through the Mandelbaum Gate into Israeli Jerusalem. He ascended Mt. Zion to the Coenaculum, the hall in which the Last Supper had taken place, on a new road which had been constructed in his honor.

At this time, according to one estimate, there were about 70,000 residents in Jordanian Jerusalem, the majority of whom were Muslims and the minority, about 11,000, Christians of various sects. Most of the residents lived in the Old City. The Damascus Gate, which marked the intersection of the roads both within the city and leading out of it, was therefore the center of activity in the Jordanian sector of the city. Nearby Sallah El Din Street was its main business artery. The Mayors of Jordanian Jerusalem (between 1948 and 1967) were: Anwar Al Khatib, Aref Al Aref, Omar Ws'amar, and Rouhi el-Khatib.

During a 20-year period Jerusalem was, therefore, governed by two separate jurisdictions, with no contact between them. The Old City and a small portion of the New City (to the north of the Old City) were under Jordanian rule while almost all of the New City was under Israeli rule. The border between Israel and Jordan ran along specifically marked streets in a north-south direction and along the line of the western wall of the Old City.

This boundary line was also a military front, where each side had military positions directly facing one another. The Jordanians were stationed along the length of the north-south wall and the Israelis on the rooftops of houses directly across it. An important Israeli military post was located in a wing of the Monastery of Notre Dame De France. There were also Israeli posts in Givat Hananiah (Abu-Tor) and in Ramat Rahel in the south.

The Mandelbaum Gate, named after the owner of one of the nearby houses, was the only point on the border where it was possible to cross from one sector of the city to the other. These crossings were made by consuls, representatives, and diplomats of various countries and by a few Christian tourists, all under the supervision of the United Nations. Christian and Samaritan residents of Israel were also allowed to pass through this gate to celebrate their respective holidays in the Jordanian sector; the Christians in Jerusalem and Bethlehem crossed over during Christmas and the Samaritans crossed over to Mt. Gerizim near Nablus during the Passover (which they also celebrate). It was through the Mandelbaum Gate that the Israeli convoys also passed on their way up to the enclave on Mt. Scopus.

Under Jordanian rule no major changes took place within the immediate area of the Old City or in its road network (with the exception of the single street which ran along the border of the Jewish Quarter). Today this street is called Batei Makhase. It runs along the length of the southern wall down to the Wailing Wall and to the Dung Gate. Until the War of Independence this street had been like a staircase, but the Jordanians removed the steps and paved a smooth road, enlarging the nearby Dung Gate and removing additional buildings which were attached to it. This was done in order to facilitate military vehicular traffic moving out of the city through the Dung Gate to the Zion Gate and "The Citadel" (Tower of David) in the Old City to their military positions opposite Israeli Jerusalem. The Jordanians also set up an Arab refugee camp directly under the northern wall of the Temple courtyard.

The Jordanians paved a new road from the city to the slopes of the Mount of Olives. It branched off from the road to Jericho, at a corner of the wall and the Rockefeller Museum, crossed the Valley of Kidron, and rose steeply to the Mount of Olives. It also branched off to the north toward the hospital building of Augusta-Victoria and to the south toward the Intercontinental Hotel.

In addition, the Jordanians paved a road which forked out from the

Jericho Road, passed the length of the Kidron river bed and ascended to the Arab section of Abu-Tor. This particular road also had military value. It facilitated the transportation of Jordanian soldiers to their positions at Abu-Tor, near the Israeli military positions at Givat Hananiah.

The Jordanians improved the roads which led out of Jerusalem. The road to Jericho was widened in part and lay directly over the gravestones of Jews buried on the Mount of Olives. It became a major highway between the Holy City and the capital city of Amman on the eastern side of the Jordan River. The Jordanians also built a road which swung around southward to Bethlehem and Hebron. They were, in effect, forced to do this because a large portion of the regularly used road was inside Israeli territory and therefore inaccessible to them. The road to Ramallah and to Nablus, which passed Mt. Scopus to the north, was also widened. On the slope of the mountain the road was broadened in order to facilitate the movement of vehicles to the settlements in Samaria. This road also led to the small airport of Atarot, which previously had only been used by the British Mandatory authority. The Jordanians expanded its runways on the lands of the settlement of Atarot, which had been totally destroyed, and renamed it *Kalandia* after a nearby Arab village.

The Jordanian Army was strategically based and well fortified both within the city and around it near the "Green Line" (Armistice Line). French Hill, at the top of Mt. Scopus, was an important military position for them. Bases were set up on the side of a nearby railway line and on Ammunition Hill which commanded a view of several important Israeli sectors—Sanhedria, Tel Arza, Batei Bochrim, and Bet Yisrael.

Another Jordanian military post was located on the heights of a Jordanian village. Its main purpose was to insure Jordanian transportation to Bethlehem and Hebron along the road which passed through this village. Still another base was on a hill near the Monastery of Mar Alias opposite the Israeli settlement of Ramat Rahel. There were also military positions above the village of Beit Zefafa (which was divided between Jordan and Israel). The Israeli railroad which runs through this village marked the border between the two halves of this divided village. The northern part was in Israel and the southern part in Jordan.

The Jordanians expropriated tombstones from the Jewish cemetery on the Mount of Olives and used them to reinforce their military fortresses on Mt. Zion. These were also used to pave the roadways in an army camp near the road to Jericho.

The entire length of the "Green Line" between Jordan and Israel was a "no man's land" and a demilitarized zone. Within this area stood Government House, the headquarters of the United Nations supervisory staff. A special road leading to it was built from the Jordanian sector of Jerusalem. The Israelis have built a new road surrounding the area since the Six Day War. This road links up with the Jerusalem–Jericho Road, and a new community has been established on the slopes of Antenna Hill.

NOTES AND REFERENCES

1. *Hamagid*, III, June 29, 1858. Supplement to Issue No. 25

2. *Hamagid*, IV, February 28, 1860, Issue No. 9

3. Jews began moving out of the Old City after 1857, followed by a purchase of land by Sir Moses Montefiore, the British-Jewish philanthropist. The first new buildings (1860) were alms houses, (Michkenot Sha'ananim). Eighty families were registered for the 20 apartments available. (Ed.)

4. For an account of the British Mandatory period see "Jerusalem Under the Mandate" on pages 53–60.

5. Teddy Kollek was also the first Mayor of unified Jerusalem

III

An Economic History of Jerusalem

ALFRED E. LIEBER

Jerusalem occupies a commanding position on a high plateau to the west of the Judaean hills. Except in the north it is separated from the surrounding range by deep and steep ravines and is thus an excellent site for a fortress. Throughout its four thousand years of history as a religious center, or as a capital city, it was only to be approached in peace. For this reason the Psalmist sings of:

> Jerusalem that is built to be a city
> where people come together in unity.

The Judaean hills also provided the products of sheep rearing: wool, hides and milk. The work of the cheesemaker in Jerusalem is still recalled in the name of the Tyropoeon Valley. Olive wood and oil, an important item in the Temple economy, as well as a certain amount of fruit, were also produced. Cereal crops, however, were rare, being unsuited to the nature of the country.

With no other natural advantages, and no indigenous raw material apart from building-stone, the economy of Jerusalem was always to be primarily a consumer's economy, supported by funds and supplies from the outside, and entirely dependent on peace. Any threat to peace immediately jeopardized the arrival of supplies to the city and moreover cut off the flow of visitors from many lands, who were no less important for its economic well-being. During the pilgrimage seasons the city became transformed into a kind of fair, and this, in its turn, attracted merchants, some of whom came specially for the purpose. Under such circumstances they might hope to sell their wares at a good price and to acquire on the spot goods from other lands, to be taken back to their home towns.

The peculiar structure of the Jerusalem economy is vividly described by Josephus, who refers to the period of its heyday, before its destruction in A.D. 70. It had achieved a level of growth and prosperity which was not to return for almost 2,000 years. The city was now a political center and, above all, the religious center of Judaism; both factors which made for the prosperity of its trades and trade. The rebuilding of the Temple and the city walls, the erection of the royal palaces, and the provision of accommodation for the ever-growing number of pilgrims and other visitors, sustained a building trade quite out of proportion to the actual size of the city. All these activities, of course, depended on and stimulated an import trade in commodities from far and near, as well as a retail trade to distribute the goods, particularly during the pilgrimage seasons. In the absence of visible exports, these imports were paid for partly by the taxes levied on the country as a whole and by the Temple revenues, but also, to a great extent, by the income derived from the visitors.

The public revenue, though considerable, could not compare with the huge income of the Temple, which was made up of the *didrachma*, levied on every Jew in the country and outside, and of the sacrifices, offerings, and tithes, the income from Temple property and bequests from pious Jews all over the world. The economic life of the city was consequently always richer and more varied than that of any other town of comparative size.

The visitors and pilgrims were especially numerous at Easter, amounting to well over 100,000 persons in some years. Moreover, then as now, Jerusalem attracted not only the poor among the pious, but also wealthy persons who came there to retire.[1] At that time, the permanent population amounted to some 25,000 to 30,000 persons.[2] In relation to the restricted water supply, this was probably the maximum possible number, taking into consideration the regular influx of numerous pilgrims. Well into the present century, water was to remain an important factor limiting the growth of the city.

Some 60 years after the destruction of Jerusalem, the emperor Hadrian decided to construct in its place Aelia Capitolina, a pagan city populated entirely by foreign settlers, which was never to be more than a garrison town. Not until 200 years later did Constantine the Great start to rebuild Jerusalem and to construct the Basilica of the Holy Sepulchre. Now, as a Christian city, it was to regain some of its importance as a pilgrimage center, although its fortunes were to wax and wane with those of the rest of the Byzantine Empire. The continuous building of churches and monasteries and the presence of numerous pilgrims assured a certain degree of prosperity.

The economic position improved further after the Muslim conquest of A.D. 638, although throughout the centuries of Muslim rule Jerusalem was never to be more than a provincial center. In addition to the Christians, there were now numerous Muslim pilgrims, attracted by the construction of the two great mosques on the Temple Mount; the third most important place of pilgrimage in Islam. Moreover, Jews had again settled in the city. Arculf, a Bishop of Gaul, who visited Jerusalem in A.D. 670, especially notes the annual fair:

> On the fifteenth day of the month of September yearly, an almost countless multitude of various nations is in the habit of gathering from all sides to Jerusalem for the purposes of commerce by mutual sale and purchase.[3]

Muqaddasi, the famous Arab geographer and native of Jerusalem, who lived at the end of the tenth century A.D., describes the advantages of the city and the produce sold in its markets and then expressly notes that the majority of its inhabitants were still Christians and Jews and that most of the population was poor. According to Nāsir-i-Khusrau, Jerusalem in A.D. 1047 was still a great city, of some 20,000 inhabitants, and an important pilgrimage center. In some years up to 20,000 Muslims might be present in the first days of the month of Dhū-l-Hijjah, during the period of the pilgrimage to Mecca. Moreover, "From all the countries of the Greeks, too, and from other lands, the Christians and the Jews come up to Jerusalem in great numbers. . . ."[4]

Christian pilgrims, of course, became still more numerous during the short period of existence of the Latin Kingdom of Jerusalem, when the city was again a capital and the Italian sea-republics maintained commercial settlements there. All this seems to have led to renewed building and consequent prosperity, but unfortunately few particulars of economic activity have been recorded. Benjamin of Tudela, who visited Jerusalem between 1170 and 1173, reports the existence of a dye-works, as a royal monopoly, which was rented to Jews on an annual basis.[5]

After the conquest of Jerusalem by Saladin in A.D. 1187, Muslim rule continued until 1917, save for the short interlude of the second Latin Kingdom. Saladin's reign attracted an appreciable settlement of Jews, among them Rabbi Yehiel of Paris who, in A.D. 1257, transferred his yeshiva to the Holy Land, together with 300 French and English pupils. He sent an envoy to Jewish communities abroad to collect contributions for their maintenance and thus initiated a way of life which was to remain typical of Jerusalem Jewry until the nineteenth century.

The continuous political instability, which led to the Turkish conquest of 1516, also cast a deep shadow on Jerusalem, whose economy became that of a backward provincial town. However, there was an outburst of building under each new ruler. Between the years 1537 and 1540 Suleiman the Magnificent reconstructed the city walls, and they assumed their present form. Both town and country population suffered from the corruption of the government, which had only one concern: to extract as much revenue from taxes as possible. This policy was enhanced by the fact that the Turks only appointed the pashas, the provincial rulers, for very short terms of office, in order to prevent them from establishing themselves properly. The city thus continued to decay and to become ever less capable of supporting itself. Famines and epidemics visited the town repeatedly, and by the end of the eighteenth century, despite a trickle of pious Jewish immigrants, the population had fallen to less than 10,000 inhabitants.

Napoleon's expedition to Egypt, in the course of which he also held Jerusalem in 1799, brought the "Eastern Question" again into the limelight; a place which it has occupied ever since. For Jerusalem a new era began with Ibrahim Pasha's conquest of Palestine from the Turks in 1832. On the one hand he introduced a more liberal regime for the non-Muslim inhabitants of the country. On the other hand he was fiercely opposed by the rest of the local population, especially in the north, and the ensuing unrest brought disaster upon disaster to the Jewish population. Finally, an earthquake in 1837 destroyed Safed and Tiberias, then the main centers of the Jewish population. Many of the survivors fled to Jerusalem, which, having attracted the interest of the Great Powers, was soon to become "the Kingdom of the Consuls."[6]

Edward Robinson, an American Professor of Biblical Literature, who initiated modern archaeological research in the Holy Land, made a social survey of the country in 1838 and particularly of Jerusalem. He found that the city had 11,500 inhabitants: 4,500 Muslims, 3,000 Jews, and 4,000 Christians. One of the few manufactures was soap, which was produced by nine establishments. There also existed nine presses for the extraction of sesame oil, and a large tannery which was situated near the Holy Sepulchre. The Christians were engaged in the production of olive wood and mother-of-pearl souvenirs, which were consecrated by the priests before being taken away by the pilgrims. At Easter the pilgrims converted the town into a huge fair, which attracted merchants from as far away as Damascus.[7]

The Jewish population took practically no part in any economic activity, since it consisted mainly of those who had come to study, or to end their days in the Holy City. Occasionally, the scribes would copy a Scroll of the Law for some Jewish community overseas. Sir Moses Montefiore was one of the first to realize that Jewish settlement could not exist on a sound basis unless steps were taken to make it productive and less dependent on foreign charity. To this end he tried to acquire agricultural land in 1838: a scheme which soon came to nothing with the return to Turkish rule. He did however help Israel Bak of Safed to establish a modern printing-works and bindery in Jerusalem in 1841, by procuring a press and Latin type in England. Bak was a skilled craftsman who cast his own Hebrew letters and in Safed had established the first Jewish farm in modern times. However, after the town had been completely destroyed by the combined efforts of an earthquake in 1837 and the Druze revolt against Ibrahim Pasha, he moved to Jerusalem. The first printing press in the city had been set up in the Armenian Convent some seven or eight years earlier, but Bak's press was to remain the only purely commercial enterprise of its kind for over twenty years. Montefiore later tried to establish a textile industry in Jerusalem, but this failed, due to bad management and the high cost of production.

A fresh stimulus to Jewish settlement in the country and especially in Jerusalem, was provided by a British movement to restore the Jews to the Holy Land, which was promoted by Lord Ashley, the seventh Earl of Shaftesbury, Lord Palmerston, then Foreign Secretary, and Colonel Churchill, the British Consul in Beirut. Early in 1839, shortly after the establishment of a British consulate in Jerusalem, the consul received instructions, originating from Lord Palmerston, that it would be part of his duty to afford protection to the Jews in general, as well as to report on the state of the Jews in Palestine.[8] The Damascus affair of 1840 and the ensuing pogroms against the Jews certainly underlined the urgency of these British activities.

The second British consul in Jerusalem was James Finn who, with his wife, took a deep interest in the affairs of the Jewish community. With the outbreak of the Crimean War in 1853, the Jews, as well as the Christian churches, found themselves cut off from their overseas sources of financial support, and the Jews rapidly became destitute, having no local resources upon which they could fall back. Finn therefore organized relief work for them, first on his lands at Talbieh outside the walls, and then also at Artas near Bethlehem. With the ever-increasing number of applicants for work, he acquired a new tract of land, which was to become Kerem Abraham (Abraham's Vineyard), the first Jewish district of Jerusalem outside the walls. Here Jews were trained as building workers, and this laid the foundation for Jewish manual labor in the city.[9] Finn's activities certainly did not pass uncriticized by part of the Jewish community itself. Besides their ever-present fear of missionary influences, they resented any attempt to alter their customary way of life, especially as they felt that this might lead to the cessation of their traditional sources of income. Such sentiments became more pronounced in 1879 when attempts were made by the Rothschild family to set up schools which would also teach secular subjects. A group of pious fanatics persuaded an aged and venerated rabbi to put these schools under a religious ban. This was reported by the British consul of the day, who commented:

> Their motive seems to be a fear that the study of foreign languages would lure away the Israelitish youths from the study of their own sacred literature and imbue them with gentile ideas, which, in its turn, would interfere with

the flow of charitable donations from Europe, whose raison d'être is the supposed piety, and consequently efficacy of the vicarious prayers of the Jews of Jerusalem.[10]

This kind of opposition continued to make itself felt until well into the present century.

With increasing Jewish immigration, the housing conditions in the Jewish Quarter of the Old City had become still more cramped and squalid. In 1855, Sir Moses Montefiore had followed Finn's example and had also acquired land outside the walls, with money left in trust by the American philanthropist Juda Touro of New Orleans. Here he therefore built houses, as well as a windmill, which was the first industrial structure outside the walls. This was followed by increased building activity both inside and outside; the latter including the construction of the German Colony by the Templars, a sect of German Christians. At the same time, in 1878, Jews from Jerusalem founded Petah Tikva, north of Jaffa, as an agricultural settlement, showing that the new spirit had caught on. In fact, living in Jerusalem outside the walls was somewhat hazardous in the first decades, and many returned at night to the relative security of the walled town.

The attraction of the city as a tourist and pilgrimage center was increased by visits from European royalty, and this resulted in the construction of more hostels and hotels. Other facilities, such as hospitals and schools, were also established, not always on a basis of objective need, but because each community prided itself on maintaining its own institutions, which helped it in turn, to attract more contributions from the overseas supporters with which it was connected.

This social fragmentation was encouraged by the regime of the "Capitulations." Thus, until the outbreak of World War I, a citizen of Jerusalem could choose whether to send his mail through the Turkish, Russian, German, Austrian, French, or Italian post office, and this in a city which had only 75,000 inhabitants in 1914.

Having failed in all their attempts to induce the Powers to desist from the maintenance of separate postal services, the Turkish post office eventually sold postage stamps for foreign correspondence at half the fixed rate. They also forbade their subjects from using other postal services, and on granting the concession for a railway linking Jerusalem with Jaffa, they inserted a proviso allowing it to carry only Turkish postal matters. Despite this, the bulk of the mail went through the Austrian and Russian posts. To the horror and dismay of their home government and the local anti-Semites, the Russian post office in Jerusalem employed a Jewish postmaster. He succeeded in his task by extending credit to the numerous charitable organizations for the postage on their fund-raising letters and collecting it from the incoming donations.[11]

The stream of tourists and pilgrims increased steadily in the nineteenth century. So did the Jewish immigration, which was mainly the result of growing anti-Semitism in various countries. Some of these immigrants brought with them skills or capital, which promoted crafts and trade, as well as the building activity which was always one of the mainstays of the economy of the city. Trade, however, was never an important factor in the economy, because Jerusalem was badly served by roads and was by-passed by the main trade route from Cairo to Damascus, which passed through Ramla, farther to the west. Jerusalem merchants used to travel twice a year to Beirut to place their orders, and at Easter Syrian merchants came to Jerusalem with their wares. Once a fortnight a ship arrived at Jaffa, bringing passengers and mail, as well as goods. The journey from Jaffa to Jerusalem was always hazardous and took at least a day and a half on horseback. Only in 1869 was a proper road built, in view of the impending state visit of the Austrian Emperor, Franz Josef. In 1888 a local Jewish entrepreneur, Joseph Navon, obtained a concession from the Turks for the construction and operation of a railway over 87 kilometers from Jaffa to Jerusalem. This was opened in 1892 and cut the traveling time to six hours.[12]

Still more astonishing was the slow development of banking, for, as the British Consul Mr. Finn pointed out, the coins of all nations were current in Jerusalem:

> The great religious establishments, as the Convents, Patriarchates, Episcopates, not to mention the six Consulates, all have money dealings, and would be benefited by a banking institution, with good capital and character. . . . But almost all the money affairs here are in the hands of a few petty firms who transact their business at enormous interest, and money when obtained on loan, often costs at the usurious rates of 50 or 60 per cent per annum: 24 per cent per annum is considered very moderate.

In 1840 a group of newly arrived Jewish immigrants, together with several established Jerusalemites, set up a joint-stock trading company, which soon branched out into banking. Another private Jewish bank started up in 1848 and stayed in business until 1915. Two Swiss Protestants not only built houses for rental but also set up their own bank, which, in turn, represented the Ottoman Bank. Other foreign banks followed slowly. In 1904 the Anglo-Palestine Company started business in Jerusalem. Today, as the Bank Leumi Le-Israel, it is the biggest in the country.[13]

Charles Warren, another famous archaeologist, conducted a census of Jerusalem in 1868 and found that the population had reached 23,500 and consisted of 10,000 Jews, 7,500 Muslims, and 6,000 Christians. However, there were only 1,932 "able-bodied working men" among them. He also registered some 1,320 shops, of which 278 were normally empty, being occupied only at Easter, by merchants from Damascus and other cities. He suggested that should the city continue to grow as in the previous few years, the many empty markets could accommodate another thousand merchants. Noting the low proportion of Jewish working men, he concluded that 3,000 and possibly 5,000 Jews were without any visible means of subsistence.[14]

In 1877, according to Dr. Neumann, the director of the Mayer Rothschild Hospital, the Jewish population was 13,000, of which some 2,000 were of independent means. Among the rest, 3,000 were in need of some financial assistance, and another 3,000 were completely dependent on public assistance. This last group consisted mainly of scholars and their students, old people, and a large number of widows and orphans. Thus, nearly half of the Jewish population was dependent to some extent on charity. He also found that 1,500 Latin Christians were living on alms received from their monasteries.[15]

By 1896 a further considerable increase is recorded, with the population amounting to 45,420. The Jews were now in an absolute majority, with 28,112 persons, compared to 8,560 Muslims and 8,748 Christians. This trend was to continue until 1914.

On the eve of World War I, Jerusalem was a flourishing city with a population of 75,200, of which 48,400 were Jews, 16,750 were Christians, and 10,500 were Muslims. Its economy was still based on three factors: pilgrimage, immigration, and, above all, financial contributions from abroad. With the outbreak of war, the first two factors came to a sudden stop, while the third practically ceased. Furthermore, the town was almost entirely dependent on supplies from abroad, which also came to an abrupt halt. The situation was aggravated by the continuous depreciation of the Turkish currency, until its purchasing power was reduced to ten per cent of its nominal value. The Jews and part of the Christian community were more dependent on their foreign connections than the Muslims and accordingly suffered more from these changes. Within just over three years of war, the Jewish community shrank to little more than half its number. Immediately after Turkey's entry into the war, a large number left of their own accord to find temporary shelter in Egypt, and the hostile attitude of the Turkish authorities to Zionism led to many expulsions among the future leaders of the Jewish community. Most of the casualties, however, were caused by starvation and epidemic disease.

On December 7, 1917, the city surrendered without a fight to General Allenby, the commander of the British forces, who entered it two days later, to initiate a new era of hope. The hastily set up military administration took energetic steps to restore the life of the town to normal. It alleviated the food shortage by importing grain from Egypt and dealt with the shortage of coins. Ronald Storrs, the Military Governor of Jerusalem, did not always see eye to eye with the different population groups, but was quick to understand the unique nature of the city and worked hard to re-establish its cultural life and to conserve and restore its ancient heritage. Thus he prepared the ground for the pilgrims and tourists who were to continue to form the backbone of the country's economy. He founded the "Pro-Jerusalem Society" which, in the hallowed tradition of the city, made efforts to raise funds throughout the world. On his initiative, Patrick Geddes, the architect, produced a plan to enhance the Old City by surrounding the walls with a green belt. This was never carried out, but a similar scheme has recently been adopted by the present Town Council and is now well on the way to be completed in the foreseeable future. Storrs also proceeded to repair the walls and the medieval ramparts and to restore historical buildings and Holy Places, such as the Holy Sepulchre and the mosques on the Temple Mount. All these activities provided much-needed employment for the impoverished population. The restoration of the mosques also brought about the establishment of the first new industry. Storrs induced David Ohanessian, an Armenian master potter, to set up a pottery and produce the tiles needed for the purpose. For this other Armenian craftsmen were brought over from Kūtāhya in Asia Minor, which had long been famous for its ceramics. They also supplied and still supply the lovely name-plates for the streets of the Old City, as well as artistic ceramic wares for the market. Another new enterprise, which employed some seventy people, was a weaving shop which the American Red Cross had originally set up during the war for the relief of Armenian and Syrian weavers. Due to foreign competition it failed, however, when things returned to normal.[16]

In 1920 the military government was replaced by a British civil administration, and in 1922 the British Mandate for Palestine was formally approved by the League of Nations. Jerusalem was once again the capital of the country and this new status was reflected in important changes in the composition of its population. It became the home of a large number of officials, both expatriate and locally recruited. The Jewish Agency for Palestine set up its headquarters in the city, as did many other public and commercial institutions, including banks. The foundation of the Hebrew University on Mt. Scopus, as well as other scientific and cultural institutions, brought about further population changes, particularly among the Jewish community, and helped to reduce the burden of the impoverished and non-productive inhabitants. Insofar as the latter desired to work, there were now plenty of opportunities in the ensuing building boom and in the provision of services for the expanding population.

A large proportion of the Jewish immigrants in this period were middle-class settlers, who brought with them both skills and capital for investment. Moreover, those local residents who owned land suitable for building could now participate in the extensive building operations. Thus the Arab landowners, in particular, took the opportunity to construct entire new residential areas outside the walls, mainly as rental accommodation for British officials, and thus provided new employment for Arab workers. These new elements had much higher incomes, on the whole, than the established population and they were also used to a far higher standard of living. Their presence therefore created untold possibilities for new economic activity, apart from the provision of accommodation and services to meet their direct needs. Thus in addition to the new housing areas, a complete change came over the older districts outside the walls. Besides dwellings, public buildings were constructed to house the new government departments, as well as schools and other institutions built partly with the aid of contributions from outside. In addition, however, the period saw the construction of offices, hotels, restaurants, shops, markets, and a host of small workshops, to serve the ever-increasing number of tourists and pilgrims, as well as the local residents.

Yet all this produced no basic change in the composition of the population or the economy. Jerusalem was and remained a city of consumers, dependent for almost all its needs on supplies from other parts of the country or from abroad, without contributing any visible exports. Even the few traditional trades, such as printing, did not manage to keep in step with developments in the field elsewhere in the country. Although an English language newspaper successfully catered to the large foreign community, no Hebrew paper took root in Jerusalem and the same applied to the publication of secular Hebrew books. Practically no new industry succeeded in establishing itself in Jerusalem. Indeed the first census of industry taken by the Government of Palestine revealed that in 1928, in the 658 "industrial" establishments in the city, only 3,316 persons were employed, including the owners. Only 80 workshops possessed some kind of power-driven machinery. The average monthly wage then amounted to 3.33 Palestinian pounds, as compared with 5.95 Palestinian pounds earned at that time in Tel Aviv; a differential which should have been ample to cover the costs of transport of raw materials and still to have provided an inducement to establish industries in Jerusalem.[17] However, there was still lacking an economic climate conducive to large-scale economic activity, for which the government of the day must take a large share of the blame. In the first place it was guided by a romantic feeling that the "Holy City" was to be preserved as a living museum of the past, whether or not this would benefit the inhabitants of the day. In addition it tried to avoid taking a stand on any issue about which the various communities of the town differed among themselves. As a result, no active steps were taken to set up industrial areas or to offer any other inducement for the establishment of industries, which might have helped to widen the basis of the economy and to reduce the ever-prevalent unemployment, both open and concealed.

From 1920 onward, communal unrest sporadically troubled the city, culminating in the riots of 1929. After the terrible attack on the 3,000-strong Jewish community of Hebron, practically all the survivors settled in Jerusalem, but even so the general sense of insecurity led the Jewish merchants to abandon the Old City and to establish themselves in the so-called New Commercial Center outside the walls. The outbreak of disturbances throughout the country in 1936 immediately led to a state of permanent strife in Jerusalem, which paralyzed any economic activity.

The large immigration of Jews from Germany, which started in 1933, as the Nazi party rose to power, brought certain talents and skills to Jerusalem, but again did little to change the occupational structure of the city. Those who settled in the capital were mainly the elderly and the numerous professionals who hoped to find work at the Hebrew University and medical institutions, although the number of available posts was limited. Rather than change their occupations, they meanwhile lived on their small savings, or took temporary jobs. Persons with capital or technical skills, who planned to set up new enterprises, established themselves in the coastal plain. There they found encouragement, cheap land, and, above all, freedom from the encumbrance of an ever less sympathetic administration. By throwing themselves into the bustling activities of Tel Aviv, a purely Jewish town, or of a mixed town like Haifa, where the future seemed much brighter, they were helped to forget the traumatic experiences which they had undergone.

These settlers of course swelled the population of Jerusalem and gave rise to a good deal of new building and other economic activity, to supply their needs, but as compared with the rest of the country, Jerusalem was a stagnating city. By 1939 the number of its inhabitants had risen to 131,300 and now constituted 8.75 per cent of the 1,500,000 inhabitants of the whole of Palestine. Yet its share in the consumption of electricity for "industrial" purposes only amounted to 1.9 per cent; and this in a country which was still overwhelmingly agricultural.

With the outbreak of World War II, ironically enough, peace descended upon the city for a period of five years. Suddenly the inhabitants could once more mingle freely with one another and move about without fear. They were joined not only by the large military establishment in the country, but also by thousands of soldiers on leave from the allied forces in the Middle East, for whom Palestine, and Jerusalem in particular, had quickly become a favorite center. Moreover, British Army headquarters quickly perceived that among the many elderly immigrants from Central Europe living in Jerusalem they could find a large part of the skilled civilian personnel which they required; a pool of labor which was wholly committed to the war effort and at the same time not over military age. The civil authorities were also called upon to do their share. They dealt with the allocation and distribution of raw materials and similar matters and, above all, tried to enlist all the productive forces in the country in the war effort. In this way they ensured the local production of as many items as possible required by the forces in the area. As a result, the country, including the capital, enjoyed a large measure of prosperity, and in the constant search for further productive capacity, the army laid the foundations for a metal-working industry in Jerusalem. Thus, by the end of the war, the city's share of electricity for industrial purposes had risen to nearly 3 per cent of the total consumption of the country, while its share in the population had risen only slightly, to 8.9 per cent.

This state of prosperity was, however, accompanied by an increasing shortage of consumer goods. The cost of living, therefore, rose continuously until, by the end of December, 1944, it stood at 2 1/2 times the level at the outbreak of the war. The consequences were particularly unfortunate for that large part of the population of Jerusalem, both Jews and Christian Arabs, who still did not take part in the living economy. Moreover, just as during World War I, they were more or less cut off from the foreign contributions, both private and institutional, on which they depended for their very existence. Various brave attempts at assistance had little effect on their abject poverty.

The approaching end of hostilities naturally led to a sharp drop in economic activities connected with the war effort, while, partly due to lack of overseas transport, there was no possibility of the prompt renewal of the pilgrimage and tourist traffic. Thus the consequences of the very narrow economic basis of the city once more asserted themselves and even the resettlement of returning ex-servicemen was a more difficult task in Jerusalem than elsewhere in the country, where the possibilities of employment were more varied. Thus, when the uneasy truce within the country itself came to an end, gloom once more descended upon the city.

The civil administration revived its hostile attitude and after 1945 the affairs of the town were run on a purely caretaker basis, by an appointed Municipal Commission, wholly composed of British officials. With the approaching end of the Mandate, the administration promoted various unrealistic schemes to turn Jerusalem into a separate entity, without giving any thought to its economic structure or viability.

The ever-increasing lawlessness which now prevailed was indirectly aided by the professed efforts of the government to check this development. As a punitive measure so-called security zones were created around the government offices. This entailed the wholesale evacuation of Jewish residents and businesses from the center of the new part of the town and effectively divided up the entire city. Thus, when on November 29, 1947, the United Nations decided to partition Palestine and to "internationalize" Jerusalem, the city was in effect already "partitioned," except for a few pockets in the New City, which were still held by the British Army. Yet nobody could have imagined that within less than six months the entire Jewish population of the Old City would also have to be evacuated.

The town had now ceased to be a meeting place; there was no longer any question of pilgrims or tourists visiting the Holy Places and every productive economic activity had come to a stop. Moreover, at the beginning of 1948 Arabs burned down and pilfered the New Commercial Center, and the same merchants who had suffered heavily in the riots of 1929 were once more on the brink of ruin. It was not long until the Jews of Jerusalem found themselves entirely cut off from the centers of Jewish population in the coastal plain. This was partly a long-term result of the Land Transfer Regulations of 1940. These regulations had prevented Jews from acquiring land in the hill country and thus from establishing settlements which would have secured communications and supplies for Jerusalem in time of crisis. As no outside supplies reached the Jewish population, all essentials soon had to be rationed. The water supply of the Jewish part of the New City, which came from the coastal plain via a number of pumping stations, first became irregular and then finally broke down, so that even water had to be doled out in pails. This added to the worries of the under-fed and over-tired population, which was subjected to constant shelling by the Arabs from the surrounding hills. Finally the supply situation became so precarious that by April, 1948, only the convoys of food that were brought in, under a hail of bullets from Arab guns, extended the lease of life of the population. For want of fuel many went for weeks without a cooked meal, or a hot drink, up to the truce of July, 1948.

On May 14, 1948, the British Mandate came to an end, almost unnoticed by the population. On the afternoon of that day it was announced, however, that the State of Israel had been proclaimed at Tel Aviv, and increased shelling began by the Arab Legion, reinforced by Egyptian guns.

With the lifting of the siege in July, supplies again started to come in. For this a new road had been hastily constructed, as the old road was still dangerous, and part of it near Latrun was in fact soon lost. By the same route, many inhabitants who could no longer make a living in the town left to start a new life in the plain, together with a large number of former civil servants who went to Tel Aviv with their families to join the new government service of Israel. This exodus was preceded by a steady trickle of people, mainly the aged and infirm, who had left before the siege began in earnest and it was reinforced by the departure of the youth to join the Israeli forces. As a result, the Jewish population of Jerusalem, which had numbered 100,000 in 1947, was down to 70,000 at the beginning of 1949, with a greater proportion than ever unable to support themselves and the large families which so many of them possessed. Numerous dwellings and offices had been badly damaged by the shelling which had pounded the town for over seven months. Nor was Jerusalem any longer the capital, for the government and all ministries sat in Tel Aviv. Above all, practically all tourist sites lay within the walls, on the other side of the now completely divided city. These walls, immediately overlooking the New City, were topped with sandbags, through which protruded the guns of the Arab Legion; a clearly visible reminder to the Jewish population of the constant peril under which they lived. Thus the outlook for the future was grim, despite the determination of the citizens to restart civil life and to restore Jerusalem to its rightful position as "the City in Israel."

The Israel Government, although still occupied with the prosecution of the war, decided that the revival of the town was of prime importance. Besides the construction of a permanent highway, which shortened travel time between Jerusalem and the rest of the country, and the restoration of the railway link, which had remained entirely in Israeli hands, immediate attention was given to the provision of adequate water and electricity supplies; all prerequisites for the restitution of the economy.

In 1949 Jerusalem was proclaimed the capital of the State of Israel and steps were taken to transfer all government ministries to Jerusalem. At the same time it was clear that if the city were to become a living entity with a viable economy, efforts would have to be made to alter its economic basis. At a very early stage a Reconstruction Commissioner was appointed. His task was to plan a more varied economy than the town had ever before possessed, by the encouragement of new industries and the reconstruction and development of existing enterprises. For this purpose, the Jerusalem Economic Corporation, which had been set up in 1947, erected a number of industrial estates. The new industries included a shoe factory, which soon employed some 300 operatives, metal and printing works, textile plants, and the expansion of existing pharmaceutical works. No less important was the construction of new hotels in the city, with the aim of attracting a large share of the increasing number of tourists who were coming to visit the new state. It was also hoped that in due course an understanding would be reached with the Government of Jordan, which had annexed the eastern part of the city, whereby pilgrims to the Holy Land might at the same time visit sites on both sides of the border; a hope which was only partly to be fulfilled.[18]

These endeavors were greatly assisted by the onset of mass immigration to Israel, which followed immediately the gates were opened in May, 1948. In 1950 alone, 30,000 immigrants were settled in Jerusalem, so that the population again achieved its prewar level. With continuous immigration and a high rate of natural increase, the population reached 195,700 on the eve of the Six Day war in June, 1967.

This rapid influx of new residents brought with it a host of new problems. However, the Jewish town was now a living entity, with a more solid and more varied economic basis than it had ever possessed before, and above all with hope for a still brighter future.

The Arab part of the divided city had suffered less in the period preceding the end of the Mandate, as all its communications with the Arab hinterland had remained open. Moreover, its water supply was unaffected, for most houses had always relied mainly on their own rain water cisterns, while some of the lesser sources of the piped supply were entirely in Arab-held territory. However, with the intensification of hostilities many of the inhabitants left to await the outcome of the struggle in purely Arab towns, especially as in this part of Jerusalem too all economic activity had come to a halt. This was particularly the case within the walls of the Old City, which had been completely dependent on the pilgrim and tourist trade. It now became a refuge for Arabs from the western part of Jerusalem. On the whole, however, the population in the Arab part of the town dropped sharply from 65,000 on the eve of hostilities in 1948, to 46,000 in 1956.[19]

With the end of the fighting in 1948, the Old City and its adjacent suburbs became part of the Hashemite Kingdom of Jordan, and, nominally, its second capital. In fact it reverted to a provincial town, living on its past glory and with a very reduced tourist trade. For political reasons the government endeavored to shift the point of gravity east of the Jordan, and to Amman the capital, in particular. Thus all economic relations with the outside world had to be conducted through Amman. Transport problems added to the difficulties, as the Israeli forces held certain vantage points which cut off the eastern part of Jerusalem completely from Bethlehem, thus damaging the tourist trade. A new road to Bethlehem was constructed after some years' delay, so that the two most important Christian pilgrimage sites were again connected with one another. A new, more direct highway to Amman, via the Abdullah Bridge over the Jordan, did little, however, to strengthen the connection between these two towns, but served as one-way route for the departure of the economically and politically active elements, most of whom were young men. These were attracted by the boom conditions in Amman, where not only the Government of Jordan and all its departments were located but also the head offices of the banks and other economic institutions.

To add to its plight, the eastern part of Jerusalem remained for some years without electricity, for the power station of the Jerusalem Electric Corporation was situated in the western section. Finally a new power station was erected. Gradually, building activity in the part of the eastern sector outside the walls picked up again, with the construction of a new commercial center and a number of hotels. However, there was an almost complete absence of any economic activity unconnected with the tourist trade, and the only large enterprise was a cigarette factory.

The Christian population was, on the whole, more affected than their Muslim neighbors by the changes of 1948 and after, since the more prosperous among them had tended to live in mixed Arab-Jewish areas outside the walls, or in districts adjoining Jewish neighborhoods. Many crowded into the Old City, where the churches and monasteries had huge properties, which, in normal times, were meant to serve pilgrims. Those whose livelihood was connected with the churches and their institutions, including a large number of schools, printing presses, and hospices, could more or less continue to follow their traditional way of life, but matters were different for the merchants and others who depended on the languishing tourist trade. Morever, a large number of Christian Arabs had been employed in Mandatory times by the government and the municipality (partly on account of their generally superior education) and they found that their employment possibilities were limited in a purely Muslim state. Nor did the road to Amman hold out for them the same hope as for a young Muslim Arab with equal skills. Many therefore emigrated overseas in the tradition of their forefathers; Christians from the Middle East having always taken a greater part in such migration than their Muslim neighbors. A census taken by the Jordanian Government showed that the Christian population of Jerusalem, estimated at between 25,000 and 31,000 in 1948, had dropped sharply to 11,000 by 1961.[20]

In June, 1967, the illogical and artificial division of the Holy City came to an end. It again assumed its traditional, multi-national and multi-religious character, as "a city where people come together in unity." With the tearing down of the barriers and the cleaning up of the no-man's-land between them, the two border towns merged again into one, and immediately the gates of the Old City were thrown open the populations started to mix freely. Moreover, foreign visitors soon found that Jerusalem was one of the safest cities in the world, by day and by night.

The Israeli visitors were avid purchasers of all kinds of souvenirs and oriental wares, but also bought agricultural produce and consumer goods. In the beginning, the Arab traders replenished their stocks of foreign imports from other Arab towns in Israeli-administered territory, but soon they began to purchase Israeli-made goods and the products of new Arab enterprises set up throughout the occupied areas. In special demand were the footwear and other leather goods produced in small workshops in the Old City itself.

Soon the Israeli authorities adopted a so-called "open bridges" policy, a unique innovation which allowed the Arab population to maintain their economic connections with the Arab world, despite the continuous state of war. Thus consumer goods started to be imported openly from Jordan and other Arab states. The boom extended even to the Arab bookstores, for Israeli Arabs, Jews from oriental countries, and, above all, the universities were insatiable customers of Arabic literature. Thus many Arab merchants were now doing the best business of their lives.

The Arabs, for their part, looked at the brightly lit shop windows of the Jewish part of the city and especially at the supermarkets, which, together with the parks, were an innovation for them. They also saw their former lands and houses, which they had abandoned in 1948.

The effect of the unification of the city on the tourist industry was much more than the sum of the customary tourism of each side alone. Over five years, the number of tourists to the city had more than doubled. Moreover, while in previous years Jewish tourists came to Jerusalem only for the day, now they tended to make it the base for their stay in the country. In the Jewish part of the town this has led to a great increase in the occupancy of the hotels and to the feverish construction of new ones. In East Jerusalem the hotels did not fully participate in this growing business at the beginning, but in 1971 alone they increased their occupancy by 55 per cent on the average, while the better hotels were fully occupied.

The situation was still more hopeful in the building industry. In Jordanian times, numerous "villas" had been constructed in the suburbs and villages around Jerusalem, with the money an Arab laborer or businessman sent back from North or South America to the wife, or other members of his family, which he had left behind. With the state of uncertainty following the Six Day War, much of this construction stopped, to be re-started a few years later. In the meantime, however, all Arab building workers (some 10,000 from Jerusalem and the West Bank together) were speedily absorbed in the wave of construction which swept Jerusalem, like the rest of Israel, so that by 1972 they formed the greater part of the building labor force. Prosperity brought about a general desire for better housing, coupled with the need to accommodate the thousands of immigrants, mainly from Europe and the Americas, who flocked to Israel following the Six Day War. For the first time, Jerusalem became a coveted place of residence for immigrants and even for veteran Israelis. Arabs also started to work in Jewish hotel and service industries, so that the initial unemployment quickly disappeared.

Many white-collar workers and professional men were in a less happy position. While the united municipality and the government services took on all previous employees, including police, teachers, and health personnel, those hitherto employed in banks and law offices found themselves out of work. All the Arab banks closed down, on instructions of their head offices in Amman, and the Arab lawyers decided, to the detriment of their clients, not to appear in Israeli courts. Their former employees found it difficult to find alternative employment, mainly because they lacked a sufficient command of Hebrew for office work, but some went into the retail trade. At first the tourist agents were also badly hit, as they found that their business connections in Jordan and the Arab states were now of little value and it was not always easy to form new tourist connections in Europe and the Americas. However, as part of the "open bridges" policy, the Israeli Government began to permit Arabs from every country to visit their families in Israel or the administered territories (The West Bank of the Jordan River, the Gaza Strip, and the Golan Heights), and thus to maintain their family ties, despite the existing state of war between the Arab States and Israel. This scheme brought in 100,000 such visitors in 1972 alone, a large number of whom must have used the services of the Arab travel agencies.

Industrial development, although not as spectacular as the progress in building, was almost as promising. The floor-space of new industrial premises erected between 1969 and 1972 (again, mainly by the Jerusalem Economic Corporation) exceeded the amount of such construction in the preceding 20 years. Two new textile plants, set up jointly by local and foreign investors, employed together over 500 workers; the majority being Arab women from Jerusalem and the surrounding villages. In addition there are modern printing plants, publishing houses, and science-based industries.[21]

Jerusalem has thus played its full share in the recent upsurge of the Israeli economy, but it has also contributed to the creeping inflation. For the Arab population the changes are obviously far-reaching and have led to a complete change in economic structure and the distribution of incomes; so that in this and other ways a social revolution has quietly taken place. The workers have benefited from full employment and from the higher Israeli wage-rates. As their real wages have risen sharply, despite the higher cost of living and the increased taxation, their standard of living has also risen and they have acquired durable consumer goods which were hitherto entirely out of their reach. Many of them have enjoyed paid vacations for the first time, and they are eligible for Israeli medical insurance and all National Insurance benefits, including allowances for large families.

The Arab landlords and the middle class have also been deeply affected from the social, as well as the purely economic point of view. In the first place, the old Jerusalem families lost their social position overnight. They had played a very active part in politics under Jordanian rule, and thanks to their high standards of education, as well as their family ties, they had occupied leading positions in government service, in the professions and in the economy. They suddenly found themselves living in an alien society, in which they had no wish to play an active part, and even boycotted municipal elections by refusing to vote or to put up candidates of their own. They have also been affected by the steadily rising cost of living, the much heavier Israeli taxation, and last, but not least, by the ever-rising wage-bills for their retainers and laborers, who now have the choice of alternative employment. On the other hand, their properties and the produce of their lands bring them greater incomes. The merchant class has certainly increased their real incomes, despite their complaints of high wage-bills and heavy taxation, which are voiced no less frequently and loudly by their Israeli counterparts. For the first time, however, the Arab employers have suffered strikes for the improvement of working conditions and wages. These have been backed by the Histadrut (the General Federation of Labor), which has helped to organize the Arab workers, in order to improve their lot, and at the same time to protect Jewish labor by preventing unequal conditions of employment.

In a truly unfortunate position, however, are the younger, educated Arab men and women who see no scope for their ambitions, whether political, social, or economic, and who feel themselves cut off from the main foci of Arab culture. This sense of isolation is obviously increased when they compare their own economic position with the achievements of the Arab working class.[22]

The economic boom has also cast its shadow on a certain section of the Jewish population which, rightly or wrongly, feels that it is deliberately being left out in the cold and discriminated against. This group consists, on the whole, of that part of the youth whose parents immigrated to Israel in the early years of the State and who were themselves born in Israel or arrived at an early age. Mass immigration in those years came mainly from other countries in the Middle East or from North Africa, where very large families were the rule and the average standard of living was low. Many of these families were further handicapped by severe physical or mental illness, and of these a large proportion were deliberately settled in and around Jerusalem, due to the proximity of the Hadassah and other hospitals and their auxiliary services. In their countries of origin the breadwinner of the family had usually been a petty trader or artisan and the family had often been partly or wholly dependent on charity. Even the healthy among them had rarely been engaged in heavy manual labor, yet this was the main type of employment available to them at the time. Casual employment meant, in effect, frequent spells of unemployment, and, in any case, a laborer's wage was insufficient to maintain the average family of this type, with some six children of school age or below. Such families consequently became more and more dependent on social assistance, adding their numbers to the numerous "old" clients under care, many of whom had been evacuated from the Old City or from the border areas in the 1948 fighting.

The immigrants were first housed in transit camps. Housing was finally built for them which, though comparable with that of the veteran population at the time, was usually too small for the size of the family. These constant upheavals and changes entirely upset their traditional way of life and in particular broke up the "extended family," on which they had hitherto been able to rely for social and financial support in time of trouble. Completely bewildered, they turned to the already overburdened social welfare authorities, who could do little more to help them than to provide the minimum of material support to stave off starvation. Nor were the education services prepared for such an extraordinary emergency. The children ran wild, lost years of schooling, dropped out of school, and, worst of all, few learned a trade. In the meantime the social and educational services have improved, but the damage has been done. These young men and women, now often with families of their own, are embittered and disgruntled. In the years following the Six Day War, when any healthy person has had no difficulty in finding employment, many of these young people still find it difficult to hold down a job for any length of time. Any work they obtain is obviously uninteresting and relatively poorly paid and, above all, its social status is low. It is clear, moreover, that such jobs will never provide the money required to achieve the standards of housing and other material benefits attained by the better-educated members of any of the Jewish communities in the city, including their own.

This impasse is attributed by many of the youth themselves to communal discrimination in all fields, including housing, education, and employment. Their bitterness increased in the past few years, when they saw that many of the recent immigrants from the Western world and from the Soviet Union quickly found well-paid jobs, in line with their better qualifications. They have also seen that huge new housing estates, with spacious apartments, have been erected for these relatively small families. They have even claimed that the attempts by the municipality to improve the Arab areas of the city by large-scale public works and to beautify the surroundings of the Old City have diverted means which might otherwise have benefited them. In fact, these were relief works instituted soon after the Six Day War, in order to help the large number of Arab workers who became unemployed when Arab building ceased. Their efforts made Jerusalem still more attractive for tourists and thus benefited all groups of the population. More serious was the dismay of these unfortunate young people when faced with the large number of gaily dressed foreign university students who appeared not to be working, and yet were looked after and received accommodation; and the many young tourists, whose presence has now become a feature of the city.

Clearly, only a few of these youths would be able to pull themselves out of the rut by their own efforts, and their reactions were predictable. Some continued to drift, sometimes took to crime, often under the influence of drugs. The more energetic banded together in protest movements to vent their grievances against society, sometimes influenced by similar movements abroad. One group has even adopted the name "Black Panthers," although it is obvious that only a small part of their problems are in any way similar to their U.S. counterparts. They have organized demonstrations, often violent in nature, to draw public attention to their case but, like most other such movements, these have died down as quickly as they appeared. The problems, however, remain, and these past activities in a time of prosperity provide a warning of what might happen during an economic recession. In 1972, 19 per cent of all Jerusalem families were still on welfare, and 16.9 per cent had more than seven children, while 39 per cent of the population were of school age.[23]

Fortunately, the extension and diversification of economic activity in the city has widened its economic basis and made it more stable; but huge tasks still lie ahead. Only an imaginative social policy for all groups of the very mixed population, providing for slum clearance and suitably planned, cheap housing, as well as adequate educational and cultural facilities, will guarantee the happiness and peace of all the communities and bind them together in a common search for a better future.

NOTES AND REFERENCES

1. Jeremias, Joachim, *Jerusalem in the Time of Jesus* (London, 1969).

2. Jeremias, Joachim, "Die Einwohnerzahl Jerusalems zur Zeit Jesu," in: *Abba, Studien zur neutestamentlichen Theologie und Zeitgeschichte* (Göttingen, 1966), pp. 335–341.

3. "Arculf's Narrative about the Holy Places, written by Adamnan." *The Library of the Palestine Pilgrims' Text Society*, III, (London, 1897).

4. Le Strange, Guy, *Palestine under the Moslems* (London, 1890), pp. 84 ff.

5. *Benjamin of Tudela, The Itinerary of*, ed. by Marcus N. Adler (London, 1907), translation, p. 22.

6. Warren, Charles, *Underground Jerusalem* (London, 1876), pp. 82 ff.

7. Robinson, Edward, *Biblical Researches in Palestine, Mount Sinai and Arabia Petraea* (London, 1841), II, pp. 83 ff.

8. Hyamson, Albert N., *The British Consulate in Jerusalem in relation to the Jews of Palestine* (London, 1939–1941), No. 2, p. 2.

9. Finn, James, *Stirring Times or Records from Jerusalem Consular Chronicles*. 2 vols. (London, 1878).

10. Hyamson, *op. cit.*, No. 295 ff., pp. 404 ff.

11. Lindenberg, Paul, *Das Postwesen Palästinas vor der Britischen Besetzung* (Vienna, 1926); Pollack, F. W., *The Turkish Post in the Holy Land* (Tel Aviv, 1962).

12. Grunwald, Kurt, "The Origins of the Jaffa-Jerusalem Railway," in: *Wissenschaft, Wirtschaft und Technik. Studien zur Geschichte, Festschrift W. Treue* (Munich, 1969), pp. 245–254.

13. Grunwald, Kurt, "Jerusalem Banks in the Last Century," *Bulletin of the Jerusalem Chamber of Commerce*, No. 1, (1964), pp. I–V.

14. Warren, Charles, *op. cit.*, pp. 490 ff.

15. Neumann, Bernhard, *Die Heilige Stadt* (Hamburg, 1877), pp. 376 ff.

16. Ashbee, C.R., ed., *Jerusalem 1918–1920 being the Records of the Pro Jerusalem Council during the Period of the British Military Administration* (London, 1921); Ashbee, C.R., ed., *Jerusalem 1920–1922 being the Records of the Pro Jerusalem Council during the first two years of the Civil Administration* (London, 1924).

17. Government of Palestine, *First Census of Industries* (Jerusalem, 1929).

18. Abbadi, I.A., ed., *Jerusalem Economy* (Jerusalem: Jerusalem Chamber of Commerce, n.d., [?1950]).

19. *Encyclopaedia Judaica* (Jerusalem, 1972), Vol. 9, *sub voce* Jerusalem.

20. The Hashemite Kingdom of Jordan, Department of Statistics, *First Census of Population and Housing 18 November 1961. Interim Report No. 7. Jerusalem District* (1963).

21. Michaelis, A.P., "Jerusalem Economy 1967–1972," *Bulletin of the Jerusalem Chamber of Commerce*, No. 5, (1972), pp. VIII–XIII.

22. Kanovsky, Elyahu, *The Economic Impact of the Six Day War. Israel, the Occupied Territories, Egypt, Jordan* (Praeger Special Studies in International Economics and Development [New York, 1970]), pp. 163 ff. *Encyclopaedia Judaica* (Jerusalem, 1972), Vol. 9, *sub voce* Jerusalem.

23. "Jerusalem Issues and Perspectives," Israel Information Services, n.d., n.p., (?Jerusalem, 1972), p. 25.

IV

Jerusalem Under the Mandate

TERENCE PRITTIE

The tragedy of the period of British rule in Palestine, from 1918 to 1948, was that, starting with such high hopes—which seemed entirely justified —it ended in an atmosphere of sour and bitter failure. What was true for Palestine as a whole was very specially true for Jerusalem, the very heart of the Holy Land. For the British Mandate restored Jerusalem, after long centuries, to the status of a capital city with a hugely important role to play as the meeting-place of three great religions, Jewish, Christian and Muslim, and as a half-way point between the civilizations of the Western and oriental worlds. The Balfour Declaration of 1917 had promised the creation of a Jewish "National Home" in Palestine, without prejudice to the rights of existing Muslim and Christian communities in the country. As the seat of Mandatory rule, Jerusalem was to witness the failure of an experiment which was founded on contradictions of policy and, even more, on imperialist power on the wane.

The first British Governor of Jerusalem, Sir Ronald Storrs, was the former "oriental secretary"—synonym for long-service diplomat—of the British administration in Cairo. His remark—"After Jerusalem, there is no promotion"—indicated his supreme satisfaction in his post there. Something of a dilettante, a lover of the oriental way of life, Storrs was in no way depressed by the outward appearance of his heritage. The population of Jerusalem had fallen by roughly a third during the war years, and was faced with a state of near-starvation. Water, as well as food, had to be strictly rationed. In the Old City, which was the heart of

53

Jerusalem, there was next to no sanitation or electricity supply. Only three good roads ran out of the city. There was widespread, often heart-rending poverty.

Jerusalem had been a neglected outpost of the Turkish Empire for four centuries past. The war had been a body-blow to the Jewish community which had constituted an absolute majority in the city since the early 1870s. From 45,000 in 1910 the Jewish population sank to 26,000 in 1919—the result of expulsions, disease, and the ineptitude of wartime Turkish administration. By 1922 it had crept up to 34,000, out of a total of 62,500. Outside Jerusalem, the only cities in Palestine in which there was a Jewish majority were Tel Aviv and Tiberias.

Britain's ability to fulfill the pledge contained in the Balfour Declaration was vitiated by the attitudes of her first two chief administrators in Jerusalem. Storrs had no sympathy with the concept of a Jewish National Home. He liked to quote Dryden's couplet as applicable to the Zionists—"God's pampered people whom, debauched with ease, no King could govern and no God could please"—although there had been little enough ease or pampering in the lives of the Jews for nearly two thousand years past. Hopes were immediately raised when Storrs' military government was replaced by a civil administration under Sir Herbert Samuel in 1920. On a Sabbath soon after his arrival Sir Herbert, himself a Jew, attended the Grand Synagogue in Jerusalem and read from the Book of Isaiah—"Comfort ye, comfort ye my people, saith your God. Speak ye comfortably to Jerusalem and cry unto her, that her warfare is accomplished." Hope and fulfillment reigned briefly; an era of peace seemed to lie ahead.

Sir Herbert, however, was one of those Jews who were most at pains to show no "favoritism" to his co-religionists. He was unimpressed by Jewish complaints at being under-represented in municipal government—with an overall majority of the population, the Jewish community contributed two out of six members of the municipal council and the mayor was, by tradition, a Muslim Arab. Nor were members of his staff noted for friendliness towards the Jewish community. More importantly, Samuel made one of the worst mistakes of the whole period of the Mandate by appointing Hajj Amin el Husseini to be Grant Mufti of Jerusalem. This was in 1921, only a year after Husseini had fled from the country after stirring up civil disorder and had been sentenced in absentia to 15 years imprisonment. Samuel, again, did nothing to prevent the detachment of Trans-Jordania from the rest of Palestine and its erection into an independent emirate—which much later became the Kingdom of Jordan.

By then, the short period of peace in Palestine had already ended. The 1920 Arab-inspired riots resulted in five Jews being killed and 211 wounded. The 1921 riots did not reach Jerusalem but caused destruction and death in other parts of the country. The long chapter of escalating disorders was under way. In 1925 there was an Arab general strike, accompanied by looting. In 1926 there was another strike, ostensibly against the visit to Jerusalem of the French High Commissioner in Syria, de Jouvenel. In 1928 there were disturbances at Jerusalem's Wailing Wall. In August, 1929, there were Arab attacks on Jews all over Palestine; in Jerusalem, Jewish merchants abandoned the Old City and established a new commercial center outside its walls. There were Arab strikes again in 1931 and 1933, and only a short breathing-space of civil peace thereafter.

Like the proverbial pig-in-the-middle, the British authorities were caught in the cross fire of the warring communities. They were bitterly blamed by both Jews and Arabs. The former believed that Britain was failing in her promise to sponsor a National Home and was, in particular, discouraging Jewish immigration and ignoring Jewish civil rights. The Arab view was that Britain was introducing an alien element into Palestine and automatically favored the Jews as "Westerners" and Europeans. Leaving the appointment of the Grand Mufti apart, British administrations suffered from the lack of decisiveness of governments in Westminster, as well as a failure to improvise policy on the spot. Typical of the latter was British non-intervention when the 1928 riots took place, following the introduction at a portion of the Wailing Wall of a Jewish "screen" which was designed, quite simply,to separate men and women. Further riots were provoked by the arrival in the city of Arab mobs recruited from the countryside, whom the British-commanded police observed but failed to disarm. The pig-in-the-middle is sometimes conscious of the weakness of his position.

The chief British failure was to distinguish between Arabs bent on trouble and violence, and Jews who wanted merely to go about their business. As so often with Middle East disputes, the British way was to apportion blame equally, and act too late and with too little authority to keep both sides apart. Lack of firmness was not mistaken for impartiality and was roundly condemned by both Arabs and Jews. Both were to turn increasingly against the British as their frustration and sense of uncertainty mounted. Thus in 1933 Arab riots and demonstrations were more anti-British than anti-Jewish. In 1936 an Arab campaign of violence and intimidation began which was undiscriminating, and continued throughout 1937. British military posts and Jewish transport and communications were the chief targets. In 1938 the Old City lapsed into a state of banditry and sabotage.

By this time the Jewish community had rejected their former policy of "Havlagah," or passive resistance. Watchmen's services had developed into the home guard, or "Haganah." Its extreme activist offshoots, Irgun and the Stern Gang, were to employ the same methods of terror and violence as the Arabs—as they believed, in justified retaliation only. In 1939 Jewish activists carried out their first major act of sabotage, when they set fire to the Department of Migration in protest against the British White Paper limiting Jewish immigration into Palestine. After World War II was over, the Irgun blew up the King David Hotel, killing 91 people, and attacked numbers of other British installations. This was, of course, during the final period of chaos and disaster before the Mandate ended in May, 1948.

Looking back over these politically sterile years, when plans for creating a more democratically aware, mixed Arab-Jewish community were first aired, then dropped because of Arab opposition, and finally abandoned, one is struck by the strange, almost dreamlike purposelessness of the British Administration. It would seem that the Mandate never foresaw any other role for itself than a purely functional one, and found itself toying aimlessly with concrete plans for settling the future of a community which resembled nothing so much as a witches' cauldron. There was never any real drive behind these pragmatically evolved ideas—because in Westminster itself nobody had worked out what was wanted, and because the great mass of the British public remained opaquely disinterested. British democracy has only worked when the average British citizen has felt himself to be involved; where the Middle East was concerned the British citizen, in vulgar parlance, could not have cared less. In accepting the Mandate, Britain had taken on a responsibility which was a leaden dead-weight.

It was inevitable that plans began to be put forward, either by British commissions or by people sponsored by the British Government, for jettisoning an increasingly tiresome burden. The British Colonial Office encouraged the production of a partition plan in 1933, which envisaged "cantonization" of Palestine. A northern canton would have been Jewish, a southern canton Arab, and Jerusalem, Bethlehem, and Nazareth would have been given some form of international administration. The Colonial Office had taken over responsibility for Palestine from the Foreign Office twelve years earlier. This was its first essay at a "solution," and it was proposed through a certain Ahmed Khalidi, of the Government Arab School. The Colonial Office was certainly not prepared at that stage to accept full responsibility on its own account.

Fresh plans for "cantonization" were put forward in 1935 and 1936. As new versions of the Khalidi blueprint were produced, they tended to become more complex, involving divisions and sub-divisions, enclaves and exclaves, areas retained under British administration, and a special entity for Jerusalem which could include an "economic" hinterland, partly agricultural but even stretching down to the Dead Sea with its potash deposits. The thought was thrown out by one British Colonial Office expert, Mr. Archer Cust, that what is today known as the "West Bank" should be attached to Transjordan—today's Kingdom of Jordan. Mr. Cust was ahead of his time; this was in fact to take place after the 1948–1949 Israeli War of Independence.

Much taken with the idea of cantonization, the British High Commissioner, Sir Arthur Wauchope, offered up his own version on September 25, 1936, at a meeting of the Palestine Executive Council. Noted for brawn rather than brains, Wauchope could still draft a good dispatch, full of practical suggestions. These were forwarded to the Royal Commission, led by Lord Peel, which the British Government had appointed to look into the future of Palestine and which came forward with its own proposals in 1937. These were more definite; there should be a small Jewish state, a larger Arab one, and Jerusalem along with Jaffa should be a mandated territory with a special administration of its own. The Woodhead Commission of 1938 (led by Sir John Woodhead) reached similar findings, save that the Jewish state became smaller. Jerusalem, again, would be in mandated territory. But the Woodhead Report was, in effect, a minority view —various members of the Commission disagreed and the document which was eventually produced was one of the most useless in British colonial history. The apathy and listlessness infecting British life at the time was plainly apparent in Britain's administration of Palestine; after 1938 no further serious British effort was made to solve the thorny Palestine Question.

Briefly, the League of Nations—an organization dead in all but name —took a hand in 1941, with a report which favored federation in place of partition. Jerusalem would have been the capital of the Federation, and the Negev Desert—for reasons which were never specified—would have been a special Federal Territory. The League's backroom boys wanted a "strong central government" in Jerusalem; how it could possibly have functioned was not adequately explained. The League's notions, at any rate, died stillborn, for the United Nations Special Committee formed early in 1947 reverted to partition. Its plan, yet again, foresaw Jerusalem belonging neither to a Jewish nor an Arab state, but being in "neutral" territory. This was even more indefinite than the Anglo-American proposals drawn up by Mr. Herbert Morrison and Ambassador Henry Grady a year earlier, placing Jerusalem fairly and squarely under British rule.

It can be seen that most planners regarded Jerusalem as a "special" problem. Because of that, they felt that the city should be detached from the overall framework of a solution of the Palestine Question. Jerusalem has, if you like, a peculiar mythology attached to it; because of its associations as a Holy City, it is generally felt that it cannot function as a normal capital. Yet Jerusalem had been a capital, and exclusively of a Jewish state, during its early history. No Arab state had ever considered making it the capital of anything more than a small, outlying province. It can be seen, too, that other "holy places" were linked in people's minds with Jerusalem; most planners wanted Bethlehem, Bethany, Solomon's Pools and other outlying holy places included in an area of "Greater Jerusalem." UNSCOP (U.N. Special Committee on Palestine) added the proviso that this Greater Jerusalem area should be demilitarized. Behind this was the vague, unexplained thought that Jerusalem should be a "city of peace." Jerusalem, in fact, was continually removed from the context of exact planning; the Christian world, given its disproportionately powerful voice in deciding the city's future, preferred to be imprecise and impractical where Jerusalem was concerned. It is significant that Jerusalem was not even mentioned in the terms of the original British Mandate.

All the many plans for Jerusalem's future came to nothing, and it was to be physically divided as a consequence of the Arab-Israel war of 1948. The Jews of the Old City were to be driven from their Quarter of it, after an almost continuous presence there lasting thousands of years. Barbed-wire fences and machine-gun posts were to be erected through the heart of the so-called "city of peace." The division of Jerusalem, which lasted from 1948 to 1967, was unnatural and in some respects absurd.

It also appeared to represent a final blot on the sad story of British Mandatory rule in the Holy City. Yet British rule, as has happened so often elsewhere, did bring certain benefits in its train. The story of those three decades is not one of total failure.

First, there was steady economic progress under British rule, although it could be argued that this was primarily the work of the growing, vigorous, and increasingly affluent Jewish middle class in the city. Rising living standards brought an increase in the population. By 1922 Jerusalem had roughly recovered to its prewar population of over 60,000. By 1931 there were over 50,000 Jews and a total population of 90,000. When its War of Liberation began, the Jewish population of Jerusalem and its suburbs had doubled to around 100,000 and there were 60,000 Arabs in the city. In Jerusalem, as elsewhere in Palestine, the stimulus of Jewish-organized trade brought new Arab settlers and an increase in the Arab as well as the Jewish population.

A great deal of building went on during the Mandatory period, and it was the first governor, Storrs, who laid down that it should be carried out with all new buildings being faced with mellow Jerusalem stone. This rule was seldom broken, and it resulted in the singular beauty of whole sections of city built at the time. Suburbs sprang up too, notably at Atarot (1920), Neve Yakov (1925), and Ramat Rahel (1926). An airstrip was constructed close to Atarot, at Kalandia. The major new buildings of the era included the Hebrew University, opened by Lord Balfour in 1925, the Hadassah Hospital, the John D. Rockefeller Museum, the Government Printing Press, the American Y.M.C.A., and the first hotel of international standard in Jerusalem, the King David, which was opened in 1930.

Municipal services were vastly improved. The pipeline from Solomon's Pools was relaid in 1919. Then a reservoir was built in the Romema Quarter and the city's water supply was finally safeguarded by the pipeline from Ras al Ayn, in the coastal plain. Electricity supply was likewise developed and was taken over in 1928 by the Jerusalem Electric and Public Services Corporation, operating with both Jewish and British capital. There was steady improvement of roads and sanitary services, new schools were built, and the Palestine Broadcasting Service began operating in 1936, with its transmitting station at Ramallah. The Hebrew daily *Ilaaretz* first appeared in Jerusalem and only moved later to Tel Aviv, and the *Palestine Post* (today *Jerusalem Post*) began publishing in Jerusalem in 1931.

In spite of Arab riots and British lack of sympathy, the Jewish community was able to establish institutions in Jerusalem which provided an organizational basis for a measure of self-rule and, in the long term, for self-government. They included the Chief Rabbinate, the Zionist Executive, the Jewish National Fund, and Keren Hayesod, the settlement aid office, and Vaad Leumi, the national council of the whole Jewish Community in Palestine. These institutions acquired permanence, whereas Arab bodies like the Muslim Supreme Council and the Higher Arab Committee were either dissolved or moved elsewhere. British rule, however laissez-faire and inchoately liberal, at least enabled the Jewish heritage in Jerusalem to be strengthened and consolidated. And British justice, with the Supreme Court as its chief example, established precedents which were not rejected when the State of Israel came into being.

The bitterness of the last three years of the Mandate left a scar on Anglo-Israeli relations. It is a sad thought that the Jewish population joined readily with the British in celebrating VE Day when the war ended. That sense of solidarity which the celebrations demonstrated was to be rudely shaken when the British authorities turned away "illegal" immigrants from Palestine's shores, when Jewish patriots were arrested and executed, and when the men of Irgun and the Stern Gang retaliated fiercely. The virtual blockade of Jerusalem by the Arabs from December 1947 to the end of the Mandatory period in May, 1948, was not the least of the causes of Jewish complaint; for the roads to the coast should, plainly, have been kept open by British military action. Instead, the lightly armed Jewish convoys had to fight their way through to the beleaguered city, and Jewish volunteers had to construct the improvised "Burma" relief road which bypassed the Arab strongholds on the way to the coast. Nor should one forget that it was British officers who led the Arab Legion across the river Jordan into the heart of Jerusalem, forcing out the Jewish population of the Old City and recapturing the Sheikh Jarrah Quarter whose retention would have given virtually total control of Jerusalem to the Jews.

On the other side, one should remember that there were at least four attempts on the life of the British High Commissioner, Sir Harold Macmichael. He bore no ill will, remarking later only that the Balfour Declaration had put British administrators into an impossible position—they had first to satisfy Jewish demands to create a National Home, and then try to give effect to the clause of the Declaration which sought to safeguard the Arab population. As so often in recent colonial history, the British fell between two stools and the manner of their falling was inglorious.

Yet the superstitious, at least, would reckon that the hand of God played its part in the Mandatory period in Jerusalem. Under British rule, the Jews learned to defend themselves. The desperate struggle in 1947–1949 to retain their foothold in Jerusalem was part of the process of the rebirth of a Jewish State. Without the Mandate, the Jews would not have been able to reestablish their identity in this fullest sense of the word. Out of chaos should have come a worthwhile lesson for Britain too; the greater tragedy for her was that the failure in Palestine was not by any means to be the last in the story of an empire's decline and dissolution.

Why did the British fail quite as badly as they did? The Balfour Declaration and its implicit contradictions was only one contributory cause. The anti-Semitism of the British Foreign Secretary, Ernest Bevin, was perhaps another. More important was the British habit of equating one warring faction with another, and not trying to sort out a solution on the basis of justice and common sense. Important, too, was the British failure to understand the deep and fervent Jewish belief in the sanctity of Jerusalem and its place in the Covenant. Britons were apt to remark that Jerusalem was equally holy to the Jewish and Muslim worlds. It was not; technically, it was the third city of the Muslim world, whereas it was wholly unique in Jewish tradition and religious belief.

Finally, it was an era of very particular British indecision—just as the present is one of British indifference to foreign policy issues. Nobody could say that the British did not try to consider a solution of the Palestine problem; the trouble was that British governments failed to trust the commissions which they appointed or to abide by their findings. Any of half a dozen plans might just have worked, had they been given unconditional British official backing. Instead, the last British High Commissioner, Sir Alan Cunningham, folded up the Union Jack and left silently, almost as a thief in the night, for Haifa and his passage home. That, possibly, was the most miserable episode of all in an experiment in colonial rule which had promised so well.

V

The Siege of Jerusalem

MARIE SYRKIN

When the British left Palestine, the new State of Israel faced invasion by seven Arab armies. The extraordinary heroism of Jewish Jerusalem during nearly two months of total siege—from April 22, 1948, when the last convoy and reinforcements reached the beleaguered city, till June 11, the beginning of the first truce—was all the more astonishing because of the unique character of the city. Its 100,000 Jewish inhabitants included scholars, religious zealots, civil servants, and a conglomerate of the various tribes of Israel who had gathered from the old Jewries of Europe and the Orient to pray, study, or simply dwell in the city of peace. This population, ranging from the academic elite of Mt. Scopus to illiterate stone-hewers, was singularly unprepared for the demands of the coming war. The pioneer settlements and young towns of Jewish Palestine had developed a sturdy tradition of self-defense. But over Jerusalem hung the Holy City's peculiar aura, fashioned of its ancient stones and more ancient dreams. Aesthetically, spiritually, the city cast its quiet spell, pervasive as its radiant starlight.

The native youth of Jerusalem, except for the students at the Hebrew University on Mt. Scopus, tended to drift away. Robust, idealistic young men and women went to the settlements; more worldly spirits preferred Tel Aviv. Consequently, Jerusalem was psychologically less prepared for battle than many a small pioneer village. Besides, the population stubbornly believed that Jerusalem would be inviolate.

Despite Arab riots and disturbances, which broke out immediately

after the passage of the U.N. Partition Resolution in November, 1947, the
city was sustained by the faith that its sacred character would safeguard
it from outright attack. As elsewhere in Palestine, the youth of Jerusalem
enlisted for secret military training with the Haganah[1], but because of the
paralyzing conviction that the international community would protect
Jerusalem the boys of Jerusalem were stationed on the borders and in the
heart of the imperiled new state of Israel.

Consequently, the Jews of Jerusalem found themselves unarmed, un-
trained, and, except for a small Haganah unit, virtually helpless in the
face of mounting Arab outrages which began in December, 1947. The
British police, instead of protecting Jews, dismembered Jewish Jerusalem
through the creation of so-called "security zones" and kept arresting any
members of the Haganah they could discover. They also systematically
sought to disarm the Jews. While the Arabs accumulated huge stocks of
arms in the Mosque of Omar, safe from British search as a sanctuary, the
"neutral" British police would confiscate any pocket knife longer than
four inches a Jew might possess.

The policy of the Mandatory Power obviously called for the surrender of Jerusalem to Abdullah;[2] secret steps for defense had to be taken.
Though the Jewish community still nursed the illusion that an international force would intervene in the event of a full-scale Arab invasion, the
citizenry began to create a home guard which in time would involve
every man, woman, and child. Colonel David Shaltiel, Haganah commander of Jerusalem from February to August, and his small staff had the
tough task of welding the city's baffling aggregate of Israel's tribes, each
resolutely clinging to its particular pieties, into a secret fighting force
which would voluntarily accept the stern discipline and shadowy authority of the Haganah. But the miracle took place.

At first, all males between the ages of 17 and 45 had to give 24 hours
of service a week. This was quickly changed to 48 hours. When a general
mobilization was declared in the beginning of May, everybody, men and
women, old and young, was on full-time duty.

Industriously and ingeniously, the home guard strove to barricade the
Jewish quarter with a barbed-wire network, particularly after the Ben
Yehuda Street bombing. Though a little of the scarce barbed wire had
been bought from British soldiers willing to drive a good bargain, most
had to be gotten by other means. In March all available wire around
private homes and factories was confiscated. Even after barriers had been
erected, there was always the likelihood that British tanks would roll in
to destroy the protection the Jews had devised. Only as the British withdrew to their bristling "Bevingrad"[3] in the center of the city, did Haganah defensive measures have a chance to stand.

Even more difficult to endure than the deliberate destruction of the
improvised barriers was the Mandatory regime's relentless hunt for

weapons. At a time when Jewish homes were being bombed, Jewish traffic ambushed, and Jewish civilians attacked without the benefit of government protection or redress, the British still maintained the fiction that they were responsible for the maintenance of order, and that any Jewish attempt at self-defense was lawless.

The morale of every inhabitant of Jerusalem was subjected to a prolonged test. For months before the shelling of the city started on May 15, there was no respite from the terror of violent death. Every day brought fresh casualties. The incidents were of a monotonous regularity: a grenade hurled into the Zion cinema, a bomb thrown at a bus or through a window in Rehavia, a passerby stabbed or shot.

The attack on Jerusalem was directed primarily against the civilian population. Arab snipers, entrenched in the heights overlooking the Jewish quarters, imperiled the movements of every pedestrian. Women and children were not exempt. Not only were they victims of random explosions, but no silhouette was too small for the Arab sharpshooter who was troubled neither by the size nor sex of his target. The home guard drew sacking across the open spaces between houses to foil the aim of Arab sharpshooters, but every day the snipers claimed new victims among housewives who had ventured out to get their food ration, or children who had run out to play.

This indiscriminate, unceasing sniping was periodically punctuated by equally indiscriminate bombings. In addition to constant attacks throughout the city, three major disasters followed each other in swift succession: the dynamiting of the *Palestine Post*[4] on February 2, 1948; of Ben Yehuda Street on February 23; and of the Jewish Agency on March 12. Of these, the Ben Yehuda Street explosion, with 54 dead and over a hundred wounded, was the most frightful. The blast wrecked Ben Yehuda Street from Zion Circus to King George Street, brought down three- and four-story buildings, and maimed and killed entire families asleep in their homes. The assault was carried out by men in British uniform driving British army lorries.

Still another major Arab terrorist outrage was to strike the community: the slaughter of the Hadassah Convoy[5] on April 13, when 67 doctors and nurses were massacred. The mass murder of Palestine's leading physicians and scientists was perhaps the most monstrous result of the vacuum caused by the British abdication of responsibility while denying its assumption by the Jews.

But the Arab attack on the civilian population was to assume an even more ruthless form. The Arabs had a cheap formula for victory: the reduction of the city through famine and thirst. Jerusalem was in a particularly vulnerable situation. Surrounded by thickly populated Arab villages, the 100,000 Jews of Jerusalem were completely isolated from the rest of Jewish Palestine. Their sole link to the coast ran almost entirely through Arab-held territory; Arab strategy concentrated on breaking this link. Neither water, food, arms, nor men could reach Jerusalem if the road to Tel Aviv were cut and the pipeline from Ras El-Ein severed.

The Battle of the Roads began early in December, even though the Mandatory Power had promised to maintain freedom of traffic on the Tel Aviv–Jerusalem highway. The British gave their customary interpretation to this undertaking. Jewish buses would be painstakingly searched for arms while Arab attackers enjoyed a minimum of interference. The disarmed Jews then had the privilege of fighting it out.

This concept of "neutrality" resulted in the repeated massacre of unarmed civilians, forced to ride the gauntlet of Arab bands crouching in the hills. The skeletons of overturned buses, which could long be seen all along the winding Jerusalem highway, testified to the ambushed convoys whose passengers were murdered by Arabs. It was in one such convoy that Hans Beyth, the head of Youth Aliya,[6] was shot down in cold blood on December 28, 1947.

Nevertheless, the contact with Jerusalem had to be maintained. The inadequately protected convoys of Egged buses set out regularly on their perilous journey accompanied by Palmach[7] girls with Sten guns hidden under their skirts. As a rule British soldiers did not search women.

Primitive devices to reinforce the buses came into being. Since Jews had no armored plate, they used metal sheets so thin that the buses were derisively called "sardine tins." To make matters worse, the thin sheet would be wedged between layers of wood to save precious metal. The economy made the buses cumbersome as well as readily penetrable.

Between December and February, these lumbering convoys continued to crawl through the deep gorges and up the steep hills. The effort to reach Jerusalem at whatever cost went on doggedly. In February, however, the Arabs blew up a mountainside between Babel-Wad and Castel, covering a stretch of the road with debris.

This huge natural roadblock meant the virtual isolation of Jerusalem. Neither supplies nor reinforcements could reach the city. The desperate situation of Jerusalem prompted "Operation Nachshon"[8] (named after the Biblical hero who plunged in first when Moses divided the Red Sea) for the purpose of opening the road.

The question of water for Jerusalem was perhaps the most crucial of all. No measure of valor could avail if the Arabs succeeded in their scheme to cut off the water supply. Water had always been a serious problem. Even in the best of times, the Jerusalem householder had to husband water.

As late as 1919 Jerusalem had depended on rain water, stored, as in Biblical times, in cisterns and pools. King Solomon had constructed huge reservoirs for collecting the water of several springs in addition to rain water from the hills, and had built an aqueduct which the Romans later improved. The Turks also laid a pipeline. These had been adequate as long as the population of the city was small and its hygienic standards primitive. With the spurt in population and a rise in its hygienic requirements, modern methods had to be introduced. Since 1880, the city had grown from 20,000 to 100,000; a large proportion of the increase consisted of Westernized householders who insisted on modern plumbing and refused to promenade to the well with pitchers gracefully poised on their heads.

During the Mandate, pipelines were laid which greatly increased Jerusalem's water supply. In 1947, when hostilities broke out, Jerusalem was serviced by three sources, chief of which was Ras El-Ein, near Latrun, 70 kilometers west of Jerusalem. From the east flowed spring water from Ein Farah, and to the south near Bethlehem was the pumping station at Solomon's Pools which had been used as a storage supply since the days of Herod. These three sources supplied Jerusalem with its normal requirement of 2 1/2 to 3 million gallons of water daily. During the dry summer months, temporary shortages might be experienced but these were not serious. There was only one drawback. All three pipelines ran through Arab territory and could be readily cut.

After the outbreak of Arab disturbances, Dr. Zwi Leibowitch, the Jewish Manager of the Water Department of the Jerusalem Municipality, realized under what grave threat the Jewish community labored. The attitude of his British and Arab colleagues in the municipality left no room for the illusion that he could expect cooperation in protecting Jerusalem's water supply. The memory of the 1936 riots, when Arab gangs had tried to sabotage the water plant, was still fresh. As Dr. Leibowitch put it, the knowledge that all three pipelines could be readily tampered with gave him "one big headache." He knew that there was no point in discussing the problem with the British representatives, and even less with the Arab members of the Municipal Council.

The only practical solution was to store an emergency ration within the city itself. Water, like arms, would have to be stored secretly. Fortunately, Jerusalem was a city of cisterns and wells. But while almost all Arab homes had cisterns, in Jewish Jerusalem only old houses were so equipped. New buildings were blessed with modern plumbing. The first step, therefore, was to locate cisterns, most of them long abandoned, wherever they might be, and determine the amount of water they could hold.

A clandestine survey was made in the houses and courtyards of the city. Two thousand old cisterns, with a total capacity of 22 million gallons, were discovered in the Jewish area. On the basis of ten quarts daily per individual the supply could last three months.

The cisterns could not be used in their present condition. Dirty, neglected, they first had to be cleaned and repaired. A volunteer force, working secretly, managed to restore them with great rapidity. The next problem was to fill the cisterns without arousing British or Arab suspicions and precipitating hostile action. By February, Dr. Leibowitch and his volunteers had scored a great coup. The cisterns, some in private homes and others in public institutions had been filled and sealed. An emergency ration of water was now at hand, which could be tapped in the hour of need.

It was obvious that when such an extremity arose, the population would not be able to move about freely. Since the cisterns were located in various parts of the city, some of them not readily accessible, a system had to be devised which would bring water to the consumer. The town was, therefore, divided into districts according to the number of cisterns within the area, so that the water would be equitably apportioned. Each district had its own supervisor who was responsible for the distribution of water. Ration cards for water were drawn up and printed to insure fair distribution. Special carts to transport water were allocated by the Emergency Committee, under the chairmanship of Dr. Dov Joseph, despite the already desperate shortage of transport and gasoline. Fortunately, everyone understood that preparations for the supply and distribution of water rated top priority.

Nothing was left to chance or to last-minute improvisations. Designated individuals knew that they would have the task of transporting the water from street to street. A driver and two attendants were assigned to each cart. Provision was even made for delivering the water inside the dwelling. Each cart was provided with a long rubber hose so that water could be piped from the curb into the hallway in case exceptionally heavy shelling made it impossible for a woman to step out on the sidewalk with her pail.

Another problem was to keep the water in the cisterns from stagnating, and a staff of technicians and bacteriologists, recruited from the Hebrew University, inspected and chlorinated the water to keep it potable.

The plan, worked out in every detail, was ready to go into effect at 24 hour's notice. It was soon to be tested.

On May 8, 1948, the Iraqis cut the pipeline from Ras El-Ein; the other two pipelines were also quickly sabotaged. Despite the critical situation in which 100,000 helpless civilians now found themselves, the British authorities neither repaired the pipe themselves, nor offered protection to Jewish engineers willing to do so. The emergency ration, which if carefully hoarded in the summer heat could last a maximum of 90 days, now had to be tapped.

The first time that the inhabitants of Jerusalem opened their faucets and no water flowed was terrifying despite the fact that the population had been carefully coached in the procedures to be followed. For weeks the citizens had been preparing for just such an eventuality, but now the children had to be told that there was no water for a bath, or even for a drink. On the first day there were a few scattered attempts to break the sealed cisterns. The primitive terror of death by thirst in the desert broke out hysterically in some sections of the city but the panic was rapidly stilled.

By May 9, within the scheduled 24 hours, the water carts began their service to the reassurance of the population, and the bafflement of those who had anticipated swift capitulation. From that day till the end of the siege, the water carts appeared regularly even in the midst of the heaviest shelling. Not a day was missed even though drivers and householders were often struck by flying shells, and more than one life was lost in the effort to give and get water. The citizens of Jerusalem could well add another verse to their prayers: "Blessed are they who bring water."

Siege conditions had prevailed in Jerusalem for months before the actual Arab invasion. Already in February the food supply was precariously low. At the beginning of March the city had food for only three weeks, and the intervals between the supply convoys which succeeded in battling their way through to Jerusalem kept growing longer. As the situation continued to deteriorate, the provisioning of Jerusalem was entrusted to Dov Joseph, Chairman of the Emergency Committee, set up to prepare specifically for a siege. The spare stocks of barley, beans, and flour husbanded in this period were to prove the mainstay of Jerusalem when the city was completely cut off. "Joseph, the Provider," as he came to be known, commandeered trucks and lorries throughout the country, despite the acute need for transport in all parts of the country. Tel Aviv stores denuded their shelves of non-perishable foods to send to Jerusalem. The result of this swift action was that on the morning of March 26 a huge convoy with food reached the city. Each of the trucks bore the Biblical pledge: "If I forget thee, oh Jerusalem." The last convoy to reach Jerusalem arrived on April 20, the eve of Passover, after the Nachshon operation had temporarily opened the road. It carried matzohs and arms.

There were 2,000 infants in Jerusalem who would have perished without milk powder. In the beginning of April, a primitive air field was constructed in the Jewish quarter of Rehavia. A small moth plane, known as "primus," flew regularly between Tel Aviv and Jerusalem, bringing milk powder, drugs, and desperately needed ammunition. There were ten weeks when this tiny plane, shuttling back and forth under constant shelling, was the sole contact between Jerusalem and the rest of Palestine. It was Israel's air-lift.

Hand in hand with the efforts to provide water and food for the threatened siege, measures were being taken to create a military force capable of repelling an invasion. For the reasons already mentioned, the Haganah was particularly weak in Jerusalem.

The number of rifles and grenades on hand was absurdly small. Of heavy arms there was none. In the whole Jerusalem area there were some 500 rifles, 400 Sten guns, 28 machine guns, three heavy machine guns, five three-inch mortars, and 20 two-inch mortars. There was a growing pile of "homemade" ammunition. Only a fraction of the required ammunition could be spared by the central authorities in Tel Aviv, and of that only a small percentage managed to reach Jerusalem before the siege. Nevertheless, secret preparation proceeded within the tightening ring of the Arab armies converging upon the city.

As the day of the Mandate's close approached, British military interference with Jewish defense efforts slackened. It was obvious that they expected the city to fall easy prey to the Arab armies. To protests against the lawlessness engulfing the city still under their tutelage, they had a stock answer: the bland counsel to "evacuate" or surrender. When, on April 30, Palmach and Haganah units succeeded in storming the Arab quarter of Katamon, from which Iraqis had been firing incessantly, the British did not at first intervene. Two days later, in the face of continuing Jewish victories, British military barred further advance.

On May 1, as the British retreated to their "security zones," Colonel Shaltiel ordered a general mobilization of all citizens. This meant the shutting down of schools, shops, offices, factories, and laundries. Only bakeries and food stores remained open for stated intervals daily. Such all-inclusive mobilization had been hotly debated because the measure meant the total paralysis of the city, but the Jewish authorities knew that all available fuel and electric current had to be conserved for the essentials of life and for defense. Every person had to be available for service in the home guard.

The full-scale invasion of the Arab States on May 15 completed the encirclement of Jerusalem. Enemy armies lay entrenched on the hills surrounding the city, and a large Arab force held Latrun, midway between Tel Aviv and Jerusalem, and the seat of the pumping station of the Jerusalem water pipeline.

The agony of Jerusalem had begun. The plan to starve the city into submission and reduce it by thirst appeared to be diabolically easy of execution. All the sections of the young state were reeling under the impact of invaders on every border. Tel Aviv was being bombed by Egyptian planes. Syrian and Iraqi tanks were battering at the settlements in Galilee. Egyptian battalions were marching up the dusty roads of the Negev. The scant arms and men available had to be divided among many fronts, each of which was in a desperate position, each of which was vital to the defense of the country. The same brigades of Jewish youth had to answer the call for help which came from northern settlements in Galilee, from the southern outposts in the Negev, or from the heart of the Sharon. And over the whole land lay the shadow of the besieged citadel.

Two battalions of Palmach, a total of 1,200 men, got through to Jerusalem in the last weeks before May 15, and their presence heartened the population. Together with the locally mobilized Haganah and the home guard capable of bearing arms, Jerusalem now had a force of about 6,000 men of whom 35 per cent had arms. Success in building up this makeshift army under the very nose of the British had been considerable.

It was essential to prevent the British "security zones," including "Bevingrad," from falling into the hands of the Arabs. These zones cut Jerusalem into islands which had to be linked up without delay. The British positions, as well as their large camp, the Allenby Barracks, were seized by the Haganah as soon as the British withdrew. Since most of the New City was already in Jewish hands by May 15, this meant that the Haganah had to concentrate on preventing the juncture of Arab forces coming from the north and the south. In addition, the Haganah was trying desperately to re-establish contact with Mt. Scopus and to break through to the Old City. It failed in the last two objectives but the main thrust against Jerusalem was checked.

On May 15, the columns of the Arab Legion started advancing against the city. Smoke and fire could be seen at the Dead Sea: the cottages of Beth Ha-Aarava (the House in the Desert), directly in the Legion's path, were burning.

Mine fields had been laid on the road to stop the tanks of the Legion. To the surprise of the watchers, the Arab columns, instead of continuing to march against Jerusalem, turned at Jericho and went toward Nablus and Ramallah.

On May 19, however, the Legion made a determined attempt to capture Jerusalem from the north. It succeeded in taking the Sheikh Jarrah quarter, whose defense had been entrusted to the Irgun,[9] this meant the continued isolation of Mt. Scopus.

The whole population rallied to stop the further advance of the Legion. At the first rumble of the tanks on the outskirts of the city, there had been momentary panic. But it was short-lived. Even the old Jews of Orthodox Mea Shearim joined in improvising tank-traps. Before dawn, a crier had awakened them, calling: "Arise and save Jerusalem." Half dressed, they had rushed out into the dark to dig up their streets and pile stones across the roads.

When light broke, the Haganah majestically drove three armored cars (acquired from departing British soldiers for a price) through the streets to encourage the people. The sight of "Jewish tanks" raised drooping spirits.

On May 20, the Arab attacks started. Characteristically, the Arab columns led with tanks instead of infantry. After several Arab tanks had been put out of commission, and two others had been captured, the Arab columns retreated. No further direct onslaught was attempted. To enter a built-up area with mechanized armor was costly, and apparently the Arab command was not prepared to storm the city with infantry.

However, what the attackers failed to achieve on the field of battle they hoped to encompass by terrorizing the population at long distance. The bombardment of Jerusalem started at once. The British-led Arab Legion pounded the Holy City unremittingly with heavy mortars. Day and night shells hailed down on the streets, struck the improvised shelters, or exploded in homes. The shelling was wanton and savage, directed at no military objective, but striking at random through the city.

The Jewish defense units had no heavy artillery with which to silence the Arab guns, but wherever they encountered the invaders in combat, they drove them back. Though the Arab Legion and the Egyptians had ravaged the outlying Jewish settlements of Kfar Etzion and Ramat Rahel, they could not advance into the heart of the city. Instead, the Haganah kept progressively clearing the New City of the enemy. The fortitude of the citizenry was its chief ally.

Between May 15 and June 11, every person who ventured out into the street did so at the peril of his life. The heavy stone houses of Jerusalem afforded some protection, but outside of their walls death struck wantonly. But because the people understood the intent of the enemy, they refused to be cowed. A proud code developed, according to which housewives went at stated hours to collect their ration of bread and beans, and over-age men went to their posts or to work in such institutions as were kept open. The *Palestine Post* was issued daily. Doctors and nurses made their way on foot to the makeshift Hadassah Hospital in the city, no matter how thickly the shells fell. Individuals developed a technique for figuring out the number of minutes between shells in the course of which one could advance along the street. Within one fortnight the civilian casualties exceeded 1,000, a heavier proportion than in the fiercest times of the London blitz.

The shells were not only killing men, women, and children; they were destroying the city. No shrine in Jerusalem was safe from the havoc unleashed by Glubb Pasha's[10] Arab Legion.

At Lake Success, the representatives of Israel kept requesting that action be taken to protect Jerusalem. On May 22, the Truce Commission transmitted to the Security Council an appeal signed by the President of the National Jewish Council, the Mayor of the Jewish area of Jerusalem, and the Chairman of the Jewish Community Council of Jerusalem. The cable read:

> *For past 5 days. . . . Jerusalem, including old city, subjected indiscriminate attacks and nightly shelling by mortars of Arab legion. Among attacked are hospitals, religious and social institutions including Hadassah Medical Center on Mount Scopus and mainly non-combatant citizens. Does world intend remaining silent? Will United*

Nations who expressed fears for peace Holy City permit this to continue? In name Jewish Jerusalem we demand immediate action to patrol Holy City.

The appeal was disregarded. Nevertheless, when the Security Council called for an immediate cease-fire without demanding the withdrawal of the aggressors, the Government of Israel immediately agreed to order a cease-fire on all fronts. The Israeli order to its commanders called for "particularly scrupulous observance" of the cease-fire in Jerusalem.

The Arab States, however, still dreaming of conquering Jerusalem and placing it under Arab rule—a dream openly abetted by the former Mandatory Power—rejected the cease-fire order. Mr. Eban warned the members of the Security Council of the imminent danger of destruction to which Jerusalem was now exposed because of the violent attacks of the forces of Egypt and Transjordan:

> The State of Israel does not shrink from its own defense, and now that its offer of cease-fire has been rejected, it sees its duty shining clearly before it. But it did yield Jerusalem to the International community upon which now devolves the responsibility for protecting that City.
>
> We cannot forbear to ask ourselves again whether the United Nations, even at this late hour, will not take cognizance of the effects on its own authority and prestige if within the next forty-eight hours, or thereafter, the Arab Legion manages to complete the devastation which it hoped to achieve in the last forty-eight hours.

In the New City, the Haganah was holding off the tanks of the invaders and clearing out the Syrians and Iraqis. But within the Old City a handful of old men, women, and children were waging a brave but losing struggle. Some 2,000 Orthodox Jews, living beleaguered among 30,000 Arabs, had been cut off from the New City since February when the Arabs blocked Zion Gate. The British had declined to remove the barrier or let the Haganah do so. As usual they offered to assist in "evacuation." But the venerable inhabitants, their wives and children, clung to the crooked alleys of the ancient city. For 2,000 years Jews had prayed near the Wailing Wall and studied the Law within its precincts. The old men and their families refused to abandon their sanctuaries.

The Mandatory Power finally agreed to permit the passage of food convoys which were carefully checked for arms and "non-residents." No such checks were exercised to curtail the activities of 30,000 Palestinian Arabs as well as Syrians and Iraqis who were openly buying arms and brandishing weapons in the Arab quarter adjoining the Jewish section. Within this armed camp the Jews of the Old City continued their traditional unworldly existence. The broom-maker and the sandal-maker plied their crafts as long as they could. Prayers could no longer be said at the Wailing Wall itself, but the great Hurva Synagogue was still filled with worshippers.

A small Haganah force managed to smuggle its way behind the thick walls to defend the Jewish quarter but it was wholly inadequate. Without ammunition and manpower, the Jewish quarter held out for two weeks against the Arab onslaught unleashed May 15.

The inhabitants of the Old City were actually besieged from February till their surrender May 28, 1949. I heard many strictures about the morale of the "old men" from professional soldiers. The old men, they complained, were not eager to fight. They kept babbling that the outcome was in God's hands. Some even protested that the Messiah would come in his own good time and that secular efforts to hasten his arrival were impious. A few had cared so little as to which national flag hung over the walls that they had been ready to raise the white flag. All that mattered to them was the Torah, which they were willing to study under any Caesar.

"A real ghetto mentality gripped some of these Jews. They said they wanted to live for God, not die for a Jewish State," complained an Israeli commander.

No doubt the charges were partly justified. In the New City, as well as in the Old, there existed clerical extremists who saw in all earthly measures to affect the course of events opposition to God's will. In the darkest days of the siege, a small fanatical sect known as the "Neturei Karta" (Watchers of the City) had demonstrated in the streets of Jerusalem with placards calling for food, modesty in dress, and surrender. The Haganah broke up the procession without establishing the comparative value of the three demands. The more mundane citizens of Jerusalem, despite their troubles, had a chance to smile at the infinite variety of their fellows. As one woman, still haggard from the months of semi-famine, put it to me:

"That's all they had to worry about, modesty in dress! It would have been funny if not for that talk of surrender."

Though it is not hard to understand the vexation of the Haganah commanders or the more worldly civilians, one cannot readily agree with the contemptuous charge of cowardice frequently whispered. On the contrary, anyone who has seen the winding streets, the huddled court-yards, the narrow passages of the Old City, intertwined like a bee-hive and compressed by the Arab quarter directly adjoining, must marvel that any group could have held out in such unlikely surroundings. The age distribution and special mentality of the inhabitants made their endurance even more startling.

In normal times the tumult of the world did not reach the Old City. Even the revolution in speech, which transformed Hebrew, a sacred tongue reserved for prayers and religious study, into a secular language, had not affected many of the inhabitants. One could find children born in Jerusalem who spoke Yiddish to their parents and knew Hebrew only as a holy script. The young people, for the most part, would leave for the pagan world outside the great walls as soon as they were able. The old folks and children remained behind, reinforced periodically by a residue of their own youth or by zealots from the outside. That such a population whose "quaint" manners and exteriors were a standard tourist attraction before 1948, should have displayed the physical stamina to withstand the siege for any period of time is cause for more surprise than reproof.

As early as December, Arabs began to block the gate leading to the Jewish quarter. When they succeeded in blocking Zion Gate completely, the population found itself encircled and cut off from Jewish Jerusalem, which in turn was encircled and cut off from Israel. Permission to leave the Old City and safe convoy were offered by the British but only with a one-way ticket. Those who had affairs to transact in the New City could not get out except on the understanding that they would make no attempt to return home. On the other hand, inhabitants of the Old City who had been caught outside the walls on the day when the gate was blocked could not get back. Mothers separated from small children, who were left helpless and untended in the Old City, begged in vain for permission to re-enter. Finally, after lengthy negotiations with the Haganah, the British allowed special cases to return with the food convoys.

The problem of defense was more crucial than that of food. Before May 14, the Haganah succeeded in smuggling in about 100 men. In addition, one local platoon (consisting of 40 men) had been mobilized. This was the sum total of those who could be expected to fight. All one could ask of the rest was that they endure patiently. As Zion Harush, aged twenty, born in the Old City said charitably when recounting the details of the struggle after his return from imprisonment in Trans-Jordan: "Old people, what did they understand about war?"

Between December and May 14, the aim of the Haganah was to keep the people occupied and to prepare for the attack. Food was rationed and distributed. Work details were organized to prevent demoralization in the virtual imprisonment of the tight Jewish quarter. Some of the men cleaned the narrow streets daily; others baked bread with the available flour. Occasionally it was possible to purchase arms from an Arab acquaintance who came secretly from the nearby Arab market whose stalls were now full of guns as well as the usual knives. The chief defense measure was the digging of underground cellars to unite the houses whose courtyards were in full view of the Arab snipers.

Whenever the British spotted Haganah soldiers they would expel them from the Old City. The Palestine government which had declined to remove the Arab roadblock from Zion Gate kept pressing for the disarmament of the Old City and branding the presence of the Haganah as a "menace to peace." The British professed to believe that the Arabs would not assail unarmed Orthodox Jews, a belief which the Jewish Agency in Jerusalem termed as "dangerous nonsense" taking occasion to remind the Mandatory Government of the Arab massacres of Orthodox communities in the Old City, Safed, and Hebron in the years before the Haganah had undertaken their defense.

The British capture of several Haganah commanders added to the terror of the increasingly terrorized population. One must understand in what a palpable sense the Old City was isolated to appreciate the feelings of the inhabitants. All Israel was an encircled pinpoint in an Arab world, but the individual Israeli saw the world not from the point of view of a map but from within his Jewish environment. Around him, or in back of him, were Jewish villages. Even in besieged Jerusalem, cut off from the rest of the land, there were friendly streets and avenues which stretched around his house for blocks. In the Old City, however, the enemy was on the other side of the wall. One could hear him breathe and move. One could only escape by retreating further back along the alleys to the last Jewish house of a dead-end street.

On April 27, a Hadassah team under the charge of Dr. Abraham Laufer, consisting of three doctors, a nurse, and an orderly, entered the Old City. Medical headquarters were set up in the two-story building of the old Misgav Ladach Hospital, which adjoined a synagogue. Preparations were made, but, as Dr. Laufer put it later, the prognosis was bad and the staff was doing its duty automatically, without real hope that a successful defense could be waged.

Measures to prevent epidemics were taken. Flies were beginning to breed and it was urgent to spread D.D.T. The water in the cisterns was chlorinated. A list of blood donors was compiled. Clean linens were stored, and by May 14, 50 white beds and a frigidaire with plasma stood in readiness.

The Arab attack started promptly. On May 15, the Arab Legion in the Old City began shelling the Jewish quarter. By May 16, the Haganah radioed to the command in the New City: "Our position is desperate; they break through from every side." And another message, sent several hours later read: "Send help—Arabs are attacking Misgav Ladach" (the hospital whose name meant "Help to the Destitute").

From May 16 to May 28, the agonized messages were received sometimes at intervals of 20 minutes. And to the plea for help would come the stern injunction: "Hold out." The exchanges of May 16 were typical of the next ten days. At 4 P.M. the message read: "Arabs have broken into the houses, some want to surrender." At 6 P.M. of the same day: "No munitions whatsoever; send help; we cannot hold out; how long are you going to wait." And the answer came: "Hold out one more hour; help will come."

On May 17, at 11:30 A.M., the message from within the Old City announced: "Arabs inform us that if we don't surrender by 12 P.M. they'll repeat massacre of Kfar Etzion." To which came the calm rejoinder: "The Arabs see our preparations and know that you are not alone. Don't lose your nerve and think of the seriousness of the situation."

The appeals for help included directions as to specific localities to be shelled so as to stem the Arab advance. But the Haganah command outside the Old City was unable to take advantage of the information for fear that their shells would strike a shrine or church. This failure added to the torment of the besieged who could not sympathize with a regard for religious edifices when their lives were at stake.

Despite the threats of surrender, the Old City continued to hold out, but the messages grew more desperate and peremptory: On May 17, at 5:30 P.M. they radioed: "The one hour for which you asked yesterday is over. If you want to find fewer people massacred, let us know when help comes."

And 20 minutes later: "There is no sense repeating 'hold out a little while.' Help should come at once. Where are our forces? The messages from the town are ridiculous. Thirty-six hours have passed since this hour yesterday. Bomb and shell [names position]."

In the meantime, the Haganah in the New City was trying desperately to break through Zion Gate and effect a juncture with the Jewish quarter. Not only were the Jewish forces handicapped by a lack of arms and men at a time when all Jerusalem was under Arab attack, but, in addition, the Arabs knew that the only possible place for a breakthrough was at Zion Gate. The mighty walls of the Old City were too thick to be stormed. This meant that the Jews lost the advantage of surprise. Nightly the Harel Brigade of the Palmach, which had fought its way to Jerusalem, strove to breach the gate, while the Arabs, entrenched behind the shelter of the thick walls, shot at them through loopholes.

As the Arabs captured house after house in the Old City, the Jews converged to the small cluster of buildings formed by the hospital and the synagogue. They overflowed the courtyard, the rooms, and the shelter. Though the courtyard was not safe, they hoped that the Red Cross flag raised over a hospital would protect them. The hope was ill-founded; the Red Cross flag was shot to ribbons almost immediately by snipers from the Haram esh Sharif Mosque.

The burial of the dead presented a special problem. According to religious tradition there may be no interment within the walls of the Holy City. At first bodies were stored in the hospital's mortuary, but this soon overflowed. Neither was cremation permitted. Finally, to avert an epidemic, the religious injunction was waived and a common grave was dug in an open square. To the rigorously observant Jews of the Old City this was profanation.

The children were as brave and lively a lot as elsewhere in Israel. Boys of ten and eleven maintained communication between the posts of the defenders. Little boys with ear-locks and skullcaps carried messages under fire as efficiently as their shortcropped counterparts in the collective settlements.

But whatever the morale of the young and active, the endurance of the old people was being strained to the breaking point. They huddled in the last refuge of the ancient Yohanan Ben Zakai synagogue, where wards for the wounded and dying had been set up after the second story of the hospital proved unsafe. The operating room was lined with holy books; medicines and dressings had to be placed in closets reserved for the scrolls. The medical staff had the unenviable task of ejecting unwounded women and children from the comparative safety of the wards because medical treatment became impossible in the congestion.

The latrines were in the courtyard. When the shelling reached a point where people either had the choice of practically certain death by venturing into the midst of falling shells or defiling the precincts of the synagogue, the limit had been reached. (As always in such conditions, dysentery was rampant.)

Outside the synagogue the hundred-odd fighters tried to push back the Arabs swarming into the streets. They shot from the rooftops in a manner reminiscent of the Warsaw ghetto battles of 1943. The Arabs then began to dynamite the houses, one by one. Like the Jews, the Arabs knew each square foot and hole of the Old City; the few streets of the Jewish quarter were familiar territory.

On the midnight of May 19, the awaited "miracle" took place: the Palmach broke through Zion Gate and brought in reinforcements and munitions.

The Palmach operation had been in the charge of the legendary Uzi, the twenty-five year-old youth who had commanded the forces that captured Castel. His order to the troops had a special ring:

"You stand before the walls of Jerusalem. For 1,870 years no Jew has climbed them. Tonight you will mount them."

It had taken the Legions of Titus three years to break through one of the massive ramparts. Now the commandos of Palmach were trying to blast Zion Gate, through which the main drive had to be made. The *Palestine Post* of May 20 described the operation:

> At exactly 3:15 two young Palmach sappers crawled across the faintly moonlit field to Zion Gate itself, planted their charge, and crawled back under cover of the heavy fire their comrades maintained. This operation is laconically referred to as "withdrawing" but was, in this case at least, a full military operation demanding the utmost training and steel nerves if it is to be carried out without exposing oneself to the enemy's return fire.
>
> Within five minutes, when the smoke had cleared enough for the men

to see that the Arabs' sandbags and towering curtain of barbed wire blocking the gate had been properly blasted away, members of the Palmach, the "Portzim" (those who break through), stormed into the walled area, and within 15 minutes had tossed their grenades into the ring of Arab defense posts opposite them and cleared the path to the Jewish Quarter, 150 meters away. Seconds later, when the wireless operator shouted to us "they're inside," we heard the rumble of an armored car as it toiled up Mt. Zion road, bringing supplies.

At 4:15 A.M. the radio from the Old City flashed the joyous news: "We have met."

But the joy was short-lived. Tanks and cannon were rolling against Jerusalem from Jericho. The Palmach could not be spared. The Portzim had to return after storming the gate. The men they had brought with them were members of the civil guard, brave and willing but with little training and experience. Not many hours later, a radio complained: "The men you sent are inadequate. Send the Palmach; the whole quarter has to be stormed."

At 8:15 P.M. of May 20 came the despairing message: "The Arabs have taken the Nissim Bek Synagogue. We cannot drive them out." And again from the outside came the insistent: "Hold out; reinforcements will arrive in time; be strong."

On the morning of May 21, more arms reached the defenders by parachute but also the news that reinforcements had not succeeded in breaking through again.

On the same day an Arab broadcast was picked up which boasted:

The Jews have renewed their desperate attempts to save the encircled Jews in the Old City by attacking churches . . . all these attacks have been repulsed with heavy casualties. The great synagogue of the Jews has been stormed after clearing out the evil Jews.

The rabbis within the Old City asked for a cease-fire to evacuate the wounded, women, and children. But the question had to be brought before the representatives of U.N.O. who had to negotiate the terms of a truce. This meant further delay.

The monotonous drama continued. At 2 A.M. of the 25th, the news came from the outside: "Our men have broken through," but at 4:15 A.M. it was followed by the announcement, "They did not succeed in establishing a link and we are returning."

The commander in the Old City radioed back at 10 A.M.: "Last night's failure has broken people's spirit altogether. At least parachute munitions." And at 11:30 A.M., came the terse tidings: "No commanders left."

On the morning of May 26, a plane circled the quarter four times and dropped munitions by parachute, but apparently nothing reached the defenders. They radioed: "We have not received anything; send plane again."

At 10 P.M. the Arabs tried an old trick. Through loud-speakers and amplifiers—the words could be heard even in Yemin Moshe, the orthodox quarter outside the walls—they threatened: "Surrender within seven hours because all the Jews of Jerusalem are about to surrender." To the dispirited population, the false information that all Jerusalem was on the verge of surrender was the last blow.

A cease-fire could not be negotiated because one of the Arab demands was that the Haganah abandon Mt. Zion, a position vital to the defense of Jerusalem. Messages from the outside kept heartening the population: "We prepare a large operation for your rescue. Fire only at targets (to save ammunition)."

At 10:20 P.M. the Old City sent out the news: "The Hurva Synagogue has been destroyed; there is no bread."

At 6 A.M. on the 28th, the outside commander was still urging: "Hold out for a day; we shall try again at night," but at 1:30 P.M. he agreed to a cease-fire. The situation was hopeless. The Yohanan Ben Zakai Synagogue was completely encircled, and the munitionless defenders knew that they would be unable to prevent a wholesale massacre of the wounded and civilians once the Arabs broke into this last retreat.

Permission to surrender had been given reluctantly; preparations for the long-promised "large operation" were actually being made for that night because the first onslaught of the Arab armies on New Jerusalem had already been withstood. But from Mt. Zion, the Haganah commanders could see the hopeless case of the surrounded synagogue. The risk of waiting another 24 hours was too great.

When the Legion commanders entered, after the surrender terms which called for the imprisonment of all those of military age and the release of women and children had been signed, they found it hard to believe that this pathetic handful had withstood the Legion for two weeks. Even for the Arabs it was not a glorious victory.

Long lines of women, children, and old men staggered through Zion Gate to the Haganah lines. 294 men of military age, a group which included the surviving soldiers and all civilian males except the very aged, were led into captivity to Amman.

The medical staff remained behind with 120 seriously wounded who were to be evacuated the next day to the Armenian Convent. A guard of the Arab Legion had been provided. Nevertheless, Arab mobs surrounded the hospital, striving to break in and savor the triumph to the full. The rabble could be seen through the windows armed with rifles, daggers, and hand grenades. While looting the surrounding houses, they had set fire to the buildings. Fire began to sweep toward the hospital and the choice seemed to be that of burning to death or being massacred by the mob.

An Arab officer went out to the mob and fired into the air. The mob recoiled and held back till more soldiers of the Arab Legion arrived. According to witnesses, the Arab soldiers bravely carried out the wounded, saving them from being burned to death and protecting them from the excited mob.

The Legion had also protected the sad-eyed lines of civilians who had filed through Zion Gate. "It was quite a job protecting these Jews from the thousands of Arabs, but the Legion saw to it that not a single Jew was harmed on the way out," proudly said the Legion commander to the correspondents who watched the surrender.

The same could not be said for the Jewish quarter. The 27 synagogues had been systematically dynamited by the Arabs and the Jewish homes reduced to rubble. "Like Stalingrad or Berlin" reported the neutral correspondents who had been permitted to roam among the shell-torn remains of houses and of rubbish which were all that was left of homes, religious schools, and ancient sanctuaries.

The devastation was total. It should be noted again that while Arab shells exploded in the narrow streets, close to the holiest shrines of Christendom, no move was made to stop the destruction. For the first time in centuries the site of Solomon's Temple was without Jewish worshippers, but the old Jews who departed bearing whatever Holy Scrolls they could rescue, vowed to return to the "City of David, the Tower of Zion."

In the meantime, within the New City, the military success of the Haganah in holding off the invaders was accompanied by a progressive deterioration in the condition of the civilian population. The water carts delivered water under the heaviest shelling, but the woman who waited for her pail of water never knew if she would leave the doorway alive. Great ingenuity was displayed in regard to the use of the meager daily ration. Charts were distributed to every household indicating how the ten quarts should be utilized. Only two quarts—for drinking and cooking —could be "wasted." The other eight had to be used successively for washing, laundry, and finally for flushing the toilets. Naturally, there was no water for baths or showers in the summer heat, but the supply could be stretched out for 90 days provided that no cisterns were demolished by Arab shells.

The distribution of food had to be controlled with equal rigor. During the last weeks of the siege the population was subsisting on 600 calories daily. Toward the end, the food ration consisted of three slices of bread; by then families had long used up whatever stock of cans or biscuits they might have had at hand at the beginning of the siege. The only fresh greens were dandelion leaves which venturesome women and children picked in the empty lots.

There was no fuel with which to cook the dry beans or the occasional potatoes. Bonfires would have to be made in backyards or gardens with whatever wood could be found; furniture was being burned. But the people scraped together whatever they could and shared.

There was no light. Electric power could be used only for vital necessities such as the public bakeries concentrated in one section of the city so as to simplify the provision of current. To make certain that the population would at least have its bread ration of three slices, the electricians' team, organized by Dov Joseph, developed a special technique for repairing electric lines damaged by the shelling. During the day, they would cruise about the city in an armored truck, looking for broken wires through a peephole and memorizing their exact location. At night they would return and make the repairs in the dark.

This combination of courage and ingenuity was practiced in every department of life. All kinds of devices were used to eke out the waning food supply. A diary kept by the young inmates of a children's home at Motza, a few miles outside Jerusalem, gives a vivid glimpse of life in the besieged city. The children had been evacuated from the exposed suburb where the institution was located in February. As early as April 4, an entry reads:

> We are always hungry soon after meals. We must be very careful with water and use every bit over and over again. We write letters to our friends but get no answers. Every day we go out into the fields and pick wild leaves and thistles which our cook prepares for meals.

After an attack on April 11, the diary notes:

> Today we went out to gather the shrapnel and spent bullets of last night's attack. We have quite a collection of many kinds by now. The mortars and cannon shells are made in England; it says so on them.

And they add: "Women go about gleaning everywhere like Ruth in the Bible."

The day after the invasion, on May 16, we read:

> Heavy shelling, day and night. From the room of our house we can see the smoke of the cannon at Nebi Samuel. We went out to glean wood again today, for we have nothing to eat but beans and we must cook them . . . . Every day we ask our teachers who has advanced, and, thank God, it is usually us. We can no longer play freely outside as shells might strike at any moment and we must be ready to dash into shelter quickly at all times. For the past days we have had hardly any classes because so much time is taken up getting water, fuel, food. So we too feel as though we are full-time soldiers.

The teachers were apparently doing a good job. There is only one break in the resolutely optimistic tone. On May 30 came bad news: "We have just heard of the fall of the Old City! How terrible! How very terrible! The children are all crying."

Happier notes were to be struck later: On June 1, the children rejoice: "Oh what good news! We have just heard of the Burma Road."[11]

Many more shells were to fall before the children could write on September 15, 1948 (after the second truce):

> Our new year of studies has begun again. We go to school in town and we all have new school bags and pencils and notebooks and books. This is the first time we are studying outside our own home because so many teachers are in the army and classes have to double up. We keep thinking about this year which was both hard and great.

Older civilian survivors of the siege relate similar experiences, except that for them the crux of existence revolved around the effort to get to their place of work or service no matter how heavy the rain of shells. After the general mobilization, when all except services essential to life stopped, it became a matter of honor not to sit cowed in the shelters but to move about. Those engaged in a vital service had no choice. Bakers were obliged to report daily to the central bakery no matter what the chance of getting through alive or unmaimed might be. The city had to have its minimal bread ration; if a baker were afflicted with a nervous wife who urged him to skip a day, she was likely to be reminded that he was "mobilized."

And there were less obviously vital activities for which death was risked daily. The editor of the *Palestine Post* and the Jewish manager of Barclay's Bank walked daily from Rehavia to their offices in the center of the city. So did their staffs. Each person knew that fear was progressive and contagious and that the fight against panic had to be won by each individual daily.

A technique reminiscent of battlefields was worked out by those who made their way along the streets. People learned to distinguish the sounds of the shells and to estimate the intervals between their falls. In the intervals of a minute or two they would dart along the street and rush into a hallway just before the next shell. By this process a distance normally covered in ten minutes might take over an hour, depending on the intensity of the bombardment, but usually the destination would be reached, though a number of casualties were inevitable.

The housewife going for her bread ration; the Yemenite charwoman going to help her mistress; the fourteen-year-old boys reporting for work on fortifications alike become expert students of the traffic signals provided by the shells.

Every survivor of the siege has his favorite "miraculous escape" story: the shell that missed by a hair's breadth as one lay in bed, or sat near a window, or darted into a hallway "just in time." And each has his favorite tale of civilian valor.

A professor's wife, herself not Orthodox, told me how heartened she would be on Saturdays to see her pious old neighbor, dressed up in his Sabbath best, setting out for synagogue as usual, walking unhurriedly to the morning service no matter how fierce the bombardment. But nerves grew tauter and bodies thinner.

The dead could not be buried save at the risk of further death. Religious law forbade cremation (the dead must rise whole on Mt. Zion at the trumpet call of the Last Judgment). In obedience to the religious injunction that graveyards must not be located within the city, funeral processions had to brave Arab attack on the way to the cemetery on Mt. Zion. Amid the mounting casualties the question of the unburied dead became as oppressive as that of the living.

The Arabs waited for the moment when thirst, hunger, and unremitting shelling would force the population to surrender; but the unspectacular heroism of plain men and women proved as unpredictable as the spectacular feats of the Haganah. However, the Jewish military authorities knew that the flour had been used up, and that there were no more munitions for the homemade "Davidkas," the improvised mortars of the army.

There was a period when the men and women of Jerusalem believed that they had been forgotten by the rest of embattled Israel. As the weeks drew on and neither food, water, nor reinforcements reached the city, the sense of abandonment grew. But it was in these weeks that the attempt to break through to Jerusalem was assuming its most dramatic form. A way to Jerusalem was being hewn through the rocky hills. The Burma Road was a neat chart. It was born, foot by foot, and remained to the last a living thing.

Through "Operation Nachshon" much of the Tel Aviv–Jerusalem highway had already been cleared. Only Latrun remained in the center blocking traffic; or waiting to be by-passed.

On the night of May 5, three Palmach scouts set out on foot from Jerusalem to discover whether they could link up with the nearest Jewish outpost from the Tel Aviv side. They threaded their way through the Judaean hills following ancient foot-tracks and camel paths which usually followed natural contours and utilized easier grades.

The scouts returned with the message that a road suitable for jeeps might be made along the wadis and camel paths. The very next night a small convoy of jeeps carrying desperately needed flour and munitions began to make its way up the dirt track traced by the scouts. On some stretches the jeeps had to be carried. One incline was too steep to be negotiated by any type of vehicle, and even the small jeeps had to be hauled up by means of a windlass. Since the road was within plain view of Latrun and within easy range of Arab shells, all construction had to take place at night. In the meantime, heavy engagements, under whose cover the building of the alternative road could proceed, were fought.

The construction of this road and its use proceeded simultaneously. From both the Jerusalem and Tel Aviv ends the work went on, and while the gap narrowed, the jeeps continued to clamber around the hair-pin turns and up the steep rock mountainside. Where jeeps could not go, donkeys went. On one precipitous incline soldiers and civilian volunteers would trudge up the three-quarter-mile stretch carrying sacks of flour and guns on their backs. At the foot of the hill, the sacks would be piled into trucks which had been sent from Jerusalem.

The road grew like a living organism advancing tenaciously forward in the wake of the men, mules, and jeeps. Finally, by the beginning of June, the sixteen kilometers of this so-called "Burma Road" were completed. A truck from Tel Aviv could reach Jerusalem.

While the road was being built, a new pipeline was being laid alongside it. Those jolting for the first time on this road had the added thrill of seeing the new pipeline which drew its water from Hulda. Soon water would again flow from the taps of Jerusalem.

With the coming of the first truce, the worst was over.

There are moments whose significance becomes apparent only in retrospect. During the siege of Jerusalem each individual knew that he stood at a climactic point in Jewish history. Each was prepared to concede that he, the individual, might be struck by a splinter, or that his son would be killed in battle, but the City would live. Men have died for cities before, but this was far beyond patriotism. For many, Jerusalem was not the city of their birth or childhood. A large percentage of the population consisted of immigrants. Yet both for the girl recently arrived from Yemen and for the veteran it was equally the meeting point of the prophetic past and the Messianic future—the city holy and beloved.

For centuries, the name *Yerushalaim* had been pronounced by Jews with a special reverence. Since the siege both a new awe and intimacy had been added.

"Those were great days," the survivors said, and one got the impression that to have been in Jerusalem during the dreadful time had been the crown of life. In Israel's aristocracy of valor, the highest rank was awarded to those who held Zion itself.

NOTES AND REFERENCES

1. ("Defense") Palestinian Jewry's underground defense organization, founded in 1920, which functioned, under the Jewish Agency's jurisdiction, until the creation of the Israeli Army on May 25, 1948.

2. King of Transjordan and grandfather of King Hussein.

3. One of a number of British "security zones" to which the Mandatory authority's forces retreated while engaged in liquidating the Mandatory administration prior to their departure from Palestine. Palestinian Jews called these zones "Bevingrads" in ironic reference to the role of British Foreign Secretary Ernest Bevin.

4. Jerusalem's English language daily, today called *The Jerusalem Post.*

5. On their way to the Hadassah Medical Center on Mt. Scopus.

6. Child Rescue Program, sponsored by the Jewish Agency.

7. *Plugot Mahatz* ("shock companies")—the commando units of Haganah.

8. Launched by the Haganah during the first two weeks of April.

9. Irgun Tz'vai L'umi—an independent military underground Palestinian Jewish extremist organization created in 1931.

10. Brigadier John Glubb, the British Commander of the Arab Legion.

11. Reminiscent of the road constructed by the retreating British in Burma during World War II.

VI

The Divided City: 1948–1967

GABRIEL PADON

In 1947, Jerusalem was a flourishing city of 165,000 inhabitants, of whom 100,000 were Jews and 65,000 were Muslims and Christians. The city was the political, administrative, religious, and cultural center of British Mandatory Palestine. The majority of its inhabitants derived their livelihood, directly or indirectly, from the presence there of the central government offices, the central institutions of both the Arab and Jewish communities, the country's central institutions of higher learning, and the Holy Places and historic sites, which drew pilgrims and tourists.

By the end of May, 1948, the city was ravaged by the intense fighting which had been initiated by the Arabs and which caused heavy casualties and suffering on both sides. The economy was at a virtual standstill. The British, before leaving on May 14, endeavored to create chaos by simply dissolving the entire administrative machinery. The central Jewish institutions moved to Tel Aviv, which became, temporarily, the capital of the State of Israel, while the Palestine Arab Higher Committee and many leading Arab families fled to the safety of neighboring countries, thus dealing a heavy blow to the morale of Arab Jerusalem and generating a substantial Arab exodus from the City. The institutions of higher learning ceased to function, and the flow of pilgrims and visitors dried up.

The plan for the internationalization of Jerusalem, provided for in the U.N. General Assembly's partition resolution on November 29, 1947, was overtaken by the course of events in the city and in Palestine in general, where newly created factors radically transformed the situation. In 1947

Jerusalem was a single administrative and economic entity; by May, 1948, the city had become divided into two units, each with its own public services, economic life, and political and military authorities. While the speed of this physical transformation had many far-reaching consequences, the psychological impact was perhaps of even greater importance. Neither the Arab nor the Jewish inhabitants of Jerusalem had ever favored political separation from the rest of the country, but in November, 1947, most of the Jewish population had been prepared, albeit reluctantly, to accept the international regime for the city as the price for the establishment of a Jewish state and of the peaceful implementation of the partition plan. The Arabs had actively opposed internationalization and the very concept of partitioning Palestine under any circumstance. By the summer of 1948, after the bitter experience of war and hardship, during which the United Nations had been conspicuously unable to exercise the authority which it had formally assumed, all faith in internationalization had been lost.

When, on June 11, 1948, the four-weeks truce ordered by the Security Council came into force, the frontlines in Jerusalem had been stabilized as a result of a military stalemate. The Jewish forces had succeeded in consolidating a continuous zone in the city by capturing a number of Arab quarters and had been able to withstand heavy artillery shelling and the assaults of Arab irregulars and, later, of the Arab Legion and the Egyptian forces. The Arabs, on the other hand, had succeeded in capturing the Jewish Quarter of the Old City and a number of Jewish villages north and south of Jerusalem and had repulsed Jewish attempts to break into the Old City and to link up with the besieged enclave on Mt. Scopus. The major Arab military achievement at that time was the imposition of an effective siege on Jewish Jerusalem by cutting off its only road link to Israel. Repeated Israeli attempts to lift the siege by capturing the fortress of Latrun (guarding the road west of the city) all ended in failure, but a few days before the truce came into effect they succeeded in establishing a lifeline to the beleaguered city by constructing a rough track (named the "Burma Road") through the hills south of Latrun.

During the truce, the U.N. Mediator, Count Folke Bernadotte, negotiated with both parties for the demilitarization of the city but without success, but achieved a limited agreement on the Mt. Scopus area. This was later incorporated into the Israel-Jordan Armistice Agreement.[1]

Hostilities were resumed in Palestine on July 8, 1948, when the Arab states, sure of their imminent victory, refused to comply with the Security Council and the Mediator's appeals for the prolongation of the truce. During the short period of fighting which preceded the second truce (which was imposed by the Security Council for an indefinite period from July 18) the New City was again subjected to indiscriminate Arab artillery shelling and, for the first time in its history, to an air-raid.

When the second truce came into force the military situation in Jerusalem had undergone no important change. The military stalemate which had crystallized by the beginning of the first truce remained unchanged and became the basis of the territorial partition of the City, endorsed by the Israel-Jordan Armistice Agreement.

This agreement, signed at Rhodes on April 3, 1949, under U.N. auspices, was designed to be of temporary duration and according to Article 12 was to ". . . remain in force until a peaceful settlement is achieved."[2] In the absence of a peace treaty between Israel and Jordan the Armistice Agreement in fact sanctioned the partition of the City in accordance with the lines established at the end of the fighting and came to govern the relations between these two states until June 5, 1967.

Two separate cities, existing side by side, thus came into being.

The demarcation lines which, for 18 years, were to be the borders between the two Jerusalems were defined by Article 5 of the Agreement, on the basis of the cease-fire agreement for the Jerusalem area signed by the two parties on November 30, 1948. Israel thereby held the greater part of the New City while the Jordanian sector included the Old City, the Northern suburbs of Sheikh Jarrah, the American Colony, Bab Zahara, and Wadi el Joz and parts of the Musrara and Deir Abu Tor quarters. There were two demilitarized zones, (1) around Government House—the seat of the U.N. Truce Supervision Organization—and (2) the Mt. Scopus area, where the Hebrew University and the Hadassah Hospital formed an Israeli enclave in Jordanian territory only a mile from the demarcation line.

In order to alleviate the inconveniences of this arbitrary partition, Article 8 of the Armistice Agreement provided for the creation of a Special Commission, composed of two representatives of each side, to work out a satisfactory modus vivendi on such matters as free access to the Holy Places and free traffic on essential roads, but this Committee never functioned properly.

In 1950, following a number of sterile meetings, Israel complained to the Security Council about Jordan's obstructive tactics in implementing Article 8 of the Armistice Agreement. The Commission ceased to meet by the end of November, 1950.

The only provision of Article 8 actually implemented was the resumption of the railroad operations to Jerusalem, and this was achieved by the Israel-Jordan Mixed Armistice Commission in an agreement concluded on April 25, 1949.[3]

Notwithstanding the many differences between Israel and Jordan, both states were in tacit agreement in opposing any plan for the internationalization of the City, and both were determined to consolidate their positions in their respective sectors.

The U.N., nevertheless, was unwilling to recognize the fundamental changes which had occurred since November, 1947, and the General Assembly reiterated the principal of internationalizing the City at its third and fourth sessions. Attempts to carry out its resolutions proved fruitless, however, owing to the consistent opposition of the two states involved and the reluctance of the Great Powers to compromise their relations with them or to tamper with an explosive situation for the sake of giving effect to U.N. resolutions.

Jerusalem's religious significance and symbolic character had prompted the Christian world to call for its internationalization but these were also the main factors which prompted the State of Israel and the Hashemite Kingdom of Jordan to hold on to their two sectors. Political, economic, and strategic considerations were very much present in the Israeli and Jordanian leaders' minds. The fact that these two states effectively controlled the City lent great weight to their arguments, and the Great Powers' reluctance to enforce internationalization enabled the two states to carry out their policies with relative success. Both Israel and Jordan strove to impress upon the world that Christian religious interests in Jerusalem were adequately protected and that, consequently, there was no essential conflict between their control of the City and those interests.

THE ISRAELI POSITION AND POLICIES

A brief recapitulation of the events leading to the division of the City will serve to explain the Israeli and Jordanian positions.

The prospect that Palestine would be partitioned and that Jerusalem would be excluded from the Jewish State had, since 1937, been a feature in the discussions on the future of the area as a whole. The Jewish reaction had been extremely hostile to excluding Jerusalem and was one of the main reasons for the *yishuv*'s (The Jewish Community in Palestine) refusal to accept the partition proposals made by the Palestine Royal Commission in 1937, for (as even the Archbishop of Canterbury had realized at the time) a Jewish State without Zion was but the parody of an ideal.[4]

The tragedy of European Jewry during the Hitler era and the plight of the displaced Jews emerging from the former death camps at the end of World War II and prevented from immigrating to Palestine by the restrictive British policies, impelled the Jews of Palestine and the Zionist Organization to press for the immediate establishment of a Jewish State. To the Zionist leadership, the urgency of this need justified their acceptance of partition and it is in this context that Jewish support for the Partition Plan proposed by the U.N. Special Committee on Palestine should be considered.

When this partition plan was discussed at the Second Session of the U.N. General Assembly, the representatives of the Jewish Agency for Palestine (backed by the almost unanimous support of the Palestinian Jews) severely criticized those provisions that called for the exclusion of Jerusalem from the Jewish State.[5] Realizing, however, that the adoption of partition by the General Assembly depended on the affirmative vote of many states who felt that the internationalization of Jerusalem was indispensable, the Jewish representatives accepted the Partition Plan in its entirety.

Their acceptance was nevertheless, qualified, and, in general, the idea of excluding Jerusalem from the Jewish State was regarded by the *yishuv* as a "sacrifice for the sake of peace and international understanding."[6] The Jews believed that this would contribute to the peaceful settlement of the Palestine problem, or at the least, that the U.N. would protect Jerusalem in the event of a military conflict. Also, the international regime proposed for Jerusalem in Resolution 181 (II) was not envisaged as permanent. It was to be reviewed by the Trusteeship Council after ten years, following a referendum in the City. Since the population of Jerusalem, in 1947, consisted of 100,000 Jews and 65,000 Arabs, the Jewish leaders were confident of the outcome of such a referendum. Thus the exclusion of Jerusalem was regarded as a necessary evil which would in any event be only temporary.[7]

After the adoption of Resolution 181 (II) by the General Assembly, on November 29, 1947, the Jewish Agency in Palestine (Palestinian Jewry's unofficial government until the creation of the State of Israel) cooperated closely with all the various U.N. bodies in the task of implementing the partition resolution.

The Jewish Agency continually appealed for the enforcement of the resolution and especially for international action for the protection of Jerusalem, but the U.N. made no serious effort to assume control of the City or to protect its inhabitants, and Jewish Jerusalem was thus left to fight it out or surrender. The Jews chose to fight and, during the last weeks of the British Mandate, defeated the main body of Arab irregular troops in the southern part of the City.

The ordeal of the siege, its liberation by the Israel Army and the absence of concrete international efforts to protect Jerusalem all had a tremendous impact on Israeli public opinion. In Israeli eyes, the sacrifice they had made in accepting the internationalization of Jerusalem had been in vain, since the U.N. had proved unable and unwilling to provide even a minimal degree of protection for the City which it had undertaken to administer. Jewish opinion no longer saw any justification for accepting the sacrifice of Jerusalem, and pressed for the incorporation of the City into the State of Israel.[8] The hardening of the Israeli position on Jerusalem occurred after the publication of Count Bernadotte's proposals, on June 27, 1948, in which he advocated the inclusion of the whole City into the Arab State. This plan shocked even moderate Jewish opinion. The Israel Government rejected it in the most emphatic terms.[9] It was the decisive factor in Israel's decision to strive for the incorporation of the city into the State of Israel.

On August 2, the Provisional Government of Israel issued two proclamations. The first declared that Jewish Jerusalem was "Israel occupied territory," and extended Israeli legislation to it. The second appointed Dr. Dov Joseph as Military Governor.[10] The first proclamation noted that the U.N. had failed to provide a legal framework for Jerusalem and that therefore the void was being filled to regularize the situation in terms of international law (it was, therefore, made retroactive to May 15, 1948).

In fact, the situation in Jewish Jerusalem needed regularization. The Jerusalem Committee, which had governed the City since the termination of the Mandate, had no proper legal authority. It had been constituted in December, 1947, by the Jewish Agency and other Jewish institutions in order to administer the City pending the establishment of the international regime, and it maintained its authority on a voluntary rather than on a legal basis.

During the last phases of the war, Israeli forces had captured territory in excess of the boundaries laid down in the partition resolution, and the Provisional Government was determined to hold on to these territories. Therefore Israel concentrated her efforts at the Third Session of the General Assembly on defeating the territorial revision proposed in the Mediator's Progress Report, but in pursuit of this aim her diplomats found that they had a most delicate case to defend. They had to invoke the partition resolution as the basis of their claim to the Negev (which was now proposed as part of the territory of the Arab State) but argued that Resolution 181 (II), which had envisaged a peaceful settlement, had been superseded and morally invalidated by the war waged by the Arab States.

The Israeli delegation rejected the Mediator's suggestions for an international regime for Jerusalem. In view of the experience of the war, they asserted, the New City must become an integral part of Israel. International religious interests could be adequately safeguarded by the internationalization of the Arab-occupied Old City, which contained almost all the Holy Places.[11] The Israeli Government maintained this position until spring of 1949, when it was superseded by the principle of functional internationalization.

The main outcome of the debates of the General Assembly's Third Session, (Resolution 194 [III]) afforded partial satisfaction to Israel, since the territorial clauses of the Mediator's plan were not endorsed. But the Israeli thesis on Jerusalem was not accepted. Instead, the General Assembly recommended the establishment of a permanent international regime for the whole City.

The Israeli Government then took certain practical measures to consolidate its position in Jerusalem without, however, formally proclaiming its annexation. The City's Jewish population participated in the new State's first general elections on January 25, 1949. On February 2, the new Israeli Government declared that Jerusalem was no longer considered "occupied territory" and that the military government was abolished. Preparations were made to move government offices from Tel Aviv to Jerusalem.

This policy suffered a setback when all foreign diplomats (with the exception of the Soviet Union, Poland, and the Netherlands) refused to attend the Knesset's inaugural session and Dr. Chaim Weizmann's investiture as Israel's President in Jerusalem on February 14 and 17, on the grounds that their attendance would imply recognition of Israel's claim to the City.[12]

The government nevertheless continued to implement its policy. "Jerusalem is in the heart of the Jewish people, and we would have made an historic mistake had we held the first session of the Knesset and the election of the first President elsewhere" contended the Foreign Minister, Moshe Sharett. Israel understood and respected the concern of other nations over the Holy Places, he said, but since all these were situated in the Old City, internationalization should be limited to that part of Jerusalem.[13]

In the spring of 1949, Israel withdrew its proposal for the establishment of an international regime confined to the Old City and initiated a new approach—that an international regime be limited to the Holy Places only. This remained Israel Government policy.

There was an exhaustive debate on Jerusalem at the Fourth Session of the General Assembly. The Israeli delegates (Moshe Sharett and Abba Eban) rejected the Palestine Conciliation Commission's proposal as "anachronistic and unacceptable"[14] and introduced a counter-proposal based on the principle of functional internationalization. This plan, which was not fully discussed by the General Assembly, was presented in the form of a draft resolution and called for a formal agreement between the U.N and Israel whereby the U.N. would assume responsibility for the supervision of the Holy Places in the Israeli sector of the City.[15] Sharett was prepared to approve an alternate scheme by Sweden and the Netherlands which, he felt, would uphold U.N. authority over the Holy Places but ". . . not at the expense of the established government, but with its full and willing support."[16]

Israel was charged with duplicity, illegal occupation, and even aggression. The Israeli delegates argued that the integration of Jewish Jerusalem into the State of Israel was beyond reproach, since Israel had been compelled to come to the rescue of the City when the U.N. failed to do so.

On December 5, 1949, Israel's Prime Minister told the Knesset that

Israel would not give up Jerusalem of her own free will. Following the General Assembly's adoption of Resolution 303 (IV) Mr. Ben-Gurion told the Knesset:

> . . . We respect, and shall continue to respect the wishes of all those states which are concerned for the freedom of worship and the free access to the Holy Places and which seek to safeguard the existing rights in those Holy Places and the religious buildings in Jerusalem. Our undertaking to preserve these rights remains in force and we shall gladly and willingly carry it out even though we cannot lend ourselves to take part in the enforced separation of Jerusalem, which violates without need or reason, the historic and natural rights of a people which dwells in Zion.

He announced the transfer of the Government and its offices to Jerusalem, and suggested that the Knesset do so too.

The move to Jerusalem was followed, on January 23, 1950, by the Knesset's adoption of a motion proclaiming that "Jerusalem was and had always been the capital of Israel."[18]

The government nevertheless continued to explore the possibilities of a compromise solution with a view to obtaining the revision of Resolution 303 (IV) at the next session of the General Assembly. It offered a degree of limited cooperation to the Trusteeship Council, despite the fact that the Council was still engaged in drafting a Statute on Jerusalem which was entirely unacceptable to Israel. Israel's counter proposal, based on the principle of functional internationalization, was that effective U.N. control should be limited to the Holy Places, and that the contractual agreement proposed at the Fourth Session should be replaced by a statute to be adopted by the General Assembly.[19]

At the Fifth Session a similar proposal by Sweden in amended form was accepted by both Israel and Jordan, but it was never put to a vote.

The deadlock reached on the Jerusalem issue at the Fifth Session induced the Israel Government to avoid further discussion at the U.N. The question of the City's future status remained in the background and the Israel Government was content to leave it there.

Meanwhile, the Ministry of Religious Affairs had established good relations with the Christian communities. The local Israeli authorities, in cooperation with Jordan, had organized an efficient procedure for the free passage of pilgrims and religious personnel between the two sectors, and the Church hierarchies declared they were satisfied with their treatment inside Israel.[20]

The Jerusalem issue surfaced again on July 12, 1953, when the Foreign Ministry was transferred from Tel Aviv to Jerusalem. Its location in Tel Aviv was inconvenient and had been vehemently criticized by the Opposition and the Israeli press. In what appeared to be a concerted action, the U.S., Britain, France, Italy, Turkey, and Australia had protested against the proposed move on May 4, 1952, but the Israel Government now stood firmly by its decision.

The major Western governments announced that their embassies would remain in Tel Aviv, declared a boycott of the Foreign Ministry, and banned all visits by diplomats to Jerusalem for any official or social functions.[21] The countries of the Soviet bloc made no comment on the move and did not participate in the boycott, but they did not transfer their diplomatic missions to Jerusalem.

On June 17, 1953, in a major foreign affairs address to the Knesset, Mr. Sharett, the Foreign Minister, explained that the transfer of his office was an administrative move essential to the proper functioning of the government. He pointed out that Israel provided free access to the Holy Places while Jordan barred access to Jews. He said that the only satisfactory solution for the City's security would come from a definite and comprehensive peace settlement between Israel and Jordan.[22]

The Israel Government was to abide by this policy until the war of June, 1967. Israel stood firm on Jerusalem's status as its capital. All official functions were held in the City. The diplomatic corps relaxed its boycott over the years and a flexible modus vivendi was achieved. Many governments came to recognize Jerusalem as Israel's capital, and by 1967 40 percent of the diplomatic missions were located there.

As has been pointed out, all the major Jewish, Christian, and Muslim shrines, including all those to which the Status Quo of 1852 applied, were situated in the Jordanian-controlled part of the City. The only Christian shrine in Israeli Jerusalem was the Coenaculum, situated on Mt. Zion in the same complex of buildings as the Tomb of David, which is venerated by Jews and Muslims. The sanctity of all Christian shrines in Israel was scrupulously observed, and the position of Christians in the Coenaculum was even improved. They gained free access to this site at all times and were free to pray there, whereas previously the Muslim guardians of the Nebi Daud Family Waqf (which belonged to the Dajani family) had allowed Christians to visit the Coenaculum only occasionally and for substantial payments, but had forbidden them to hold services there or even to kneel in private prayer.[23]

Israel never formally withdrew her proposal for functional internationalization, which has lapsed with the passage of time.

No complaints were ever raised by the churches against Israel's treatment of the Holy Places under her control. In June, 1967, even the Superior General of the Franciscan Order charged with guarding the Catholic interest in the Holy Places declared himself satisfied after 19 years experience of Israeli rule.[24]

Jews and Israeli Muslims were denied access to their Holy Places in the Old City. This situation, Israel believed, could only be remedied by convincing Jordan to honor her commitments under Article 8 of the Armistice Agreement, but all Israeli endeavors to this end were in vain.

The overwhelming majority of Israeli public opinion (and for that matter, Jewish opinion in general) strongly supported the government's stand. The only Jewish pronouncement in favor of territorial internationalization came from the leaders of the Neturei Karta in 1948. This sect had always rejected Zionism on the grounds that the establishment of the State of Israel was a profanation of Judaism and that Israel's redemption can only come about by Divine Act. They refused to acknowledge Israel's existence and sent a number of appeals to the U.N. to internationalize Jerusalem, where their community resided.

Israeli Jerusalem developed tremendously during the years of the city's division, keeping pace with the growth of the country as a whole. The number of its inhabitants, which had fallen to 84,000 by the end of 1948 due to the war and the resulting loss of its central role in the country's life, began to augment quickly in 1950 when Jerusalem once more became the capital and considerable numbers of immigrants settled there. The population increase was about 40,000 between 1948 and 1952. On the eve of the reunification of the city it was 196,000.

A complex of new residential quarters was built to house immigrants, government officials, and other newcomers to Jerusalem. New government offices, the Knesset building, cultural, religious, and public institutions were constructed and new parks were laid out. When it became clear that the Jordanians would not permit the use of the institutions on Mt. Scopus, a complete new university campus was built in the suburb of Givat Ram, and a new Hadassah medical center, including a faculty of medicine, was constructed in Ein Karem. Many new hotels were built and light industry was developed, making Jerusalem once again the political, administrative, and spiritual center of the country.

THE JORDANIAN POSITION AND POLICIES

Jordan's categorical opposition to any form of international control over Jerusalem can best be understood in the context of the plans and ambitions of her first ruler, King Abdullah. Emir—by the grace of Britain—of the backward and dismal territory of Transjordan (which had been truncated from Mandatory Palestine in 1922) Abdullah was rewarded for his loyal services to the British Crown in March, 1946, when he obtained nominal independence for his country. He immediately proclaimed himself king and (significantly) changed the name of his realm to "The Hashemite Kingdom of Jordan."[26]

While granting independence, however, Britain still retained a special position in Jordan by virtue of a treaty of alliance, revised in March, 1948.

As a result, Jordan's applications for admission to the United Nations were repeatedly rejected by a Soviet veto and Jordan was only admitted to the U.N. at the end of 1955. For this reason, Jordan's newly won independence also encountered caustic criticism in the Arab world.

King Abdullah nurtured the ambition of uniting Jordan, Syria, Lebanon—and, if possible, Palestine—under his throne. This "Greater Syria" scheme, as a principle of Jordan's foreign policy, was formally announced by the king in a Speech from the Throne on November 11, 1946. It incurred the opposition of Lebanon and was rejected by most Syrians as well as by Egypt and Saudi Arabia, but the king's idea of a "Greater Syria" as a means of containing Zionism appealed to a number of Palestinian notables who were opposed to the leadership of the Husseini clan, and he did, therefore, gain some influential supporters in Palestine.

Although rent by mutual distrust and rivalry, all the Arab States agreed in principle that Palestine should be "saved from the Zionist designs." The Arab League failed to organize a coordinated plan of campaign, but their opposition to Abdullah's "Greater Syria" scheme forced the Hashemite monarch to agree to the resolution adopted by the League on April 12, 1948, providing that once Palestine was "saved" it would be handed over to the Palestinian Arabs. When the Arabs failed to "save" Palestine, however, King Abdullah regarded this resolution as no longer binding, and proceeded to absorb that part of Palestine which his forces had occupied.[27]

Possession of Jerusalem seemed to have been of particular importance to King Abdullah. He was aware that the Hashemite family derived nearly all its prestige and importance in the Arab world from the position it had held in Ottoman days as Sharif of Mecca. As the "Guardians of the Prophet's Flag" and "Custodians of Mecca and Medina" they had enjoyed the support of the British during World War I. King Abdullah was well aware of the prestige incurred by the possession of a Holy City and he hoped to possess at least the third holiest in Islam—Jerusalem. In addition, his father, Hussein, ex-Sharif of Mecca and King of the Hejaz, was buried in the precincts of the Haram esh Sharif.[28] Also, the city's exclusion from Jordan was seen as strategically disadvantageous. There was the danger that it could serve as a convenient base for fomenting opposition by Palestinian leaders hostile to Jordan's annexation of Arab Palestine. It would also deprive Jordan of important sources of revenue from pilgrims and from the tourist trade.

Jordan's Arab Legion invaded Palestine on May 15, 1948. It concentrated on conquering Jerusalem three days later. The occupation of Jerusalem was of such importance to King Abdullah that he overruled the strategic objections of the Legion's Commander, General Glubb, and deliberately sacrificed important positions in other sectors in order to secure control of the city.[29]

The king proceeded to consolidate his conquests even before the con-

clusion of the armistice agreements. He was aided by a number of prominent traditionally anti-Husseini notables, mainly from the Nablus and
Hebron areas, who campaigned extensively for union with Jordan. The
defeat of the Arab armies caused shock and consternation among the
Palestinian Arabs, who had been promised a rapid and easy victory by
their leaders, and thus the relative success of the Arab Legion strengthened the hand of the pro-Hashemite faction and many began to look to
King Abdullah for protection, not out of sympathy but despair, believing
that only he could prevent the Israeli army from capturing the whole of
Palestine.

On July 9, 1948, the Political Committee of the Arab League, fearing
the annexation of Arab Palestine by Jordan, and acting on Egyptian
initiative, set up an "Administrative Council for all Palestine," which on
September 23 became an "Arab Government of all Palestine" with its seat
in Gaza, which was under Egyptian occupation.

The king's reaction was prompt. On October 2 a "Palestine Arab
Congress" claiming to represent all the Arabs of Palestine met in Amman
and, denouncing the Gaza Government, called for Jordan's protection.
Later that month, after efforts to conciliate the king and Hajj Amin el
Husseini (The British-appointed ex-Grand Mufti of Jerusalem) had
failed, the Hashemite monarch barred the agents of the Gaza Government from the territory controlled by his forces. Finally, on December
1, a second "Palestine Arab Congress" met in Jericho under the leadership
of the Mayor of Hebron, Sheikh Muhammad Ali Al Ja'abari. It proclaimed King Abdullah "King of Palestine" and invited him to unite
Jordan and Palestine under his crown. The Jericho resolution was approved by the Jordanian Parliament on December 13, and the Prime
Minister, Tewfiq Abul Huda, announced that the union would be put
into effect according to constitutional procedures.[30]

The *de facto* annexation of Arab Palestine took place on March 17, 1949,
when the military government was replaced by a civilian administration
centered in Jerusalem. On May 7, three Palestinian Ministers were included in the Jordanian Cabinet. These steps were followed in 1950 by a
decree conferring Jordanian citizenship to all Palestinians. Parliamentary elections on both banks of the River Jordan were held on April 11
and the process was completed on April 24, 1950, when the new Jordanian
Parliament formally ratified the annexation.[31]

King Abdullah's Palestine policy placed him at odds with the rest of
the Arab States. Fearing complete isolation, the king tried to seek a
separate peace settlement with Israel. He too was opposed to Jerusalem's
internationalization. As he told the London *Times* correspondent on February 21, 1949, he saw no reason why the Holy Places could not be adequately safeguarded by his government. He wished to retain the Old City
and the Arab quarters but laid no claim to Jewish Jerusalem.[32]

The sudden enthusiasm of the other Arab governments for internationalization in 1949 drew the bitter comment in his memoirs that "The demand for the internationalization of Jerusalem was one of the most unbalanced declared Arab aims. . . ."[33] In 1949, he joined Israeli spokesmen in denouncing a Catholic plan for internationalization (although on the grounds that no "infidel" should control the city).[34]

Israel and Jordan had, since the end of 1949, been negotiating secretly for a separate peace settlement. Abdullah made several proposals—such as that he be given control of the former Arab quarters of Jerusalem in exchange for free access by Israel to the Western Wall and the Mt. Scopus areas—which were rejected by Israel. All negotiations ended by March, 1950, when the Arab States became apprised of the talks and threatened Jordan with expulsion from the Arab League.[35]

Despite the Arab League's Resolution 319 of April 13, 1950, that the presence of the Arab armies in Palestine should be considered temporary and that once Palestine was liberated it should be handed over to its people,[36] the Jordanian Parliament, on April 24, 1950, ratified the annexation of Arab Palestine, to which Britain promptly extended her military guarantee. Egyptian efforts to have Jordan expelled from the Arab League failed.[37]

At the Fifth Session of the U.N. General Assembly, the Jordanian observer, Ahmad Tuqan Bey, repeated his government's opposition to any international control over Jerusalem or the Holy Places. Like the Israelis he claimed that the U.N. had lost all moral justification for imposing its control over the city since it had failed to do so while Jerusalem was being menaced by destruction. The Holy Places, he argued, were being as adequately safeguarded by Jordan as they had been under the consistently tolerant Muslim governments since the days of Omar.[38]

Because of the growing difficulties he experienced in Arab Palestine, King Abdullah appears to have discarded, or at least postponed to a distant future, his original idea of transferring his capital to Jerusalem, or of making it his alternate capital. There was great agitation against his person and his policies, fomented by his Palestinian opponents and by hostile Arab rulers. This was centered in Jerusalem and forced him to eliminate his enemies and fight the Palestinian separatist tendencies by stiff police measures. In August, 1950, the administrative autonomy which the West Bank had enjoyed under its own Governor General was abolished.[39]

As is reflected in his memoirs, King Abdullah's special attachment to the city did not weaken. Although he was fully aware of the danger to his life, he continued his regular attendance at the Friday morning prayers at the al-Aqsa Mosque. He was assassinated there on July 20, 1951.[40]

At his death, Jordan, for a time, moved closer to the Egyptian-dominated Arab League. This did not, however, affect Jordan's determination to keep Jerusalem and the West Bank. This was accelerated by the gradual liquidation of the remaining separate institutions and government offices and the elimination of their distinct character. The centralization of government in Amman also made that city the economic and commercial center of Jordan, so that Jerusalem was gradually drained of its intellectual elite and of its economic life and was relegated to the role of a provincial city; a center of tourism and pilgrimage.[41]

Palestinian leaders criticized the Jordanian Government for its deliberate discrimination and neglect of Jerusalem and the West Bank. Until the end of Jordanian rule, in 1967, the government was dominated by politicians from the East Bank, who naturally tended to favor their own region and were inclined to regard the Palestinians with suspicion and distaste and Jerusalem as a hotbed of opposition and trouble. Whenever anti-government riots occurred in Jordan, the most violent were in Jerusalem.

King Hussein did not appear to be favorably disposed towards Jerusalem, where he had witnessed the murder of his grandfather as a young boy, and this may account for the restrictions he placed on the city's political role. The Jordanian Government directed all major investments to the East Bank, discouraged the development of industries in the Jerusalem area and blocked the creation of a university and other cultural institutions in the city.[42] The only investments or economic activities encouraged were those directly or indirectly connected with tourism, and the city became the main source of Jordan's foreign currency earnings. This attitude is reflected in the archives of the Muhafaza (District) of Jerusalem.[43]

The resentment of the Arabs of Jerusalem against the government's "... neglect, subjugation and humiliation of the Holy City"[44] was all the more increased as they witnessed the tremendous development efforts made by the Israeli Government in its sector of the city. When Israel transferred its Foreign Ministry there, a public outcry in Arab Jerusalem called for "the reinforcement of the Arab character of the city in the face of the Zionist expansionist aims."

In response, the Jordanian Government held a Cabinet meeting in the city (on July 27, 1953), resolved to hold further meetings there periodically, and proclaimed Jerusalem the "alternate capital of the Hashemite Kingdom." Parliament followed suit and on August 6 held a session in the city, passing a resolution affirming that Jerusalem was an integral and inseparable part of Jordan.[45]

In November, 1954, when the British and American ambassadors to Israel decided to present their credentials in Jerusalem, King Hussein announced that he would build a palace in Jerusalem and reside there a part of each month.[46]

However, all these declarations and resolutions remained (as intended) verbal demonstrations only, made to placate Arab opinion. The Jordanian Cabinet only met twice and Parliament only once in Jerusalem while more than ten years passed before the foundations of the royal palace were laid at Tel al-Ful, north of Jerusalem.

Nevertheless, the Jordanian Government emphasized the Muslim character of Jerusalem and made it a center of Muslim pilgrimage. In 1953, the Muslim feast of Al Isra W'al Mi'raj (the "Nocturnal Journey" and the "Ascension to Heaven of the Prophet") became a special Jerusalem event and the occasion for pilgrimage. There were special decorations and a military parade. The Muslim Brotherhood undertook to organize an annual pilgrimage to Jerusalem for this feast, to collect funds for the restoration of the al-Aqsa Mosque, and to remind all Muslims of their sacred duty toward Palestine and Jerusalem.[47]

A "World Islamic Congress" was convened in Jerusalem in December, 1953, with delegations from the Arab World, Africa, Asia, the Soviet Union, and China. It endorsed Jordan's sovereignty in Jerusalem[48] and met again in 1960 and 1961, maintaining a permanent bureau there.

When the creation of the Palestine Liberation Organization (PLO), reviving the concept of a Palestinian identity, gave rise to renewed agitation threatening to undermine the unity of the kingdom, the Jordanian Government began to pay more attention to Jerusalem. It allocated more funds for development projects, invited the Arab governments to open consulates there and to contribute to building and restoring Muslim institutions, and nationalized the Rockefeller Museum. The king himself came to Jerusalem to discuss development projects.[49]

In July, 1966, the Government officially declared the city its "Spiritual Capital" and invited all Arab organizations to hold their conventions and meetings there.[50] This coincided with the inauguration of the Knesset's new building in Israeli Jerusalem, which had a great impact on Arab opinion.

If Jordanian Jerusalem developed during the years of the city's division it was rather in spite of the policies of the Amman government and entirely the result of local initiatives. According to official government sources, the population of Arab Jerusalem was about 42,000 at the end of 1948, 47,000 in 1952, 60,000 in 1961, and almost 70,000 on the eve of the June, 1967, war. Amman, which became the political, administrative, economic, and educational center of the kingdom, grew at the expense of Jerusalem, draining it of substantial numbers of intellectuals, students, businessmen, and political leaders. There was also an important exodus to other Arab countries and to the Americas, especially of Christians. This exodus was compensated for, to some extent, by the influx of newcomers, mainly artisans, laborers, and small merchants from the Hebron area (nicknamed locally "the Scots of Palestine").

No public housing and few government development projects were carried out in Jerusalem, with the exception of some designed mainly to help develop pilgrimage and tourism, which became a most important source of revenue for Jordan. Most of the developments of hotels and tourist services arose from local initiative. The boom in tourism brought relative prosperity to the city, especially in the 1960s and encouraged an important private building movement which transformed neighboring villages such as Shufat, Beit Hanina, and Al Azariye into beautiful garden suburbs.

Jordan always asserted that the question of the Holy Places was a purely domestic affair and consistently refused to accept international control or to admit outside intervention. Immediately after assuming control of Jerusalem, the Jordanian Government had adopted the Mandatory Orders in Council relating to the Holy Places and announced that it would maintain the status quo.[51] King Abdullah took them under his personal protection, and in 1950, with the stalemate at the U.N., proceeded to assert his direct control over the Holy Places. On January 5, 1951, he appointed Ragib Pasha Al Nashashibi, the former Mayor of Jerusalem under the Mandate and Governor General of the West Bank and Minister of Refugees under Jordan, as "Protector of the Haram esh Sharif and Royal Custodian of the Holy Places."[52]

Nashashibi was ceremoniously installed in Jerusalem on January 15, but the Catholic consuls and church dignitaries boycotted the ceremony on the ground that this infringed upon the status quo.[53]

When Nashashibi died he was succeeded by Dr. Hussein Fakhri Al Khalidi (on April 19, 1951). His investiture was boycotted by the entire consular corps as well as by the Catholic hierarchy.[54]

Dr. Khalidi nevertheless succeeded in reconstituting many lost records on the status quo, and achieved an agreement among the major communities (Orthodox, Latins, and Armenians) on several controversial issues. Though he was the final arbiter in all disputes, the Jordanian Cabinet, in July, 1952, reversed his ruling on a controversy concerning the Church of the Nativity. Dr. Khalidi appealed to the prime minister to reconfirm his powers, but Tewfiq Pasha Abdul Huda refused to do so. As a result, Dr. Khalidi resigned on August 23, 1952.[55]

The post of Royal Custodian of the Holy Places lapsed, and his duties again reverted to the Governor (Mutassarif) of Jerusalem. A Ministerial Committee, consisting of one Muslim and two Christian ministers, was created to discuss and hand down final decisions on appeals by the Christian communities, but this committee also lapsed. Heads of communities thus had to appeal to the cabinet, the prime minister, and sometimes directly to the king. In 1955 the Jordanian Government renamed the Governor of Jerusalem "Muhafiz [District Head] of Jerusalem and the Holy Places." The Catholic consuls and some of the Christian hierarchy refused to recognize the second part of the title.[56]

Disputes, and sometimes even serious brawls (as in Bethlehem in 1961 and in Deir al Sultan in 1966 and 1967), in the Holy Places continued, but the Muhafiz of Jerusalem generally settled them according to the principles of the status quo, which was only infringed upon when it suited the government. (In February, 1961, for instance, when relations between Egypt and Jordan were strained, the government dispossessed the Copts of the Monastery of Deir al Sultan in favor of the Ethiopians.)[57]

Jordan's remarkable achievement, nevertheless, was to promote an agreement, in June, 1961, between the Orthodox and Armenian Patriarchates and the Custody of the Holy Land, for the restoration of the Church of the Holy Sepulchre.

While the Jordanian Government respected and treated Christian Holy Places relatively well, Jewish shrines and holy sites were desecrated and destroyed. Under Article 8 of the Armistice Agreement, Jordan had undertaken to allow free access to them and to make possible the use of the ancient cemetery on the slopes of the Mount of Olives, but it consistently refused to implement this provision. Jordan even barred access to non-Israeli Jews, requiring all tourists to present a certificate of baptism before visas were granted. The synagogues of the Jewish Quarter in the Old City were wantonly destroyed; their remains were used as stables, hen houses, rubbish dumps, and even latrines. The Western Wall itself was not damaged (it is also the outer wall of the Haram esh Sharif) but the Tomb of Simon the Just was used as stables.

The worst acts of desecration occurred at the cemetery of the Mount of Olives, where prophets, holy men, and eminent rabbis from all over the world were buried (in keeping with the Jewish tradition that the resurrection of the dead would begin there). An Inter-Ministerial Commission appointed by the Israeli Government to assess the damage to this site reported, in October, 1967, that it had been deliberately destroyed and desecrated by the Jordanian Government and the Municipality of Arab Jerusalem. Graves had been ripped open and bones scattered; thousands of tombstones had been smashed or removed by the Jordanian Army to build fortifications, footpaths, army camps, and latrines. The Jerusalem Municipality had granted concessions to merchants who destroyed graves and sold the gravestones to building contractors.[58]

Christian Arab emigration increased, spurred on by the climate of Muslim domination and discriminatory practices in employment and business, coupled with occasional harrassment. (Christian leaders cite, among others, such incidents as the hasty erection of a mosque on a plot of land near Jerusalem which had been given to Pope Paul in January, 1964, by King Hussein for the purpose of building a church to commemorate the Pontiff's visit.)

In 1953, two laws (Numbers 36 and 61) gave the Jordanian Government strict control over Christian institutions. The first required all foreign institutions to dissolve themselves and to register in accordance with Jordanian law, with government rights of inspection. The second regulated and limited the acquisition and possession of real estate by religious and charitable institutions and forbade them to acquire any property in the vicinity of the Holy Places.[59]

Following worldwide protests, the government, while refusing to withdraw the laws, suspended the application of some of their provisions, and later amended others.

Renewed Muslim clamor against foreign religious institutions resulted in the promulgation of Law Number 4 of 1965 (amending Law number 61 of 1953) further limiting the rights of the Christian Churches and institutions to possess or acquire real estate, banning their acquisition of property within the Old City, and making the acquisition of property within the municipal area of Jerusalem conditional on the approval of a special government committee.[60]

Christian religious leaders protested, to no avail, but most of the time managed to circumvent the new restrictions by personal appeals to the king or to friendly ministers, paying bribes or registering new property in the names of trusted individuals.

The Jordanian Government also actively intervened in the internal affairs and disputes of the Christian communities. It twice deported the Armenian Patriarch Archbishop Tiran Nersoyan, in order to secure the election to the Patriarchal throne of the candidate whom it favored, and intervened in the conflict between the Greek hierarchy and the Arab laity in the Greek Orthodox Patriarchate—a conflict which flared up again in 1965 after the death of His Beatitude Timotheos.

In general, however, the heads of the Christian communities in Jordan succeeded in defending their interests by inducing the government to suspend the application of adverse measures. The king took a paternal interest in Jordan's minorities and was occasionally prepared to intervene in their favor, and cabinet ministers, politicians, and civil servants were open to all sorts of inducements. It was a system, however, that did not afford the Christian communities much security.

THE MODUS VIVENDI IN JERUSALEM

The Armistice Agreement which governed the relations between Israel and Jordan until June, 1967, was never fully respected and this period was rich in border incidents, sabotage incursions, and retaliatory raids. There were periods of great tensions, and some grave incidents occurred even in Jerusalem, although both governments made special efforts to contain and prevent incidents in the city because of its special character and importance.

On certain issues, such as the Holy Places and the Christian minorities, both Israel and Jordan sought to prove to the world that an international regime was not necessary since its main objectives could be satisfactorily achieved by their governments.

This required the close cooperation of the two governments and they succeeded in reaching a modus vivendi. Before the conclusion of the Armistice Agreement, the Israeli and Jordanian authorities made special arrangements to permit Christians to cross the demarcation lines to celebrate Christmas and Easter, but these were only temporary arrangements and, except to members of the consular corps and the Christian clergy, the right of free passage between the two sectors of the City was granted only occasionally.

At the start of the Catholic Holy Year of 1950, the Israel Government proposed to Jordan the establishment of a regular procedure for the free passage of pilgrims and tourists through the demarcation lines. Negotiations were conducted through the Armistice Commission, and an agreement was reached creating a permanent frontier post, although Jordan stipulated that foreign pilgrims and tourists should be permitted to cross the demarcation lines in one direction only.

This permanent frontier post, which came to be known as the "Mandelbaum Gate," began to function on January 12, 1950. It permitted the crossing into Jordan of pilgrims and tourists, local clergy, the consular corps, and Israeli Christians (mostly Arabs) during Christmas and Easter.[61]

Only Jews and Israeli Muslims were consistently denied a crossing by Jordan—in direct contravention of Article 8 of the Armistice Agreement.

A special body, which was not dependent on the Armistice Commission, was set up by mutual agreement to regulate the flow of pilgrims and tourists between the Israeli and Jordanian sectors of Jerusalem. It consisted of the Israeli District Officer and the External Liaison Officer of the Jordanian Foreign Ministry. From 1952 until 1967, they held regular weekly meetings at the Mandelbaum Gate and worked closely together. In due course, this body also came to deal with matters which, in normal times, would have been regarded as consular functions, such as regulating the repatriation of Arab refugees to Israel and the emigration of Israeli Arabs to Jordan within the scope of the Family Reunification scheme. They also arranged twice weekly meetings at the Mandelbaum Gate between the Israeli and Jordanian halves of Muslim families and even weddings were occasionally performed there to enable the divided families of the couple to be present at the ceremony. Requests by Jordanians to be allowed to visit Israel for medical or compassionate reasons, the transfer of documents and affidavits required by the courts or citizens of one state from the other side, etc., were also handled.[62]

It is important to note that the smooth working and the spirit of friendly collaboration of this body were never affected by border incidents, retaliatory raids, or periods of intensified hostility between the two states.

Both Israel and Jordan repeatedly tried to persuade foreign governments to modify their policies and to regularize the situation of their consuls in Jerusalem, which functioned without proper accreditation. Though these efforts met with no success, the attitude of the two governments remained unchanged. They upheld their claims to full sovereignty over Jerusalem while the consular representatives continued to regard both Israel and Jordan as occupying powers whose de facto control over their respective sectors of Jerusalem was of a temporary nature only pending the City's internationalization.

Because Israel established her capital in her part of the city while Jordan, though declaring her sector to be a second, alternate or spiritual capital, never took any steps to that effect, the measures taken by foreign governments to emphasize their non-recognition of Israeli and Jordanian sovereign rights in Jerusalem affected Israel more than Jordan. These measures limited the scope of normal diplomatic activities in Jerusalem without prejudicing the countries' friendly relations with Israel. Every embassy had its own set of rules, but the diplomatic corps often had a concerted approach to specific problems of protocol.

The Israel Government was determined to attain recognition of Jerusalem as Israel's capital, but tried to avoid serious clashes on this issue.

Most of the newly established diplomatic missions in Israel were set up in Jerusalem, thus recognizing its status as Israel's capital. These were mainly the embassies of Latin American and African states, and their number slowly increased until, at the beginning of 1967, out of the 54 diplomatic missions in Israel, 21 were in Jerusalem and 33 in Tel Aviv.[63] The U.N., as an international organization, established the office of the Resident Representative of the U.N. Development Program for Israel there in May, 1952. The only official functions in Jerusalem from which some of the Western ambassadors continued to absent themselves were the Independence Day military parades of 1958, 1961, and 1967.

During the last years prior to June, 1967, the outward signs of the doctrine of non-recognition were reduced to the refusal by some governments to put the Jerusalem address on congratulatory messages to Israel's president or official messages or notes to the prime minister and foreign minister. When Israel made her displeasure at this practice known, some governments adopted the ingenious device of addressing their message to "Israel" without specifying the name of the capital, or of transmitting them through their embassies with no address.

This ill-defined modus vivendi suited all the parties concerned (with the exception of the Arab States). Israel and Jordan exercised sovereign rights over their sectors of the city without any real outside challenge.

Foreign governments were satisfied that Christian interests were secure and regarded internationalization as impracticable. For most it was also considered unnecessary, though some remained attached in principle to the U.N. resolutions. The three Western Powers were anxious to freeze the territorial status quo in order to preserve the armistice regime. Thus, to the relief and satisfaction of all parties (except the Arab States) the question of the status of Jerusalem was, until June, 1967, relegated to the background, pending the conclusion of a final peace settlement.

For 18 years the modus vivendi between Israel and Jordan in Jerusalem survived all crises because both governments were determined to maintain it for political, economic, and military reasons. Israel, though dissatisfied with Jordan's refusal to permit free access to the Jewish Holy Places and sites and to the institutions on Mt. Scopus, was prepared to acquiesce to the status quo and to continue to maintain the Armistice Agreement with Jordan. When, in the early morning of June 5, 1967, Egypt forced a war of self-defense on Israel, the Israel prime minister sent an urgent message to King Hussein assuring him that he had no intention of initiating military operations against Jordan provided that she did not attack Israel.[64]

Yet Jordan ignored this message and launched an attack. Jerusalem was shelled by Jordanian artillery and thus the Armistice Agreement and the modus vivendi, which for nearly 20 years had survived all vicissitudes, were irrevocably shattered.

NOTES AND REFERENCES

1. United Nations G.A.O.R., Third Session, Suppl. 11, p. 35 (A/648—Progress Report of the Mediator).

2. Israel-Jordan Armistice Agreement in: *U.N. Treaty Series*, Vol. 42. p. 303.

3. Hebrew University, *Israel and the United Nations*, pp. 109–110.

4. Parliamentary Debates, House of Lords, Vol. 106 (1937) Col. 649.

5. U.N. G.A.O.R., Second Session, Ad Hoc, pp. 16–17.

6. Israel Office of Information, *Jerusalem and the United Nations*, p. 19.

7. W. Eytan, *The First Ten Years*, p. 130.

8. Eytan, *op. cit.*, pp. 70–71; *Israel and the United Nations, op. cit.* p. 131; *Haaretz*, 30 June 1948.

9. G.A.O.R., Third Session, Suppl. 11 (A/648), pp. 9–10, 19–26.

10. *Iton Rishmi* No. 12 of 2 August 1948 (The Official Gazette of the Provisional Government of Israel).

11. Y. Shimoni, "Israel in the Pattern of Middle East Politics," *Middle East Journal*, July, 1950; cf. speeches of the Israeli representatives in G.A.O.R., Third Session, Part I, First Committee, pp. 640–647, 711–712.

12. *The Times* (London), 14 February 1949; S. McDonald—*My Mission to Israel*, p. 128.

13. *The Times* (London), 14 February 1949.

14. U.N. G.A.O.R., Fourth Session, Ad Hoc, Appendix I, pp. 32–44 (A/AC31/L34).

15. *ibid.*, p. 46 (A/AC.31/L. 42).

16. *ibid.*, Plenary, p. 600.

17. *Divrei HaKnesset* (Israeli Parliamentary Debates), III, p. 221; *The Times* (London), 6 December 1949.

18. *ibid.*, III, p. 603; *The Times* (London), 24 January 1950.

19. U.N. G.A.O.R., Fifth Session, Suppl. 9 (A/1286), pp. 29–33.

20. For the statements of Church leaders on Israeli policy, see: Ministry of Religious Affairs, *Christian Communities In Israel, 1950–1951*, pp. 5–24.

21. *The Times* (London), 11, 22, and 30 July 1953; *Le Monde*, 13 and 15 July 1953; *New York Times*, 11, 12, 17, and 29 July 1953; *Neue Zuricher Zeitung*, 26 July 1953.

22. *Divrei HaKnesset*. XIV, pp. 1640–1645.

23. Great Britain, Public Records Office—Colonial Office File CO/733/152/57202 of 1928.

24. For the declaration to the press by Father Constantin Koser, see: *Le Monde*, 7 July 1967.

25. N. Bentwich, *Israel*, p. 178; cf. F. Bernadotte, *To Jerusalem*, p. 142; E. Marmorstein, *op. cit.*, pp. 358–359.

26. *Jarida Rasmiyya lilmamlaka AlUrduniyya AlHashamiyya* (Jordanian Official Gazette) No. 886 of 1 February 1947.

27. M. Khadurri, "The Scheme of Fertile Crescent Unity," in Frye, *The Near East and the Great Powers*, p. 155.

28. Bernadotte, *op. cit.*, p. 112; Bilby, *New Star in the Near East*, pp. 196–197; For the king's own explanation of his ideas, see: *Memoirs of King Abdullah of Trans-Jordan* (edited by P. Graves).

29. J. Kimche, *Both Sides of the Hill*, p. 112; Kirk, *The Middle East 1945–1950*, p. 281.

30. *The Times* (London), 2 and 14 December 1948; cf. Dearden, *Jordan*, pp. 76–80.

31. Khadurri, *op. cit.*, pp. 168–169; cf. Dearden, *Jordan*, pp. 83–84.

32. *The Times* (London), 22 February 1949.

33. A. Abu Sha'ar (ed.) *Mudhakirat al Malik Abdallah Ibn al Hussein-Al Takmil*, p. 339, cf. P. Rondot, "Le Probleme des Lieux Saints," in *L'Afrique et L'Asie*, No. 1 (1950), p. 13.

34. *Filastin*, 9 December 1949.

35. McDonald, *op. cit.*, pp. 192–194; Kirk, *op. cit.*, pp. 309–310; Eytan, *op. cit.*, pp. 42–43; *The Observer*, 5 February 1950; *New York Times*, 1 and 3 March 1950.

36. The Arab League, *Collection of the Resolutions of the Arab League*, I, pp. 62–63, 68; cf. B. Ghali, *The Arab League 1945–1955*, p. 413.

37. *ibid.*

38. U.N. G.A.O.R., Fifth Session, Ad Hoc, pp. 471–473.

39. E. Wright, "Abdullah's Jordan," in *Middle East Journal*, August, 1951.

40. King Hussein of Jordan, *Uneasy Lies the Head*, pp. 1–9.

41. N. Sofer, "The Integration of Arab Palestine into Jordan," *Hamizrach Hechadash* ("The New East"), Vol. IV (1955), No. 3.

42. A. Abidi, *Jordan, A Political Study 1946–1957*, p. 180.

43. These are now in the State Archives of Israel.

44. See the statement of the Vice Mayor of Jerusalem in *Filastin*, 19 May 1953;

cf. *Filastin*, 28 May 1954; A. Sarich, 21 November 1954.

45. *New York Times* and *Filastin*, 28 July 1953; *Filastin*, 7 August 1953; *Proche Orient Chretien*, Vol. III (1953), p. 265; cf. M. Rousan, *Palestine and the Internationalisation of Jerusalem*, p. 99.

46. *Filastin*, 31 October 1954; *New York Times*, 1 November 1954.

47. *Proche Orient Chretien*, Vol. III (1953), p. 167.

48. *Filastin*, 10 December 1953; *a Difa'a* 12 March 1954.

49. *A Difa'a*, 3 July 1966; *Jerusalem Times*, 28 July 1966; *Filastin*, 31 August 1966; *Al Manar*, 21 September 1966.

50. *A Difa'a*, 10 July 1966.

51. Dearden, *op. cit.*, pp. 184–185.

52. *Filastin*, 31 December 1950; cf. *The Times* (London), 29 December 1950; *New York Times*, 3 January 1951; The text of the Royal Decree is reproduced in: King Abdullah, *My Memoirs Completed* (Al Takmila), pp. 102–103.

53. *The Times* (London), 16 January 1951.

54. *New York Times*, 19 April 1951; *Filastin*, 20 April 1951.

55. *A Difa'a*, 10 September 1952.

56. Dearden, *op. cit.*, p. 190.

57. *The Times* (London), 4 and 12 April 1961; *New York Times*, 3 April 1961; *La Bourse Egyptienne*, 7, 8, 11, 14, 15, 19, 27 March and 3 April 1961.

58. Israeli Ministry of Foreign Affairs, *Desecration*; Israeli Ministry of Religious Affairs, *Report of the Inter-Ministerial Commission for the Examination of the Desecration of the Burial Grounds on the Mount of Olives and at Hebron*; cf. *Al Jihad*, 3 May 1955, 23 April 1962 and 1 July 1962; *Al Manar*, 22 March 1962; *A Difa'a*, 10 April 1962.

59. *Proche Orient Chretien*, Vol. III (1953), pp. 267–268.

60. *Jarida Rasmiyya* (Jordanian Official Gazette) No. 1818 of 18 February 1965; cf. *Filastin*, 11 January 1955. *A Difa'a*, 19 January 1955; *The Times* (London), 18 January 1955; *Egyptian Gazette*, 7 August 1964, *Proche Orient Chretien*, Vol. V (1955), pp. 63–64.

61. *New York Times*, 21 February 1959; Dr. M. Mendas, "Pilgrimage to the Holy Land" in *Christian Communities in Israel, 1950–1951*.

62. Information given by Mr. Raphael Levi who was the Israeli Representative in these meetings from 1952 until 1967; cf. *New York Times*, 21 February 1959.

63. *Israel Government Yearbook, 1966–1967*, pp. 168–172; *In Jerusalem:* Bolivia, Central African Republic, Chile, Colombia, Congo (Brazzaville), Congo (Kinshassa), Costa Rica, Dahomey, Dominican Republic, Gabon, Greece, Guatemala, Honduras, Ivory Coast, Malgasy Republic, Netherlands, Niger, Panama, Upper Volta, Uruguay and Venezuela. *In Tel Aviv:* Argentina, Australia, Austria, Belgium, Burma, Brazil, Bulgaria, Canada, Cuba, Czechoslovakia, Denmark, Ecuador, Finland, France, Germany (Federal Republic), Ghana, Great Britain, Hungary, Italy, Japan, Liberia, Mexico, Norway, Peru, Philippines, Poland, Rumania, Sweden, Switzerland, Turkey, U.S.S.R., U.S.A., and Yugoslavia.

64. Israel Information services, *Jordanian Belligerency*, pp. 1–2; D. Kimche and D. Bavly, *The Sandstorm*, p. 191.

VII

The Juridical Status of Jerusalem

YEHUDA Z. BLUM

On June 27, 1967, the Knesset passed the Law and Administration Ordinance (Amendment) Law, 5727–1967, Section 1 of which provides that "the law, jurisdiction and administration of the State shall extend to any area of Eretz Israel designated by the Government by order."[1] Pursuant to this provision, the Israel Government the following day proclaimed new municipal boundaries for the City of Jerusalem, incorporating within the limits of the unified city, *inter alia*, those parts of Jerusalem that had been under Jordanian rule in the years 1948–1967, including the walled city, commonly referred to as the "Old City" of Jerusalem.

These legislative measures evoked instant reaction by the deadlocked United Nations General Assembly which had been convened, at the request of the Soviet Union, on June 17, 1967, for an emergency special session to discuss the situation in the Middle East. On July 4, 1967, the General Assembly adopted a Pakistan-sponsored resolution in which it expressed its deep concern "at the situation prevailing in Jerusalem as a result of the measures taken by Israel to change the status of the City," considered that "these measures are invalid," and called upon Israel "to rescind all measures already taken and to desist forthwith from taking any action which would alter the status of Jerusalem."[2] Ten days later the General Assembly adopted a further resolution in which it took note "with the deepest regret and concern" of Israel's noncompliance with its resolution of July 4, deplored Israel's failure to implement the said resolution, and reiterated its call to Israel to rescind all measures already taken and to desist from taking any action which would alter the status of Jerusalem.[3] This approach has also been echoed in three resolutions adopted by the Security Council in 1968, 1969, and 1971, respectively.[4]

Apparently, then, both the General Assembly and the Security Council regarded the situation that had obtained in Jerusalem between the termination of the British Mandate in May, 1948, and the outbreak of the June, 1967, hostilities as one worthy of preservation. It is not without irony that the international community which denied recognition of Jordanian rights of sovereignty over Jerusalem while the Jordanians controlled the eastern part of the city[5] should have become aware of the existence of such rights only after the Jordanians were ousted from Judaea and Samaria[6] (including Jerusalem). Yet it has to be remembered that both the General Assembly and the Security Council are *political* organs of the United Nations and their decisions are political decisions motivated by political considerations of the majority of membership. It would therefore seem appropriate to subject the questions regarding the status of Jerusalem also to a *legal* analysis, in order to ascertain what precisely was the status of Jerusalem (and, more specifically, of the formerly Jordanian-held part of the City) on the eve of the Six Day War of June, 1967, since the restoration of that status is the declared objective of the two United Nations organs referred to above.

It will be recalled that during the Mandate period Jerusalem formed an integral part of Palestine, and served as its administrative capital throughout the 30 years of British rule. In its well-known resolution 181 (II) of November 29, 1947, the U.N. General Assembly recommended that the British Mandate be terminated, and that Palestine be partitioned into a Jewish State, an Arab State, and the City of Jerusalem (as a *corpus separatum*), the three regions to be linked by an economic union. The Jewish Agency,[7] representing the Jewish side in the deliberations concerning the future of Palestine, expressed its readiness to accept the partition resolution as a compromise between the conflicting national aspirations of Jews and Arabs despite the fact that it involved a second and very considerable reduction in the size of the territory earmarked for Jewish rule, compared with the original "Jewish National Home" of the Palestine Mandate.[8] No less painful for the Jewish side was the fact that Jerusalem, with its Jewish majority[9] and with the unique place that the City of David has occupied in the hearts and minds of Jews for three millenia, was to be excluded from the territory of the projected Jewish State and was to become—as an internationalized territory—an enclave within the contemplated Arab State. However, all these concessions of the Jewish side were made conditional on the reciprocal acceptance of the partition "package deal" also by the Arabs. No such acceptance was forthcoming. The Arabs of Palestine as well as the neighboring Arab States categorically rejected the partition plan, and were not prepared to settle for anything less than an independent State of Palestine to be ruled by the Arabs. Thus, at the meeting of Premiers and Foreign Ministers of Arab League States held in Cairo between December 8 and 17, 1947, following the adoption by the General Assembly of the partition recommendation, it was decided that the Arabs were "determined to enter battle against the United Nations decision to partition Palestine and, by the will of God, to carry it to a successful conclusion."[10] At the same meeting it was also agreed to take "decisive measures" to prevent the partition of Palestine, and the General Assembly's resolution on the matter was defined as "a violation of the principles of right and justice."[11]

The juridical aspects of the Arab refusal to accept the partition plan are aptly summed up by Lauterpacht:

> While, of course, it is unfortunate that the Arabs rejected the resolution, they were to some extent correct in their incidental assertion that the General Assembly was not able by resolution to dispose in a binding manner of the whole or any part of the territory of Palestine. Palestine was not the property of the U.N. to give or withhold as it pleased. The role of the U.N. was a restricted one. Its acquiescence in the termination of Britain of its obligations as a Mandatory was . . . a legal necessity. Moreover, the Assembly could, by putting forward a plan which the interested parties might accept, provide the legal basis for the settlement of the future government of the country. But resolutions of the General Assembly do not normally create legal obligations for the members of the U.N. (even if Israel and the proposed Arab State had been members at that time, which they were not); and the Partition Resolution did not have a legislative character. The Assembly could not by its resolution give the Jews and the Arabs in Palestine any rights which either did not otherwise possess: nor, correspondingly, could it take away such rights as they did possess.[12]

Consequently, when the Palestine Mandate was terminated on May 14, 1948, the Partition Resolution had already been overtaken by events and had been effectively frustrated, as has been pointed out by Lauterpacht, "in three out of its four major elements. No Arab State was established within Palestine; there could thus be no economic union of the Arab and Jewish States. Further, the physical attack by the Arab forces upon the Jewish State as such, left the Israeli forces with no option but to respond in kind and maintain such hold as they could upon the areas then in Jewish possession, to the point—by way of defensive rationalization of their position—of moving in places beyond the lines laid down in the Partition Resolution."[13] Since the Resolution failed to be implemented, "its description of specific boundaries ceased to be fully relevant. . . . As a description of a particular boundary they became worthless. . . ."[14] Thus, "the coming into existence of Israel does not depend legally upon the Resolution. The right of a State to exist flows from its factual existence—especially when that existence is prolonged, shows every sign of continuance and is recognized by the generality of nations."[15]

It is certainly not without interest to recall here the deliberations that took place on May 14, 1948, some two hours before Israel's proclamation of independence, in the "People's Council" which transformed itself, upon the accession to independence of the new State, into the "Provisional Council of State" (the forerunner of the Knesset until the latter came into being following the first parliamentary elections in January, 1949). Several members of the People's Council enquired why the draft of the Proclamation of Independence failed to make any reference to the boundaries of the State as laid down in the U.N. Partition Plan. David Ben-Gurion, Chairman of the "People's Administration" (that was soon to become the Provisional Government of Israel), replied to these enquiries in the following words:

> There was a discussion on this in the People's Administration. There was a proposal before us to fix the boundaries and there was also opposition to this proposal. We have decided *to evade* (and I deliberately use this term) this question, for a simple reason: if the U.N. will stand by its resolutions and obligations, will preserve the peace, will prevent bombardments, and will carry out by its own force its decision, we on our part . . . will respect all these resolutions. So far the U.N. has done nothing of this kind and this burden has fallen on us. Therefore, not everything is binding on us and we have left the matter open. We have not said: 'no U.N. boundaries;' we have not said the opposite either. We have left the matter open for future developments.[16]

Less than ten hours after Mr. Ben-Gurion's statement was made, developments started to unfold rapidly and dramatically. The neighboring Arab States (aided by Iraq, Saudi Arabia, and the Yemen) who during the closing months of the British Mandate had actively supported, trained, financed, and equipped the Arab guerrilla forces operating in Palestine with a view to frustrating the U.N. partition plan (in fact, a large proportion of the persons engaged in these guerrilla activities had been of non-Palestinian stock), now openly moved into the field by invading Palestine with the declared purpose of liquidating the newly born Jewish State. The Jewish population of Jerusalem soon found itself besieged by the advancing armies of Transjordan, Egypt, and Iraq. The Arab Legion of Transjordan captured the eastern part of the City. Armed forces of Egypt and Iraq joined them in indiscriminately shelling the Holy City. The civilian casualties alone on the Jewish side approximated 2,000. An even worse fate befell the Jewish Quarter in the Old City of Jerusalem which, after a prolonged siege and bombardment, was captured by the Arab Legion, its adult male population, irrespective of age, taken prisoner, while most of the Quarter's buildings—including scores of ancient synagogues with their invaluable scrolls and other religious relics—were systematically destroyed and razed to the ground.

In those days there was little doubt indeed in the minds of jurists and statesmen alike as to the apportionment of blame for all these events and as to the proper legal evaluation of the acts undertaken by the Arabs upon the termination of the Palestine Mandate. The non-Arab world was virtually unanimous in its condemnation of the very presence of the military forces of the Arab States on Palestinian soil, since the forcible entry of those armies into Palestine and the resulting military intervention was regarded as use of force in violation of the rule embodied in Article 2(4) of the U.N. Charter.[17] The use of force by the contiguous Arab States having been illegal, it naturally could not give rise to any valid legal title. *Ex injuria jus non oritur.*

The initial justification given by the Arab States for their armed intervention was that they had to enter Palestine "to establish security and order in place of chaos and disorder which prevailed. . . . In face of . . . brutal crimes against humanity in a contiguous country . . . they deem it their bounden duty . . . to intervene in Palestine with the object of putting an end to the massacres raging there and upholding law and principles recognized among the United Nations. . . ."[18] They also asserted that they "were compelled to enter Palestine to protect unarmed Arabs against massacres."[19] King Abdullah of Transjordan spoke of his awareness of "our national duty towards Palestine in general and Jerusalem in particular."[20]

The Ukrainian representative in the Security Council countered these attempts to justify the illegal Arab intervention in Palestine by rightly rejecting "the assertion . . . that the intervention has no other object in view than the restoration of security in order in Palestine,"[21] because "it is known . . . that according to the rules of the international community each Government has the right to restore order only in its own territory."[22] He further stated:

> . . . none of the States whose troops have entered Palestine can claim that Palestine forms part of its territory. It is an altogether separate territory, without any relationship to the territories of the States which have sent their troops into Palestine.[23]

On May 27, 1948, the Ukrainian representative invited the Council to note "the unlawful invasion by a number of States of the territory of Palestine, which does not form part of the territory of any of the States whose armed forces have invaded it."[24]

When the Arabs became aware of the inherent legal weakness of their initial argument, they sought to shift it and to justify their armed intervention by reference to the provisions of Chapter VIII of the U.N. Charter concerning regional arrangements. Under this modified version of their argument, the Arabs maintained that "Palestine being a member of the Arab League and the Arab League constituting a regional arrangement . . . Article 52 of the Charter applies,"[25] and that "the neighbouring Arab Governments which are members of the Arab League consider themselves responsible for the maintenance of security in their area as a regional organization in corformity with the provisions of the United Nations Charter."[26] This reliance by the Arab States on Chapter VIII of the U.N. Charter to justify their armed intervention in Palestine was shown by the United States representative to be devoid of any legal merit. He stated:

> Their statements are the best evidence we have of the international character of this aggression. . . . They tell us quite frankly that their business is political. . . . Of course, the statement that they are there to make peace is rather remarkable in view of the fact that they are waging war.[27]

Referring to the reply sent by King Abdullah of Transjordan to questions addressed to him by the Security Council, the United States representative stated that the king's answer

> is characterized . . . by a certain contumacy towards the United Nations and the Security Council. He has sent us an answer to our questions. These were questions addressed to him, as a ruler who is occupying land outside his domain, by the Security Council, a body which is organized in the world to ask these questions of him. . . . The contumacy of that reply to the Security Council is the very best evidence of the illegal purpose of this Government in invading Palestine with armed forces and conducting the war which it is waging there. It is against the peace; it is not on behalf of peace. It is an invasion with a definite purpose. . . . Therefore here we have the highest type of the international violation of the law: the admission by those who are committing this violation.[28]

The United States representative also reminded the Arab States that their intervention in Palestine could not be characterized as an action taken under Chapter VIII of the Charter, for Article 53 required for any enforcement action taken under regional arrangements or by a regional agency the prior authorization of the Security Council, and no such authorization had been given to their armed intervention in Palestine.[29]

The concerted Arab attempt to crush Israel by unlawfully invading Palestinian soil eventually failed, although some Palestinian territory (including East Jerusalem) remained in the hands of the invading Arab armies. The military realities prevailing at the time were reflected in the

Armistice Agreements concluded between Israel and each of her Arab neighbors between February and July, 1949.[30] However, those Agreements did not remove—and were not intended to remove—the illegality of the presence of the invading Arab armies on the territory of the former Palestine Mandate. We do not need to enter here, for present purposes, the controversial questions relating to the nature and scope of armistice agreements in general.[31] It is sufficient to confine ourselves here to a specific provision contained in the Israel–Jordan General Armistice Agreement concerning the matter here under consideration. Article II(2) of that Agreement stipulates, *inter alia*, that:

> no provision of this Agreement shall in any way prejudice the rights, claims and positions of either Party hereto in the ultimate peaceful settlement of the Palestine question, the provisions of this Agreement being dictated *exclusively by military considerations*.[32]

It follows that the effect of the Israel–Jordan Armistice Agreement (similar provisions may be found also in the Agreements concluded with Egypt, Lebanon, and Syria, respectively) was to freeze, as it were, the rights and claims of the parties as they existed on the day of the Agreement's conclusion. In consequence, no subsequent unilateral act could, as long as the Agreement remained in force, improve, affect, or alter the rights of any party as they existed when the Agreement was concluded. The purported annexation by the Kingdom of Jordan of the "West Bank" in April, 1950, was, therefore, from the point of view of international law, devoid of any legal effect.

This conclusion is warranted not only by the just-quoted provision of the Israel–Jordan General Armistice Agreement, but also by legal considerations of a more general nature.

For the reasons elaborated above, the most favorable construction—from the Jordanian viewpoint—that can be placed on the presence of armed elements of Transjordan on Palestinian soil after May 15, 1948, is that they enjoyed there the rights of a belligerent occupant,[33] within the meaning of this term under international law. According to Stone, "the position of the State of Jordan on the West Bank and in East Jerusalem itself, insofar as it had a legal basis in May, 1967, rested on the fact that the State of Transjordan had overrun this territory during the 1948 hostilities against Israel. It was a belligerent occupant there."[34] It is a cardinal rule of the international law of belligerent occupation that:

> occupation does not displace or transfer sovereignty. The occupant is entitled to exercise military authority over the territory occupied, but he does not acquire sovereignty unless and until it is ceded to him by a treaty of peace (which is the commonest method), or is simply abandoned in his favor

without cession, or is acquired by him by virtue of subjugation, that is, extermination of the local sovereign and annexation of his territory. . . .[35]

Castrén, likewise, points out on this matter that *"sovereignty* over occupied territory . . . is not transferred to the occupying Power. . . . [O]ccupied territory may not be *annexed*, and unilateral declarations to this effect are consequently void of legal effect."[36]

Stone expresses the same view stating that "an Occupant is not legally entitled to annex until the state of war out of which the occupation arose has ceased."[37] And Kelsen, in somewhat different terms, seems to agree:

> It is a rule of general international law that by mere occupation of enemy territory in the course of war the occupied territory does not become territory of the occupying belligerent, or—as it is usually formulated—the occupying belligerent does not acquire sovereignty over this territory. . . .[38]

Another consideration to which regard must be had is that, according to the prevailing view, an armistice agreement does not affect the status of the belligerent occupant who—unless it is otherwise stated in the agreement—remains bound in respect of the occupied territory by the Hague Regulations. Thus in von Glahn's view, "the Hague Regulations would apply to . . . [armistice] occupation, subject to such modifications as might have been included in the armistice agreement."[39] And, according to Greenspan, "The situation in occupied territory during an armistice remains unchanged from that during hostilities."[40]

It follows from all this that, just as the annexation of occupied territory by a belligerent occupant is obviously prohibited before the cease-fire or the armistice, it is equally prohibited, under international law, after the cease-fire or armistice, as long as this remains in force. Thus, it should not occasion surprise that the resolution adopted on April 24, 1950, in a joint session of both Houses of the Jordanian Parliament, proclaiming "its support for complete unity between the two sides of the Jordan and their union into one State, which is the Hashemite Kingdom of Jordan,"[41] has not met with international recognition. In fact, there are only two States who seem to have recognized this extension of the territory of the Kingdom of Jordan, namely, the United Kingdom and Pakistan.[42]

Israel's reaction to this purported annexation by Jordan of Judaea and Samaria (including East Jerusalem) was expressed by the Israel Foreign Minister of the day, Mr. Moshe Sharett, who told the Knesset:

> This is a unilateral act which in no way binds Israel, we have concluded an Armistice Agreement with the Government of [the] Hashemite [Kingdom of] Jordan and we are determined to abide strictly by its provisions. How-

ever, this agreement does not constitute any final political arrangement; and
no such arrangement is possible without negotiations between the parties
and the conclusion of peace between them. It must therefore be clear that
the question of the Arab [-inhabited] territories west of the Jordan [River]
remains . . . open.[43]

While Israel's negative reaction to the purported annexation by Jordan of Judaea and Samaria, was, of course, not unexpected, the same
cannot be said about the reaction of the Arab States to these measures.
They too voiced their strong opposition to the Jordanian annexation
measures. On April 13, 1950, that is, 11 days before the adoption of the
Jordanian parliamentary resolution referred to above, the Council of the
Arab League decided that "annexation of Arab Palestine by any Arab
State would be considered a violation of the League Charter, and subject
to sanctions."[44] Three weeks after the said proclamation—on May 15, 1950
—the Political Committee of the Arab League, in an extraordinary session in Cairo, decided, without objection (Jordan herself was absent from
the meeting), that the Jordanian annexation measure constituted a violation of the Council's resolution of April 13, 1950,[45] and considered the
expulsion of Jordan from the League; but it was decided that discussion
of punitive measures be postponed to another meeting, set for June 12,
1950.[46] At that meeting of the League Council it had before it a Jordanian
Memorandum asserting that "annexation of Arab Palestine was irrevocable, although without prejudice to any final settlement of the Palestine
question."[47] This formula enabled the Council to adopt a face-saving
resolution "to treat the Arab part of Palestine annexed by Jordan as a
trust in its hands until the Palestine case is fully solved in the interests
of its inhabitants."[48] The Council thereupon constituted itself as the
League's Political Committee,[49] and invited Jordan to agree that the
annexation should cease to be valid if the frontiers of Palestine as they
existed under the British Mandate were restored.[50]

Some 17 years later, on May 31, 1967 (that is, less than a week before
the outbreak of the Arab-Israel hostilities of June, 1967), Jordan herself
seems to have called in question—unwittingly, perhaps—the validity of
her annexation measures of April, 1950, when her representative, Mr.
El-Farra, told the Security Council:

There is an Armistice Agreement. The Agreement did not fix boundaries;
it fixed the demarcation line. The Agreement did not pass judgement on
rights—political, military or otherwise. Thus I know of no boundary; *I know
of a situation frozen by an Armistice Agreement.*[51]

If the analysis here submitted is correct, the Kingdom of Jordan never
acquired the status of a legitimate sovereign over Judaea and Samaria

(including East Jerusalem); on the interpretation most favorable to Jordan, her rights in these territories could not exceed those of a belligerent occupant. Consequently, Jordan is not entitled in respect of these territories to the reversionary rights of sovereignty which international law confers on the legitimate sovereign *vis-à-vis* the belligerent occupant. Thus, whatever Jordanian rights existed in Judaea and Samaria (including East Jerusalem) on the eve of the June War of 1967, within the framework of the Israel–Jordan General Armistice Agreement of 1949—and it must be remembered that that Agreement was the only source for the existence of any Jordanian rights in those territories—ceased to exist when the Jordanian forces were ousted from the said territories as a result of the hostilities of June, 1967. This conclusion is warranted by the fact that the Jordanian attack on the morning of June 5, 1967, along the Israel–Jordan Armistice Demarcation Line in general and in Jerusalem in particular,[52] was in the nature of a "material breach" of the Israel–Jordan General Armistice Agreement, Article I(2) of which had provided that "no aggressive action by the armed forces—land, sea, or air—of either Party shall be undertaken, planned, or threatened against the people or the armed forces of the other." And it is an accepted principle of international law (which has now also found expression in the 1969 Vienna Convention on the Law of Treaties) that "a material breach of a bilateral treaty by one of the parties entitles the other to invoke the breach as a ground for terminating the treaty or suspending its operation in whole or in part."[53]

The initiation by Jordan on June 5, 1967, of large-scale hostilities against Israel—as a result of which Jordan lost control of Judaea and Samaria, including East Jerusalem—was unqestionably in the nature of such a "material breach" following which Israel announced—as she was entitled to do—that she regarded the Armistice Agreement with Jordan as terminated because of its violation by Jordan.

While Israel thus seized control of East Jerusalem in 1967 in lawful exercise of her inherent right of self-defense which is recognized also under Article 51 of the U.N. Charter,[54] the origins of Jordanian rule in East Jerusalem lay—as has been amply shown above—in the aggression committed by Transjordan in 1948 against the newly born State of Israel, in the course of which aggression Transjordan invaded Palestinian territory (including East Jerusalem). Schwebel has succinctly pointed up the important legal consequences flowing from this difference in the origins of the respective rights in East Jerusalem (and in the other regions of Palestine which were overrun by the Arabs in 1948) of Israel, on the one hand, and of the Arab States, on the other:

> Having regard to the consideration that . . . Israel . . . [acted] defensively in
> 1948 and 1967 . . . and her Arab neighbors . . . [acted] aggressively in 1948 and

1967 . . . Israel has *better title* in the territory of what was Palestine, including the whole of Jerusalem, than do Jordan and Egypt. . . .[55]

Schwebel's assertion that Israel can show a *better* title than Jordan or Egypt to any territory that lies within the boundaries of the former Palestine Mandate rests on solid legal foundations. For it must be remembered that title to territory is normally based not on a claim of *absolute* validity (few such claims could be substantiated), but rather on one of *relative* validity.[56] Thus, for example, in the *Minquiers and Ecrehos* case, the International Court of Justice, when called upon to adjudicate in the territorial dispute between the United Kingdom and France, decided "to appraise the *relative* strength of the opposing claims to sovereignty."[57] Since, in the present view, no State can make out a legal claim to Judaea and Samaria (including East Jerusalem) that is equal to that of Israel, this relative superiority of Israel may be sufficient, under international law, to make Israeli possession of those territories virtually indistinguishable from an absolute title to be valid *erga omnes.*[58] The fact that Israel has so far refrained from making full exercise of these rights beyond the municipal limits of Jerusalem is perhaps best explained by the Israel Government's reluctance to close *political* options in any future negotiations with Jordan.

It is against the background of these *legal* considerations—as distinct from the *political* considerations underlying the resolutions of the political organs of the U.N.—that the questions surrounding the juridical status of Jerusalem have to be viewed. In fact, in passing the law of June 27, 1967, and in proclaiming the following day the municipal unification of Jerusalem and the extension of Israeli law and jurisdiction to the unified city, the Knesset and the Israel Government, respectively, only followed the pattern set in 1948 and consistently resorted to ever since. Thus, in Section 1 of the Area of Jurisdiction and Powers Ordinance, 5708–1948, passed by the Provisional Council of State on September 22, 1948, it had been provided that "any law applying to the whole of the State of Israel shall be deemed to apply to the whole of the area including both the area of the State of Israel and *any part of Palestine* which the Minister of Defense has defined by proclamation as being held by the Defense Army of Israel."[59]

It was in virtue of this conception that the law and jurisdiction of Israel were extended to all those parts of the former Palestine Mandate held by Israel which lay beyond the boundaries envisaged under the partition plan of the U.N. General Assembly, including the western part of Jerusalem and the "Jerusalem Corridor" that between 1948 and 1967 linked Israel's capital to the rest of the State. Likewise, it was in this spirit that the then Prime Minister of Israel, David Ben-Gurion, told the Provisional Council of State on November 11, 1948:

The Government is not bound by the [U.N. General Assembly] Resolution of November 29, [1947], and the Foreign Minister has repeatedly stated that account has to be taken of the new situation. . . . The Government is well aware of the fact that the areas held by us [which are situated beyond the boundaries proposed under the partition plan] have been *liberated* from enemy hands by the Israel Defense Forces.[60]

This conception was also echoed some 19 years later by the Minister of Justice Ya'akov Shimshon Shapira when, in tabling the bill that was to become the law of June 27, 1967, he told the Knesset:

What needs to be stated—for the purpose of the bill which I am now introducing . . .—is that the Israel Defense Forces have liberated from foreign yoke considerable areas of Eretz Israel . . . which have now been for more than a fortnight under the control of the Israel Defense Forces.

The legal conception of the State of Israel—an organic conception adjusted to the practical political realities—has always been based on the principle that the law, jurisdiction and administration of the State apply to all those parts of Eretz Israel which are *de facto* under the State's control.

It is the view of the Government—and this view is in conformity with the requirements of international law—that in addition to the control by the Israel Defense Forces of these territories there is required also an open act of sovereignty on the part of Israel to make Israel law applicable to them. . . . It is for this reason that the Government has seen fit to introduce the bill which I now submit to the Knesset.[61]

NOTES AND REFERENCES

1. 21 *Laws of the State of Israel* (authorized translation from the Hebrew, prepared by the Ministry of Justice), p. 75. "Eretz Israel" (literally "the Land of Israel") is the Hebrew designation of the Holy Land, and served also as the Hebrew name of Mandatory Palestine.

2. General Assembly Resolution 2253 (ES-V).

3. General Assembly Resolution 2254 (ES-V).

4. In its Resolution 252 (1968) of May 21, 1968, the Security Council considered that "all legislative and administrative measures and actions taken by Israel, including expropriation of land and properties thereon, which tend to change the legal status of Jerusalem are invalid and cannot change that status," and "urgently" called upon Israel "to rescind all such measures already taken and to desist forthwith from taking any further action which tends to change the status of Jerusalem."

In its Resolution 267 (1969) of July 3, 1969, the Council reaffirmed its previous resolution, censured "in the strongest possible terms all measures taken to change the status of the City of Jerusalem," requested Israel to inform the Council of its intentions with regard to the implementation of its resolution, and determined that, in the event of a negative response or no response from Israel, it would reconvene without delay to consider further action.

In Resolution 298 (1971) of September 25, 1971, the Council again resolved that Israel actions "to change the status of the city of Jerusalem, including expropriation of land and properties, transfer of populations and legislation aimed at the incorporation of the occupied section are totally invalid and cannot change that status," and called on Israel to rescind all previous measures and to take no further steps in the "occupied section" of Jerusalem "which may purport to change the status of the City, or which would prejudice the rights of the inhabitants and the interests of the international community, or a just and lasting peace." The Council also instructed the Secretary-General to report within 60 days on the implementation of the resolution.

In his report to the Council of November 19, 1971 (S/10392), Mr. U Thant stated that he had been unable to fulfill his mandate. For Israel's reply to the Secretary-General, see the said report, as reproduced in the U.N. *Monthly Chronicle* for December, 1971, 108, pp. 112–115.

5. See footnotes 42, and 44 to 50 below.

6. The geographical designation "Judaea and Samaria" is preferred throughout this article to the commonly employed political term "West Bank," which in actual fact prejudges the issue here under discussion by implying that the areas in question constitute the "west bank" of the Kingdom of Jordan. The inaccuracy of this political term from the geographical point of view is only augmented by the fact that the whole of Palestine (and consequently the whole territory of Israel, including Tel Aviv, Haifa, and the coastal plain) is situated on the "west bank" of the Jordan River.

7. Under Article 4 of the Palestine Mandate, under which Great Britain was made responsible for "the establishment in Palestine of a national home for the Jewish people," and recognition was given "to the historical connexion of the Jewish people with Palestine and to the grounds for reconstituting their national home" therein, the Jewish Agency was recognized "as a public body for the purpose of advising and cooperating with the Administration of Palestine in such economic, social and other matters as may affect the establishment of the Jewish national home and the interests of the Jewish population in Palestine."

8. The original Palestine Mandate comprised both Palestine and Transjordan, with a total territory of approximately 42,000 square miles, of which slightly more than 10,000 square miles (about one-fourth) were situated to the west of the Jordan River, the rest being to the east of that river.

Under Article 25 of the Palestine Mandate, Great Britain was empowered "to postpone or withhold application of such provisions of this mandate as . . . [she] may consider inapplicable to the existing local conditions" in the territories "lying between the Jordan and the eastern boundary of Palestine."

Pursuant to the said provision, Great Britain in 1921 decided, with the consent of the Council of the League of Nations, to exclude the territory of the Palestine Mandate lying to the east of the Jordan River (*i.e.,* Transjordan) from the application of the Mandate provisions relative to the establishment of the Jewish national home. As a result of this decision—the main purpose of which was to offer the Emir Abdullah of Hejaz (the later King Abdullah) the possession of Transjordan and to remove the danger of an Anglo-French conflict because of Abdullah's threatened march on Damascus to reinstall there his brother Feisal (later King Feisal of Iraq) who had been driven out by the French—the territory earmarked for the Jewish national home was reduced to about one-fourth of its original size. Only slightly more than a half of this remaining one-fourth (*i.e.*, about one-eighth of the original Palestine Mandate) would have become the Jewish State under the Partition Plan of the U.N. General Assembly.

9. Jerusalem has had continuously a Jewish majority for the past century. According to the Rev. James Parkes (*Whose Land? A History of the Peoples of Palestine* [Pelican-Penguin Books, rev. ed., 1970], p. 230), "In 1872 the Jewish population [in Jerusalem] just outnumbered the combined Christian and Muslim inhabitants (Jews 10,600, Christians 5,300, Muslims 5,000). In 1899 the comparable figures were: Jews 30,000, Christians 10,900, and Muslims 7,700."

The figures for 1948 were 100,000 Jews, 25,000 Christians, and 45,000 Muslims. In 1967 there were 195,000 Jews, 10,800 Christians, and 54,900 Muslims, showing a sharp decline of the Christian community in East Jerusalem during the 19 years of Jordanian rule. In 1970 there were 215,000 Jews, 11,500 Christians, and 61,600 Muslims, the Jewish population thus constituting about three-quarters of the population of the unified city.

10. 6 (1946–1948) *Keesing's Contemporary Archives*, p. 9244.

11. *Ibid.* Numerous decisions to this effect were taken by the Arab States during the first months of 1948, while the Palestine Mandate was rapidly approaching its end. Thus, for example, on April 22, 1948 (*i.e.*, less than one month before the Mandate's termination), King Abdullah of Transjordan declared that the Arab world must take "joint action against Zionism," and issued a call to the Arab countries to join with the Transjordanian army "in a movement to Palestine to retain the Arab character of that country."

12. Lauterpacht, E., *Jerusalem and the Holy Places*, 1968, p. 16.

13. *Ibid.*, p. 22.

14. *Ibid.*, p. 21.

15. *Ibid.*, p. 19.

16. 3rd session of the People's Council, *Records of the People's Council and the Provisional Council of State*, I, p. 19; in Hebrew. Emphasis in original.

17. Article 2(4) stipulates that "all Members (of the U.N.) shall refrain in their international relations from the threat or use of force against the territorial integrity or political independence of any State, or in any other manner inconsistent with the Purposes of the United Nations." Transjordan was not a member of the U.N. in 1948. However, the rule embodied in Article 2(4) is commonly believed to be one of general international law and thus applicable to *all* States, whether or not members of the United Nations. According to Kelsen (*The Law of the United Nations*, 1950, p. 107), "non-Member states are obliged by the Charter, just as Members are, ... to refrain in their relation to other states from the threat or use of force." See also Soder, *Die Vereinten Nationen und die Nichtmitglieder*, 1956, pp. 156–157. See further Goodrich, Hambro and Simons, *Charter of the United Nations*, 3rd ed., 1969, p. 60.

18. Egyptian communication to the Security Council of May 15, 1948; Doc. S/743.

19. Cablegram by King Abdullah to the Security Council, Doc. S/748.

20. *Ibid.*

21. Security Council, *Official Records*, 292nd meeting of May 15, 1948, p. 25.

22. *Ibid.*,

23. *Ibid.*, 297th meeting of May 20, 1948, p. 5.

24. *Ibid.*, 306th meeting of May 27, 1948, p. 7.

25. *Ibid.*, 299th meeting of May 21, 1948, pp. 13–15. Article 52(1) of the Charter provides that "nothing in the present Charter precludes the existence of regional arrangements or agencies for dealing with such matters relating to the maintenance of international peace and security as are appropriate for regional action, provided that such arrangements or agencies and their activities are consistent with the Purposes and Principles of the United Nations."

26. *Ibid.*, 301st meeting of May 22, 1948, p. 7.

27. *Ibid.*, 302nd meeting of May 22, 1948, pp. 41–42.

28. *Ibid.*

29. *Ibid.*, pp. 42–43.

30. The Israel–Egypt General Armistice Agreement may be found in 42 *United Nations Treaty Series*, p. 251; the Israel–Lebanon Agreement, *ibid.*, p. 287; the Israel–Jordan Agreement, *ibid.*, p. 303; the Israel–Syria Agreement, *ibid.*, p. 327.

The name of the "Hashemite Kingdom of Transjordan" was changed in 1949 to the "Hashemite Kingdom of Jordan," the reason for this change being the fact that "the country today includes a large part of Arab Palestine . . . thus extending geographically on both banks of the Jordan River." (Official announcement of the Jordan Government of June 2, 1949, reproduced in 7 [1948–1950] *Keesing's Contemporary Archives*, p. 10050). In view of the fact that the official announcement regarding the change of name was made only on June 2, 1949, it is not clear why the Armistice Agreement with Israel was signed on April 3, 1949, by "Jordan," rather than by "Trans-Jordan."

31. See Rosenne, *Israel's Armistice Agreements with the Arab States*, 1951, pp. 24–32; Levie, "The Nature and Scope of the Armistice Agreement," 50 (1956) *American Journal of International Law*, p. 880; Feinberg, *The Legality of a "State of War" after the Cessation of Hostilities*, 1961.

32. 42 *United Nations Treaty Series*, p. 306; emphasis supplied.

33. Stone, *The Middle East under Cease-Fire* (A Bridge Publication) 1967, p. 12. Some writers even go so far as to question the right of the aggressor to enjoy the benefits of the international law of belligerent occupation. Thus, for example, Seyersted maintains that "*it can no longer be maintained that the laws of war apply equally in all respects to the aggressor and the defenders.* Basically the aggressor could not derive from his illegal act any rights under the customary laws of war." (Seyersted, *United Nations in the Law of Peace and War*, 1966, p. 224; emphasis in original).

34. Stone, *loc. cit.*

35. McNair, *The Legal Effect of War*, 3rd ed., 1948, p. 320.

36. Castrén, *The Present Law of War and Neutrality*, 1954, pp. 215–216; emphasis in original.

37. Stone, *Legal Controls of International Conflict*, rev. ed., 1959, p. 720.

38. Kelsen, *Principles of International Law*, 2nd ed. (ed. by Turner), 1967, p. 139.

39. von Glahn, *The Occupation of Enemy Territory*, 1957, p. 274.

40. Greenspan, *The Modern Law of Land Warfare*, 1959, p. 390. See also Castrén, *op. cit.*, p. 214; see further Stone, *op. cit.*, p. 696, n. 14.

41. 8 (1950–1952) *Keesing's Contemporary Archives*, p. 10812.

42. Three days after the Jordanian parliamentary resolution, on April 27, 1950, Mr. Kenneth Younger, Minister of State, announced in the House of Commons that "His Majesty's Government have decided to accord formal recognition to the union," excluding, however, Jerusalem from this recognition, since "His Majesty's Government . . . are unable to recognize Jordan sovereignty over any part of it." (Hansard, *Parliamentary Debates, House of Commons*, 5th series, vol. 474, cols. 1137–1138). See also Stone, *The Middle East under Cease-Fire*, 1967, p. 13.

43. *Divrei HaKnesset* (Parliamentary Records), vol. 5, p. 1282, col. 1; in Hebrew.

44. 8 (1950–1952) *Keesing's Contemporary Archives*, p. 10812.

45. *Ibid.*

46. Schwadran, *Jordan—a State of Tension*, 1959, p. 298.

47. 8 (1950–1952) *Keesing's Contemporary Archives*, p. 10812. The use of the term "Arab Palestine" is rather interesting, for it constitutes an oblique and indirect admission of the existence of a "non-Arab" part of the country. In view of the fact that Transjordan originally invaded Palestine "to retain the Arab character of that country" (see footnote 11 above), the terminology employed here would appear to reflect a hitherto unacknowledged change in the official Arab position.

48. Schwadran, *op. cit.*

49. 8 (1950–1952) *Keesing's Contemporary Archives*, p. 10812. The adoption of the resolution by the Political Committee rather than by the Council is explained by the fact that, according to Article 7 of the Pact of Arab States of March 22, 1945, only the Council's decisions are binding; the Political Committee's decisions, on the other hand, are only in the nature of recommendations. (See 70 *United Nations Treaty Series*, p. 254.)

50. 8 (1950–1952) *Keesing's Contemporary Archives*, p. 10812.

51. U.N. Doc. S/PV 1345 of May 31, 1967, p. 47; emphasis supplied.

52. On June 19, 1967, Israel's Foreign Minister Abba Eban told the U.N. General Assembly that "even after Jordan had bombarded and bombed Israel territory at several points, we still proposed to the Jordanian monarch that he abstain from continuing hostilities. I sent a message to him through General Odd Bull, the United Nations representative, at 12:30 P.M., some hours after the beginning of hostilities. A message to this effect reached him several hours after the outbreak of hostilities on the southern front (with Egypt). . . . Jordan tragically answered not with words but with a torrent of shells." *(General Assembly, Official Records*, 1526th meeting, pp. 12–13.) On June 26, 1967, Mr. Eban gave the General Assembly a detailed account of those developments of June 5, and told the Assembly that "Jordan opened intensive and destructive war upon Israel on 5 June, without Israel having fired a single shot against Jordanian citizens, without Israel having touched an inch of Jordan territory. . . . Even after several Jordan bombardments and bombing sorties had taken place, with loss of Israeli life and damage to our towns and cities, we offered Jordan the opportunity to disengage. . . . At noon I sent a message to the Jordanian monarch through General Bull. The message was plain: Israel will not attack any State which refrains from attacking it. The message . . . was answered by the crash of shells falling in Jerusalem's streets and buildings. For the second time in twenty years that city, whose name stirs the deepest historic memories, was wantonly converted by Jordan forces into a battlefield. Jordan . . . had gambled with destiny and incurred

the full responsibility of unprovoked war." *(Ibid.,* 1536th meeting, p. 9.) Mr. Eban's version was confirmed in substance by General Odd Bull who had been Chief of Staff of the U.N. Truce Supervision Organization until 1970, after the latter's return to his native Norway in August of that year. In an interview to the Oslo daily *Aftenposten* of August 22, 1970, General Bull confirmed that on the morning of June 5, 1967, "I was summoned to the Israel Foreign Ministry and on arrival, at about 9 A.M., I was asked to convey a message to King Hussein and the Jordanian Government. It amounted to the following: if Jordan remained passive during the war, Israel would do nothing. On the other hand, if Jordan joined Egypt, Israel would use all means in its power to fight Jordan. The message was conveyed through our cease-fire apparatus. As far as I can understand, it reached King Hussein at 10:30 A.M. and the exchange of fire in Jerusalem started about an hour later." King Hussein himself, in an interview published in the Hamburg weekly magazine *Der Spiegel* of September 4, 1967, acknowledges the receipt of an Israeli message to the effect that "if we do not attack, we shall be spared the otherwise unavoidable consequences. However, at that time we had no longer any other choice, we had to do everything [possible] to aid our allies [in Egypt and Syria]." *(Der Spiegel* of September 4, 1967, p. 97.) See also Hussein of Jordan, *My "War" With Israel* (as told to and with additional materials by Vick Vance and Pierre Laner), 1969, pp. 64–5.

53. Article 60(1) of the 1969 Vienna Convention on the Law of Treaties, 63 (1969) *American Journal of International Law,* p. 875.

54. On the question of self-defense in relation to the Six Day War, see Shapira, "The Six-Day War and the Right of Self-Defence," 6 (1971) *Israel Law Review,* pp. 65–80. Shapira points out that "Substantial majorities of the Security Council, as well as of the General Assembly, rejected all proposals designed to brand Israel as the aggressor and to order the withdrawal of its forces back to the armistice demarcation lines." *(Ibid.,* p. 79.) He therefore rightly concludes that "Even if the United Nations record on this matter falls short of establishing an affirmative finding decisively upholding the lawfulness of Israel's action, at the very least it provides solid support for Israel's claim to have acted in legitimate exercise of its right of self-defence." *(Ibid.,* p. 80.)

55. Schwebel, "What Weight to Conquest?" 64 (1970) *American Journal of International Law,* pp. 346–347. Under the Israel–Egyptian Armistice Agreement of 1949, Egypt retained control of the "Gaza Strip" in the southwestern corner of the former Palestine Mandate. Unlike Jordan, however, Egypt never purported to annex that territory, and regarded it as being merely under Egyptian administration.

56. See O'Connell, *International Law,* 2nd. ed., vol. 1, 1970, p. 407; see also Stone, *No Peace—No War in the Middle East,* 1969, p. 40; see also Brownlie, *Principles of Public International Law,* 1966, pp. 150–151; see further Blum, *Historic Titles in International Law,* 1965, pp. 222–229, 335–336.

57. International Court of Justice, *Reports of Judgments,* 1953, p. 67; emphasis supplied.

58. For a different view, see Levine, "The Status of Sovereignty in East Jerusalem and the West Bank," 5 (1972) *New York University Journal of International Law and Politics,* pp. 485 ff., and Gerson, "Trustee Occupant: The Legal Status of Israel's Presence in the West Bank," 14 (1973) *Harvard International Law Journal,* p. 1 ff.

59. 1 *Laws of the State of Israel*, p. 64; emphasis supplied.

60. 26th session of the Provisional Council of State, *Records of the People's Council and Provisional Council of State*, vol. II, 26th session, p. 5; emphasis supplied.

61. *Divrei HaKnesset* (Parliamentary Records), vol. 49, col. 2420.

VIII

Jerusalem as the Capital of Israel

HIRSCH GOODMAN

HISTORICAL PERSPECTIVE

Jerusalem has always had a unique place among the cities of the world. It is precisely this uniqueness that has fostered unending debates at international forums about the city's status.

The city's historical and religious significance for the three monotheistic religions has perennially acerbated discussion and clouded rational analysis concerning Israel's claim to Jerusalem as its capital. To Muslims and Christians the city has spiritual and religious connotations; for Jews this city has an extra dimension beyond their spiritual and religious connections with it, for Jerusalem has been the focus of Jewish national aspirations throughout the centuries.

Although Jewish rule in the city has been intermittent, the Jewish presence has been a virtually uninterrupted feature of its life since 1,000 B.C. It was the capital of King David at the peak of the greatness of the ancient Jewish Kingdom, and the site of the First and Second Temples.

The fall of the city to the Romans in A.D. 70 and the subsequent destruction of the Second Temple resulted in the loss of Jewish sovereignty over the city that was to last for some 2,000 years (apart from a brief period of Jewish rule under the Persians in the seventh century A.D.).

Nevertheless, Jerusalem continued to serve as the spiritual center during the period of the Jewish dispersion, and the Jewish return to the city is the major theme in Jewish worship. This was reinforced with the rise of secular Zionism—a movement propagating the return to Zion, the site of King David's fortress, today near the center of the modern city.

Despite its religious importance, Jerusalem under non-Jewish rule was a neglected provincial town of small population (15,000 in 1845) and little political or administrative significance in the area. However, the major world powers continuously maintained a certain degree of involvement in the area because of the presence of major religious institutions and communities of the three major religions. These communities—various Christian sects in particular—still frequently appeal to their countries of origin to maintain and protect their rights in the city.

As a result of the growth of European power in the Middle East, renewed interest in the area by the European countries in the latter half of the nineteenth century led to their more direct involvement in the affairs of the city, stimulated its growth, and resulted in the first expansion of the city outside the Old City walls.

It was at this stage that the first Jewish quarters were built, under the sponsorship of European Jewish philanthropists such as Sir Moses Montefiore and the Rothschilds. The construction of Christian institutions also flourished, and it was during this period that many of the major landmarks of modern Jerusalem, such as the Hospice of Notre Dame de France, the Church of Gethsemane (built by the Russian Royal Court), and the Soeurs de Reparatris Convent were constructed.

In the mid-nineteenth century the town also received its first hospitals built by European philanthropists and religious orders. These included the Rothschild Hospital, Bikur Holim, the Russian Compound Complex (which included hospitals, hospices, and churches) and the Italian hospital (built along similar lines).

EMERGENCE OF THE CITY

It was, however, only with the establishment of the British Mandate over Palestine at the end of World War I that the city emerged as an important capital and that the institutions and services befitting its newly acquired role were developed. This period was one of expansion, with many new suburbs being built, particularly in the western regions.

In the early 1920s, major Jewish quarters were established in Romema, Talpiot, Kiryat Moshe, Kiryat Shmuel, Bayit Vegan, and Beit Hakerem.

The British, however, mainly converted existing buildings, such as the Russian compound and the Augusta-Victoria Hospital, into administrative centers. The presence of the British government bodies in Jerusalem encouraged the establishment of the main national Arab and Jewish bodies there, such as the Arab Higher Committee and the Va'ad Leumi (the National Council of the Jewish Agency) in the city. The latter was centered in a fortresslike compound, the Jewish Agency building, which became the physical and activist nerve center of Zionist politics.

Several other major institutions were also constructed during this period, including the Hadassah Hospital, the Hebrew University on Mt. Scopus, the Young Mens' Christian Association, and the King David Hotel.

The growth of Jerusalem during this period is reflected in the rapid increase of its population, rising from 60,000 in 1905 to 165,000 in 1948. The Jewish element, already a majority of the population by the mid-nineteenth century, grew from 40,000 to slightly over 100,000 over the same period.

The rapid growth of the Jewish population inevitably led to increased tension between the Arab and Jewish sectors, resulting in serious riots in 1920, 1929, and particularly in 1936. Similar disturbances occurred throughout Palestine, but the particularly sensitive nature of Jerusalem, owing to its religious importance and the fact that its population was the most interdispersed of all the cities in Palestine, without a clear division between Arab and Jewish quarters (such as in Safed, Haifa, Tiberias, Tel Aviv, or Jaffa), heightened the conflict in the city. One of the major points of confrontation was the Wailing Wall, where severe restrictions were placed on Jews because of Arab suspicions about Jewish designs on the Temple Mount area—the present-day site of the major mosques. Jews were forbidden to blow the shofar (ram's horns) on High Holidays. Attempts to set up partitions dividing male and female worshippers at the Wailing Wall, as required by Jewish law, were regarded as a change in the status quo and ultimately led to the riots of 1929. The disturbances always centered around the Western Wall, which is adjacent to both the Jewish Quarter and to the Mosques of Omar and al-Aqsa in the Old City.

Increased Arab-Jewish hostilities after World War II ruled out the possibility of a bi-national state and made the partition of Palestine the only viable solution to the Arab-Jewish problem.

PARTITION

Under the 1947 Partition Plan eventually ratified by the United Nations, Jerusalem was designed to become an internationally administered city with the right of access to the holy places guaranteed to all. Though proposed internationalization of the city was regarded as a severe blow, Jewish leaders were prepared to accept it since they felt that the partition plan as a whole was the most realistic way of achieving a Jewish State. Only minority right-wing groups, such as the Irgun Tz'vai L'umi, were bitterly opposed to the internationalization scheme and proclaimed that "Jerusalem was and will forever be our Capital." Arab rejection of the scheme and the subsequent invasion of Palestine by the Arab armies led to the 1948 war, the results of which effectively annulled Jerusalem's status as envisioned by the Partition Plan and the United Nations decision.

During the war itself, control of Jerusalem and its approaches from the coast and of the centers of Jewish settlement became one of the primary military objectives of the Israel Army. The military effort entailed was out of all proportion to the strategic importance of the city, but Israeli leaders were adamantly convinced that a Jewish state without Jerusalem was inconceivable. In meeting the objections of his senior military commanders to mount a major offensive to clear the road to Jerusalem—an effort which entailed the mobilization of all the country's resources and left other sectors exposed to Arab attack—Ben-Gurion argued that "we have three vital centers—Tel Aviv, Haifa and Jerusalem. We can still survive if we lose one of them—provided that the one we lose is not Jerusalem." Some of the worst reverses suffered by Jewish forces during the war occurred in this theater, specifically at Latrun, the key to the city from the coast. Though the price paid was high, the Israelis managed to forge a narrow corridor, linking the city to Tel Aviv.

Jewish efforts in Jerusalem itself were less successful. Unable to provide the city's defenders with either arms or material, the newly emergent State of Israel found itself faced with the loss of the Old City and the Jewish quarter and its holy sites to the Jordanian Arab Legion.

The cease-fire arrangements, based on the military realities of the moment, created the partition of Jerusalem that lasted from 1948–1967. A north-south cease-fire line was drawn up—running roughly along the western wall of the Old City. The Arabs retained control over the Old City and its northeastern suburbs while the Jews retained the so-called "New" City. The Jordanians, who had entered the war primarily to gain territory, unilaterally annexed these sectors, which became an integral part of Judaea and Samaria, in 1950.

JERUSALEM UNDER ISRAELI RULE

After the war, measures were quickly taken to integrate the Jewish controlled sector of the city into the State of Israel. Ben-Gurion's government proclaimed Jerusalem the capital of the new state in 1948 and rapidly proceeded to transfer national institutions to the city.

These actions were carried out despite the ambiguous status of the city under international law. The United Nations and the major powers refused to recognize Israel's action and continued to maintain their embassies in Tel Aviv. Apart from several South American and African countries, 24 of the 46 foreign embassies are situated in Tel Aviv to this day. The major powers and most European countries have confined their representation in Jerusalem to the consular level.

Israel's position in the immediate postwar period remained tenuous due to security considerations, for it was basically an island of Jewish settlement surrounded on three sides by Arab villages. The war also had a disastrous effect on the Jewish population of the city. Some 30 per cent of the residents had left the city in the face of the lack of adequate food supplies and the open warfare in its streets.

Once Jerusalem became the capital of Israel, however, precedence was placed on linking the city with other centers. Within a few years a new road had been built by-passing Latrun, which remained in Jordanian territory. Regular railway services were instituted and the city was linked to the national power and water networks. In addition, many new settlements were established along the narrow corridor linking Jerusalem with the rest of the State. These settlements were mainly moshavim (cooperative farm villages) populated by new immigrants, who were coming up to the country in substantial numbers during this period. These measures were in line with the government's policy of maintaining a physical presence along the country's long and vulnerable borders, and served the purpose of providing protection to the city's approaches.

JERUSALEM AS THE CAPITAL OF ISRAEL

Despite the importance of Jerusalem on a religious and nationalistic level its emergence as the capital of the new state was far from certain in the immediate post-1948 period. Ravages suffered during the war, the difficulties of communications, and the serious decline in population all served to cloud its future.

Also, during the Mandate period, Tel Aviv became the primary center of Jewish settlement and the place where most major Zionist affairs were transacted. Tel Aviv was in the heartland of Jewish settlement, easily accessible from all parts of the country and thus in a position to provide the services and security for Zionist activities, and it was also the home of most of the leading Zionist activists. Jerusalem, on the other hand, had been under close supervision of the British, and the population, on the whole older and traditionalist, had been less involved in and dedicated to modern Zionist affairs, since they regarded the city as a religious rather than a political center. Thus, under British rule, although the main Zionist organs such as the Jewish Agency, the Jewish National Fund, and the National Executive maintained their headquarters in Jerusalem, most de facto business had been conducted in Tel Aviv, and in many respects, this relationship between the two cities, in which Jerusalem played a nominal, symbolic role and Tel Aviv served as the true center of power, has remained much the same.

Following the government's firm resolve to make Jerusalem its capital, sessions of Israel's Parliament (the Knesset) were transferred to the capital immediately after the cessation of hostilities, and were held in a temporary premises in the city. Other institutions, including government ministries, were transferred more gradually. It is interesting to note that Chaim Weizmann, the first President of Israel, continued to live in Rehovot (near Tel Aviv) beside the scientific institute he had founded, and did not take up residency in Jerusalem. The succeeding presidents of Israel have all, however, made Jerusalem their home.

By the late 1950s construction was started on a new government center, the *Kirya*, which today houses some of the major ministries. The *Kirya* is situated in the western part of the city, next to the Knesset and an array of other national buildings, which together comprise an impressive complex, visibly symbolizing Jerusalem's role as the nation's capital.

Thus far, 19 out of Israel's 21 government ministries have permanent head offices in the city. The major exception is the Ministry of Defense —the largest single government body—which is still in Tel Aviv, primarily for reasons of security. Israel Army Headquarters, too, are still situated in Tel Aviv.

THE WAR OF 1967 AND ITS AFTERMATH

The Six Day War of 1967 which resulted in the reunification of the city under Israeli rule and the establishment of Israeli control over the surrounding territory in Judaea and Samaria has had a profound effect on Jerusalem.

Geographically, the city is no longer an isolated outpost with no significant hinterland, but has become a major regional center. This fact, coupled with the removal of the security threat and easier access has led to an unprecedented new growth. Tourism in particular has flourished, stimulating the growth of the services industry, and the city has also benefitted from government-sponsored immigration.

The second major result of the war was the reunification of Jerusalem itself. Within a few weeks of the end of the war, the Knesset unilaterally declared Israeli sovereignty over the Old and eastern sections of the city, and government policy has unequivocally stated that the status of Jerusalem is not negotiable in any peace treaty with the Arab states, and that the city must remain one, and under Israeli control. Israel's unilateral moves have not gained international recognition and have been soundly

condemned by the United Nations, but its actions are a logical consequence of the national attitude towards the city, as Israel's historic capital.

The reunification of Jerusalem has also meant that for the first time
in 20 years the city had a considerable non-Jewish population comprising
some 30 per cent of the total population. Yet although on the administrative and services level the city is unified, it has remained in many respects
still divided, since contact between the Arab and Jewish sectors is still
minimal.

To ensure its continued control and in an attempt to ring the city with
Jewish settlement, the state has initiated a vast building program in what
was, between 1948–1967, Jordanian territory and in the confines of the "no
man's land" area of that period. Other steps to ensure cohesion have also
been taken. Thus, for example, Arabs living in Jerusalem who opt to do
so are free to enjoy full citizenship rights, including the progressive
Israeli social benefits, voting rights, government business loans, and the
right to travel and work freely throughout Israel.

JERUSALEM'S ROLE IN ISRAEL TODAY

From the socio-economic point of view, Jerusalem's population differs
considerably from that of other major Israeli cities. Apart from the significant non-Jewish minority, Jerusalem has also had faster population
growth as a result of immigration. This has grown since 1948 by some 250
per cent and stands today at 291,000—76,000 of whom are Arabs. Over 50
per cent of the city's Jewish residents were born outside Israel, and a
majority of these come from the Afro-Asian countries. The occupational
breakdown of the city's population reflects its character as a government
and service center. 75 per cent of the labor force is employed in administration, education, health, tourism, and various services, while only 17 per
cent is engaged in industry (as compared with 32 per cent in Tel Aviv and
Haifa).

Apart from the Knesset, government ministries, the Supreme Court,
and the Bank of Israel, many other Jewish institutions have made Jerusalem their headquarters. As is to be expected, most religious organizations,
including the Chief Rabbinate, the Rabbinical Law Courts, and other
important institutions of religious learning are to be found in Jerusalem.
Other major Israeli institutions include the Hebrew University—the first
and still primary institute of higher learning in the country—the Hadassah Hospital, the National Insurance Institute, and the Jewish Agency.
The latter has been instrumental in forging the role of Jerusalem as the
capital not alone of Israel but of world Jewry as well—a process further

reinforced by the multitude of international Jewish congresses held in Jerusalem annually.

ECONOMIC AND SOCIAL PROBLEMS

Several factors have, however, hindered the emergence of Jerusalem as the capital of Israel. Primary amongst these has been the fact that Tel Aviv, which has remained the financial and industrial hub of the country and its main center of population, has continued to dominate not only the economic, but also the cultural life of the country as a whole.

Many important private organizations maintain their headquarters in Tel Aviv. Prominent amongst these are virtually all political party related organizations. An interesting example is provided by Histadrut —Israel's Trade Union Federation—which despite the fact that it built its headquarters in Jerusalem recently, still continues to transact most of its affairs in Tel Aviv.

In addition, most government ministries have important offices in Tel Aviv where much of the day-to-day work is done. Thus, for the greater part of the week, government ministry personnel are not to be found in Jerusalem, while ministers too spend several days a week outside the capital on the conduct of party and government affairs. (The position of Knesset members in Israel differs from that of Representatives in the United States or in Britain, because the Israeli system of elections is proportional and not constituent, and thus members of parliament and ministers do not need to maintain a regional base or to keep in contact with their constituents.)

In recent years, government policy of encouraging the transfer of national institutions and large public organizations to the capital has been down-played, in keeping with the freeze on all public building in the capital, so as to divert manpower and building resources to immigrant housing. As a result, office space is unavailable, and many ministries are housed in temporary office space scattered throughout the city. The Ministry of Health, for example, recently moved to a new apartment block in the suburbs from its temporary offices in the annex of one of the city's larger hotels.

CONCLUSION

Despite the many problems, the trend toward Jerusalem's emergence as the capital of Israel cannot be denied. If, in the early 1950s, much of government policy was motivated by nationalistic considerations and was often symbolic in nature, recent developments—and specifically, the war of 1967—have created a situation which makes government from Jerusalem actually viable and not merely symbolic.

International recognition has, however, not been achieved, and the sensitive nature of the city and the conflicting demands of Israel and Jordan, and also of the religious authorities of all the three great religions would appear to preclude any solution to the problem in the foreseeable future.

II

THE COMMUNITIES

IX

The Jewish Presence in Jerusalem
Throughout the Ages

MENASHE HAREL

Throughout history, and particularly under Jewish rule, Jerusalem has been the main city in the Judaean Hills and the chief reason is its geography. Jerusalem stands atop of a range of hills, encircled and protected by deep valleys, at the junction of mountain highways, and has always enjoyed an excellent economy, between grainfields to the west and the desert to the east, and with a good supply of water.

THE CANAANITE PERIOD (330–1200 B.C.)

The city is called "Rushalmam" in Egyptian execration texts of the nineteenth century B.C.; Kathleen Kenyon discovered a nine-foot-thick wall of this period near the Spring of Gihon. In the days of the Patriarch Abraham, Jerusalem was governed by Melchizedek, described in Chapter 14 of Genesis as "King of Salem" and "the priest of the most high God," a description suggesting its importance and holiness even in Abraham's time and hinting at identification with Mt. Moriah. It probably gained its sacred character from the Spring of Gihon, the largest source on the hilltop and held by the ancients to be of miraculous property, as its waters rise and fall at regular intervals. Hence, too, several kings of Judah were crowned beside it.

Jerusalem is mentioned in the Tell el-Amarna letters, written in the fourteenth century B.C., as the principal town of Canaan. At the time of the Israelite entry into the Promised Land in the following century, its Amorite king, seemingly a vassal of Egypt (Josh. 10), led an alliance of the kings of the mountains and the plains, banded together to fight the Tribes.

THE FIRST TEMPLE PERIOD (1200–586 B.C.)

In the reign of David, Jerusalem was a Jebusite city (II Sam. 5:6). David brought the Ark of the Covenant from Kiryat Ye'arim to Jerusalem, and bought a threshing-floor from Araunah the Jebusite as site of an altar (II Sam. 24:24). By this act, he made Jerusalem the center of worship of the Tribes, but the Temple was built by his son Solomon, and thenceforward Jerusalem became the unique focus of Jewish creed and nationhood. Solomon did more: he launched a vast building program and concluded pacts with the kings of Egypt, Ammon, Moab, Tyre, and the Hittites that gave the city international renown. From its foundation and throughout the Canaanite period, Jerusalem had been a provincial capital and no more; only under the kings of Israel did it become the national and political capital of Jewry, the very heart of its faith and philosophy, symbolizing the unity of the Tribes.

THE SECOND PERIOD (586 B.C.-A.D. 70)

Jewish authority in Jerusalem and Judah became firmly entrenched again after the return from the Babylonian Exile. Under the Hasmonaeans, sovereign Jewish sway was extended over the entire Land. Nehemiah had repaired the city walls in 52 days (Neh. 4), Hasmonaean Hyrcanus rebuilt them and their watch towers. Ten thousand builders and a thousand priests toiled to build Herod's Temple, a thousand chariots hauled the building materials. The courtyard and colonnades took eight years to finish, the Sanctuary itself only 18 months (Ant. 15:11,12; 2:5,6). The Sages could rightly say, "Who has not seen the Sanctuary has not seen a magnificent building." But the total rebuilding of Jerusalem and its walls in Herod's days took approximately 46 years (John 2:20).

During the Second Temple period, a span of about 600 years, Jerusalem drew the prayers and commanded the allegiance of every Jew in the Land and the Diaspora alike; the First Temple had been a center of veneration and national liturgy for Jews in the Land alone. The sanctity of the city was evident in learning of the Torah, pilgrimages, the establishment of schools and synagogues. Synagogues were built for public worship, but the Temple was the hub of communal life in Jerusalem and the supreme national institution of Jewry throughout the world. Jews were under religious commandment not alone to make pilgrimages to the Holy Land but to settle there; Christians and Muslims were content with pilgrimage. Even when the Temple stood no longer, Jews everywhere regarded it, nonetheless, as a Divine behest to make their devotions in a Jerusalem that lay in ruins.

THE ROMAN PERIOD (A.D. 70–324)

Jews lived on in Jerusalem and worshipped their God amid the wreckage of the Temple Mount. Such was the strength of this passionate attachment that, when the emperor Hadrian sought to establish a Roman town upon the Mount, defiling the holy city, rebellion broke out under Bar Kochba, and the Jews recaptured it for a space (A.D. 132–135). The revolt was bloodily suppressed, and the Romans forbade Jews to dwell in Jerusalem, on pain of death. Yet, the lament entitled *Arzei Levanon* ("Cedars of Lebanon"), written immediately after the rising collapsed, tells that a certain "Rabbi Hanina Ben-Taradion gathers after him congregations in ravished Zion," an index, perhaps, that the anti-Jewish decree was not, in fact, enforced, and the soil of the Land was still sacred to Jews. Rabbi Meir ordained: "One may not lease them [the Gentiles] houses in Eretz Israel or, it goes without saying, fields," and, defying Roman edicts, synagogues were established in the third century on Mt. Zion in Jerusalem itself and throughout the Land, particularly in Galilee.

THE BYZANTINE PERIOD (324–637)

Jerusalem had become holy to a rising Christianity, and early in the fourth century Constantine the Great and his mother Helena built magnificent churches there, but now Jews were excluded, and for a time Jerusalem was the only city in the Land with a Christian majority. Jerome, writing in the fourth century, mentions that Jews might only enter on the Ninth of Av, to mourn the quenching of past glory: "Silently they come and silently they go, weeping they come and weeping they go, in the dark night they come and in the dark night they go," as the Sages told. The Traveler of Bordeaux, writing in 333, speaks of that marked stone on the Temple Mount whither Jews went to pray. In 362, at last, the emperor Julian promised a delegation of Syrian and Silician Jewry: "I shall rebuild the Sanctuary of the most high God with all vigor." But a mysterious fire that broke out on the Temple Mount during the early stage of the building operation brought this project to an abrupt halt, and it was never renewed. In 443, heartened by the goodwill of the empress

Eudocia, Jewry again dreamt of the Day of Redemption, and from Jerusalem a message went out to the Diaspora:

> The time of the Exile of our people has already passed and the Day of the Ingathering of the Tribes come. The kings of the Romans have bidden that our city, Jerusalem, be returned to us. Make haste and come up to Jerusalem for the Feast of Tabernacles, for our Kingdom in Jerusalem shall be established.

Manifestly, Jews were being vouchsafed to dwell peacefully in Jerusalem. St. Cyril of Scythopolis records that St. Sabbas journeyed to Constantinople in 512 to persuade the emperor to exempt the poor of Jerusalem from taxation while a certain Marianus went to the emperor to denounce the exemption of the Jews: it may be inferred that the Jewish population enjoyed a modicum of equal rights.

But Justinian, in the early sixth century, enacted discriminatory laws, and Jews were denied the holding of government office; humiliation was carried to such lengths that their stone of prayer on the Temple Mount was littered with garbage.

THE LATER PERSIAN PERIOD (614–629)

Upon the Persian conquest of Palestine, a pact was concluded between the Persians and its Jews, one mutually desirable: the Jews hoped for the restoration of Jewish autonomy, the rebuilding of Jerusalem and the Temple; the Persians needed Jewish help to gain control of the Eastern Mediterranean. A Jewish administration was, indeed, established in Jerusalem and worship renewed. But, in 629, the Byzantine emperor Heraclius seized the city and decreed the expulsion of the Jews to a distance of three miles. In 638, it fell to the army of the Caliph Omar.

THE EARLY MUSLIM PERIOD: THE UMAYYAD CALIPHATE (638–750)

Jewish soldiers had served in Omar's victorious army, and he countenanced the renewal of Jewish settlement in Palestine and Jerusalem, declaring that the Muslims had come to the country because they were kinsmen of the Israelites, both being scions of Abraham. Contemporary Arab writers record that stones were piled on the Temple Mount by the Jews, in readiness for the rebuilding of the Temple; the Muslims did, in truth, deliver the Mount into Jewish hands, and Jews could celebrate the Feast of Tabernacles upon it.

So now Jerusalem was a city holy to three faiths, if not in equal measure. It was Arabia that was to Islam what the Land of Israel was to Judaism, and, in any event, Palestine was never independent under Muslim aegis; its governance throughout that period was entrusted to overlords in Damascus, Baghdad, Cairo, or Constantinople.

But Omar at least proclaimed the Temple Mount to be a place of Jewish prayer. By the Jews, this was eagerly and happily interpreted as a sign of the beginning of Redemption.

> Omar asked the Jews—where do you wish to live in the city? and they answered—At the southern end of the city, which is the Jews' market. And [the reason for] their plea was the proximity of the Temple and its relics and the waters of Siloam for immersion. And the Emir of the Faithful gave this to them.

The Jewish quarter—or market—lay near the Western Wall.

Under the Umayyad Caliphate, Syria and Palestine were the major provinces of the Muslim empire with its capital in Damascus. Between 691 and 697, Abd al-Malik built the Dome of the Rock in Jerusalem as monument rather than mosque, and his elder son al-Walid built the mosque of al-Aqsa beside it, and in al-Aqsa, since Mecca was far away, the Muslims of Syria and Palestine began to hold their festal services. Mughir ad-Din says that Jewish families were actually appointed guardians of the Haram of Abd al-Malik. Suleiman, his second son, chose to live in Palestine and built Ramla to be its capital, relegating Jerusalem to humble provinciality. The townsfolk of Palestine consisted of Jews, Arabs, Persians, and Samaritans, all living side by side—in Tiberias and its surroundings, in Dan, Haifa, Jaffa, Jerusalem, and Hebron, and as far south as the Jewish settlement of Eilat. Jews flocked to Jerusalem after the Muslim conquest, and their community had quickly become the most important in the country, so that Jewry everywhere looked no longer to Tiberias but to Jerusalem.

THE ABBASID CALIPHATE (750–969)

Baghdad, not Damascus, was the capital now. In the Abbasid heyday, the importance of Jerusalem dwindled by reason of its remoteness from the "metropolis," and Mecca became the magnet of the Muslim devout. Haroun al-Rashid made that pilgrimage every second year, but never once to Jerusalem, for the Abbasid caliphs, in general, neglected Jerusalem; only al-Mamun (813–833) gave money to repair Muslim institutions on the Temple Mount. The viceroys of the Abbasids and of their successors, the Fatimids, governed Palestine from Ramla. Meanwhile Jewish life went on. It is of this period that Rabbi Ben Meir, principal of the

Palestinian Academy, tells that the courtyard of the Temple Mount was a meeting place for Jews.

THE FATIMID CALIPHATE (969–1071)

Al-Hakim, Fatimid despot of Egypt, first ordered that the synagogues and churches of Jerusalem be destroyed, but in the end relented, and Jews and Christians were permitted to rebuild them. Salmon Ben-Yeruham, the Karaite, writes in the middle of the tenth century:

> When the Kingdom of Ishmael appeared, Israel was given license to enter and live there [Jerusalem] and the courtyards of the House of the Lord were handed back to them and there for years they prayed.

The Seljuks took Jerusalem in 1071 in an assault of unbridled devastation. As Seljuks and Fatimids fought thereafter, the citizenry of Palestine grew less and less. The Arab historian, al-Muqadassi, who lived in Jerusalem in that century, writes that, after 400 years of Muslim rule in Palestine:

> The scholar of religious law is forsaken, and the secular scholar is not to be seen . . . the Jews and the Christians have long since superseded them, and the mosque is empty of worshippers and of the secret of study.

Sahal Ben Matzliah, a resident in Jerusalem at the end of the previous century, writes:

> Our brothers knew that Jerusalem in this time was a sanctuary for every fugitive, a comfort for every mourner and a repose for every pauper, and the worshippers of the Lord congregate within it, one from the town and two from the family [meaning, in large numbers]. . . .

Never again—from the Seljuk conquest until the twentieth century —was Jerusalem to be under Arab hegemony.

THE EARLY CRUSADER PERIOD (1099–1187)

Crusader Jerusalem was circumscribed in area, and its walls followed the lines of those standing today. Godfrey de Bouillon always stressed that the territory which he had conquered was the Land of Israel: the letter in which he informed the Pope of his taking of Jerusalem bore the superscription: "de Terra Israel." But in the ravaging of Jerusalem, the Crusaders slaughtered Muslims and Jews indiscriminately, and set fire to the Jewish quarter, in those days sited to the north of the Temple Mount, burning its synagogues, one of them with all its worshippers. A Crusader ordinance specifically banned Jewish and Muslim settlement in Jerusalem as profane, and the wrecked and deserted Jewish quarter was given over to Syrian Christians. But Benjamin of Tudela (1170) could report:

> And there is a dye-factory there, which the Jews rent yearly from the king, so that no man but the Jews shall do any dyeing work in Jerusalem, and there are about two hundred Jews living below the Tower of David at the limits of the [city-] State.

THE LATE CRUSADER PERIOD (1187–1260)

The Ayyubid Sultan Saladin and his successors favored the dwelling of Eastern Jews and Christians in Jerusalem. That great soldier and statesman recognized the Jewish right to the Land, but was also mindful that Jews had fought in the Arab ranks to take Jerusalem from the Crusaders. Alharizi (1170–1235) recounts that, after Saladin's proclamation, "three hundred rabbis" from France and England came to live in Palestine, and Jews from North Africa, accompanied by Muslims, to live in Jerusalem itself.

THE MAMELUKES (1260–1516)

Saladin had permitted Muslims and Jews once more to live at least in the hilly parts of Palestine, and the ban on Jewish residence in Jerusalem was formally lifted, but Jews did not begin to return in any numbers until the coming and encouragement of Nahmanides. In 1267, he had found two lonely Jewish families, and wrote to his son:

> Only two Jews, brothers, dyers by trade, did I find. And behold, we pressed them, and we found a ruined house with marble pillars and a beautiful dome, and we took it [to serve] as a synagogue . . . and they already began to build, and we sent to the town of Shechem [Nablus], to bring thence the Scrolls of the Law, which had been in Jerusalem and had been smuggled out when the Tartars came, and, behold, they built a synagogue and they will pray there, for many come to Jerusalem all the time, men and women, from Damascus and Tsova and all the provinces of the country, to see the site of the Temple and weep over it. . . .

A. Lunz notes that "the Jews then established a special quarter in the south of the Old City near Mount Zion, and the life of the Jewish settlement centered around the synagogue of Nahmanides, which the Muslims sought to seize from them."

The Mamelukes ruled Jerusalem from Cairo. In the course of time, accordingly, many Jewish citizens left what was again a provincial city and went to Damascus and Egypt, and on, thence, to Turkey.

Earthquake, epidemic, drought, locust plagues, and famine precipitated this migration; but there were, as well, the tyranny of the court in Cairo, persecution by petty satraps governing from Syria, and the cruelty of local emirs, whereof the upshot was anarchy, peasant uprisings, and Bedouin raids. Arab writers speak of Mameluke recognition of the links between the Jewish people and its Land, and of Mameluke plans to discuss the restoration to it of the whole of Palestine. All the same, Jews had to wear yellow turbans, Samaritans red ones, and Christians blue ones; the Muslim turbans were white. But the Mamelukes oppressed their Muslim subjects in Palestine no less: according to a Muslim account, the fate of a slave was preferable to a farmer's. When Rabbi Ovadia of Bertinoro (1415–1510) settled in Jerusalem, things improved for the Jewish community under his inspiring leadership, and there was an influx from Spain and Portugal. At this stage, the Ottoman conquest of Constantinople, the end of the Byzantine empire, and the expulsion of the Jews from Spain marked a turning-point in the history of the Jewish congregations in the Land of Israel, and signified the onset of a numerous return.

THE OTTOMAN PERIOD (1516–1917)

The Turks ruled Palestine for 400 years. Though still denied autonomous statehood, Palestine now entered the global scene of merchant and trader. Suleiman the Magnificent repaired and rebuilt the walls and gates of Jerusalem (1537), restored the Citadel of David, and improved the city's water supply; like his predecessor, Selim, he employed Jewish physicians at his court. In the late sixteenth century, Sultan Bayezid II called upon Jews to settle in his new domain; Spanish Jews from Salonica, Constantinople, Adrianople, and other Turkish centers responded to the call, settling in Tiberias, Safed, and Jerusalem. Palestine's status as the spiritual home of Jewry rose momentously.

With the arrival of Spanish refugees, the Jewish population rose, and this Sephardic element was to characterize Jewish settlement for virtually the next four centuries. It was now that the splendid complex of four Sephardic houses of worship came into being on the traditional site of the Academy of Rabbi Yohanan Ben Zakkai. Yet the community in Jerusalem began to contract as a result of burdensome taxation and confiscation of property, until only the poor were left; the Ottomans levied a poll tax, a watch-and-ward tax, a tax on gifts at festivals, a government-aid tax, and a land tax.

After the massacres in the Caucasus in 1648 and 1656, Jews made their long way to Palestine from Russia and Poland. In 1700, Rabbi Judah Hehassid, assembled his disciples and set out for Palestine with 1,500 of them, to hasten the coming of the Redemption. He bought the plot of land upon which Nahmanides had built his synagogue, and on it set up his own conventicle, which, after his death, came to be known as the "Hurva." In 1721, the Arabs burned it down with its 40 Scrolls of the Law, and the Ashkenazi Jews then prayed in the principal Sephardi place of worship; the "Hurva" was rebuilt in 1837.

In 1777, the Hassidic Rabbi Menahem Mendel of Vitebsk brought 300 of his followers from the Ukraine, Lithuania, and Rumania to Safed and Tiberias, and thence to Jerusalem.

After Sir Moses Montefiore visited Palestine in the mid-nineteenth century, the condition of the Jews of Jerusalem became better and their area of settlement wider. The first Jewish quarters were established outside the city walls, and Jewish hospitals and educational institutions were founded.

Yitzhak Ben-Zvi wrote:

> There were periods of devastation and ruin in Jerusalem, as occurred in Safed; yet the Jewish population withstood the onslaught, and settlement was never abandoned even for a short period, as in Tiberias, or even for a few years, as in Safed.

For, in truth, no town in Palestine could be like unto Jerusalem. Jerusalem was the only city in which Jews had succeeded in holding out for 2,000 years after the fall of the Second Temple, despite religious and economic sanctions, pain of death for entry, and widespread havoc. The Jews always believed that they were but regaining what had been taken from them by force. Under alien domination Jerusalem was never a great city; on the contrary, it lost size. Only under Jewish rule did it expand and its population, Jewish and non-Jewish, increase.

POPULATION AND EXTENT OF THE CITY THROUGHOUT THE AGES

Under Melchizedek, in the days of the Patriarchs, and under the Amorites in the time of Joshua, Jerusalem was the capital of the southern region of the Hills of Judah and the plain. Jebusite Jerusalem covered only ten acres. Under Solomon, it was the capital of the Land of Israel, and, under the kings of Judah, the upper and lower cities extended over an area 16 times as large. Jerusalem was constricted under Persian rule, but expanded again under the Hasmonaean dynasty, and attained its zenith in the late Second Temple period, to cover 450 acres and house a population of 200,000 (equal to the total population of Palestine at the end of the nineteenth century). It was on its highest level of development in respect of water supply and neighborhood farming. After the death of Herod, and until the Bar Kochba revolt, the Roman governors ruled Judaea from Caesarea, and, from Hadrian's reign onwards, the limits of the neglected city shrank to 200 acres.

The Byzantines, too, dignified Caesarea as the capital of Palestine, although Christendom held Jerusalem—now peopled by only 80,000 souls—in holy regard. The Muslim conquerors shifted the capital to Ramla, as we saw, and, at its peak as a Muslim city, under the Fatimids in the eleventh century, Jerusalem's population was no more than 30,000 and its area less than a square kilometer, not half its dimension in Second Temple days. When the Crusaders entered, the count of citizens was about the same—Arabs and Jews, but thereafter it dropped to a handful of 3,000, even including Syrian Christians and the Christian Bedouin attracted to Jerusalem by Baldwin by pledges of tax-exemption. True, the Crusaders had regarded Jerusalem as a sacred city, and expelled its Jews and Muslims, but they chose Acre as their political and economic capital. At its peak Crusader Jerusalem's population reached 30,000.

Under Mameluke control, Jerusalem's fertile hinterland was ruined by systematic robbery, plunder, and exploitation, so that, from the final Mameluke period, and throughout the era of Ottoman rule up to the eighteenth century, the population of the city swung sparsely from 10 to 15,000.

The Sublime Porte did practically nothing to develop Palestine; no new roads, no new settlements, except for Jewish villages in early Zionist days. By the end of the nineteenth century, the total population was only 200,000, a density lower than any since the Canaanite period.

From 1860 onward, Jewish and Christian quarters were established outside Jerusalem's walls. The city was linked to the telegraph network and a carriage-way built to Jaffa and other towns. In 1892, the Jerusalem–Jaffa line, one of the earliest railways in the Middle East, began to run. Toward the end of the nineteenth century, Jerusalem had a population of 25,000; with Zionist aliya it rose to 75,000, 50,000 of them Jews. At the close of the century, 60 percent of all Palestinian Jewry lived in Jerusalem. Thereafter, the Arab population also rose, both in Jerusalem and in formerly derelict areas in the hills of Judaea, as well as throughout Palestine and Transjordan.

At the termination of the British Mandate in 1948, there were 165,000 residents in Jerusalem as a whole, of whom 100,000 were Jews; of the Arabs and others, 33,000 lived in the Old City. The area of the Jewish city was 25.76 square kilometers, double its size at the beginning of the twentieth century. The Arab part had an area of 2.6 square kilometers, of

		Settlement in Jerusalem in the Nineteenth and Twentieth Centuries			
Year	Jews	Muslims	Christians	Total	% of Jews
1844	7,120	5,000	3,390	15,510	45.9
1876	12,000	7,560	5,470	25,030	47.9
1896	28,122	8,560	8,748	45,420	61.9
1905	40,000	7,000	13,000	60,000	66.6
1913	48,400	10,050	16,750	75,200	64.3
1922	33,971	13,413	14,669	62,578	54.3
1931	51,222	19,894	19,335	90,053	56.6
1948	100,000	40,000	25,000	165,000	60.6
1967	195,000	54,963	12,646	263,309	74.3

which the Old City constituted a third. Twenty years later, in a reunified Jerusalem, the Jewish population had doubled to approximately 200,000, equal to the population in the late Second Temple period; the Arab population was unaltered at 65,000, 24,000 residing in the Old City.

		Jewish Population of Jerusalem and the Rest of the Land of Israel[1]	
Year	Jerusalem	The Land of Israel	Jerusalem Jews in Total Jewish % of Population
1833	3,000		
1856	5,700	10,500	54
1895	28,000	47,000	60
1913	45,000	85,000	53
1916	26,000	56,000	46
1922	33,970	83,800	41
1931	51,220	174,000	29
1934	64,500	300,000	21
1939	80,800	475,000	17
1946	100,200	625,000	16
1967	200,000	2,500,000	8

NOTES AND REFERENCES

1. Statistics compiled from the *Encyclopaedia Britannica, Calendar of Palestine,* the *Palestine Government Yearbook,* Government Census of Palestine, and other sources.

X

The Arabs in Jerusalem

ORI STENDEL
(Translated from the Hebrew by Mordecai S. Chertoff)

i. A History of the Arabs in Jerusalem

The Arab presence in Jerusalem was particularly sparse prior to the Muslim conquest of Palestine. Although wandering tribesmen did occasionally break out of the Arabian peninsula and reach the city, apparently few of these actually settled there.

Early in A.D. 638 the troops of Omar appeared at the gates of Jerusalem, but the circumstances of the city's surrender are not known. The text of the surrender document has been lost, and the clauses known today as "Omar's Covenant" must be attributed to a later period.

Arab settlement in Jerusalem began following the conquest, although it was many years before they constituted more than a minority in the city.

It is to this early period that the leading Arab families attempt to trace the roots of their respective family trees.

The al-Khalidi family, which is centered to this day in Jerusalem, traces its beginnings back to General Khaled Ibn Alwalid, conqueror of the city. The Nusseibeh family, keepers of the keys to the Church of The Holy Sepulchre, preserves a tradition according to which the heavy keys were given into their keeping by Omar himself, supreme ruler of the Muslims. Other ranking families also try to weave their histories into the events of those remote days from which they draw inspiration from the glory of the conquest.

In point of fact, this period in the history of the Arabs in Jerusalem is shrouded in obscurity.

The conquest did open a new chapter in the history of the city. The Arab settlement there grew, with the Arabs enjoying the benefits of their status as rulers and their exemption from the poll-tax (jizyah) which was imposed upon the Christian inhabitants.

Against this background the Arabization of the local populace began, although it was, apparently, a very slow process.

Jerusalem was not designated the capital city of the early Muslim kingdoms. And her religious attributes in Arab consciousness developed only gradually, with the development of the tradition of the nocturnal journey of Muhammad, the Prophet of Islam, to the Temple Mount in Jerusalem. In time, this site was marked by the building of the al-Aqsa mosque, within which, according to Muslim belief, the miraculous ascent of Muhammad to heaven took place.

It appears that during this early period the Arabs, too, still called Jerusalem by its Roman-Byzantine name, Aelia. The other names began to appear only later on: Medinat Bet Almakdas (City of the Temple), then Almakdas, and the final transformation—Al Quds, which is what the Arabs call Jerusalem today. The city acquired increased sanctity among Muslims as a result of the widespread building activity which began, in effect, only 50 years after its conquest.

The caliph Abd al-Malik (685–705) is, to all intents and purposes, the father of the Muslim construction in Jerusalem. In 691 he built the Dome of the Rock Mosque, later attributed to Omar. It would seem that during the reign of his heir, al-Walid (705–715), al-Aqsa Mosque was built. Following the Six Day War, archaeologists uncovered a large palace in the southwest corner of the Temple Mount, also built during the reign of these same caliphs.

The mosques on the Temple Mount brought to Jerusalem special status, making it the third among the Muslim holy cities, after Mecca and Medina. Despite this status, it never became the capital city of the Umayyad Caliphate, nor was it ever considered the capital of Palestine. On the contrary, the city of Ramla, built by the caliph Suleiman (715–717), was declared the capital of the district of "Palestine."

Toward the end of the Umayyad regime a tendency to strengthen the Muslim character of Jerusalem is discernable, resulting in oppression of the Christian residents. The Muslim Arabs were obviously still only a minority of the city's population. The process of Islamization was not rapid, and meanwhile a Jewish population returned to the city, accompanied by members of various Christian sects.

During the period of transition from Umayyad rule to the rise of the Abbas dynasty, Jerusalem was ravaged by a rebellion of the Muslim residents against the caliph Meroan. In 746 a punitive campaign was mounted, during which the walls of the city were destroyed. The same year the Dome of the Rock was damaged by an earthquake.

With the rise to power of the Abbas dynasty, the capital was even further from Jerusalem, but interest in the city grew. The first Abbasid caliphs invested a great deal of effort in repair of the walls and caring for the holy sites.

The caliph al-Mamun (813–833) conducted a survey of the Dome of the Rock, and seized the opportunity to "correct" the inscription attributing the construction of the mosque to the days of Abd al-Malik, but neglected to "correct" the date. This "error" of his provides eternal evidence of the forgery in the dome of this magnificent mosque.

In the days of al-Mamun famine struck the city, and the overwhelming majority of its Muslim residents fled. In 841, some years after his death, a peasants' revolt erupted and quickly turned into a campaign of plunder and desecration of Jerusalem. Mosques, churches, and synagogues were looted and destroyed. Masses of residents, of all sects, fled the city in panic. In the tenth century, again, the city was subjected to extreme tension. In 966 the Church of the Holy Sepulchre and the Church of Mt. Zion were set afire by Muslims, and the Patriarch Johannes was put to death at the instigation of the local administration.

Fatimid control of Jerusalem brought about a change in the city, one which led to its economic growth, although the Abbasid Caliphate did not make its peace with Shi'ite control of the holy city. The Seljuk Turks conquered Jerusalem in 1071. Their internal struggles racked the city by fierce battles.

From the Seljuk conquest down to the twentieth century, Arabs no longer ruled over Jerusalem. While the city was taken by the Fatimids in the summer of 1098, just one year later the Crusaders stormed the gates.

At the time of the Crusader conquest Muslim life in Jerusalem was limited to the spiritual center of the Temple Mount. There had been academies for the study of Islamic law there, but during this period they, too, were deserted. The geographer, al-Muqadassi, complained: "The mosque is empty, there are no religious scholars and no intellectuals; there are no debates, and there is no instruction." But Jerusalem remained a Muslim religious center, even though the Arabs as such were not central.

The real carriers of Islam in Jerusalem, as in many other centers in Muslim countries, were from other nations, particularly Persians. The wanderings of the famous Muslim philosopher al-Ghazali is symbolic: he reached Jerusalem in 1095, to be a recluse there.

During Crusader days the number of Muslim residents of Jerusalem dropped sharply because of the ban imposed on their living in the city. Their mosques were converted into churches. Christian Arab immigrants from Transjordan began to settle in Jerusalem, encouraged by the Crusaders.

The wheel turned with the conquest of Jerusalem by Saladin Al-

Ayubbi in 1187. He banned Christian residence in the city and renewed the Muslim community within its borders. He turned the churches back into mosques, or other Muslim religious institutions. Thus, the Church of Saint Anne, near the Lion's Gate, was turned into a Shafite academy and named Salahia, after Saladin.

This Muslim hero became engraved deeply in the historical consciousness of the Jerusalem Arabs. His reign constitutes a central historical chapter and serves as the axis of leadership-family traditions. He repaired the al-Aqsa mosque, destroyed the Templar buildings around it, and installed the pulpit (Minbar) made of beautifully carved Syrian wood. (In the summer of 1969 this fine piece of work was burned in a fire started by a crazed tourist who arrived in Israel obsessed with messianic delusions.)

During the third Crusade another attempt to conquer Jerusalem was made, but it was unsuccessful. However, the Crusaders achieved their objective through negotiations in the Tel Ajul Concord of 1229, between Al Malki Al Kamel, the hostile ruler of Egypt, and Kaiser Frederick.

According to this agreement Jerusalem was divided between Muslims and Christians. Actually, the Muslims were restricted to the Temple Mount area, while the rest of the city was assigned to the Christians. This was during the second reign of the Crusaders over Jerusalem (1229–1244). Renewed attempts at Christian settlement were made during this period but the results were meager compared to the successes of the twelfth century.

In 1244 Jerusalem was pillaged and sacked by an army of nomad Khwarizmian Turks from Central Asia. A few years later the Mamelukes rose to power in the city.

During the Mameluke period Jerusalem deteriorated both politically and economically. Her economy sagged. Heavy taxes were imposed upon her residents. At the same time, a cultural renaissance began. The Mamelukes excelled in the building of Muslim religious institutions. Mosques and academies were built, zavis (Dervish sanctuaries), savils (ritual baths), and Muslim cemeteries were developed. This construction gave the city a definite Muslim ambience. Muslim religious fanaticism grew, bringing with it estrangement from other religious groups, Jews, and particularly Christians.

During the Mameluke period the festive religious processions from Jerusalem to Nebi Musa, on the way to Jericho, were instituted.

A new chapter in the history of Jerusalem was opened in 1516 with the conquest of the city by Sultan Betmani Selim I. For 400 years it was ruled by the Ottoman Turks. At the beginning of this period Suleiman the Magnificent repaired the walls of Jerusalem, reconstructed the "Tower of David," the city's fortress, and repaired the aqueducts bringing water from Solomon's Pools. Suleiman's wife set up charitable institutions, particularly for academy students. The results of all this construction are visible in the city to this day even though the city sank into lengthy stagnation after Suleiman's death.

During the Ottoman period there was the progressive development of elite families who rented key positions in the city from the Sublime Porte in Istanbul. For a fee, they acquired administrative posts, became tax collectors, judges, and religious teachers.

Through the conduct of these offices they made back their investments and provided a firm foundation for their status in the city.

During this period some of the leadership families began their migrations to the city: the Dajanis, also called "Daudi" because of their claim to David's Tomb on Mt. Zion. According to a family tradition, their rights to the Tomb go back to the days of Saladin, although it appears that it was not until the Ottoman period that their claim to this holy place was firmly established.

The Hal'di family also seized its place in the power structure at that time. Alha 'Aldiyah, the family library, reflects their period of glory. To this day its treasures include ancient manuscripts, rare books, and documents from the Ottoman period. (The library is now locked, its keys held by Hiyder Alh'Aldi, current head of the family. About a year ago I was among the few who were permitted to enter. The library has been neglected and shows considerable disorder, but undoubtedly contains much valuable research material.)

It was during the Ottoman period that two other families migrated to Jerusalem, families which later seized the very top leadership: the Husseinis and the Nashashibis.

Until the nineteenth century the Ottoman regime accorded Jerusalem no particular importance. Its population dwindled, and almost no pilgrims were prepared to brave the dangers. Those in power exacted a "Protection Tax" from all who came to the city.

At the beginning of the nineteenth century Jerusalem had an estimated population of 9,000 people, Muslims, Christian, and Jews. The city was neglected, and lacked the most basic services.

The change came during the reign of Ibrahim Pasha, who conquered Jerusalem toward the end of 1831. A City Council was set up, restrictions against Jews and Christians were abolished, and security was established.

A peasant uprising against the Egyptian regime erupted in 1834. The rebels broke into Jerusalem through the Dung Gate and succeeded in trapping Ibrahim Pasha's garrison troops in the Citadel. He did manage to retake the city from the rebels, but his own rule lasted only another few years. In 1840 the Egyptian troops withdrew and Ottoman rule was restored. This time, attempts were made to improve the administrative order. Jerusalem became a sanjak (district) ruled by a government subject to the Wali (general governor) of Damascus, until 1887.

During the second half of the nineteenth century the importance of Jerusalem gradually increased, as a result of the growing interest of the Great Powers in the Ottoman Empire, including Palestine. The holiness of the city for Christianity attracted foreign consulates and Christian pilgrims. One consequence was the creation of religious and charitable institutions by both Christians and Jews. Another was a proportional drop in the Muslim Arab presence in the city.

Jerusalem began to grow beyond the walls of the Old City in the 1860s, the new sectors being settled mostly by Jews and Christians.

By 1873 the Muslims were actually a minority in Jerusalem: 5,000 residents, as compared to 5,300 Christians and 10,600 Jews.

In the '70s and '80s Arabs began to settle outside of the walls too. Abu Tor developed alongside the Bethlehem road and Katamon grew up south of the Old City. At the same time, the construction of Muslim religious institutions stopped almost completely. The Mograbi Mosque was built in 1871 in the Old City, the only Muslim religious construction in many generations, in contrast to the widespread building of religious institutions by Christians and Jews. Thus, the city lost more and more of its Muslim character, so much a feature of the Mameluke period.

In 1887 Jerusalem underwent a political transformation. It became the capital of an independent sanjak, directly accountable to the imperial capital. A mixed Council—Muslims, Jews, and Christians—was established to serve with the governor.

At the beginning of the twentieth century the population of Jerusalem had reached 45,600, of whom 8,600 were Muslims, 8,700 Christians, and 28,200 Jews. The Arabs constituted the smallest group in the city, although national consciousness at that time was relatively unimportant. The basic divisions, which were responsible for the fundamental loyalties, depended upon sentimental attachments and religion.

On the eve of World War I, in 1912, Jerusalem's 72,000 residents consisted of about 10,000 Muslims, 16,000 Christians, and 46,000 Jews. Most of the Jews settled in the new sections of the city, while the Arab population was concentrated, by and large, within the Old City; although there was a well-developed Jewish Quarter in the Old City too.

During the war Jerusalem was an important center for Turkish troops, and the civilian population suffered from hunger, epidemics, and government pressure. Many residents abandoned the city, and by the end of the war its population had shrunk to 55,000.

The first British troops reached Jerusalem on December 9, 1917, and two days later General Allenby entered the city, through Jaffa Gate. During the summer of 1920 a civil administration assumed control over Palestine, and Jerusalem was established as its capital. The high commissioner took up residence there in the Augusta-Victoria building, which had been taken from the Germans.

With the establishment of the British administration the country was no longer under Muslim rule, although Ragheb bey Nashashibi was made mayor of Jerusalem itself, and remained in that post until 1934. He was succeeded by Dr. Hussein Fahri Alhaldi, who ran against Nashashibi and was elected with the help of the Jewish voters who constituted a majority in the city.

Toward the end of the Mandate the administration of Jerusalem was turned over to an appointed City Council, made up of six Arabs and six Jews.

The sociopolitical alignment of the Arab community during the Mandate was characterized by a fierce struggle between two camps: one headed by the Mufti, Haj Amin el Husseini, chairman of the Supreme Muslim Council, the other by the Nashashibis and their supporters.

In Jerusalem the central institutions of the Palestine Arabs developed during the British administration. Most important of these was the Supreme Muslim Council, which controlled the funds of all of the religious bodies and so acquired tremendous financial power which was utilized to finance the Husseinis' political struggles against the Nashashibis, and against the Jewish community as well.

In 1936 the Arab Higher Committee was formed, with representatives of the Husseinis and Nashashibis sitting together under the chairmanship of the Mufti of Jerusalem, Hajj Amin el Husseini. In this framework of internal unity the banner of rebellion against the British regime and the Jewish community was raised, but within a very short time the rift between the Husseinis and Nashashibis was again exposed. Meanwhile, the Mandatory regime dispersed the Arab Higher Committee. Hajj Amin el Husseini was dismissed from his post as Mufti of Jerusalem and chairman of the Supreme Muslim Council and forced to flee from the country. Other upper-echelon Jerusalem Arab leaders were exiled to the Seychelles Islands.

The constant tension between Jews and Arabs following the disturbances of 1936–1939 resulted in the separation of their respective residential areas. Segregated neighborhoods developed, and business contacts dwindled. A purely Arab commercial center developed near Damascus Gate. The Old City was the focus of the Arab population, and Arabs lived throughout the Old City except for the Jewish Quarter.

Following the passage of the U.N. Partition Resolution of November, 1947, Arab gangs seized control of the Arab sectors of Jerusalem and launched a bloody struggle against the Jewish community, hoping to conquer the entire city.

The British High Commissioner for Palestine left his official residence in Jerusalem in May, 1948, and the battle intensified. On the 28th of May the Jewish Quarter of the Old City was taken, after a bitter siege. Homes were destroyed, and the surviving Jewish male residents were taken prisoner.

In the course of the war, during 1948, many of the Arab residents of Jerusalem fled, and the exodus continued even after the fighting died down.

The Old City of Jerusalem was taken by the Arab Legion, and Jordan's King Abdullah set up a military government in the city. The war split Jerusalem in half. In the east, a Jordanian municipal council was set up, headed by Aref el-'Aref, who had previously served as a senior official with the British Mandatory regime. In the west, the Jewish city flourished. The boundary between the two sections was a winding one, in some sections marked by a high wall. From time to time firing broke out across this artificial boundary.

The Temple Mount, with the Muslim holy places, remained under Jordanian control. Jews were barred from access to the Western Wall, in clear violation of a specific provision in the Rhodes Armistice Agreement between Israel and Jordan.

During the Jordanian occupation there occurred a complete sociopolitical transformation within the Arab community in East Jerusalem. The Hashemite Jordanian regime tended to build upon the Nashashibis. Shortly after the conquest of the West Bank, the head of the family, Ragheb bey Nashashibi was appointed its ruler.

With that appointment the tension of the struggle between the Husseinis and Nashashibis faded. Old enmities seemed to disappear. The old allegiances no longer counted, and new personalities became prominent.

The focus was now on Amman, where local dignitaries became ministers, senators, and representatives in the Hashemite Kingdom government. Simultaneously, the power of the old leading families was weakened in keeping with deliberate policy.

The Hashemites considered Jerusalem a base of hostile forces and imposed upon the city close supervision, aided, generally, by the naming of non-Jerusalemites to rule the city.

Ostensibly, the Jerusalem Municipal Council was elected by the city's residents, but according to Article 34 (1) of the Municipalities Law of 1955 (#29), the Council was dependent upon the central government, which did not refrain from involving itself even in the electoral process. Furthermore, in accordance with Jordanian law, the mayor of the city was selected by the Council of Ministers, rather than by the residents of the city or even the members of the municipal council.

Economic growth in the city was blocked in a variety of ways by the Jordanian government: It banned the establishment of major enterprises in Jerusalem (most of the banking centers were concentrated in Amman); employment opportunities for intellectuals were minimized, and many were forced to move to Jordan or even farther away to other Arab countries. The Jordanian government hampered cultural life in the city, too, refusing to permit the opening of secondary schools. Anwar Nusseibeh, who served as Minister of Defense in the Jordanian Government, points out that Amman deliberately saw to it that attempts to establish an Arab university in Jerusalem were frustrated. Toward the end of 1966 a devastating blow was dealt the Arab press in Jerusalem: it was nationalized. Long-established newspapers stopped publication and many able newspapermen left the city. Only two papers remained, both completely subservient to the official line.

In the socio-economic sphere, the Jerusalem landed aristocracy became involved in trade, banking, and tourism without being severed from the political arena, although the relative importance of land in conferring status in the socio-economic status diminished drastically.

During this same Jordanian period the migration of Hebronites to Jerusalem grew significantly, and their importance in the socio-economic and political arenas increased.

Judges, attorneys, and many senior government officials in the city administration were Hebronites, including the last Jordanian mayor of Jerusalem, Rouhi el Khatib. Hebronites were also prominent in the trade department and the municipal council.

During this period the difference between Hebronites and Jerusalemites became a fundamental social gap.

In June, 1967, Jerusalem's eastern sections were conquered by the Israel Defense Army, and the city reunited. The wheel of history was turned back, as it were, and Jerusalem once more became a unified whole.

Unification of the city created a bustling two-way traffic, accompanied by renewal of the relationships that had been severed 20 years earlier, and the weaving of a whole network of new relationships.

Since the Six Day War there has been a rapid rise in employment. Among the lowest wage earners income doubled and, in some cases, even trebled. Laborers, officials, and other employees acquired additional benefits, totally new to them. Prices rose, but for most wage-earners income rose even faster, so that their real income did increase.

In the course of this process there was a diminishing of the polarization of income between the upper classes and the bulk of the population. Today, the Arab population of East Jerusalem is about 72,000, with an average annual growth rate of four per cent. Muslims constitute a majority of the Arabs—83 per cent, as compared to 16 per cent for the Christians, in their various sects. One of the more remarkable features is the return of former residents to the city within the framework of the Israel Government's family reunification plan.

For the past few years there has been a daily Arab newspaper appearing in East Jerusalem, *Al Quds*, edited by Muhammad Abu Zuluf, and *A Sha'ab* another daily.

The first signs of a socio-political transformation within the Arab community are reflected in the publication of *Alfaghr* (the Dawn), a weekly edited by Yussef Nazr and Jamil Hamada, young Muslims who are challenging the "Old Establishment" of Jerusalem society and trying to create an independent Palestinian entity.

The Arab population is gradually being absorbed into the life of the unified city, but there is no question that the process is not complete. In contrast to the rapid economic development, the effects of a social barrier are still felt, although even in this area there is growing contact and an increase in joint ventures.

In the political arena the Arabs of Jerusalem still consider themselves aliens in Israel. Many of them did, indeed, vote in the last municipal elections, but leading Arab personalities did not respond to Mayor Teddy Kollek's invitation to accept membership on the Municipal Council.

The Arabs of Jerusalem consider themselves, by and large, still Jordanian citizens, and are not eager to seize the opportunity open to them of becoming Israeli citizens.

The absorption of the Jerusalem Arabs into Israel is slow—gradual—but unquestionably this is only the beginning of a process that is growing and deepening.

ii. Christians in Jerusalem: 1948–1971

GENERAL BACKGROUND

DEMOGRAPHIC TRENDS OF THE CHRISTIAN POPULATION AT THE TIME OF THE BRITISH MANDATE

Jerusalem has loomed large as an object of Christian concern and veneration during most of the two-millennial history of the Church. It was a major goal of the medieval Crusades; it has been a focus of pilgrimage from the fourth century until today. The faithful of diverse denominations, drawn to Jerusalem's shrines, settled in their vicinity, mainly in the Christian Quarter of the Old City.

In the nineteenth century, when the city began to develop, its Christian population grew proportionately, and, while at all times a numerical minority, it has consistently played an important part in Jerusalem's religious life. The flow of Christian pilgrims and the many Christian institutions have opened up a variety of occupational and trading possibilities and given the Christian community an economic status exceeding that which might be expected from its numbers alone. In addition, the interest displayed in the Holy City by Christian Powers has strengthened Christian standing there.

The following table shows the demographic development from 1844 and during the first years of the British Mandate. The figures are drawn from the sources noted below:

		JERUSALEM POPULATION: DEVELOPMENT FROM 1844 TO 1951		
Year	Population	Jews	Muslims	Christians
1844 a)	15,510	7,120	5,000	3,390
1876 b)	25,030	12,000	7,560	5,470
1896 c)	45,420	28,112	8,560	8,748
1905 a)	60,000	40,000	7,000	13,000
1910 d)	73,600	47,000	9,800	16,400
1922 e)	62,578	33,971	13,413	14,699
1931 f)	90,503	51,222	19,894	19,335

a) *Encyclopaedia Britannica.*
b) *Liévin de Homme, Guide Indicateur de la Terre Sainte,* 1876.
c) *Calendar of Palestine for the year 5656* (1895–6).
d) *Calendar of Palestine for the year 5670* (1909–1910).
e) Government Census of Palestine, 1922.
f) Government Census of Palestine, 1931.

Until the end of the first decade of the twentieth century, the Christians constituted a tiny minority in Jerusalem. Then, within a few years, their number grew to almost double that of the Muslims, although it dwindled somewhat in World War I, when the Turkish Government expelled Jews and Christians not of Ottoman nationality. Under the Mandate, the count of Christians and Muslims was approximately even, despite differences in the birth rates. Toward the end of the Mandatory period, in 1946, there were 31,300 Christians, compared to 33,680 Muslims.

Two basic demographic characteristics of the Christian population in the Land of Israel, including Jerusalem, became apparent at that stage: 1) a relatively low birth rate with a high level of family planning, as compared to the Muslims; and 2) a tendency to emigrate, especially to Europe and the United States, for the manifold skills of the Christians and their knowledge of Western languages enabled them to find remunerative employment abroad.

CHRISTIANS IN EAST JERUSALEM DURING JORDANIAN RULE

DEMOGRAPHIC TRENDS

A Jordanian census taken in 1961 recorded 11,000 Christians within the Jerusalem municipality's jurisdiction, as compared to 31,300 in 1946. There is no doubt that, under Hashemite rule, when the city took on a preponderantly Muslim character, and "Arabization" was the official aim, a great number of Christians emigrated.

According to a census of 1967, the number of Christians living in the city area as defined before the Six Day War was 8,500, which was 21 per cent of the total.[1] The proportion is higher if we exclude the village of Silwan from the city area: while Christians were a quarter of all of Jerusalem's population within the city area, their percentage in the surrounding villages was lower.

A TABLE SHOWING THE CITY AREAS IN WHICH CHRISTIANS WERE CONCENTRATED[2]			
District	Population	Christians	Muslims
Christian Quarter	4,246	3,630	478
Armenian Quarter	2,391	1,354	793
Jewish Quarter[3]	3,500	13	3,481
Muslim Quarter	13,538	1,573	11,929
Entire Old City	23,675	6,570	16,681
Wadi Joz	3,418	297	3,073
Sheikh Jarrah	1,743	349	1,362
American Colony	4,432	1,091	3,252

In the areas not included within the urban jurisdiction in the Jordanian period, the distribution of the population by religions was this:

District	Population	Christians	Muslims
Shu'afat	3,400	375	2,975
Beit Hanina	3,609	923	2,553
Silwan (including Mt. Zion)	7,243	164	7,038
Abu Tor	3,853	24	3,800

Thus it is evident that, under Jordanian authority, the Christians by and large kept to their own areas, although there were no hard and fast rules as to where members of this or that community might reside. There were not a few Christians in the Muslim Quarter and vice versa. Harat A-Nassara was indisputably a Christian sector, but most of the shops in it were owned by Hebron Muslims, called Khalaile: the census does not show this movement, as there is no record in it of registration of shops. It was a conspicuous fact, nevertheless, which led to complaints that the area ought to be renamed Harat Al-Khalaile, and the busy Sundays and quiet Fridays pointed this up. Outside the walls, Christians lived mainly in the upper sections of the town, in Sheikh Jarrah, the American Colony, and Beit Hanina, with only a handful in the other sections.

The Status of Christians in the City

The Christians formed a social unit that was distinct from the Muslim by virtue of divergent cultural and religious backgrounds. By mutual consent, differences were played down, and extreme cases of religious disputes were rare, but there was always tension between the communities, which waxed and waned according to extraneous circumstances. The social groupings, diverse organizational activities, and closed marriages all served to keep Christians and Muslims apart. There were rumors among the Muslims that the Christians' principal mission was secretly and slowly to acquire all the land.

Indeed the Amman government took the rumors so seriously as to pass a law which forbade the transfer of any land to corporate bodies without official sanction. It seems, however, that the Christians still found ways and means of getting round the embargo, with the connivance, no doubt, of acquisitive Muslims who cared little for the derisive gibe—"He sold land to the Church"—that their profitable heresy drew down upon them from their more law-abiding kin.

At times of tension, Muslims were apt to emphasize the foreign aspect of Christians and to identify them with the West or with the Hashemite king. But no conclusions can be drawn from this, and many old established Christian families were held in high regard. Moreover, Muslim attitudes towards Christians varied greatly, depending on social and political views.

The division between Christians and Muslims in the city was manifested in several ways:

(a) There were no blood ties. Mixed marriages were of the rarest and, at the upper end of the social scale, almost unheard of. Muslims were equally exclusive, and the daughters of one of the most progressive and eminent Muslims of the city told me that their father had left their choice of husbands entirely to them, except that he had insisted that they be Muslims.

(b) Special seats were reserved for Christian representatives of the Jerusalem area in the Jordanian House of Representatives by a secondary partitioning of the area according to religion. This principle was in force throughout the Jordanian period, but the extent of Christian representation changed with the overall rise in the number of Jerusalem members of the House.

Years	Representatives Jerusalem district	Muslims	Christians
1950–1958	3	2	1
1958–1961	4	3	1
1961–1967	5	3	2

The number of reserved Christian seats was larger when representation in bodies of local government, such as the municipality and the Chamber of Commerce, was more extensive: in those bodies no seats were reserved by law for Christians, and a study of the period shows a decline in Christian membership. The second elections to the Jerusalem municipality in 1955 show a marked setback for the Christian representatives as compared to the elections of 1951, when three Christian candidates received a third of the votes cast for the entire municipal council. In 1955, there was a sharp drop: whereas the Christian candidates received 4,860 votes in 1951, only one Christian was elected in 1955 and by no more than 836 votes. No Christian members were elected at all in the following years, for all the communal endeavors exerted. The government in Amman thereafter used its authority to appoint Christian councilmen.

THE CHRISTIAN SCHOOLS

These took their religious character from their association with the churches and the institutions connected with them. Children of all Christian classes were sent to these schools, which aimed at developing Christian awareness, and whose syllabus emphasized religious instruction. Notwithstanding, some of the Muslim élite sent their children there, too, on account of the high scholastic level. All the schools taught foreign languages, which was very useful to Christians who later left the country to study or to better themselves—departures that were often a prelude to permanent emigration.

SOCIO-ECONOMIC TRENDS

Below are outlined certain socio-economic trends that were to be found among Jerusalem Christians of all denominations:

(a) A close family nucleus was the basis of all social life.

(b) Most of the Christians were merchants, shopkeepers, engaged in all branches of tourism, travel agents, hoteliers; in the lower strata, they were clerks and tourist guides. The printing trade and import and export occupied many, as did the running and upkeep of Christian institutions.

(c) There was a great shortage of Christian young men, because so many went abroad in search of work or to study. This naturally limited the chances of marriage for young women, not seldom critically—they frequently married late in life and sometimes not at all, a prospect that induced apprehensive girls equally to go away to the Lebanon or the West.

(d) One general characteristic of the younger Christian men and women was their superior level of education. The schools prepared their pupils for university entrance and even in the poorer classes the standard was commendable. Lack of a local university and the resultant exodus made the average age of the Christian population of Jerusalem relatively high.

Trends among the Christian Population after the Six day War

On June 29, 1967, East and West Jerusalem were reunified. Road blocks and barriers were removed. Arabs flocked to West Jerusalem and Jews to East Jerusalem. The two nations mingled with one another in mutual curiosity. A new reality was born and, with it, the nature of relations altered. The Arabs, however, were bewildered by the suddenness of the change and found it hard to accustom themselves to it. Gossip among them had it that the change was temporary, a passing wind. The situation slowly returned to normal, but the economy had suffered a grievous shock in those first months. What with the stoppage of the tourist trade and the closing of the banks, hotels were empty and the travel bureaus did no business. Many Christian families felt the brunt of this and some were forced to consume their savings. But by degrees, the tension lessened, fears vanished and stability was restored. The population as a whole began to get used to the new state of things and even found elements in it to their advantage. Business in cafés, restaurants, hotels, bakeries, and garages recovered, and the shops attracted throngs of Israelis. Money spent by the municipality in rehabilitating the public services did much to put the economy back on its feet, so that it has expanded, within the last two years, incomes have gone up, and there is now less polarization between classes, wages having risen. Christian businessmen were quick to establish contacts with the Israeli economy and to take it into account. Frequently, partnerships and friendships of Mandate days were renewed. Socially, there has been a rapprochement between Christians and Jews, many Christians having learned Hebrew. Relations between the Israel Government and the heads of the Christian denominations are much improved. Thus:

(a) On June 27, 1967, the Knesset passed a law ensuring the sanctity and inviolability of Holy Places. Notices have been posted marking the shrines and guaranteeing their immunity to damage.

(b) A committee was formed to settle claims of the churches to be indemnified for damage caused during the 1948 and 1967 wars. Although most of the damage had actually been done by the Jordanian army, 6,000,000 Israeli pounds have already been paid over to the churches, monasteries, and Christian establishments of education, religion, and welfare out of Israel's exchequer. Building and repair work has been under way ever since the fighting ended in 1967.

(c) in May, 1970, the Evangelical-Episcopalian community (the Anglican Church) was granted the status of a recognized religious community, a status withheld from it by the Ottoman and Mandatory regimes.

(d) The churches have been granted certain exemptions from taxes and duties.

(e) The government scrupulously refrains from intervention in the conduct of Christian schools.

The many Christians whom I have conversed with have expressed respect for the Israel Government and seem to be more secure under its aegis. The consequence is that fewer Christians are leaving the city than during Jordanian rule. According to the census of 1967, there were about 11,000 Christians in Jerusalem at that time, 17 per cent of a total Arab population of 68,500; now there are 11,500, suggesting that the birth rate balances the rate of emigration, which is certainly lower than it was in the Jordanian period. All the same, Christians still go abroad to study and work and, as always, their knowledge of languages and their talents make them much sought after. Their birth rate is relatively low compared to the Muslims, and this means that they are always proportionately fewer, but, socially, their influence is widely and deeply felt and they may be expected to play an integral part in the life of reunified Jerusalem.

NOTES AND REFERENCES

1. Following the Six Day War, the urban area was enlarged to include Shu'afat and a section of Beit Hanina. In the extended precincts there were 10,800 Christians, 17 per cent of the total.

2. These facts, based on an Israeli census of 1967, illustrate the situation as it was at the end of the Jordanian period, with minor changes due to the change in government.

3. Under Jordanian rule, this was the Jewish Quarter in name only; Muslims had taken over all the property of the Jews.

XI

The Role of Histadrut in East Jerusalem

GIDEON WEIGERT

In 1967, Aharon Becker, Secretary General of the Israel Labor Federation (Histadrut[1]) at that time, formally opened the first Histadrut office in a pink stone building on A-Rashid Street in East Jerusalem. The brief history of the subsequent activities of the Israel Labor Federation among Jerusalem's 70,000 Arab residents constitutes a record of trial and error; a mosaic of achievements and failures.

Six years are but a drop in the ocean of human achievement, yet these years formed a long, turbulent period as far as labor organization in the Holy City is concerned.

Four major factors account for this state of affairs. The first is the peculiar position in which the Jerusalem Arabs found themselves after the June, 1967, war. Since 1948 they had been Arabs in an independent Arab society and part of the local and regional administration. Then, almost overnight, they found themselves transformed into a minority living in occupied territory, faced with the loss of every feature of self rule and—against their wishes—"annexed" to Israel. There had been, technically, an annexation, yet there were also many loopholes in this annexation and these still create a high degree of frustration. Jerusalem's Arab residents live in the capital of Israel while retaining Jordanian citizenship and belonging, for all legal purposes, to a nation with which Israel is still at war.

The second factor serving to increase the difficulties and tensions was that labor and trade union organization has always been a weak spot, not alone in Jordan but in the Arab world as a whole. Consequently the western trade union concepts of "class consciousness" and labor discipline, so integral in Israeli labor thinking, were almost non-existent in East Jerusalem prior to June, 1967.

A third factor was that the Arabs of Jerusalem had not been living in a political, social, or economic vacuum prior to the Six Day War. They had been part and parcel of a larger population living next door in Ramallah, Bethlehem, and Jericho. What affected the inhabitants of Samaria to the north or of Judaea to the south affected them just as much.

The fourth and last factor was Israel's total lack of preparedness, before June, 1967, to deal with what it had never expected to encounter —the great variety of problems created by the annexation of such a large concentration of Arabs as in Jerusalem (which is by far the largest Arab center in Israel) and more especially with the great variety of problems and the diversity of fields in which the working population was employed. These were compounded by the total lack of experience on the part of Histadrut officials in dealing with the special problems found in Jerusalem, which were totally unlike any experienced in organizing the Israeli Arab population.

From the very beginning then, these four factors had their great impact in Jerusalem as a whole and on its Arab working population (amounting to over 20,000 persons aged fifteen and above) in particular. They have almost the same impact today. They created a series of obstacles for Histadrut from the very start of its activities in East Jerusalem. Some of these obstacles have, very gradually, begun to disappear, yet their existence over the past six years has largely contributed to shaping that mosaic which the Histadrut in East Jerusalem has formed. Only when these basic factors are kept in mind can one understand and evaluate the problems of labor organization in East Jerusalem today.

Prior to 1967, labor organization in East Jerusalem, according to reliable sources, was in extremely poor shape. No central body existed for the 16 Arab trade unions in this sector, although each of these trade unions included several hundred workers. The activities of these trade unions were restricted. There were few, if any, educational, social, or cultural activities, and few of their members received the full range of social benefits.[2] Worse still was the situation with regard to child labor. According to the same source, ". . . children worked in subhuman conditions, 12 hours per day for one Israeli pound [roughly 29¢—1967] without a paid day of rest or any social benefits whatsoever. . . ."

The Israel Labor Federation's Arab Department, which by 1967 had accumulated almost 20 years of experience in dealing with Arab labor and trade union affairs, put out its first "feelers" to the Eastern sector of Jerusalem in July, 1967, when it sent one of its most able men, a native-born Jerusalemite, to establish contact with the former Jordanian trade unions. This particular official had distinguished himself by several years of successful activity as the head of Histadrut's regional office in Nazareth.

The first move was to organize a visit by key men in the former Jordanian trade unions and cooperative societies to the Jerusalem Labor Council. Thirty-five Arab trade union leaders participated in the visit. This was followed by a whole series of exchange visits, initiated by the Jerusalem Labor Council, the Arab Department of the Histadrut, and Mo'etzet HaPo'alot (which is concerned with issues of special interest to women members of Histadrut and to working women in general) in Tel Aviv.

One month later, on the occasion of a special festive session in Jerusalem of Histadrut's Executive Committee (this Committee is permanently situated in Tel Aviv), the Secretary General of the Federation expressed his hope that "within two years 20,000 East Jerusalemites, *i.e.* the entire working force in the Arab sector, would become members of the Federation."[3]

Soon after the official opening of Histadrut's East Jerusalem branch on August 23, 1967, however, an interdepartmental dispute erupted between Histadrut's Arab Department in Tel Aviv and the Jerusalem Labor Council, each claiming sole jurisdiction in East Jerusalem. This dispute delayed all substantive activities for a number of valuable months and it was not before December, when the Jerusalem Labor Council gained sole control over Histadrut activities in East Jerusalem, that the real work began.

Histadrut's first struggle in East Jerusalem began in the shadow of campaigns emanating from the neighboring Arab countries and the various Palestinian organizations inciting the Arab population against cooperation. Not surprisingly, therefore, few East Jerusalem workers were ready to commit themselves politically at the beginning of 1968 by joining so purely Israeli an organization as Histadrut—an act which, of course, would have meant that commitment. They were afraid, not unaturally, that joining Histadrut would cost them their former jobs; that they themselves and their families in the Arab countries would be branded as traitors to the Arab national cause. And the same consideration was still in force five years later.[4]

Nevertheless, 12 East Jerusalem drivers employed by the National Bus Company (an Arab owned enterprise) embarked on the first labor dispute with Histadrut support in March, 1968. When the company was warned that the workers would go on strike unless it agreed to negotiate on the men's demands (for a six-day work week, a day off per week, and overtime pay) its first reaction was to order bus drivers from the West Bank to step in and take the places of the men on strike. This the West Bank drivers refused to do. Negotiations commenced within 24 hours. The 12 East Jerusalem drivers won their demands, and the change in their working conditions also affected the wages of the drivers on the West Bank who were employees of the same company.

Some East Jerusalemites joined Histadrut ranks from the very beginning, and these people have since done much to overcome the initial mistrust. They strove to enlist the cooperation of their fellow Arab workers in the formerly Jordanian sector of the city in a common effort to raise their conditions of employment to the level enjoyed by the Jewish workers in the western sector of the city.

One of these East Jerusalemites is Fa'ez Jaber, who played a leading role in bringing about the successful outcome of the National Bus Company labor dispute. Fa'ez, a veteran trade-unionist, had been the secretary of a trade union under Jordanian rule. He had a great deal of experience in organizing Arab drivers and metal plant workers, and he has, since that first successful strike, been active in organizing East Jerusalem's workers into Histadrut-affiliated trade unions. Ghazi Alam e Din is another such East Jerusalemite. His activities began in mid-1968. By that date the Histadrut's East Jerusalem branch had become geared to providing regular cultural activities for its members. A Histadrut Health Fund clinic (Kupat Holim), a Working Women's Council club, a vocational training center and a Working Youth's branch were already operating in East Jerusalem. A branch of Hapoel, ("the Worker"—Histadrut's sports organization) was then opened. Ghazi Alam e Din had been the foreign news editor of the Jordanian daily, *A-Diffa*. He found that journalism was much akin to cultural activities and went to work for Histadrut, which put him in charge of its cultural activities in East Jerusalem. The extent of his success in the course of his first year-and-a-half of work (mid-1968 through 1969) was demonstrated by the fact that over 13,000 East Jerusalemites participated in the cultural activities he organized during that period. Some of these were solely Histadrut activities, others were organized in conjunction with the Civic Information Center and the Jerusalem municipality's Department of Cultural Affairs. When Ghazi left, his job was taken over by another young East Jerusalem intellectual. Some of the earlier activities (such as a film club) were dropped, but most of the other activities Ghazi had initiated were continued, while new features, such as a permanent "Arab Jewish circle" (for an on-going interchange of views) and Arab-Jewish meetings in the homes of East Jerusalem workers, were added.

The first actual Histadrut-led strike in East Jerusalem took place at the Grand National Hotel, where the management had fired three employees who had been the first to join Histadrut. This occurred in February of 1968. Histadrut called for the strike which was quickly joined by all the hotel's employees. As a result, management finally agreed to arbitration. A similar dispute, with the Gloria Hotel, followed later that year —with the same results. These developments constituted the first "turning point." After that, hundreds of East Jerusalem workers flocked to

Histadrut's local office to register for membership. At that time the Histadrut still had many obstacles to overcome, such as raising wages and the whole question of providing social benefits for its Arab members. It faced these difficulties by changing its tactics in the course of time. As one official declared in 1969:

> Having run into political difficulties with traditional trade union tactics, an effort was now being made to see whether "gentle persuasion" would not be more suitable in trying to get East Jerusalem employers to raise wages. . . .[5]

HISTADRUT'S CULTURAL ACTIVITIES IN EAST JERUSALEM IN 1973
(Average monthly activities, conducted partly in conjunction with the municipality and the civic education center)

Type	No. of Participants	Frequency of Meetings	Comments
Discussion groups in Homes	220	18 per month	(held in Arab homes in East Jerusalem)
One Day Seminars	50	once monthly	
Three Day Seminars	150	3 times per yr.	
May Day & Histadrut anniversary celebrations.	2,000	2 times per yr.	(30% of participants come from W. Jerusalem)
Lectures and films	100	twice monthly	
Lectures at places of work	500	6 per month	(in plants in West Jerusalem)
Excursions	45	once per month	(one bus load for a day long trip)
Hebrew language courses	50	twice weekly	(two classes)
Jewish-Arab at home meetings	400	16 per yr.	(40% of participants Jewish)
Permanent Arab-Jewish discussion group	360	6 per yr.	(30% of audience Jewish)

(The material for this chart was especially prepared for the author by the Director of the East Jerusalem branch of the Jerusalem Labor Council.)

At present (1973), six years after unification, 8,000 East Jerusalem workers, (male and female) are members of Histadrut. 5,500 of these are wage earners and the remaining 2,500 are housewives. This constitutes about 30 per cent of the labor force in the Arab sector of Jerusalem. 70 percent of these Arab members are employed in West Jerusalem.[6] To add a note of explanation: the East Jerusalem labor scene is composed of three layers. There are: 1. the local workers, who live in the city; 2. workers who live on the West Bank and who commute to Jerusalem to work but return to their villages and towns every day; and 3. the members of East Jerusalem employers' families, who, of course, look after the "family interests" of the establishment and oppose any kind of labor organization which is contradictory to those interests. Since the Six Day War, East Jerusalemites have become more "class conscious" (as we have seen above) and have pressed for better conditions of employment. Local employers have begun to employ more and more members of their own families and also workers from the West Bank whom the Histadrut cannot organize since they are not Jerusalemites and the Israel Federation of Labor does not operate in the occupied territories. These West Bankers work in the Arab sector of Jerusalem where their status of non-protection is exploited by the local employers. This is particularly true in East Jerusalem, but also pertains in many work places in West Jerusalem. As a result of this trend, the percentage of East Jerusalemites working in East Jerusalem enterprises dropped from 60 percent to 40 percent in 1968, while the percentage of West Bankers working in East Jerusalem enterprises rose from 40 percent to 60 percent, as more and more of Jerusalem's Arab workers, fed up with the poor employment conditions afforded in their own people's establishments, began to look for permanent employment in enterprises in the Jewish sector of the city where Histadrut-guaranteed social conditions exist, while more and more West Bankers flocked to the Old City to take up the vacancies resulting from this switch.

A hopeful new drive has been launched in the direction of setting up cooperatives in East Jerusalem. The first attempt, to set up a cooperative printing shop, Matba'at e-Salem (the "Peace Printing Press") was made in 1969 and proved to be a total failure, since the preparatory groundwork was insufficient and no fundamental investigation into the economic viability of such an enterprise had been made. Two new cooperatives have recently been registered; one is a 300,000 Israeli pound capital cooperative printing society, A-Sharq ("Orient"). Its 12 members have been promised loans by Histadrut and an Israeli bank. A-Taliah ("The Pioneer") is a 20 member cooperative of Arab teachers who are planning to build a cooperative housing project for themselves at Shuafat, in the northern outskirts of Jerusalem.

The East Jerusalem branch of the Jerusalem Labor Council has also been instrumental in persuading unskilled Arab laborers in East Jerusalem to enroll in vocational training courses run by the Israel Ministry of Labor. In 1973, some 100 East Jerusalemites participated in these courses, lasting an average of ten months each, to become waiters, carpenters, locksmiths, electricians, construction workers, draftsmen, mechanics, etc.

Six years after the unification of Jerusalem, the labor scene is a mosaic of light and shadow, achievement and stagnation. For thousands of Arab workers, whether they are members or not, Histadrut has become a permanent, well known address, a force to be relied upon, a source of confidence, particularly among those East Jerusalemites who are permanently employed in the western sector of the city.

Only recently a first break-through was achieved in one of the largest East Jerusalem establishments, the Intercontinental Hotel, on the Mount of Olives, which employs over 250 workers. Here the first ever collective labor agreement between Histadrut and an East Jerusalem employer was signed.[7] It provided, *inter alia*, for a new grading scheme, pay raises and social benefits, and enabled the staff to elect their own Labor Committee to represent them in dealing with management. This is the first committee of its kind to be set up in East Jerusalem. No other East Jerusalem establishment has a Collective Labor Agreement providing similar concessions to the staff.

Many grave problems still remain unsolved. The external pressures on East Jerusalem's workers against being organized by Histadrut, still exist. In many cases, this pressure, which essentially is based on economic considerations on the part of the employers, takes the form of a political motivation, as was the case in the labor dispute at the printing press of East Jerusalem's national newspaper *Al Quds*.[8]

Only about 40 percent of East Jerusalem's salaried workers, and hardly any self-employed workers, artisans, or members of the free professions, are organized in Histadrut. The East Jerusalem branch of the Jerusalem Labor Council continues to suffer from serious financial difficulties, which prevent it from extending its activities. A reliable source told this author that but for this consideration, the scope of activities would today have been much wider and the results would have had a much greater impact.[9] A notable shortage of manpower is also apparent. The same five members of the staff deal with the problems of the 8,000 members of the East Jerusalem branch today as they did four years ago, when Histadrut Arab membership amounted to less than half this number. The same source pointed out that there are still ". . . hundreds of East Jerusalem workers employed in small workshops of up to five employees, both in the eastern and the western [Jewish] sectors of the city whom we have not yet even contacted." These workers are not paid according to Histadrut wage scale and do not enjoy the required social benefits. The same source added that "while 90 percent of the East Jerusalemites employed in Jewish firms in the west receive their full rights, only 10 percent of those employed by Arab establishments in East Jerusalem receive similar rights. So far only three East Jerusalem employers have signed labor contracts with the Federation."

WORKING WOMEN

Histadrut began the task of organizing East Jerusalem's women in the summer of 1968, when the Working Women's Council opened a vocational training center in East Jerusalem. In addition to providing two courses in sewing and hairdressing (the courses were largely subsidized by the Ministry of Labor) Hebrew language courses were also provided for the some 40 women students, as were, also, monthly lectures and occasional excursions. The impact of these activities was, naturally, limited. At the end of 1968 the Women's Council's officials attempted to organize a women's dressmaking cooperative, a task for which they were not equipped. A group of 20 young girls was organized into a society, but without much advance study of the economic soundness of the planned project or the suitability of the candidates from the point of view of social coherence, and thus the scheme was launched into a void. Created in a hurry, the whole experience resulted in utter failure less than a year later. Since 1969, Histadrut has not again attempted to set up a women's cooperative in East Jerusalem.

The Arab women's group in East Jerusalem is today part of the local branch of the Tel Aviv-based Working Women's Council, but its activities are extremely limited, and its courses reach no more than 100–150 women at intervals of ten months (the duration of the vocational training and parallel Hebrew courses). This means that in the last five years no more than at most 600, out of a potential female labor force of some 10,000, have benefited in one form or another, from these activities. A spokeswoman for Mo'etzet HaPo'alot in Tel Aviv admitted that "if not for financial shortcomings much more might have been achieved."[10] The hairdressing course has been discontinued. Instead, every three months or so, a group of female members spends half a day in a kibbutz and half a day visiting a textile or food processing plant in Israel. At similar three-monthly intervals, a new venture has recently been introduced, of Arab-Jewish women's gatherings. Groups of East Jerusalem women and girls are invited to spend the day in the homes of Jewish women or in Israeli women's centers.

KUPAT HOLIM—WORKERS' HEALTH FUND

Histadrut's Health Fund in East Jerusalem has not been able to extend its facilities to keep up with the growth of its membership. Its clinics are small and cramped and the medical staff has not been increased in proportion to the ever-growing demands of the Arab members and their next of kin, although they are fully entitled to free medical services as dues-paying members of Histadrut.

YOUTH

According to the 1967 East Jerusalem census there were about 6,000 youth aged between fourteen and nineteen. 50 percent were students and 50 per cent were employed. Since then, the figure is believed to have gone up to 10,000. By the end of 1969, 300 East Jerusalem youth had joined the local branch of Histadrut's Working Youth Organization. Special vocational training courses were started for them, as well as Hebrew language evening classes, lectures, excursions, and sports facilities.

Out of an estimated number of 2,000 Arab working youth in East Jerusalem aged between fourteen and eighteen in 1973, 850 were members of Histadrut's Working Youth Organization. This figure included 160 girls. The two secretaries of the Organization's East Jerusalem branch have more work than they can cope with. They organize day-long seminars for boys and girls in the eighth grade elementary classes in all of East Jerusalem's government schools to discuss working youth, Histadrut, and juvenile labor laws before the start of the summer vacation. During the vacation they take prospective new members on a one-day tour of various places in Israel. According to a reliable source, the number of East Jerusalem youngsters who join the local manpower reservoir each year is estimated at 300.[11] Not all of East Jerusalem's young people register with the Working Youth Organization immediately upon leaving school. Some are organized later, in the course of visits to work places or during the bi-annual census taken among working Arab youth in both sectors of the city. However, this census does not include such establishments as restaurants, cafes, print shops, etc., where some 800 of the total 2,000 young workers are employed. In 1972 a summer camp for 100 East Jerusalem working youths was organized in a nearby forest and lasted for three days. There are twice-weekly Hebrew and Arabic language classes, attended by some 40 teenagers, and weekly film shows (and a lending library) are provided in the club room. The Tel Aviv headquarters of the organization publishes an attractive Arabic-language monthly, *Sawt e-Shabibah* ("The Voice of Youth"), which has 500 subscribers in East

Jerusalem. A new feature has now been added to the range of cultural activities for East Jerusalem youth: Arab-Jewish youth meetings, and, in particular, meetings with kibbutz youth which have proved a great success. Small groups of Arab youth mingle with the sons of the kibbutz in work, social gatherings, and entertainment.

However, the secretary of the organization's East Jerusalem branch has complained that his school for apprentices has no inspector, which is *de rigueur* for all such schools in Israel. As a result, only 50 per cent of those who (according to Israeli law) must attend classes one day per week (for ten weeks) are actually attending. The rest are either playing truant or working, and this is illegal according to Israeli law. The same source added that Israeli law, which prohibits juveniles from working the night shift, is not being enforced in Jewish bakeries in West Jerusalem which employ East Jerusalem youth.

The six years that have passed since the unification of the Holy City, in 1967, are but a drop in the ocean of human history, and no time at all in the 5,000 year chronicle of the Jewish people, but they signify a long road of trial and error for the Israel Labor Federation in its efforts to organize the labor force in East Jerusalem. No revolutions have been made, no startling results have been achieved, yet slowly—very slowly—the idea of a conscious labor class, of people who know their rights and are ready to defend them, is penetrating into Arab society in Jerusalem. The road is still long—very long indeed—but those who lead the caravan are confident that the goal will be reached. With enormous patience and a great deal of deep psychological insight, progress will be made. As one of the Arab intellectuals working for Histadrut in East Jerusalem has put it:

> I am convinced that through systematic cultural, social and trade union work among East Jerusalemites, much can be achieved, in the long run, toward better understanding between the inhabitants of the two sectors of the Holy City. . . .[12]

Notes and References

1. The General Federation of Labor in Israel (Histadrut—"the Organization") was founded in 1920. Its national headquarters are in Tel Aviv, where its Executive Committee (Va'ad HaPoel—"Labor Council") is situated. The headquarters of Histadrut's Arab Department and of *Mo'etzet HaPo'alot* ("Working Women's Council") are in the same building. The Jerusalem Labor Council is one of Histadrut's local branches. It is composed of elected local officials who are responsible for all local activities, but takes its direction on general policy from the central body. The administration of the East Jerusalem Labor Council is mainly Arab.

2. G. Weigert, *The Arab members of Histadrut,* International and Arab Departments, General Federation of Labor (Histadrut), (Tel Aviv, 1971).

3. *The Jerusalem Post,* August 24, 1967.

4. The employers of the printers of the East Jerusalem press of the Arab national daily *Al Quds* in November, 1971, used slogans such as "Arab interests" in their fight against the Histadrut-supported printers who threatened to strike in a labor dispute.

5. David Lenon, "Gentle Persuasion in East Jerusalem," *The Jerusalem Post,* May 15, 1971.

6. An interview with Shlomo Shoshani, Director, East Jerusalem branch of the Jerusalem Labor Council. Material especially prepared for this article.

7. *Ba'Moezah* ("In The Council"), Jerusalem Labor Council monthly, May, 1973.

8. See footnote 3.

9. See footnote 5.

10. Interview with Violette Battat, Secretary, Arab Department of *Mo'etzet HaPo'alot,* Tel Aviv. Material especially prepared for this article.

11. Interview with Elias Jirjis, Secretary, East Jerusalem Branch, Working Youth Organization. Material especially prepared for this article.

12. Ziyad Khazen, Member, National Secretariat, Working Youth Organization, Tel Aviv. See also G. Weigert, *Israel's Presence in East Jerusalem,* (Jerusalem: [published by the author] 1973), pp. 76–78. . . . In September 1973, 2500 of the 6,000 eligible east Jerusalem Arab voters participated in the Histadrut elections. Two Arab men and one women were elected to the Jerusalem Labor Council. The Arab-Jewish Discussion Circle is again functioning. In April 1974 a large new Kupat Holim clinic opened, staffed by five doctors, two nurses and two pharmacists, all Arab.

XII

Jerusalem Planning: A Progress Report

NATHANIEL LICHFIELD

The year 1967 saw, for the first time in 2,000 years, the whole city of Jerusalem as a Jewish capital. But the Jewish State of which it was the capital was certainly different, and very different also from what it had been at the time of the creation of the State in 1948. With this fact came many problems for the new administration, one of which is discussed in this paper: measures for the planning and development of the united and growing city in accordance with contemporary views, skills and practices in these matters.

TOWN PLANNING IS NOT NEW IN JERUSALEM

One of the many features in which Jerusalem is fortunate has been the recognition for most of this century that this city should be planned on contemporary lines. That the Turks did not recognize this was perhaps understandable, in view of their failure to apply such measures elsewhere. But the British did recognize this need, and before the fighting of World War I had ceased in Palestine General Allenby[1] had commissioned the first modern town planning scheme from W. McLean, a leading British architect. His scheme, of 1918, was followed by others of 1919, 1922, 1930, and 1944,[2] prepared under the British Mandate. With the creation of the State of Israel, planning continued on both sides of the borderline in the divided city. For West Jerusalem, the new state commissioned the plans of 1950 and 1959 and a further plan in 1962. In East Jerusalem the Jordanian Government also continued to plan with the help of Henry Kendall, who had been the Chief Town Planner during the Mandatory period.

The planners working in the early 1960s were primarily concerned with West Jerusalem, but with the unification of the city in 1967 extended their work to cover the whole city and published their plan accordingly.[3]

In this way they continued the tradition of Jerusalem planning, in the periodic adaptation of the town plans for the changing situation, and for the first time in 30 years offered a plan for the whole city. Ironically enough, this plan itself, already six years in the making, began to be eroded by the rapidly changing circumstances of Jerusalem following the reunification.

URBAN EXPLOSION

Even the casual visitor to Jerusalem in the 1970s will notice the rapid change in pace and style of its urban development. The more informed observer of future plans will know that this is only a beginning. While such change, against the backcloth of historical Jerusalem, is regrettable, it is certainly inevitable in the context of the history of the State of Israel.

Since the foundation of the State, Israel has seen dramatic transformation in terms of population, economic growth, and urbanization pattern. In 25 years it has changed from an area of colonial occupation to a modern developed state. However, Jerusalem remained largely unaffected in all this time. It was divided. West Jerusalem was at the end of a cul-de-sac looking to the west and East Jerusalem was at the edge of Jordan. West Jerusalem was overshadowed by Tel Aviv in its capital-city functions and East Jerusalem was unimportant in the urban hierarchy of Jordan.

Israel's determination to make the united city its capital—and the opening up of the West Bank—have introduced the ingredients of urban explosion, which may be modest in absolute terms compared with many cities around the world but is not so modest relative to the growth capacity of Jerusalem. Following are some indicators of the changes that are taking place.

(a) The unification of the city was accompanied by its enlargement, from 8,750 acres in West Jerusalem to 27,500 in the total city, comprising the former West Jerusalem and ten former Arab municipalities.

(b) All at once Jerusalem has a hinterland from which there is access in all directions, in contrast with the limited situation in the past.

(c) Within the city, even though West and East Jerusalem are recognizable, there is a breaking down of the barriers in terms of social, economic, and government activities.

(d) The transfer of activities from Tel Aviv to Jerusalem, both consistent with building the capital and in associated ways, is growing.

(e) The road access to Tel Aviv has been considerably improved, with travel time down almost to one of daily commuting.

(f) The growth of Jerusalem is wider in geographical spread than is justified by the actual population numbers, with major new public housing developments on the outskirts, with urbanization in outlying villages, and the more recent possibility of large-scale development in the territories to the west of the city. The population itself has been growing at the rate of 3 per cent per annum, included in which is a very high natural increase rate for both Jews and Arabs (2.8 per cent per thousand for the former and 4.25 per cent for the latter in recent years). This amounts to 10,000 extra people per annum and is likely to grow to 15,000 per annum by the early 1980s.

(g) The actual rate of housebuilding is faster, having reached 6–7 per cent in 1971 to allow for the more rapid formation of households and housing shortage.

(h) To cope with the rate of urbanization, some 15,000 people were in the construction industry in 1971. Of this considerable total, some 70 per cent were Arabs who, mainly, commute to Jerusalem from the surrounding territories, and often stay in the city during the week. There is thus a heavy element of transient population.

(i) There is growth in economic activity of all kinds, including factory development, commerce, government, and the Hebrew University.

(j) There is a rapid rise in motor vehicles, associated with the growth of population and also with the rapid growth in private vehicle ownership from the low datum of 45 private cars per thousand people in 1968.

(k) New commercial developments under construction show the high rise tendencies found in developed cities, with hotels, residential blocks, and offices aiming between 10 and 20 floors.

(l) While the center of Jerusalem looks much as it has for decades (apart from the isolated projects just mentioned) there are some 30 projects on paper which would transform the situation if built, and some of which already have permission for development.

(m) Consistent with all these pressures and heavy inflation and speculation, property and land prices have escalated and are continuing to rise.

PLANNING NEEDS

While these future pressures were predictable and to some extent predicted in the late 1960s, it took, in the nature of things, some time for the actual development to manifest itself, and for the implications of the expected changes to be appreciated in the planning and development of

Jerusalem. This realization was stimulated by the conclusions, in December, 1970, of the Town Planning Sub-Committee of the Jerusalem Committee. This committee consisted of an international group of architects and planners who had been invited to provide their advice and suggestions by the Mayor of Jerusalem, Teddy Kollek, and who critically reviewed the situation of planning in this city. In the early 1970s, as a result, the municipality proceeded to take stock of its position as a town planning and development authority with a view to strengthening its capacities. Heretofore, in line with other municipalities throughout the country, it had confined itself to its statutory duties of controlling development under the machinery of issuing town planning permits and building licenses, and had relied for plan preparation on outside consultants and the Ministry of the Interior.

In place of this approach, the municipality proceeded to set up a municipal planning organization under the control of the City Council as the local planning commission, with the aim of strengthening its capacities. These moves resulted in the creation, in 1972, of a Planning and Implementation Division of the City Engineer's Department (he being also responsible for the city's infrastructure and public buildings). The new Division took over the municipal personnel heretofore concerned with varying aspects of the planning and development activities, comprising plan making, planning control and implementation, control of buildings, administration, etc. In August, 1972, came the appointment of the Chief City Planner to head this Division in conjunction with the City Engineer.

A priority task of the new organization was to bring into effect as quickly as possible a plan for the development of Jerusalem, enforceable under the law. This was clearly necessary in view of the pressures which have been outlined and seen against the inadequacy of the instruments which were then currently available for the containment of such pressures. The inadequacy stemmed from the fact that while the Master Plan of 1968 covered the whole of the city, it was advisory only and not legally enforceable, with only part of the city (West Jerusalem) being covered by a legal operative scheme. Furthermore, since this dated from 1959 it needed to be reviewed in the light of the changes since that time, and it had in fact already been altered in many of its details through the introduction of detailed town planning schemes under the law.

However, this inadequacy could not be solved by translating the Master Plan itself into a legal document. The reasons for this were varied. The Master Plan needed review, since it had been prepared during the 1960s and its ruling data was of 1966. Its proposals had come under criticism from several quarters, and many facts created since its completion in 1968 had come to be at variance with it. Thus there was the need to review the Master Plan proposals in the light of all these and other changes.

This alone was not enough, and for quite another reason also. The Master Plan had not been conceived as an operational plan, devised for the purposes of implementation. In accordance with Israeli practice, this would be in the legal plan which had to follow. In the light of contemporary planning practice, the form of the Israeli legal plan is dated. It was very closely based on the practice in Britain between the wars initially introduced by the Mandate Government and not significantly altered by the new State. Therefore it was thought necessary to carry out the review of the Master Plan in terms of a more contemporary process of planning —that which is currently being used in Britain, which has had 25 years of experience of this form of planning and has replaced the inter-war practice that had, in the main, been adopted in Israel. The central features of such contemporary planning are the concept of the plan as a plan for development, geared to a time and resource scale, supported by a style of planning which attempts to combine social, economic and physical policies in the one planning system.

Against this background, the planning process now being carried on comprises the following: a) utilization of established survey and study material in order to save the time that would otherwise be needed for its revision; b) review of the Master Plan proposals and subsequent events in order to consolidate and build-up on past thinking without attempting to introduce an entirely new plan at this stage; c) the carrying-out of this consolidation in the form of a contemporary kind of planning borrowed from Britain; d) the restructuring of the Master Plan in accordance with this process; and e) on this basis, the introduction as early as possible, of legal outline plans for the whole city, based upon the proposals which emerge.

In brief, the process is regarded as an emergency one: to try, by the end of 1973, to introduce the kinds of policies that are needed in Jerusalem if the future growth and development of the city is to be promoted and controlled in accordance with the goals and objectives which do and should guide this future.

But the planning process for a city involves more than the preparation of a plan. This is only a guide to the policies which should be in force, and unless these are influential in shaping growth and development as it takes place, then the exercise, however technically efficient, is wasted. Accordingly, supplementary means are necessary if the planning and development of Jerusalem is to be put upon a sound and enduring basis. Such other means are listed below, and efforts are being made to advance them concurrently with the plan preparation.

(a) Within the framework of the plan and policies being formulated as already described, it is necessary to provide an ongoing basis for the implementation of the development and renewal of the city. These include the various means available for control of the planning and development initiated by outside private and public agencies, together with the positive implementation of development and policies to be undertaken by both the municipality and other bodies, it being remembered that in Jerusalem as in the rest of Israel investment by public agencies comprises a major part of the total.

(b) From the last it follows that there must be co-ordinated decision-making by all those agencies who are concerned in the problems of planning and development of the city. This is practicable under Israeli law, for since 1965, all Ministry development requires the permission of the local commission, as does private development. But in practice there needs to be more than legal observance, there needs also to be a basis for co-operative decision-making and adjustment of individual programs.

(c) If work of this kind is to be based upon a municipal organization there needs to be an efficient professional, technical, and administrative machinery which is operating smoothly for the purpose. Unhappily, there are no parallels for such a local planning organization in other cities of Israel, and while Jerusalem is fortunate in having a good basis already established for the purpose, the creation of such an efficient organization is an uphill job; it would be so in any city of the world which decides to undertake serious planning at the municipal level, and it is particularly difficult in a city which has so much to protect as has Jerusalem, where the growth and problems have suddenly accelerated over a short space of time and where the whole world is interested in what is going on.

(d) But this alone is not enough. As has been discovered around the world, the planning of a city is too complex and important to be left to a municipality, however efficient its professional organization and well-disposed its elected members. The issues involved are important to all the people of the city; they demand to be involved, and the price of their non-involvement is a heavy one in terms of the difficulties of implementation of the plans and policies. In Jerusalem, this issue is compounded by the fact that the city is not only important for the whole State of Israel but also for people throughout the world. Jerusalem is the home of two of the leading monotheistic religions, Judaism and Christianity, and of great significance also for the Muslims. Jerusalem is a magnet for continuing generations of visitors and tourists seeking manifold activities.

SOME PLANNING ISSUES

So far, we have dealt with the nature of the recent changes that are taking place in the city, the needs which arise in its planning and the manner in which this is being undertaken. We now close by enumerating some of the planning issues which arise.

The issues to be described will have a familiar ring, for they are to be found in cities the world over. But it is also true of all cities that the common issues need to be considered for the unique situation which each city provides. This is especially true of Jerusalem for it is a very special kind of city. This is said so often that there is a danger in not realizing how very true it is. A few points will illustrate. The city has the special significance for the great religions, as has been mentioned above. It has a long and enduring history, which has left its relics. It has superb natural endowments, in its topography, landscape, stone formation, elevation, climate, light, and sky. It has the very special qualities of the built environment contributed by successive generations of civilizations. It is a symbol of modern Israel. It is a divided city in which peaceful co-existence is a necessity if the Eternal City is to fulfill its promise to mankind.

It is against these qualities, this special spirit and character, that the following everyday issues must be considered.

(a) Bearing in mind the present functions of the city (as capital, a university town, a religious center, a tourist center, etc.), what should these be in future? How will these special functions accord with the everyday role of providing a contemporary life for its residents?

(b) Currently the city has some 320,000 people (240,000 Jews and 80,000 Arabs). It is growing steadily and the question of size limitation arises. Unrestrained growth will threaten the qualities of the city and in particular those of the Old City and its surroundings. Unrestrained growth will also damage the city visually because of the peculiar topography which offers a plateau surrounded by steeply sloping mountains. Thus there is the possibility and desirability of size limitation. Something of the order of half a million people is considered to be a reasonable size for physical growth with extension planned in a satellite manner to be determined.

(c) In addition to too great a size, a threat to the city could also come from too rapid a rate of growth. As indicated above, this has been at around 3 per cent per annum and was visualized as such in the Master Plan. More rapid rates of growth, of up to 7.5 per cent, have been advocated with the aim of rapid achievement of a large city. However, analysis has shown that the implications for this rate of growth would be severe on all the city's resources and a more modest target is preferred. Currently this is of the order of 3.7 per cent per annum.

(d) Another sensitive area of Jerusalem is its central area—that part of the city where the accumulation of city-wide services, such as shopping, business, government, and recreational facilities are to be found. Currently, the city has two such centers; the larger one in West Jerusalem and the smaller in East Jerusalem, each virtually adjoining the Old Walls and spreading away from them. While these are the twin cores of the city, the central area activities have spread even wider, from the Givat Ram University in the west to Mt. Scopus in the east, with the government precinct, Israel Museum, and Jerusalem Theater situated outside the established core. Thus the issue here is to accommodate for the future growth of such activities contingent on the growing population and increasing functional importance of the city in the state, while at the same time avoiding over-concentration of activities in the traditional cores, which cannot be readily adjusted for great growth (in terms of use and traffic) and which should not be so adjusted because of the threat that this could bring to the Old City and its environs. Thus a policy of controlled expansion and dispersal is called for.

(e) As in all cities, a limiting factor on its central development is the need to accommodate the growth of traffic, in particular that of the motor car. As indicated earlier the potential expansion of motor vehicles is great, and if its free use is to be accommodated a large program of road building is needed. Such provisions were made in the Master Plan in 1968. However, as is beginning to be appreciated around the world, cities can be destroyed by providing for free and unfettered use of the motor car by road construction, and this particularly applies to Jerusalem, with its compelling need for protection of its spirit and character. Thus alternatives are being explored, such as restraint on the use of the motor vehicle for work and travel to the central area, the creation of more facilities to encourage greater use of public transport, controlled parking, environment and traffic management.

(f) Part of the protection of the spirit and character of Jerusalem is in the preservation of its historical heritage, whether these are archaeological sites, buildings of importance to the religions, or buildings of historical and architectural interest. As might be expected, the number of such sites and buildings runs into several hundreds. The potential threat therefore is great. The dangers from this threat have not been powerful in the past, because of the slackness in pressure and the strong institutional constraints, and the means of protection are not as advanced as in other countries. Thus there is the compelling need for the listing and categorization of the places to be protected, and for some means of ensuring that they are in fact protected when the need arises.

(g) From protection of individual sites and buildings to protection of areas is a short step. In this Jerusalem is also fortunate in having certain quarters, some dating from perhaps a century ago, which have neighborhood qualities requiring protection as a whole. Here, however, it is not practicable to think in terms of preservation but rather of conservation and rehabilitation, so as to enable these quarters to be usefully occupied and therefore maintained in a contemporary sense. Here again, knowledge of the area and the devising of means of carrying out protective policies have to be fully established as a preliminary to their successful implementation.

(h) So far we have been largely considering the established city and the problems which arise from its protection in terms of the expected changes. But there is also a new Jerusalem, growing up away from the Old City and away also from the new modern center which is developing around the government office precinct, Knesset, and Israel Museum. Here Jerusalem is spreading out onto open hills, in new residential suburbs to the north or south, and is filling and expanding established areas in West Jerusalem and the former East Jerusalem. There is the need to ensure that the new development is worthy of the older Jerusalem and yet built in the contemporary idiom suited to a Middle East society and climate. These are not only problems of layout, design, and third-dimension but also involve the familiar and vexing question of living patterns of the different peoples in the city, and not only of Jews and Arabs in general but of the different sects within the Jewish and Arab populations. The future with regard to this problem is difficult to foresee. While the city is united there is still nonetheless an East and West Jerusalem, delineated by history and topography. Will this always continue? Should it continue?

(i) In introducing these comments on Jerusalem's planning problems reference was made to the city's spirit and character, and the special features of Jerusalem were brought out in many of the issues mentioned. The concern for this element is thus all-pervading, its nature is subtle and the solutions are complex. But this theme runs throughout the whole planning process, and will be a touchstone for the development that will take place in accordance with the plans.

In brief, will the new Jerusalem damage the old? And, will the new Jerusalem be worthy of the old?

NOTES AND REFERENCES

1. General Edmund Allenby, Commander of the British Expeditionary Force in Egypt which entered Jerusalem in December, 1917, was put in charge of the provisional military administration of the occupied ex-Ottoman areas.

2. For an account of the successive plans, see: Henry Kendall, *Jerusalem: The City Plan, 1918–1948* (London: His Majesty's Stationery Office, 1948); Arieh Sharon, *Planning Jerusalem: The Old City and Its Environs* (Jerusalem: Weidenfeld and Nicholson, 1972).

3. Arieh Hashimshoni, Joseph Schweid and Zion Hashimshoni, *The Jerusalem Master Plan 1968*, Vol. I (Jerusalem, The Municipality of Jerusalem, 1973) (Hebrew).

XIII

What It Means to Be Mayor of the City of Peace

TEDDY KOLLEK

The first British Governor of Jerusalem, Sir Ronald Storrs, used to say that "there is no promotion after Jerusalem," that governing Jerusalem offers challenges unlike any other task and that the satisfaction gained in meeting them is uniquely rewarding—and I heartily agree.

According to one definition the name Jerusalem itself means "City of Peace." But while the first vision of universal peace came from Jerusalem and from the Prophets who preached here, the City has known little fruit of the message it gave to the world. In ancient times it saw a succession of conquerors, for whom Jerusalem held the key to the Holy Land. In modern times, the City has seen war in 1917, 1948, and 1967, as well as riots in 1921, 1929, 1936–39, 1946–48, 1963, and 1966. Nineteen years of truncated existence, from 1948 to 1967, brought hardships to the citizens on both sides of the armistice lines, incidents of shooting were not unusual.

I would be the last person to maintain that we have brought heaven on earth to Jerusalem. The threat of violence is still with us. The gap between the rich and poor still exists, as do the differences between Jews and Jews, Muslims and Muslims, Christians and Christians—and among these groups. Yet we have avoided any major clash, interracial or inter-faith strife. I believe that this is not a small achievement. It could be an omen for the future and an example not only for our own area of the world.

Governing Jerusalem, however, means more than keeping the peace. Before reunification, Israel's capital was at a dead end, geographically, at the edge of a frontier with hostile neighbors. Its lack of industry and capital investments placed severe restrictions and a heavy strain on the Municipality's ability to provide adequate services for its citizens. Since 1967 Jerusalem has regained its proper place at the center of the country. It has been a magnet for both Israelis and new immigrants, and has begun to suffer many of the blights of modern urban life. Even before reunification more than half of Jerusalem's population consisted of immigrants. Most of these new settlers came from the Arab countries, Asia, and North Africa. Their standard of education and economic status was lower than the Israeli or Western-born Jerusalemites and their families larger. Jerusalem had the largest number of families in the country with five or more children. It had the highest rate of natural increase—twice that of Tel Aviv. It had the greatest proportion of elderly and the highest rate of exodus of young people in search of better economic conditions.

In 1967 the problems were compounded. 70,000 Muslim and Christian Arabs were added to the city's population. The birth rate among these new residents was one of the highest in the world—almost double that of the Jews—and their social, economic, and educational conditions far below the standards of West Jerusalem. The Old City, with its unique religious and historical heritage, became a part of the Municipality's responsibility, along with the overcrowded slums it contained.

And Jerusalem became the true capital of the State of Israel. Thousands clamored to live within its borders, all seeking proper housing and municipal services.

I felt that the challenge of my first task was to make the City's services available equally to all residents, to overcome fear and suspicion and, with time, to develop a sense of civic unity and pride. Within a comparatively short time the standards of living in East Jerusalem were elevated, educational facilities were improved, there was full employment, and cooperation in the daily life and functioning of the City became commonplace. Today, as I mentioned earlier, peaceful coexistence is a fact, and no one thinks any longer in terms of partition and the redivision of the City.

The second challenge was to give practical expression to the Government's declaration regarding the complete freedom of worship to the various religious denominations, as well as unimpaired access to their holy shrines and places of worship. This was implemented immediately, and good relations and cooperation exist between the various Christian and Muslim institutions and the Municipality.

The third challenge is one which is still with us—it is the challenge of making Jerusalem a vibrant and viable city, of protecting its unique and rich past without turning the city into a museum or sacrificing progress in the late twentieth century idiom. But even more it is the challenge of providing equal opportunity, equal services, and equal status to all of the segments of the city's population. Jerusalem must not become a melting pot, a city with a mono-culture. Its ethnic and cultural diversity is a major factor in the City's charm and attractiveness. We have made every effort to ensure that Christian and Muslim cultures should flourish, alongside the traditions of the various Jewish communities, and we will continue to do so. The practical application of this principle is to ensure that the wealth of evidence of a rich past should be made the basis of vital and creative activities.

Moreover, we are trying to close the gap between the have and have nots. Where it is impossible to increase the size of a family's dwelling, we increase its living space by providing a park in the neighborhood, a community center, a youth club.

We are attempting to bridge the educational differences by establishing libraries in the poorer areas, building better-equipped schools and providing supplementary lessons. We have established joint activities between Arab and Jewish youth.

Above all, we seek to plan for the future. With an ever-present eye on the universal interests in Jerusalem, we are attempting to create a city which will meet the human, social, and economic needs of a modern urban population. I believe, along with leading figures in the fields of art and history, theology, town planning and architecture, that what people do and how they live is as organically vital to the character of Jerusalem as are its ancient buildings and landscapes.

Our sages have taught us that before reaching the heavenly Jerusalem of the spirit it is necessary to inhabit the earthly Jerusalem. It is in the latter that we live and work—but always with our eye toward the former.

This then is the challenge and the satisfaction—frustrating and elating, disappointing and rewarding, infuriating and satisfying, but always, always, alive and exciting.

III

THE HOLY CITY

XIV

The Biblical Concept of Jerusalem

SHEMARYAHU TALMON

Precis

Advancing the present dialogue demands a close look at what the Bible says about Jerusalem. The many biblical references to the city would alone show its importance to writers and readers alike. Since the Jerusalem-theme develops through various biblical strata a study of this multiform development should help one's understanding of the later divergent Jewish and Christian views on the topic.

In the Hebrew Bible mention of Jerusalem predominates in the historical books, the prophetic books, and the psalms. The article prescinds from the Jerusalem-theme in the apocryphal writers. Judaism, the Qumran community, and Christianity each put different emphases on various strata of the biblical treatment of Jerusalem, there taking place a cross-fertilization between the community and the concept. The author bases his treatment of the Jerusalem-theme upon the socio-political-historical facts as found in the Bible rather than upon any "conceptual" or "ideological" framework derived from these facts. The "mythic," in other words, must be understood in terms of the historic. The author finds much in the later Jewish Bible that mythologizes history with the result that there takes place a too-great emphasis on the "celestial Jerusalem" and a de-emphasizing of the terrestrial city. A closer look at the biblical sources would show that every example of an idealized city of Jerusalem could be matched with an example of a highly mundane city, a city not peaceful but warlike, a city not inhabited merely by pious Jews but by a mixed group of foreigners.

The biblical writing corresponds very often to the concrete historical moment that called it forth. An integral understanding must take into con-

sideration what may seem at first glance contradictory views as to the meaning of Jerusalem and in no event may the concrete, historical meaning be
set aside in favor of the mythological.

I

For the present-day controversy over Jerusalem with all its ramifications, my paper on the concept of Jerusalem in the Bible appears to be
altogether irrelevant. It may be considered paradoxical, but in fact is not,
that the basic literary and spiritual inheritance common to both Judaism
and Christianity, namely, the canon of the 24 books of the Hebrew Bible
has had little bearing on the analysis of the actualities concerning Jerusalem, and on the discussion that arises from this analysis. It seems that
since all sides concerned take their departure from the diversified image
of Jerusalem and the ideologies interlinked with it which developed in
post-biblical times and in post-biblical literature, the discussion from its
very beginning tended to become lopsided. Basing themselves on differing, and more often than not conflicting, premises, Christian theologians
and Jewish thinkers who are engaged in this discussion never even arrived at the threshold of a dialogue situation. I dare not hope that my
presentation of the matter in hand may help in improving the situation
altogether. Without attempting to actualize the biblical material as I
conceive of it, I shall nevertheless maintain that its analysis may hold
some hope, if not for closing the gap between the opposing factions in
the evaluation of the meaning of the phenomenon "Jerusalem," then at
least for furthering a better understanding by Christians and Muslims of
the attitude of a Jew toward Jerusalem.

In view of the above referred to, possibly deplorable, irrelevance of
the biblical concept for the actual theological and socio-political differences of opinion, I can present my conception of Jerusalem in the Bible
sine ira though *cum studio.* Being an exegete and a philologian by training,
by profession, and maybe also by conviction, I shall try to base my case
on as objective a presentation of the biblical material as can be expected
of a student of the Bible who approaches his topic armed with the tools
of his trade, but at the same time bearing the weight of his beliefs and
his own existential situation.

Let me begin with some simple statistics. The city name Jerusalem is
mentioned in Hebrew Scriptures some 750 times. Zion appears about 180
times. There are several hundred more references to diverse appellations
of the city, such as Mt. Moriah, City of David, City of Judah, Temple
Mount, Holy City, Shalem, Jebus, Ariel, The City, and so on. Altogether
there must be some 2,000 mentions of Jerusalem in the Hebrew Canon.
This figure stands no comparison with the number of references to

Jerusalem in inter-testamental literature, for which, though, we lack a complete concordance, or in the New Testament. The statistical imbalance becomes even more prominent if one considers the fact that the collection of the 24 Old Testament books, by sheer bulk, is heavily outweighted by the above corpus of later literature. To complete the picture, it has to be stated that similar conclusions can be drawn from such a numerical comparison of mentions of Jerusalem in the Old Testament Canon with its occurrences in Rabbinic literature.

It is readily admitted that word counts in literature do not necessarily convey a true impression of the relative importance of the words counted in a given context. But often the quantitative check may be taken as a pointer to qualitative values. The preponderance of certain words, which are employed not only in one basic meaning but also serve as vehicles which carry sentiments and ideas derived from that meaning by diverse associations, frequently are a tangible indicator of the centrality of the sentiments and ideas in the thought processes which motivated the writers of the literature under review. At the same time this preponderance gives evidence to the importance of those words in the world of ideas of the audience to whom the authors address themselves.

This statement certainly is applicable to the employment of the name Jerusalem and its parallel appellations in the Hebrew Scriptures. In this instance it can be easily shown that quantity spells significance. The word count reveals to us the focality of Jerusalem in biblical thought. The plethora of references to Jerusalem discloses the importance of the city and the ideas connected with it in the minds of the biblical authors and their audience alike.

We can now proceed further with our analysis. It is commonplace to state that the Bible is not a "book" in the accepted sense of the word, but rather a collection of books, or an anthology of ancient Hebrew literature which grew over a thousand years. Therefore it is imperative not to stop short at presenting a general all-embracing statistical picture, but to try further to find out how the references to Jerusalem are distributed among the various and varied components of the biblical canon, *i.e.*, among diverse major literary genres or strata, and among the individual books.

The results of this break-up have some bearing on the diversified development of the theme "Jerusalem" in the literature of the post-biblical period. As will yet be shown, some of the differences in stress and evaluation of the theme and the motif in Jewish and Christian thought can be explained as having arisen from the different measure of importance attributed to the diverse literary strata of the Jewish Bible in the theologies of Judaism and Christianity. I would maintain that in tracing this diversity of stress put on different strata of the Hebrew biblical canon by later generations, we may discover a means of finding out where and why Judaism of the late Second Temple period and early Christianity diverged from each other, even when they based their theological tenets on the Hebrew Scriptures which were their common heritage. With reference to the issue on hand, I hope to show how this different stress put on different parts of the Hebrew Bible affected the concept of Jerusalem as it developed in Jewish and Christian thought.

II

It cannot cause any surprise that there are only two possible references to Jerusalem in the Pentateuch, and not more than about a dozen in Joshua and Judges. These books present the history of Israel in a period in which Jerusalem had not yet achieved its later centrality. For other reasons, mentions of Jerusalem are altogether missing in some Wisdom writings, *e.g.*, in Job, Proverbs, and for that matter also in Esther, and are few and far between in others, such as Ecclesiastes. This rarity can in no way be explained by considerations derived from the historical and chronological setting of these books, but rather should be attributed to the marked anthropocentric nature of Wisdom literature, in distinction from the ethnocentric character of the other literary genres of the Bible. Jerusalem being first and foremost a historical entity, and being preponderantly connected with historical issues of biblical Israel, non-historical Wisdom teaching has little use for it, as a name or as a concept.

Mentions of Jerusalem are clustered heavily in the official court or temple historiographies, Samuel, Kings, Ezra-Nehemiah, and Chronicles, in the prophetic books which mirror, to a great extent, the same situations which are reported in the historiographies, and especially in the Book of Psalms, which may be considered to have been commissioned, at least in part, by the royal house of Jerusalem in order to be employed in the divine service at the Temple which had been instituted and developed by King David and his descendants. Herein may be found the reason for the ever-so-often recurring references to Jerusalem and to the Davidic dynasty in the Book of Psalms.

The distinctive distribution of references to Jerusalem in the books of the Bible again tallies, as I hope to prove, with the focal contents and meaning of the theme "Jerusalem" in biblical thought.

It appears that in the issue under review the pinpointing of the discussion on the Hebrew Bible can be fully justified. These books became a source of intense inspiration to later writers, both Jewish and Christian, who derived from them vital themes and motifs which were then incorporated into, and became fruitful within, their own complex of ideas. This process certainly was not uniform. Rather did it sub-divide into several main streams which can be identified with the major religious trends that crystallized within Judaism in the Second Temple period. In some instances, as in the case of the Covenanters from Qumran, the process resulted in the formation of distinctive sub-groups that retained in one form or another their affiliation with Judaism, and in the most notable case, that of Christianity, it culminated in a complete divorce from the mother community.

In view of the concrete historical and institutionalized literary significance of Jerusalem, of which its eschatological motif character is a secondary derivation, it seems wise to focus our view here on those developmental aspects of the theme which can be firmly connected with compact communities of the Second Commonwealth Era, and to give only peripheral attention to its more diffuse sediments in the disjointed apocryphal literature. Let me explain a little more the implications of this statement. Since I cannot conceive of Jerusalem as mainly a theme of spiritual significance and meaning, but as a theme which has definite and direct institutional affiliations, I shall refrain here from discussing the meaning of Jerusalem in the apocryphal writings simply because we cannot connect this literature with a clearly circumscribed, socially constituted body. In contrast to this, when we discuss Qumran, Judaism, Christianity, we know where we stand. Here the dual way of impact and fertilization from the community to the concept and from the concept to the community makes it much easier and better understandable to find out what Jerusalem stood for in these three religious communities.

It is submitted that the later diversification of the theme Jerusalem and the uneven importance of Jerusalem within the frames of those constituted communities at least in part can be ascribed to the fact that the different groups put different stress on distinctive strata of the Old Testament literature, strata in which were variedly highlighted diverse aspects of Jerusalem. It shall be my concern to deal especially with those biblical writings which appear to have been somewhat neglected in the quest for the significance of Jerusalem in the Bible, first and foremost the historiographies. I shall endeavor to distill from them what I consider to be the essential meaning of Jerusalem in the biblical period. This approach to the interpretation of historical facts as they are recorded in the Bible is based on the premise that we can thus discern the ideas and attitudes which the biblical writers believed to be inherent in them, or with which they had invested them.

The task appears to be more difficult than the approach usually taken by interpreters, that of scanning the prophetical writings and the Book of Psalms for a conceptual picture of Jerusalem. This picture is not always necessarily anchored in socio-political actualities but rather often mirrors "spiritual" or ideological elaborations which have been freed, so to speak, from the limitations of reality. As against this, the analysis of the historiographies could or even should convey to us concepts which have existential roots in biblical society and in its history.

III

Let me summarize in short what Jerusalem stands for in the historical books of the Hebrew Scriptures. Its very name indicates that the city initially had been built as a "foundation of [or for the deity] Shalem," to be identified with Shalmon—Shulmanu known from Assyrian sources, a deity of which further extrabiblical information has come to us during the last decades. In view of this theophoric character of the name Jerusalem, that is to say its having as a component the divine name Shalem, it may be considered as certain that also the *nomen locus* Shalem mentioned in Genesis 14, in the well-known tradition connected with the Patriarch Abraham, indeed can be identified with what was destined to become the Holy City of Israel—Jerusalem. This equivalence of Shalem and Jerusalem-Zion obviously is already taken for granted in biblical literature itself, as may be deduced from the employment of Shalem and Zion as synonyms in Psalm 76:2: "in Shalem is His tent [or his tabernacle], and His dwelling place in Zion." By means of a popular etymology, the theophoric component in both Shalem and Jerusalem, namely the divine name Shalem, was equated with the Hebrew word Shalom—"peace." This paved the way for the elevation of Jerusalem to the proverbial City of Peace, a concept which found its most stirring expression in the most probably post-exilic Psalm 122, in which "the peace of Jerusalem" is the central catch-phrase. Even more expressly, Shalem and Shalom are identified in Hebrews 7:1–2 where the above story of Abraham's meeting with Melchisedek (Gen. 14) is paraphrased:

> For this Melchisedek, King of Shalem, priest of God Most High, who met Abraham returning from the slaughter of the kings, and blessed him; to whom also Abraham divided a tenth part of all; being first by interpretation King of righteousness, and then also King of Shalem, which is King of peace.

Alas, this popular etymology which has clearly discernible roots already in antiquity cannot be considered to have either a linguistic or, for that matter, a historical basis. In actual history Jerusalem seldom ceased from being a city of bloodshed and war. Let me read just two passages which exemplify the internal strife which repeatedly rent the city. One is from Kings 21:16 where it is said that "Manasheh shed innocent blood very much, till he had filled Jerusalem from end to end." The other is taken from Matthew 23:29:

> Woe unto you, scribes and Pharisees, hypocrites, for you built the sepulchres of the prophets and garnish the tombs of the righteous, and say, if we had been in the days of our fathers, we would not have been partakers with them in the blood of the prophets.

There certainly is no need to specify the almost innumerable references to wars about and around Jerusalem from its historical conquest by David (II Sam. 5:4–9) to the battles in which it is embroiled in late eschatological vision (e.g., Zech. 14).

The pre-Israelite temple-city Jerusalem which had been ruled by the priest-king Melchisedek who officiated at the shrine of El Elyon, God Most High, was hebraised, as it were, by locating in its circumference the *hieros logos* of Isaac's sacrifice by his father Abraham (Gen. 22) on Mt. Moriah which from days of old was associated with Jerusalem.

It may be claimed with much probability that the above two traditions, which linked Abraham with Shalem—Jerusalem, like many other patriarchal traditions, in fact reflect concepts of monarchic times which were retrojected into the days of the forefathers. I cannot enlarge here on this issue. Let me just draw your attention to the very presentation of the forefathers in the Bible. By viewing them with scrutiny, you will find that many of the stories reflect in fact royal themes. Abraham is portrayed exclusively dealing with none but kings and rulers. And it can hardly be a coincidence that the two main cities in which he appears, Jerusalem and Hebron (Gen. 23), in future will serve in succession as the metropolis of King David's realm (II Sam. 5:1–5).

The twofold association of Abraham with Jerusalem, one set in a political context arising out of the war against the five foreign kings who had invaded Canaanite territory to fight against the kings of Sodom and Gomorrah and their satellites (Gen. 14), and one illustrating the religious character of Jerusalem where the patriarch had built an altar on Mt. Moriah (Gen. 22), projects the twofold significance of the city in the days of the Davidic kingdom. Jerusalem, which initially had been inhabited by indigenous Canaanites, as we know from the Amarna letters of the 14th century B.C., and from the Book of Joshua (Chapter 10), later had been ruled by another ethnic group, the Jebusites, as we learn from the Book of Judges (19:10–12), and had served in both stages as a foreign cult place (Gen. 14; II Sam. 24:18–25), after its conquest by David (II Sam. 5:6–9), became the religious and political pivot of Israel. By transforming the foreign city of Jerusalem into the metropolis of his empire, a city which had no previous affiliation with one of the Israelite tribes whom he had set out to weld into one nation, David created a new unifying political center for Israel. By building in Jerusalem the Temple dedicated to Israel's God (according to the tradition preserved in Chronicles, Chapters 15–16, 22), or at least by laying the foundations for the building operations to be carried out by his son Solomon (according to the tradition embedded in I Kings, Chapters 6–8), David also made Jerusalem the cornerstone of the religious and cultic unification of Israel.

Jerusalem thus became the symbol and the most significant exponent of the transfer from "peoplehood" to "nationhood" and "statehood." But it was never exclusively subjugated to or identified with the new social phenomenon. Therefore, when the state ceased from existing, Jerusalem did not lose its importance and symbolic meaning for the Jewish people. The city which in antiquity had experienced one decisive transformation of her significance could easily retransfer and readjust to ensuing different historical situations. She has in fact done so for many hundred years without losing her prestige and symbolic value that had been conferred on her by David.

With the conquest of Jerusalem, David and the Davidic house apparently also took over the old emblems of sovereignty and the royal epithets of Melchisedek, the former priest-king of Jerusalem. This is obviously hinted at in Psalm 110:4, the accurate translation of which, though, cannot be safely established. The Psalmist addresses himself to a typical or rather prototypical king of the Davidic dynasty: "The Lord hath sworn and will not go back on it. Thou are priest forever after the order of Melchisedek."

In the short period of Israel's unity under David and Solomon, the nation experienced an unprecedented and never again matched state of political glory, economic achievement, and cultic splendor. It is for this reason that the capital of the realm, Jerusalem, became a beacon of well-being and success for future generations. Late biblical and post-biblical Judaism made the idealized image of that historical Jerusalem the cornerstone of their hopes for a national and religious renaissance, and ultimately perceived in it the prototype of the New Jerusalem, the very pivot around which turned their eschatological aspirations.

IV

It is possible, or even probable, that into the idealized image of the real-historical Jerusalem was blended the ancient Near Eastern mythic motif of the "City on the Mountain," of which not only literary but also pictorial representations have come to us. The geographical elevation of the city whose acropolis invariably is occupied by a sanctuary, clearly symbolizes its closeness to heaven, and hence the therefrom arising claim to divine status. The Tower of Babel tradition may well be considered a variation on this basic theme. The ever-recurring emphasis on the mountainous character of Jerusalem and its surroundings which, as we all know, certainly is anchored in geographical reality, obviously is meant to confer some of the notions inherent in the City on the Mountain motif by means of historicizing a myth. The depiction of the Temple as standing on the highest mountain in the area, and being the tallest building in the city, which later tradition will not allow to be topped by any other building, further illuminates the similarity with Canaanite, especially Ugaritic, and Mesopotamian themes. These mythic elements become exceedingly prominent in prophetic and psalmodic literature which are much less reality-bound than is historiography. I refer here especially to Psalm 68:16–17, in which we have a report, as it were, on a controversy between the mountains that had been previously the chosen ones of God and now are superseded by Mt. Zion:

> A mountain of God is the mountain of Bashan; a high mountain is the mountain of Bashan. Why look ye askance, ye high mountains, at the mountain which God hath desired for his abode? Yea, the Lord will dwell in it for ever.

Mt. Sinai is not mentioned in these verses, but we find an explicit reference to it in the verse to follow, where the Hebrew text should be corrected to read: "The Lord has come *from* Sinai in holiness" (*Adonai ba' miSinai bakodesh*). This seems to imply that also Mt. Sinai is included among the rejected, or the mountains supplanted by Mt. Zion. I shall yet return to the here-implied rivalry between Mt. Sinai and Mt. Zion in which the latter tradition prevailed over the former.

In these non-historiographical strata of the biblical literature, national-religious imagination often soars high to leave behind any consideration of reality. One may be permitted to define this phenomenon, which again can be observed in the Book of Psalms, as a process of mythologization of history. It appears that this de-historization will serve later generations as a launching pad for the ideological transfer of terrestrial Jerusalem to the celestial plane, *Jerushalaim shel ma'lah* being an exalted and sublimated likeness of Jerusalem *shel matah*. The upper, the celestial, Jerusalem is viewed in a radiant infinitely refined vision which bears only a remote resemblance to the terrestrial city. However, also at its peak, the idea of the celestial Jerusalem as it was conceived by Jewish thinkers, and even by mystic fancy, never lost its touch with down-to-earth reality. A definite strand of this-worldliness, which seems to permeate normative Jewish religion in all its ramifications, effectively checked the tendencies which became rampant among Jewish fringe groups and in Christian mysticism to paint a picture of the celestial Jerusalem which is untrammelled by the image of the historical city. In contrast, normative Judaism was less concerned with the metahistorical "Heavenly Jerusalem" than with the latter-historical "New Jerusalem" which, in the main, restorative eschatology portrayed as an improved edition of its historic prototype.

This prototype, the historical Jerusalem of the Hebrew Scriptures, symbolizes the civilization and cultivation centered ideology of Israel. The post-conquest city organization of Jerusalem is the opposite pole of the pre-conquest desert culture. Its monarchic regime is set off favorably against the democratic anarchism of the Period of the Judges. Mt. Zion in many respects is opposed to Mt. Sinai. Though Mt. Sinai represents the beginning of Israel's freedom, it also retains as yet the flavor of serfdom in Egyptian bondage, religiously, morally, and politically. Mt. Zion, and the covenant that God established there with David, represent Israel's sovereignty in its full bloom, in civil and in sacred life.

I especially stress this point because I feel that the concept of a "desert ideal" has played havoc in some quarters with Bible exegesis and biblical studies. The latent nativism of the late nineteenth century brought about a rather astonishing predilection for the "desert" which is completely opposed to what the Bible advocates in reality. The trend found in Christian theology at the turn of the nineteenth and the twentieth centuries which is rooted in a modern romanticism, and which attempts to recapture, as it were, the positive essence of a surmised biblical "nomadic ideal," clashed sharply with the city-oriented culture of the Jew in those centuries. I would maintain that this contrast, based as it is on wrong assumptions with regard to biblical literature, appears to have had a definite impact on the attitude of some Christian exegetes toward the Jews and to Judaism of their times.

The above-referred-to symbolic opposition of Mt. Zion as the center of cultured, cultivated, civilized life to Mt. Sinai, which stands for primitive nomadism, is already alluded to in the Epistle to the Galatians. There, in chapter 4:22–25 we read:

> For it is written that Abraham had two sons, one by the handmaid and one by the freewoman; howbeit the son by the handmaid is born after the flesh but the son by the freewoman is born through promise. Which things contain an allegory: for these women are two covenants; one from Mt. Sinai, bearing children unto bondage, which is Hagar. Now this Hagar is Mt. Sinai in Arabia and answereth to the Jerusalem that now is; for she is in bondage with her children. But the Jerusalem that is above is free, which is our mother.

The writer had started out correctly by showing that Jerusalem is in opposition to Sinai, but in the very next verse he changes this terrestrial Jerusalem which is as terrestrial as Sinai into a heavenly Jerusalem. Taking this additional step he certainly goes further than any Jew would have done at any time. This last sentence already presents Christian exegesis.

Now, if I am correct in this interpretation, if Jerusalem symbolizes orderly civilized life, then the destruction of Jerusalem spells anarchy. This assumption indeed is borne out by biblical literature. Just think of any of the prophets. They present to you the loss of Jerusalem and its destruction as the beginning of a new chaos. Isaiah 3 shows society in complete disintegration after Jerusalem is conquered. Her fall means a return to the pre-creation state.

V

The basic realism of the presentation of Jerusalem in the Bible is further illustrated by the recording of historical circumstances which less fact-minded writers well might have suppressed. As already stated, tradition freely admits that Jerusalem had not been an Israelite city from old, that it had been inhabited by foreigners, to some degree also at the height of its occupation by the Israelites, and that it had originally served, and continued to serve, as a sanctuary of foreign cults even under the Israel rulers, Solomon, Hezekiah, Mannasseh, Josiah, and others.

One is almost inclined to suspect that the biblical historiographers put special emphasis on the fact that Jerusalem always had a mixed population, knit into one social network, without making light of an individual or group identities. Not only are we told that Jebusites, from whom David had captured the city, were permitted to continue to live in it unmolested side by side with the Israelites, but our sources also report at great length that the royal court literally was ridden with foreign warriors, Karatites, Palatites, Hittites and others, and advisers, some of whom rose to prominence in the administrative hierarchy of the realm, as for example David's and Solomon's ministers. These foreign elements apparently were economically and socially fully integrated and they in fact became a main pillar of support of the Davidic dynasty.

This resulting melting pot situation was enhanced by an apparent liberal attitude as to the admissibility of individuals and groups of foreign ethnic extraction into the Jerusalem cult. The manifold connections of the tribe of Judah, and especially of the Davidic dynasty, with originally non-Israelite elements, is amply exemplified in biblical traditions. Suffice it here to mention Tamar the Canaanite who had borne two sons to Judah, the eponym of the tribe (Gen. 38), Ruth the Moabite, great grandmother of David (Ruth 4), and Absalom's mother, Maacah, a princess of Geshur in Transjordan (II Sam. 3). It has been surmised, with much probability, that even the house of Zadok, the high priest who officiated in the Jerusalem Temple, belonged to the indigenous population of Canaan, having been initially affiliated with the local shrine at Gibeon (I Chron. 16:39).

There is, on the other hand, a recurring insistence, especially in prophetic literature, on a future purge of Jerusalem from all foreign elements who had brought pollution into the city. In a rather narrow nationalistic vision, again set in the frame of history, Jerusalem in the days to come will be inhabited exclusively by people of pure Israelite stock. They will congregate in the city and worship in its Temple to the one God, the God of Israel. This trend also makes itself strongly felt in post-exilic historiography. It would appear that this tendency attempts to balance the opposite trend, to which I referred earlier, which had prevailed in pre-exilic Israel as exemplified in early biblical historiography. In both cases a realistic historic concern is at work, namely the endeavor to cope with actual situations and the problems inherent in them. Pre-exilic monarchic Israel, as represented by the metropolis Jerusalem, saw itself settled with a numerous minority of foreigners, and could conceive of no better way of handling the situation arising from this fact than by absorbing them into the Israelite society. The post-exilic community of Jerusalem, a mere remnant of the once vigorous nation of early monarchic times, outnumbered manyfold by the population of Palestine which it encountered at the time of the Return from the Exile, saw itself forced to segregate from the peoples of the land in order to be better able to maintain its exclusive identity. Jerusalem, purified and holy, thus became the quintessence of a recessionist ideology, which shrank from any contact with those who had not gone through the purifying smelting furnace of the exile, Judaeans and Ephraimites alike.

Pre-exilic prophecy had castigated Jerusalem, its kings and inhabitants, because: "They strike hands with the children of strangers" (Isa. 2:6). Dissociation from other nations then was considered the only way of preserving the metropolis and the nation of Israel from disaster. Alliances with foreigners, and with foreign rulers, spelled catastrophe (Isa. 7:4–9). At the same time, prophecy and foremost post-exilic prophecy conceived of Jerusalem as of the center of an organized world-wide council of nations. At the end of days, Mt. Zion, which stands for Jerusalem as a whole, will become the goal of pilgrims from all the nations (Isa. 2:2; Mic. 4:2; Is. 60): "And at that time they called Jerusalem the throne of the Lord, and all the nations shall be gathered unto it, to the name of the Lord, to Jerusalem" (Jer. 3:17). Punishment will be meted out to all the families of the earth that will not go up unto Jerusalem to worship the King of lords, the Lord of hosts (Zech. 14:17).

Here one is inclined to find an expression of the significance of Jerusalem at its very peak: the city being raised from the status of the capital of the Israelite kingdom to that of the metropolis of the inhabited ecumene, which means the inhabitants of the Near East. None of the prophets had a wider horizon than let me say Cyprus in the west and Mesopotamia in the northeast, Egypt in the south, and Phoenicia in the north. So even when we talk of the prophets' cosmopolitan conceptions, we should bear in mind that they simply seem to refer to the nations that had been included in the Davidic empire or in some way or other had been affiliated with it. The eschatological picture remains earth-bound.

I have laid much stress on the former presence and subsequent integration of foreigners into Jerusalem in biblical times, in the social, political, and cultic life and institutions, because this fact may help in explaining the existence of the two seemingly contradictory tendencies which can be traced in practically all strata of biblical literature, with the pendulum swinging once in this direction, once in the other. Jerusalem being the hub of the nation, so much so that to all intents and purposes the city was identified with Israel as a whole, and its very name having become synonymous with that of the realm at large, it may be said that the biblical pronouncements which reflect the attitude of the metropolis towards foreigners in fact give expression to all Israelite concepts concerning this issue.

VI

Let me now turn to the vision of Jerusalem as the metropolis of the world. This vision is not limited to a portrayal of the future fate of the nations, but first and foremost presents Jerusalem as holding promise for every Jew, inhabitant of Palestine or of a foreign country. Indeed, the city is expected to become a place of worship for every individual human being, Jew and non-Jew alike. The sterile and the stranger, referred to in Isaiah 56:1–8, who are, I believe, in the main Jews living in foreign countries that have joined themselves to the Lord, are given an option on the city of Jerusalem and on the Temple: "For thus says the Lord: My salvation is near to come, and righteousness to be revealed, and my House shall be called an House of prayer for all peoples." The gloriously humanistic role to be played by the future Jerusalem, not any more fettered by nationalistic paraphernalia, fired the imagination of intertestamental and early Christian writers who perceived in it the apex of the spiritual development of Israel, crystallized in this noble image of the Holy City.

It would appear, however, that also in offering this flighty portrait of the latter-days Jerusalem, biblical ideology remains earthbound. Late prophets, such as Jeremiah, do not fail to present that ideal Jerusalem in an almost disturbing realistic fashion:

> Behold the days come, says the Lord, that the city shall be built to the Lord from the tower of Hananeel unto the gate of the corner, and the measuring line shall yet go out straight onward until the hill Gareb, and shall turn about after Goath. And the whole valley of the dead bodies, and of the ashes, and all the fields unto the brook of Kidron, unto the corner of the horse gate toward the east, shall be holy unto the Lord; it shall not be plucked up, nor thrown down any more for ever (Jer. 31:38–40).

This vision of the future Jerusalem could well have been written by a town-planner, but certainly was written by an author who knew the historical Jerusalem and could wish for nothing better than having it restored in the future to its one-time measurements. Even eschatological Jerusalem is envisaged in the boundaries of earthly Jerusalem as it had been in biblical times.

Jeremiah's words throw some light upon yet another aspect which has

been of decisive importance for the significance attached to the city of
Jerusalem in Jewish tradition until this very day. It is the whole
circumference of the city which is held, and will be held, holy. In distinction from other religions, that have pinned their pious reverance for
Jerusalem on select localities in her, on particular *topoi* which are connected with specific events in their *Heilsgeschichte*, Judaism has sanctified
the city as such, and in doing so has kept alive the significance attached
to Jerusalem in the Bible.

In keeping with the historical realistic overtones which echo in the
description of the future Jerusalem, the new covenant to be established
there will be preceded by great tribulations. Just as there always has been
war and bloodshed as a *sine qua non* of peace in historical Jerusalem, so
also the eschatological picture of the ultimate and final peace cannot
unfold without a preceding war, a preceding catastrophe. The era of
eternal peace to be inaugurated in Jerusalem will come after tumultuous
wars, fought out against the nations, whom God decreed to be an-
nihilated in the valley of Jehoshaphat, the valley of His judgment (Joel
4:1f). It is then that Jerusalem again will become the capital of the kingdom into which will be gathered the dispersed of Israel, who there will
find solace and comfort (Joel 3:16). At that time, if righteousness should
prevail in Jerusalem, "then there shall enter in by the gates, the gates of
this house, kings sitting upon the throne of David, riding in chariots and
on horses, he, and his servants, and his people" (Jer. 22:4). Even this
latter-day picture includes an actual king with his entourage. The visions
remain earth-bound.

VII

The fervent hope for a future restoration of Jerusalem, which signifies
the glorious revival of the nation, became the *vade mecum* of Jewry also
after the destruction of the Second Temple. This is strikingly illustrated
by a recent archaeological discovery. Just a few months ago, excavators
of the Temple area of Jerusalem chanced upon an inscription in square
Hebrew characters incised into one of the huge dressed stones of the
Western Wall, in a layer which until recently had been hidden under the
rubble that had accumulated over the centuries. The inscription consists
of the first part of Isaiah 66:14, exactly as it is preserved in the Massoretic
text, which also reflects the major ancient versions: "And ye shall see *it*
and your heart shall rejoice and your bones shall flourish like tender
grass." The "it" added in the Revised Version, which has no equivalent
in the Hebrew text, correctly refers back to the preceding verse, which
ends on the promise: "And ye shall be comforted in Jerusalem" (Isa. 66:13).

It is obvious that the ancient mason or masons who had been at work reconstructing the Temple wall, or redressing its stones, in their piety had conceived of their labor as a sign of the impending fulfilment of Isaiah's vision.

At this juncture a remark on the time of the inscription is in order, as far as it can be ascertained. The stratum in which it was discovered has been dated by the archaeologists in the 4th century A.D., in the days of Julian the Apostate. Julian became famous for his liberal attitude towards non-Christian religions, and for his zeal in restoring places of non-Christian worship. In this context also the Jewish Temple of Jerusalem was given a new lease of life, though only for a very short period. The newly discovered inscription, in spite of its pitiful shortness, reveals the sentiment of Jewry at that time. It stands to reason that the inscription could not have been incised at the whim of some obscure worker. We may safely assume that it had been commissioned, or at least sanctioned, by some Jewish authority. More than the Bible-based emanations of eschatological hopes in the solidified and codified rabbinic literature, the solitary stone inscription on the wall of the defunct Temple gives evidence of the on-going hope for an imminent restoration of Jerusalem as a renewed center of a national worship and an imminent source of rejoicing and well-being.

It is highly significant that Jews of Julian's days could find no more adequate means of expressing this complex hope, both historical and meta-historical, than by quoting a catch-phrase coined by a biblical prophet of the post-exilic restoration period. There can be little doubt that Isaiah's words indeed were understood as a catch-phrase meant to bring to the mind of the readers of this stone inscription the wider literary context in which they are set in the prophet's book. There they are preceded by a vivid description of the restored Jerusalem that again will become a metropolis in the truest sense of the word: a mother to the cities and villages surrounding her and to the people living within her confines:

> Rejoice ye with Jerusalem and be glad for her, all ye that love her. Rejoice for joy with her, all ye that mourn over her, that you may suck and be satisfied with the breasts of her consolations, that ye may milk out and be delighted with the abundance of her glory. For thus saith the Lord: Behold, I will extend peace to her like a river, and the glory of the nations like an overflowing stream. And ye shall suck thereof. You shall be borne upon her sides and dandled upon her knees. As one whom his mother comforteth, ye shall be comforted in Jerusalem.

XV

Jerusalem in Jewish Consciousness

MORDECAI S. CHERTOFF

The primary sources of Jewish law are the legal passages in the Bible, upon which the rabbinic legislators erected a superstructure so elaborate that some of its ramifications can be related to their source only with the greatest difficulty. A secondary source is to be found in the narrative portions of the Bible, which also provide precedent for later rabbinic enactments. Burial procedures, mourning customs, and the requirement for the consent of the prospective bride derive from the patriarchal narratives in Genesis, although specific procedural details are the result of later legislation.

In much the same fashion, Jewish attachment to Jerusalem derives from biblical history, although the role Jerusalem played—and still plays —in normative Judaism and in the folk tradition far transcends its biblical base.

Shemaryahu Talmon has analyzed the basic realism of the presentation of Jerusalem in the Bible, and the essential historicity of the biblical narrative. At the same time, Jerusalem came to represent far more than the temporal and spiritual capital of the Jewish commonwealth. It came to symbolize orderly civilized life. Its destruction signalized the onset of anarchy. If the conquest and establishment of Jerusalem as the capital of Judaea by David signified the establishment of a Jewish polity in Palestine, its destruction marked the end of Jewish statehood. Because that destruction was also accompanied by the destruction of the Temple, the spiritual viability of Israel was seen as inextricably bound up with the fate of the commonwealth itself. Half a century after the second destruction, by the Romans, the nation expended its last efforts in a briefly successful revolt under Bar Kochba; a desperate effort to restore Jerusalem to its dual role as temporal and spiritual center.

That revolt was only the first of many attempts at restoration. Jerusalem was the inspiring force behind the many messianic movements which sprang up, generation after generation, in every part of the far-flung Jewish diaspora. There was Moses of Crete in the fifth century, Serenus of Syria and Abu Isa of Ispahan in the eighth, David Alroy of Baghdad in the twelfth, Abulafia of Messina in the thirteenth, Asher Lemmlein of Istria at the end of the fifteenth, David Reubeni and Shlomo Molcho in the sixteenth, and Shabbetai Zevi in the middle of the seventeenth century. Whether these leaders were genuine mystics or ambitious imposters did not affect the folk response. The call for the return to Zion was as irresistible in the sixteenth century as it had been in the fifth. When Shabbetai Zevi proclaimed himself Messiah he produced a spiritual upheaval such as diaspora Jewry had never known before. Jews sold their homes, their businesses, and prepared for the Return. The Messianic ecstasy, as Abraham Joshua Heschel has pointed out, "found its adherents in equal measure among the enlightened communities of Amsterdam, Hamburg and London and among the mystically inclined Jewries of Egypt, Syria, and Turkey."[1] Even the non-Jewish world was stirred, and bets were actually taken at Lloyds of London as to the date when Shabbetai Zevi would enter Jerusalem in glory.

The significance of Jerusalem to the Jews was so much a part of the consciousness of the non-Jewish world that every plan for Jewish political restoration, from the proclamation of Cyrus in the sixth century B.C. to that of Napoleon on the eve of the nineteenth century—2,500 years later—was expressed in terms of the rebuilding of Jerusalem. The affinity was acknowledged even by the anti-Semite gripped by pogrom-fever. Mobs attacking the Jews incited themselves with the cry: *"Hep! Hep!"*, an acronym for *Hieroselyma est perdita!*—Jerusalem is lost! Why should ignorant peasants in the nineteenth and twentieth centuries have taunted Jews with the destruction of Jerusalem, if Jerusalem was nothing to the Jews?

To the Jews, Jerusalem has always been and is, The City. "Aloof, waterless, on the road to nowhere"—as George Adam Smith describes the plateau on which it stands. It had, he wrote:

> none of the natural conditions of a great city. And yet it was here that She arose, who, more than Athens and more than Rome, taught the nations civic justice, and gave her name to the ideal city men are ever striving to build on earth, to the City of God that shall one day descend from heaven—the New Jerusalem. For her builder was not Nature nor the wisdom of man, but

on that secluded and barren site the Word of God, by her prophets, laid her eternal foundations in righteousness and reared her walls in her people's faith in God.[2]

The sanctity of Jerusalem derived from the Temple, although according to tradition a prior sanctity had dictated the choice of Jerusalem as the site of the Temple—for it was on Mt. Moriah that Abraham bound his son as a sacrifice. Mt. Moriah is therefore chosen to be the site of the Temple and the Holy of Holies. In associating the Temple site with the patriarchal sacrifice, Jewish tradition is also extending the affinity to Jerusalem from David's conquest to the very dawn of Jewish history: to Abraham, founder of the people.

Because of its special holiness, Jewish law treated Jerusalem differently from other cities. It was not assigned to any of the tribes. There could be no permanent ownership of city land, for example, and certain other enactments did not apply to it. Some of the ways in which Jerusalem was unique are listed in one source as follows:

> Jerusalem's houses do not become unclean through leprosy;
> It is not to be declared a condemned city; . . . .
> The dead may not be lodged there overnight;
> The bones of a dead man may not be carried through it;
> No place is made available there for a resident alien;
> No graves may be kept there excepting the graves of
> the house of David, and of Huldah the prophetess
> which were there since the days of the early prophets. . . .
> Neither geese nor chickens may be raised there, nor,
> needless to say, pigs;
> No dunghills may be kept there because of uncleanness;
> No trial of a stubborn and rebellious son may be held
> there, such is the view of Rabbi Nathan (see Deut.
> 21:18*ff.*);
> No houses may be sold there save from the ground up
> [only the structure, not the ground, could be sold];
> The sale of houses is not valid there for longer than
> twelve months;
> No payment for a bed is accepted there [from the
> pilgrims who come for the Festivals]—Rabbi Judah
> says: Not even payment for beds and coverings;
> The hides of the sacrificial beasts are not for sale
> there.[3]

Even after its destruction, Jerusalem retained its holiness, and the special laws continued to be observed. When praying, a Jew must face Jerusalem; if in Jerusalem, he "should turn his heart toward the Temple." Entrance to the Temple Mount itself is forbidden because of ritual impurity. In Temple days Jews were obligated to make pilgrimages to the Temple. After the destruction, the law remained in force. The pilgrimages must still be made to Jerusalem, but the pilgrim is also obliged to mourn the destruction of the city (by rending his garment). Mourning for Jerusalem, in fact, was enjoined upon every Jew until the restoration, and the tradition prescribed how it was to be done. When painting a home, one small area was to be left unfinished in remembrance of Jerusalem. One item of a full-course meal should be omitted from the menu for the same reason. Some part of a woman's jewelry or make-up must be left incomplete—*zekher lehurban*—in memory of the destruction.

The Avelei Zion, "Mourners for Zion," devoted themselves to mourning the destruction of the Temple and praying for the redemption of Zion. Their customs can be traced back to the period immediately following the destruction of the Temple, and the group may have originated in Jerusalem itself. Similar groups existed in Germany, Italy, and Yemen and other Oriental countries.

Normative Judaism set aside a special period of mourning for Jerusalem. It begins with a fast on the 17th day of Tammuz when, according to the biblical account, the Babylonians breached the walls of Jerusalem, and culminates on the 9th day of Av *(Tisha B'Av)*, when the Temple was destroyed. The day is observed as a 24 hour fast day with its own special liturgy, including the very moving Book of Lamentations.

There is a legend that on Tisha B'Av a dove appears in a niche of the Western Wall, surviving remnant of the Temple, cooing its participation in the mourning of Israel for the Temple.

Mourning and the yearning for redemption infuse all of Jewish liturgy, and are characteristic of the Jewish rites of passage as well as in the day-to-day life of the Jew. When the newborn child is welcomed into the community a blessing is recited that he may be worthy to make the holy pilgrimage of the three festivals (Passover, Shavuot, Sukkot). The dead are buried with a small sack of earth from the Holy Land under their heads. To those in mourning, the prescribed words of comfort are: "May the Lord comfort you among all those who mourn for Zion and Jerusalem." To this day, the climax of the Jewish wedding ceremony is the breaking of a glass in remembrance of the destruction of Jerusalem. In the benedictions that solemnize the wedding, there is a prayer for Jerusalem:

> *O Lord our God,*
> *May there soon be heard*
> *in the cities of Judah*
> *and in the streets of Jerusalem,*
> *the voice of joy and gladness,*
> *the voice of bride and groom,*

the jubilant voice of those
joined in marriage under their bridal canopy,
the voice of young people
feasting and singing. . . .

After every meal, a prayer for Jerusalem is included in the blessings recited:

> Have mercy, O Lord our God, upon Israel our people, upon Jerusalem Your city, upon Zion the abiding place of Your glory, upon the kingdom of the house of David. . . . Rebuild Jerusalem the holy city speedily in our day. Praised are You, O Lord, Who in Your compassion rebuilds Jerusalem.

Not (as Heschel points out[4]) "who will build," but who *is* building Jerusalem. Since the obligation to help in that rebuilding rests upon every Jew, one of the Hassidic leaders said: "By our service to God we build Jerusalem daily. One of us adds a row, another only a brick. When Jerusalem is completed, the redemption will come."

The liturgy is replete with references to Jerusalem. Such references are, in fact, obligatory in all the statutory prayers. The most important is the blessing entirely devoted to Jerusalem in the daily Amidah (the silent devotion). It begins "To Jerusalem Thy city return in mercy. . . . rebuild it soon in our days," and concludes, "Blessed art Thou, O Lord, Who buildest Jerusalem." A full treatment of these references is beyond the scope of this paper; suffice it to say that there are so many prayers, petitions, expressions of gratitude, and celebrations that invoke Jerusalem that any Jew who observes even the minimal requirements of the tradition utters the name several times each day.

The structure of the Jewish liturgy harks back to the Temple service. As part of the service on the Day of Atonement (Yom Kippur), the most sacred day in the Jewish calendar, a poem is read describing that Temple service on that day, as it was performed by the High Priest. The Yom Kippur service concludes with "Next year in Jerusalem," more, perhaps, as an exhortation to the worshipper than as a petition to the Almighty. In the same spirit, the Passover *seder* (feast) concludes with the same words.

An impressive example of the longing for Jerusalem, as expressed in the liturgy, is the hymn sung at the Friday evening service to welcome the "Sabbath Queen" *(L'choh Dodi)*. Of its nine stanzas, six voice the yearning for Jerusalem.

Attachment to the Land of Israel dominates the liturgy. Even the prayers for rain and for dew are timed to coincide with the needs of the Holy Land rather than the climate of the land in which the prayer is being recited. The pilgrim festivals are both national and agricultural celebrations. While they commemorate events in the history of Israel they simultaneously rejoice over the harvest of that particular period of the year in Palestine. This affinity with the Holy Land is observed even in a minor holiday such as Tu'Bishvat ("The New Year of the Trees") when Jewish children would dig through the snow-covered, frozen earth in Eastern Europe and today in the Northeastern United States, to plant saplings, as their peers are doing at the same time—in mid January—on the Judaean hills.

There is a rabbinic tradition that Messiah was born on the day the Temple was destroyed. Certainly, the hope for restoration, and the striving for it, were born on that day, and nourished by liturgists and poets down through the ages. Eliezer ha-Kallir (in the sixth or seventh century) was one liturgist whose poems are still read in the synagogue on various festivals, including the 9th of Av. Solomon ibn Gabirol, Moses ibn Ezra, Judah Halevi, and Abraham ibn Ezra, in the heyday of Spanish Jewry, made their timeless contributions to the liturgy, and down to our own day the themes they sounded—the longing for redemption and the hope for it—persist in Jewish literature, both sacred and secular. It occurs in the historic accounts of Jewish travelers who visited the Holy Land and wept over the destruction of Jerusalem, and is echoed and re-echoed in the reborn modern Hebrew and Yiddish literatures that began to flourish at the end of the nineteenth century. *Ahavat Zion* ("Love of Zion"), the very first modern Hebrew novel (published in 1853), is an historical novel set in Jerusalem in the days of the First Temple. Poets, essayists, and novelists down to the present day have dealt and deal with Jerusalem— its past, present, and hoped-for future. Jerusalem is central in a number of the works of the classical Hebrew writer Shmuel Yosef Agnon, in the poetry of his contemporary Uri Zvi Greenberg, and in the works of the younger Hebrew poet Yehuda Amichai.

A very eloquent contemporary, the late Abraham Heschel, has summed up the meaning of Jerusalem for the Jew in these words:

> I have discovered a new land. Israel is not the same as before. There is great astonishment in the souls. It is as if the prophets had risen from their graves. Their words ring in a new way. Jerusalem is everywhere, she hovers over the whole country. There is a new radiance, a new awe.
>
> The great quality of a miracle is not in its being an unexpected, unbelievable event in which the presence of the holy bursts forth, but in its happening to human beings who are profoundly astonished at such an outburst.
>
> My astonishment is mixed with anxiety. Am I worthy? Am I able to appreciate the marvel?
>
> I did not enter on my own the city of Jerusalem. Streams of endless craving, clinging, dreaming, flowing day and night, midnights, years, decades, centuries, millennia, streams of tears, of pledging, waitings—from all over the world, from all corners of the earth—carried us of this genera-

tion to the Wall. My ancestors could only dream of you, to my people in Auschwitz you were more remote than the moon, and I can touch your stones! Am I worthy? How shall I ever repay these moments?

The martyrs of all ages are sitting at the gate of heaven, having refused to enter the world to come lest they forget Israel's pledge given in and for this world:

> *If I forget thee, O Jerusalem*
> *let my right hand wither.*
> *Let my tongue cleave to the roof of my mouth*
> *if I do not remember you*
> *if I do not set Jerusalem*
> *above my highest joys.*
>
> Psalm 137:5–6

They would rather be without heaven than forget the glory of Jerusalem. From time to time their souls would leave the gates of heaven to go on a pilgrimage to the souls of the Jewish people, reminding them that God himself is in exile, that He will not enter heavenly Jerusalem until His people Israel will enter Jerusalem here (Zohar, 1, 1b.).[5]

In the contemporary Jewish view, Jerusalem is being rebuilt by the people of Israel who kept the vision and the hope alive through the centuries of exile and suffering; who did, indeed, set Jerusalem above their highest joys.

NOTES AND REFERENCES

1. Abraham Joshua Heschel, *Israel: An Echo of Eternity* (New York: Farrar, Straus and Giroux, 1971).
2. George Adam Smith, *The Historical Geography of the Holy Land* (London, 1894).
3. *The Fathers According to Rabbi Nathan*, trans. Judah Goldin, (Yale Judaica Series [New Haven, Conn.: Yale University Press, 1955]), chap. 35, pp. 143–144.
4. *Op cit.*
5. *Op cit.*

XVI

The Sanctity of Jerusalem in Islam

HAVA LAZARUS-YAFEH
(Translated from the Hebrew by Yehuda Weiss)

Jerusalem is one of the most controversial issues in the Arab-Israel conflict. The Arabs believe that Jerusalem is a holy city in Islam, and this belief is fully shared by millions of non-Arab Muslims. The origins and the realities of this claim must therefore be examined in some detail. Why is it that Islam, which originated in the Arabian peninsula and far removed from Palestine, came to invest Jerusalem, of all cities, with an aura of sanctity? Were the sages of Islam always unanimous on this issue? Why was this belief so devoutly nurtured in the Islamic tradition? My answers will, of necessity, be only partial ones because of the complexity of the problems and traditions involved, and also because of the overabundance of material available in Arabic sources as well as in general research literature on the issue.

THE ROOTS OF THE SANCTITY OF JERUSALEM IN ISLAM

The concept that Jerusalem is sacred to Islam stems from both Judaism and Christianity. But scholars are divided on the question as to which of the two religions had the stronger influence on Muhammad and who his outstanding teachers were. Some are inclined to opt for the theory that they were Jews; others think they were non-orthodox Christian sectarians. There is no doubt however that Muhammad took some basic concepts from both Judaism and Christianity, such as the Unity of God, the Covenant between man and his Maker, man's responsibility for his own actions, the Day of Judgment, and Reward and Punishment among others. If that is true, can we not assume that he also received the idea of the sanctity of Jerusalem from the same sources? Jerusalem is not expressly mentioned in the Koran (although most Muslim interpreters—and some Islamic scholars—are inclined to consider that Sura 17 is an intimation about Jerusalem). However, the sanctity of the Land of Israel and the Divine promise given to the Children of Israel that this land would be theirs *is* expressly stated in the Koran, which cites the words of Moses in the story of the spies: "Oh my people, enter the Holy Land that has been promised to you." (Sura 5:21) (*cf.* also, the expression "Holy Land" in Zech. 2:14).

Other verses in the Koran attest, at least indirectly (as in Sura 2:136 *ff.*) to the fact that the direction toward which Muhammad and his followers turned in prayer (Qibla) was originally Jerusalem—obviously under the influence of Jewish and Christian customs prevalent in the Arabian peninsula at that time. Muslim traditionists and historiographers and commentators of the Koran have stated this expressly, and some even explain it as a Divine commandment, given in order to convert the Jews of Arabia to Islam. This is why one of Jerusalem's epithets in Islam is, to this very day, Ula-l-Qiblatain—the first of the two directions to be faced in prayer (the second and dominant one in Islam being toward Mecca). The direction in prayer towards Mecca was established later, shortly after Muhammad's arrival in Medina, and probably after the break between the prophet and the Jews. In the same period—and for the same reasons—Muhammad changed the Islamic Fast, of 24 hours on the tenth day of the first month (like the Jewish Day of Atonement) to a daily fast from sunrise to sunset, lasting the whole month of Ramadan in order to sever any association with Judaism. But the ties between Islam and Judaism were not completely broken off even after the clash with the Jews. For example, the Fast of the tenth day of the first month remained an optional one in Islam (but because of the abolition of intercalation in Islam it may fall in different seasons, unlike the fixed Jewish Day of Atonement). The basic concepts of the Ramadan fast remained similar to those of the Jewish Day of Atonement: God is asked for forgiveness; the ideas of repentance, judgment, etc. Even the idea that the Koran was revealed in the month of Ramadan may be of Jewish origin, *e.g.*, like the two Tablets of the Covenant. Even the description of the beginning of the Fast in the Koran (Sura 2:187)—". . . and eat and drink until the white thread becomes distinct to you from the black thread of the dawn."[2]— seems to have the imprint of the language of the Mishna: "From what time may one pray the Shema of the morning prayer? From the hour one can discern between blue and white" (Berakhot 7:2). In Jewish tradition this refers, of course, to the prayer shawl (*tallith*), whereas it has no meaningful background in Islam.[3] If this is the case with a basic law like the Fast, Jewish influence may have been even stronger with regard to a general idea, such as the sanctity of Jerusalem. Even after the direction of prayer was changed in Islam, the idea of the sanctity of that city, located so far away from the cradle of Islam, was maintained and cultivated, especially among circles of pious Muslims who felt attracted to the religious concepts of Judaism and Christianity.

THE ARAB CONQUEST OF JERUSALEM

The historic events that occurred after the death of the Prophet in 632 have reinforced the sanctity of Jerusalem even more by giving this concept a pragmatic meaning. The Muslim armies stormed out of the Arabian peninsula shortly after Muhammad's death. They conquered many countries and built up an empire that reached Gibraltar in the west and India in the east. Jerusalem was captured during the reign of Omar (Umar), the second caliph after Muhammad, in 638. Once far away, this city was now well within the new Arab empire.

The historical details of this conquest are still vague and even the year of the conquest seems uncertain. Both Christian-Byzantine sources and Muslim sources recount many contradictory stories and probably reflect either a pro-Christian or anti-Christian bias (as the case may be), but some common basic elements related to the concept of Jerusalem's sanctity can be discerned. At the time of the Arab conquest the Temple Mount seems to have been covered with garbage. The caliph Omar ordered the area cleaned and on it erected a temporary mosque. (For this reason the Dome of the Rock is often erroneously called the Mosque of Omar.) According to one of the Muslim traditions quoted by the famous historian Al Tabari (d. 923), a Jew named Ka'ab Al-Ahbar, who had converted to Islam, advised the caliph to build this mosque to the north of the Rock. The caliph rejected his advice because he considered it a Jewish scheme to coerce every Muslim who turns his face in prayer towards Mecca to prostrate himself at the same time to the Rock also—a suspicion grounded on the fact that the Rock is considered by Jews to be part of what was the "Holiest of Holy" in the Jewish Temple. According to Al Tabari,[4] the caliph expressly said so to Ka'ab: "By Allah, Ka'ab, in thy heart you are still a Jew, for I have seen how you took off your shoes [before entering the Temple Mount], but we Muslims were not ordered to sanctify this Rock, we were only ordered to turn [in our prayers] towards the Ka'aba [in Mecca]." Therefore Omar ordered the temporary mosque to be built to the south of the Rock so that worshippers turning their faces to Mecca should be praying with their backs to the holy Rock of Judaism. This remained the custom even after the Rock was incorporated into Islamic tradition and became holy to Muslims as well.

There is no doubt that the cleansing of the Temple Mount was the main reason (apart from Islam's general, tolerant attitude toward Judaism) why the Jews considered the Arab conquest of Jerusalem as an act of redemption, which began for them with the lifting of the yoke of the Byzantine empire. For example, the author of *Nistarot DeRabbi Shim'on bar Yohai* (an apocalyptic book written soon after the Arab conquest) writes:

> And the second king who will emerge from Isma'il shall conquer all the kingdoms and shall come to Jerusalem and prostrate himself [before the God of Israel], he shall wage war against Edom [Byzantium], they shall flee and he will be a strong ruler. He shall be a friend of Israel and help them and build up the Temple. He shall make even Mt. Moriah and call Israel to build up [there] the Temple. In his day Israel shall be saved and the offspring of David [the Messiah] shall come forth.[5]

THE MOSQUES ON THE TEMPLE MOUNT

The magnificent Dome of the Rock was built only 60 years after the Arab conquest of Jerusalem—at the end of the seventh century. This is the earliest Islamic edifice to be preserved, despite the changes and repairs it has undergone during its long history. As an inscription on the building attests, it was built by the Umayyad Caliph 'Abd al-Malik in 691. But a caliph from the later rival 'Abbasid dynasty, al-Ma'mun (831) who envied the glory of his predecessor, erased Abd al-Malik's name from the inscription and put his own name to it instead. However, since he neglected to change the year of its construction also, he failed to enter history as the builder of this magnificent Dome. Opinions are divided as to the circumstances of the erection of this Dome. For a long time the opinion prevailed (also shared by the famous Islamic scholar Ignaz Goldziher) that Abd al-Malik intended to establish a place of pilgrimage that should be equal to and compete with the Ka'aba in Mecca, which was at that time ruled by a rebel named 'Abd-Allah ibn al-Zubair. 'Abd al-Malik may not have wanted his subjects to undertake pilgrimages to Mecca, or Abd-Allah may have prevented the Umayyad subjects from entering Mecca for the Hajj. Some historiographers maintain that 'Abd al-Malik did not content himself with erecting the Dome of the Rock, but also saw to it that the traditionalists, especially one named Ibn Shihab al-Zuhri, made it their business to spread sayings (Hadith) seemingly by the prophet Muhammad in praise of worship in Jerusalem at the Dome of the Rock. The most famous and widespread Hadith of this kind was presumably handed down from the Prophet by Abu Huraira (who is not considered very reliable), and also by others. It goes as follows: "Nobody shall set out for a pilgrimage [in Huraira's words: to 'saddle up'] except for three mosques: This mosque [in Medina]; the Holy Mosque [in Mecca] and [the mosque in] Jerusalem." This pronouncement in various versions and many similar ones were widespread in medieval Muslim literature and they are still quoted today. That is why Jerusalem and the Temple Mount are also called "Thalith Al-Masadjid," the "Third of the Mosques," after Mecca and Medina. Some sources even maintain that 'Abd al-Malik also made efforts to establish some pilgrimage rituals in Jerusalem as equivalents to those at the Ka'aba in Mecca. For example, he is said to have ordered the "circling" of the Rock ("Tawaf")—but from right to left, contrary to the custom of circling the Ka'aba from left to right—and to have added some other customs, which were considered forbidden innovations in religion ("Bida' "). Nevertheless, it appears that all these stories are inventions of the anti-Umayyad historian Al-Ya'qubi, a Shi'ite sectarian whose accounts were later followed by some Muslim and Byzantine historiographers. Most of the better-known Muslim historians do not even mention such a daring attempt as the creation of an institution parallel and even competing with Mecca. Many contemporary scholars, therefore, doubt the authenticity of the whole story. S.D. Goitein,[6] for example, thinks that the reasons that prompted 'Abd al-Malik to build the Dome of the Rock were not political but religious, and of two different kinds: (1) In order to strengthen the nimbus of sanctity surrounding Jerusalem—and Palestine in general—in Islam, and especially among the pious, who were undertaking frequent pilgrimages to Jerusalem (possibly under the influence of Christian monks). They considered a stay in the Holy Land as a Divine Commandment and declared all its fruit to be "halal," meaning that these could be eaten even by the most meticulous religious Muslim without fear that the fruit was wrongly acquired or cultivated, *e.g.*, with stolen money, etc.);[7] (2) It was an attempt to compete with the beautiful Christian churches that were considered an affront to victorious Islam and to outdo these with a magnificent Muslim edifice. (Some corroborating evidence to this contention may be found in the Arabic inscriptions inside the Dome of the Rock. They contain mainly polemical verses from the Koran against Christianity.) Indeed, Abd al-Malik succeeded in his efforts, and the Dome of the Rock, built with the assistance of experts from Byzantium and other lands, became the pride of Islam.[8]

It is not clear whether 'Abd al-Malik himself or (which is more plausible) his son al-Walid was the one who constructed the second building on the Temple Mount, known as the al-Aqsa Mosque, which is believed to have been erected on the foundations of an ancient church. There is no doubt however that the two edifices were meant to be considered as an indivisible pair (even though there are traditions about competition between them, as there are between Mecca and Medina). The Dome of the Rock was meant to glorify and guard, as it were, the Holy Rock above which it rises. Any individual could, of course, say his prayers therein, but it is the second building, the al-Aqsa Mosque, which was intended as a mosque ("Djami'") for public prayer and worship, especially on Fridays.

'AL-ISRA AND AL-MI'RAJ'

The building of the two mosques, especially the second, prove that the sanctity of Jerusalem in Islam had in the interim been strengthened by still another tradition. This tradition, not yet fully crystallized at the time, was about to become the dominant one with regard to Jerusalem's sanctity in Islam. In this tradition the city derives its sanctity from the Koran, Sura 17:1 (Surat Al-Isra or Surat Bani-Isra'il) which says:

> Glorified be He Who carried His servant by night ["Asra"] from the inviolable Place of Worship ["Al-Masdjid Al-Haram" *i.e.*, Mecca] to the Far Distant Place of Worship ["Al-Masdjid Al-Aqsa"] the neighborhood whereof We have blessed, that We might show him of Our tokens! Lo! He only He is the Hearer, Seer.

This verse, as others in the Koran, may originally have been but an intimation of Muhammad's consecration to his prophetic mission, like the apocalyptic visions frequently found in Jewish and Christian scriptures of the first centuries of the Christian era. Some scholars, following Islamic traditionalists, try to connect another account of Muhammad's consecration to his mission with it. This second story is not found in the Koran, but was later derived by commentators from Sura 94:1, and is the well known story of the opening of Muhammad's chest ("Sharh-Al-Sadr") and the washing of his heart with snow by two or more angels. This story was later separated from our story of "Al-Isra" and appears in the biographical literature about Muhammad as pertaining to his early childhood, when he was about three years old.[9] If the above mentioned Koran verse indeed relates to an apocalyptical experience by Muhammad, it may be assumed that the expression "Al-Masdjid Al-Aqsa" originally meant "The Far Distant Place of Worship," *e.g.*, a kind of heavenly house of worship, but certainly not the mosque in Jerusalem, which was built much later by an Umayyad caliph, and was called "Al Masdjid Al-Aqsa" because of the later identification of Jerusalem with this name. A. Guillaume tried to find a place near Mecca (Dji'rama) to fit the description in the Koran but his suggestion has not been accepted by scholars, and certainly not by Islam.[10]

Some scholars believe that the verse in fact contains an intimation regarding both Jerusalem and Palestine, which are also depicted in the very same terms ("The neighborhood whereof we have blessed") in other parts of the Koran (*e.g.*, Sura 21:71). Therefore the Islamic scholar Joseph Horovitz assumed that the "Heavenly Temple" cited in the verse was perhaps the one in the "Heavenly Jerusalem." In his opinion this is what the early commentators of the Koran meant when they explained "Al-Masdjid Al-Aqsa" as "Beit Almaqdas" ("Beit Hamikqdash"), which is Jerusalem—but the Heavenly Jerusalem.[11] In later times these concepts became confused and people started looking for the "Far Distant Place of Worship" of Jerusalem (the heavenly city) in terrestrial Jerusalem, and that is why the mosque built by the Umayyads at the end of the seventh century was called "Al-Masdjid Al-Aqsa." Here we have additional evidence of the well known fact that it is not always the factual or the original meaning of a verse or a term which are the most important in the history of religion. Islamic oral tradition (Hadith), the commentaries on the Koran, and even articles of faith soon accepted the idea that the verse in Sura 17 meant terrestrial Jerusalem and that it was connected with a certain event in the life of the Prophet, which was believed to have occurred shortly before his flight from Mecca to Medina. The details of this story were said to be related by contemporaries of the Prophet and handed down from generation to generation, and while the early sources were cautious and short on details, later sources felt free to add many details and even fantastic stories, catering thereby to the need of the masses for miraculous events that were believed to have happened to the Prophet and Lawgiver. The story became an amalgamation of different events: the nocturnal journey ("Isra") to Jerusalem and the ascent to heaven ("Mi'raj"), with additional legendary motifs common to all religions, such as the motif of a miraculous animal or a sojourn in the upper spheres. Here is the essence of the story: The angel Gabriel appeared in the house of Muhammad's wife in Mecca one night and awakened the Prophet. He ordered Muhammad to dress and to ride with him on a miraculous animal named "Al-Buraq" (possibly derived from the root "Baraq"—lightning—and meaning a white animal, like the supposed donkey of the Jewish Messiah). This animal is described in Islamic sources as being different from all other animals; it is "more than a donkey and less than a mule." Its head is that of a human being, its body that of a horse, its eyes are like blinking stars, its mane is a carving made of precious stones . . . (in later generations a marvelous peacock's tail and eagle's wings were added [*cf.*, Persian miniatures]). Following a short and miraculous ride Muhammad and his guide, the angel Gabriel, arrived in Jerusalem. According to later versions Muhammad hitched his animal to one of the rings hammered into the Western (Wailing) Wall which were specially reserved for the animals of the prophets (therefore the Western Wall is called Al-Buraq in Arabic). Other versions relate that the miraculous animal also participated in the heavenly journey made by the Prophet and only the earliest versions of the Prophet's life make no mention of any part of this story. At the Rock, the cornerstone of the Temple so the accounts relate, Muhammad found a miraculous ladder ("Mi'radj") wrought of gold, silver, and precious stones. He ascended this ladder and guided by Gabriel was brought into the upper skies. Here he met various angels and many prophets of Islam: John the Baptist, Jesus, Abraham (with whom he also prayed), David, Solomon, Joseph, and others. He was shown the torments of the sinners, and then came before the Divine Throne. A thousand fiery veils were removed and he was granted an almost face-to-face encounter with Allah, Who revealed to him the basic precepts of Islam. Muhammad confirmed his faith with the same words that the Israelites had uttered at Mt. Sinai: "We shall do and we shall heed" and then came down from heaven, taking upon himself and his followers the obligation of 50 prayers a day. Under the influence of Moses, however, he came back several times in order to ask Allah to reduce the number of prayers, and Allah finally consented to five daily prayers in Islam instead of the original 50. Gabriel showed Muhammad Paradise and then brought him safely back to his bed in Mecca that same night and promised Muhammad that even if all his people refused to believe in his miraculous journey, Abu Bakr would accept the story as true. And so it came to pass, and that is why Abu Bakr, the first Caliph of Islam (632–634) after Muhammad's death, earned the title "Al-Siddiq," the true believer (in the Prophet's own words).

Indeed, Muhammad's first followers were not too eager to accept the truth of the story of the "Isra" and "Mi'radj." Even after the Prophet had withstood the test of credulity and had described some details about Jerusalem (as he had seen the city on his journey), only a few were said to regard this story as anything more than a dream. Even much later, rationalistic Arab theologians still maintained this attitude, but it still came to be believed as truth, and one of the basic articles of faith in Islam became the concept that Muhammad had really ascended to heaven in the flesh and that the point of ascent was the Temple Mount, above the Rock ("Al-Mi'radj Haqq"). From then on only few ventured to challenge the truth of this account—one which provided Islam with many motifs of miraculous events. Some mystics tried to explain it as a mystical allegory, as a kind of spiritual ascent made by Muhammad. Some (like the eleventh century blind heretic poet Abu-l-'Ala Al-Ma'arri) tried to ridicule it. But the story caught on in Islam (and even wielded its influence outside Islam —for example, on the Italian poet Dante) and it is this story that established the historical and theological basis for the sanctity of Jerusalem in

Islam. A day of feast was established, with a special prayer commemorating this event, on the 27th day of the month of Radjab, the seventh in the Islamic calendar. It is especially interesting to note that this day had been an ancient pagan holiday in the time of Djahiliyya (the "Days of Ignorance") that preceded Muhammad's appearance in the Arabian peninsula. The ancient traditions about the *"Mi'radj"* mention completely different dates for this event.

JERUSALEM AND MECCA—POPULAR AND PAGAN MOTIFS

From now on, new avenues were opened whereby to reinforce the concept of the sanctity of Jerusalem in Islam, and a new, mainly pagan, layer was added to the monotheistic foundation of this belief. The big Rock, for example, where the Holy of Holies of the Jewish Temple was thought to have been located, assumed a more and more central place in the Islamic belief in Jerusalem's sanctity. At first it was connected with the story of the "Mi'radj" only because Muhammad had ascended to heaven from that point, as Jesus had done before him (Christian legends also undoubtedly had some impact on the stories of the "Mi'radj" in Islam). Later, Muhammad's footprints came to be shown on the Rock and also the imprint made by his saddle and even the place where Gabriel had flattened the Rock before the Prophet's ascent (as against an earlier tradition that placed Muhammad's point of departure near the Rock but not on the Rock itself). From now on, and obviously under Jewish and Christian influence, popular tales about the Rock also included the story of Abraham and the sacrifice of Isaac (Abraham's footprints also came to be shown on the Rock), the story of Malki Zedek, King of Shalem, the story of Jacob's ladder, and accounts of David and Solomon and also many other biblical and Islamic personalities. The cradle of the child Jesus, the place where Jesus and Mary had prayed, His chair, the place of His ascent to heaven—the traces of these and many other events came to be shown on the Temple Mount. It also came to be the place where angels pray and the place where (according to some traditions) Noah's ark had come to rest after the flood. Under the influence of Judaism, Islam came to accept the tradition that the Temple Mount would be the place of Resurrection and Last Judgment, and for this reason many Muslims, like many Jews, wish to be buried in its vicinity. Some Islamic traditions also maintain that Muhammad himself had asked to be buried in Jerusalem, since the Temple Mount is the navel of the world and all the souls assemble under the Rock after death, and this is to be a corner of Paradise in the world to come.[12]

From this point on a new trend in Islamic belief and legend can be discerned. From the beginnings of its history, Islam elevated Mecca to a superior status, just as Jerusalem had been elevated in Judaism, and thus many tales from the Pentateuch, from the Jewish legends (especially tales about Abraham, Hagar, and Ismael), and from Christian sources were transplanted to the Arabian peninsula and to Mecca in particular. Thus Mecca became the place where Isaac (or Ismael) was almost sacrificed, the desert oasis where Ismael was saved by a spring of fresh water, etc. Mecca also came to be considered the center of the world, the place where Adam was created, and where many other events took place—the place that paralleled Jerusalem in Judaism. Thus the terrestial Ka'aba in Mecca was said to parallel a heavenly one *(Al-Bayt-al Ma'mar)* just as the terrestrial Jerusalem parallels the heavenly one. The Ka'aba stones were said to have been hewn out of stones from the Mount of Olives.

However, a new and opposite trend now also emerged; the effort to establish the sanctity of Jerusalem in Islam by use of legends and images connected with the sanctity of Mecca, with the Ka'aba, and with Muhammad. There was even an attempt to link both cities—the bride (the Ka'aba in Mecca) would come to the bridegroom (the rock in Jerusalem) prior to the advent of the terrible Day of Judgment. And thus the two cities became linked with the history of Islam, the life of the Prophet, and with eschatology as well as with cosmology.[13]

Pagan elements certainly linger in this glorification of a big rock under a dome which also supposedly forms the cornerstone of the Temple, where the Ark of the Covenant holding the Tablets of the Law came to rest, where Jacob lay and had a dream about a heavenly ladder, and which is the foundation of the world. This glorification probably originated with the ancient worship of stones—as can be attested to by the identification of this rock with the threshing floor of Aravanah, the pagan Jebusite. Ernest Renan already noted that man always worships at the same sites and that only the apparent historical explanations for the sanctity of these sites change from generation to generation and from creed to creed. We may add to this theory that man also always worships on the same days and at the same times and that only the explanation of the meaning of certain holidays changes (the date of "Mi'radj" on the 27th day of Rajab was a pagan holiday in Mecca long before the advent of Islam, for example).

However, the above is not meant to be derogatory. On the contrary, it is evidence of the strength of monotheistic religions like Judaism and Islam that they were able to transvaluate ancient pagan elements and to absorb them into a new, monotheistic setting. However, the primitive masses who do not comprehend the strict requirements of a pure, monotheistic religion keep on worshipping stones, fountains, trees, and holy graves—only now under a monotheistic guise, by linking the particular fetish they revere with an event in the life of the Prophet (as in the case of Islam) or with other holy men.[14] The veneration of all kinds of relics —such as a hair from the Prophet's beard, kept in a small urn on the southwestern side of the Dome of the Rock—also belongs to this type of worship. (For a long time the horns of the ram sacrificed by Abraham in place of Isaac were also "shown" as a relic on this site!)

RESISTANCE TO THE SANCTIFICATION OF JERUSALEM

As stated elsewhere in this essay, there was also some resistance in Islam to the sanctification of Jerusalem, but this resistance was never strong enough to overcome the belief. Though its premise was strictly religious, it never could successfully withstand the tremendous influence of Judaism and Christianity or the popular devotion and the miraculous tales about the life and deeds of the Prophet. The opponents of the sanctity of Jerusalem in Islam have felt and stated time and again that this sanctity is alien to Islam, that it is an imitation of Jewish tradition ("Mushabahatan li-l-Yahud") and that it could undermine the special status of Mecca (and Medina) in Islam. The proponents of this resistance cite many sayings of the Prophet (Hadith), which ostensibly clearly intend to enhance only the sanctity of Mecca in Islam. One of these sayings declares: "There are only two mosques for pilgrimage—in Mecca and in Medina." Another decrees: "Better one prayer in Medina than a thousand prayers elsewhere, except in Mecca."[15] There are many stories about those who vowed to pray or to go on a pilgrimage to Jerusalem, but were prevented from doing so by Muhammad's wife Maimuna or by Omar, who became the second Caliph of Islam. Maimuna and Omar dissuaded them from going to Jerusalem and advised them to pray in Mecca or in Medina instead. According to one of these traditions Omar even struck two men who had returned from a pilgrimage to Jerusalem and said to them, "Don't you have the Ka'aba to go to and pray?" Nonetheless, these accounts were never incorporated into the collections of oral traditions that are considered authentic in Islam. Throughout these sources Jerusalem always appears as the third holy place in Islam, and at times as even greater than third. These traditions contain "Hadith" (sayings) like the following: "Better one prayer in Medina than a thousand prayers anywhere else except at al-Aqsa," or, "Five prayers in Jerusalem will cleanse the pilgrim and he shall be pure as on the day of his birth." Many of them praise Jerusalem and mention the merit to be gained in the performance of the religious commandments there. They maintain that it is not only forbidden to commit a sin there but even that it is impossible to do so![16]

And yet, when the eleventh century Muslim jurist Al-Mawardi in his book on the *Laws of Government* ("Al-Ahkam Al-Sultaniyya") divides the lands ruled by Islam into three categories, Mecca takes the first place, Medina the second, and Jerusalem is not mentioned at all (it is incorporated as an integral part of Islamic lands without any exceptional rules and regulations pertaining to them). In Mecca, for instance, and to a lesser degree in Medina also, and in all of Al-Hidjazit it is forbidden to shed blood, to hunt, or to cut trees, and no non-Muslim can live there.[17]

Later, in the fourteenth century, the most orthodox Islamic thinker Taqi Al-Din ibn Tajmiyya (1328) came out openly (albeit unsuccessfully) against the idea of the sanctity of Jerusalem in Islam in his effort to purify Islam from alien influences, which he said distorted its original stature. However, Jerusalem was, at that time, already an integral part of Islamic tradition, perhaps to no small measure because of the many threats to which it was exposed in the course of time. In the beginning, Jerusalem and all of Palestine was in imminent danger of falling to the neighboring Byzantine Empire. Later, during the Crusades, the long-standing threat of Christian conquest became a reality. The Crusader's conquest (1099) and the conversion of the Dome of the Rock into a Christian church triggered the declaration of a holy war (Djihad) by Muslim leaders for the reconquest of Jerusalem from the Christian infidels.[17] Muslim literature in praise of Jerusalem (Fada'il Al-Quds) began to flourish greatly. It had existed before, as part of a whole literary genre in praise of various cities, but now it particularly stressed the sanctity of Jerusalem in Islam and the importance of placing the city under Islamic rule.[18] In the same way, when Jerusalem was taken back under the leadership of Saladin (Salah-Al-Din) in 1187, and particularly from the thirteenth century on, a great deal of building activity began around the Temple Mount and in the whole city—so as, obviously, to establish its Islamic character.[19] All this did not prevent Jerusalem (and parts of Galilee) from being conquered once again by the Christian Crusaders' armies (1229), but the Temple Mount remained in Muslim hands.[20]

JERUSALEM IN CONTEMPORARY ISLAMIC THOUGHT

State and religion were never separated in Islam, and political events were often interpreted in religious terms, while religious values often became crystallized in the ideologies of political movements. The sanctity of Jerusalem was thus emphasized, and particularly so after the Crusaders' conquest. A somewhat similar phenomenon occurred in the twentieth century.

Despite its sanctity and its elevated status in Islam, Jerusalem remained a decaying city of ruins during the whole of the nineteenth century. It became the focus of religious and political Arab activity only at the beginning of the present century, and only because of the renewed Jewish activity in the city and Judaism's claims on the Western Wailing Wall. Several Arab committees were established to protect the "Al-Buraq" (Western Wall) against Jewish "encroachments"—for the Arabs felt that the Jews were attempting to snatch it out of Arab hands and to change its "status quo." The former Grand Mufti of Jerusalem, Hajj Amin el Husseini, played a particularly ominous role in Arab activities. He disseminated photographs of the Dome of the Rock topped by a flag with the Star of David throughout the Arab world. This photograph had, in fact, originally been distributed at the end of the nineteenth century by the teachers of a rabbinical school, Yeshivat Torat-Hayyim, in their fund raising efforts among world Jewry, but according to the mufti it was proof of Jewish intentions to take over the Temple Mount and to rebuild their Holy Temple on it.[20]

It is interesting to note that while East Jerusalem was actually in Arab hands (1948–1967) its sanctity was never especially stressed. It is, of course, still generally mentioned in Arab school textbooks, but without special emphasis. Jerusalem's sanctity to Christianity is also mentioned, as are the Christian Holy Places in the city, but the Jewish share in Jerusalem is never alluded to.[21] Following Al-Mawardi in his description of different kinds of Islamic territories,[22] a Lebanese jurist in his lecture to the International Academy for Law in the Hague, 1966, never even mentioned Jerusalem.

After the Six Day War of June, 1967, however, Muslim leaders began once more to deplore the fall of Jerusalem into the hands of infidels and as during the era of the Crusaders began again to emphasize the sanctity of Jerusalem in Islamic tradition. The great religious university of Al-Azhar in Cairo is today especially active in producing such tracts, and literature in praise of Jerusalem seems to be flourishing once more.[23] Yet even today one can discern some Arab and Muslim voices protesting against the over-veneration of Jerusalem in Islam and depicting this veneration as an imitation of Jewish tradition. At present a modern Egyptian writer is fighting, like Ibn Taimiyya fought more than 600 years ago, for the purification of Islam from alien influences. The writer is Abu Rayya. He also takes a strong stand against the glorification of Jerusalem and al-Aqsa in Islam and maintains that pure, original Islam knew nothing of this tradition.[24]

Nevertheless, his is a minority view that will never uproot the Muslim tradition of Jerusalem's sanctity, which is now so deeply rooted in the hearts of millions of believers. It seems, on the contrary, that this tradition is being permanently reinforced by present political circumstances, and sometimes even by sheer accident (as when a Christian fanatic set fire to the al-Aqsa Mosque in 1969), mainly because, as has already been pointed out, there is no distinction between politics and religion in Islam. It appears, therefore, that the belief that Jerusalem is a holy city to Muslims, as it is to Jews and Christians, and precisely because it is holy to the latter two religions, must be accepted as fact. In principle, even if not *de facto*, Muslims too concede today that Jerusalem is a holy city not only to Islam but also to millions of believers of the two other monotheistic religions. Sayyid Qutb, a modern commentator of the Koran and a fanatical Muslim and member of the Muslim Brotherhood, who was executed in Egypt in 1966, explained the first verse in Sura 17 as follows:

> The journey [of the Prophet] from Mecca to Jerusalem brings together the [three] great monotheistic religions, from Abraham and Ishmael until the last of the Prophets [Muhammad]. It binds together the holy places for all religions, as if Muhammad, in his miraculous journey [from Mecca to Jerusalem] had validated the holy places of the Prophets who had preceded him —Prophets whom he includes in his message and with whom he thus links himself. For this journey intimates things that transcend the frontiers of time and space and that range far wider than the borders of time and space. And they encompass meanings that are much deeper than those that appear at first reading of this verse.[25]

NOTES AND REFERENCES

1. See EI v. Ramadan and cf. S.D. Goitein, "The Muslim Month of Fasting, its Early Development and Religious Meaning" in S.D. Goitein, *Studies in Islamic History and Institutions* (Leiden, 1966), pp. 90–110.

2. The translation of the verses of the Koran in this article is taken from: Mohammad Marmaduke Pickthall, *The Meaning of the Glorious Koran*.

3. See A. Geiger, "Was Hat Mohammed aus dem Judenthume aufgenomen?" (L eipzig, 1902), p.87.See also G. Vajda, "Jeûne Musulman et Jeûne Juif" in HUCA 12–13, 1938, pp. 367–385 and cf. S.D. Goitein, *Jews and Arabs, Their Contacts Through the Ages* (New York: Schocken, 1955), ch. 4, "The Jewish Tradition in Islam," pp. 46–61.

4. Al-Tabari, *Annals of Kings and Prophets* (in Arabic), ed. by De Goeje, part I, Vol. 5, p. 2408.

5. See the original Hebrew version in Yehudah Even Shmu'el, *Midreshey Geula*, Jerusalem, 1954, p. 189 and cf. *ibid* pp. 102–198.

6. See S.D. Goitein, "The Sanctity of Jerusalem and Palestine in Early Islam" in his *Studies in Islamic History and Institutions*, pp. 135–148; *idem*, "The Historical Background of the Erection of the Dome of the Rock," *JAOS* 70, 1950, pp. 104–108; cf. also, W. Caskel, *Der Felsendom u. die Wallfart* (Cologne, 1963).

7. Many stories from mystic and popular Islamic literature on this topic are quoted by Mudjir Al-Din Al-Hanbali, fifteenth century judge in Jerusalem, in his book on the history of Jerusalem and Hebron (*Al-Uns Al-Djalil fi Ta'rikh Al-Quds wa-l-Khalil*).

8. See O. Grabar, "The Umayyad Dome of Jerusalem," *Ars Orientalis* III, 1959, pp. 33–62. On the artistic elements of the Dome of the Rock see the studies by K.A.C. Creswell and M. Van Bershem.

9. cf. B. Schrieke, "Die Himmelfahrt Muhammads," *Der Islam* IV, 1916, pp. 1–30. The literature on this topic is abundant. On the evolvement of legends and miracles around the person of Muhammad see Tor Andrae, *Die Person Muhammads in Lehre und Glauben seiner Gemeinde* (Upsala, 1917).

10. See A. Guillaume, *Islam* (Pelican Book) and see M. Plessner "Muhammed's Clandestine 'Umra." in *RSO* 32, 1957, pp. 525–530.

11. See El v. "Isra" and "Mi'raj." The last was written in the first edition by Joseph Horovitz. cf. also Geo Widengren's studies of the stories of the "Mi'raj" as compared to a wider background of comparative religions.

12. Rich material of this sort was collected by R. and H. Kriss, *Volksglaube im Bereich des Islam*, I. (Wiesbaden, 1960), p. 137, ff.

13. *cf.* H. Busse, "The Sanctity of Jerusalem in Islam," *Judaism*, XVII. 1968, pp. 441–468, which deals also with the history of the city and its relations with Mecca and Medina.

14. See I. Goldizsher, "Die Heiligenverehrung in Islam" in, *Mohammedanische Studien II* (Halle, 1890), pp. 275–378.

15. See M.S. Kister, "You shall only set out for three Mosques, A study of an early tradition," *Museon*, 1969, pp. 173–196.

16. See many sayings of this kind in Mudjir Al-Din's book, mentioned in footnote 7 above.

17. See E. Sivan, *id*, "Le Caratère sacré de Jerusalem dans l'Islam aux 12e-13e siècle," *Studia Islamica* 28, 1967, pp. 149–182.

18. See two examples of this kind of literature in L.D. Mattews, *Palestine, Muhammedan Holy Land*.

19. See *e.g.* A. Ashtor (in Hebrew), "Jerusalem in the Late Middle Ages" in *Jerusalem*, V, 1955, pp. 71–116.

20. *cf.* J. Porath (in Hebrew), *The Growth of the Palestinian Arab National Movement 1918–1929* (Jerusalem, 1971).

21. See H. Lazarus-Yafeh, "An Inquiry into Arab Text Books," 1967, p. 219. *Asian and African Studies*, VIII, 1972, p. 16.

22. See S. Mahmassani, "The Principles of International Law in the Light of Islamic Doctrine," *RADI, Receuil d'Academy of International Law*, T. 117 (Leiden, 1967), pp. 250–251. cf. also N. Feinberg, *Arab-Israeli Conflict in International Law, A critical Analysis of the Colloquium of Arab Jurists in Algiers* (Jerusalem, 1970), p. 110.

23. See H. Lazarus-Yafeh, "Contemporary Religious Thought Among the 'Ulama' of Al-Azhar," *Asian and African Studies*, VII, 1971, p. 235.

24. Abu Rayya (in Arabic), *Light on Muhammad's Tradition* (Cairo: Third Edition, [n.d.]), p. 169. See also G.H.A. Juynboll, *Authenticity of the Tradition Literature, Discussions in Modern Egypt* (Leiden, 1969). Abu Rayja died recently.

25. See his voluminous commentary "In the Shadows of the Qur'an," XV, p. 12.

XVII

Jerusalem—A Christian Perspective

JOSEPH P. BRENNAN

For the Christian there are two Jerusalems. One exists in his imagination —the City of David and Solomon, the site of the Temple, the home of the priests, the scribes, and the pharisees, the city where Jesus of Nazareth preached and performed miracles, outside whose walls He was put to death, buried, and rose again. It is the city where the Spirit of God first descended with a rushing like that of wind, where the Good News was first proclaimed, where Baptism and the Breaking of Bread were first celebrated, where the early followers of Christ were first assembled as *the Church* and the city where their first major decisions were reached. From its gates the first missionary impulses of the small Christian community radiated to the surrounding districts and to the remoter parts of the then-known world. This is the Jerusalem which takes its infinitely varied shapes within each Christian reader of the Old and New Testaments. Whether his visions are as accurate as the latest archaeological evidence can make them, or as romantic and fanciful as the generations of Christian art upon which most of our piety has been nourished, *that* Jerusalem is for most Christians a remote, unreal, and unthreatening place which ceased to exist in A.D. 70. They can no longer weep over it with Jesus, nor set it above their highest joy with the psalmist. Since it has no substance, it has no power to move to tears of either joy or anguish.

The Christian's other Jerusalem is "the city of the living God, the heavenly Jerusalem . . . the assembly of the first-born who are enrolled in heaven" (Heb. 12:22–23), where there is no temple (Rev. 21:22), but where

226

a new covenant is mediated and a new sacrifice offered (Heb.12:24). This is the Jerusalem he claims as his mother (Gal. 4:26), and it is her name that he bears (Rev. 3:12). A present yet future reality, this Jerusalem has no man-made foundations, no spatially-defined limits. Its builder and architect is God (Heb. 11:10), and its citizenship is won not through birth or naturalization, but through faith. Transcending both space and time, this Jerusalem exists whenever and wherever men "receive gratefully that kingdom that cannot be shaken" by political and social upheaval (Heb. 12:28), and live in the hope of seeing that heavenly "city which is to come" (Heb. 13:14). This Jerusalem is a faltering image of his experience of the Communion of Saints.

But if for the Christian Jerusalem is an historical memory or a mystical experience, for the Jew Jerusalem is this and more. The Jerusalem of priests and prophets, of rabbis and saints is also the Jerusalem of synagogues and supermarkets. Her very stones are dear to him, and the dust of her streets has as much power over him as it had over countless generations before him (Ps. 102:15). It is for the well-being of Jerusalem that he prays at each wedding and funeral, at the beginning of every Sabbath, and at the end of every day. For the Jew there can be no personal or family joy without a prayer of longing or of gratitude for the welfare of Jerusalem.

The Christian may look upon this passionate love for what Paul calls "the present Jerusalem" (Gal. 4:25) with a degree of condescension, remembering perhaps Jesus' words that "the hour is coming, and now is, when neither on this mountain nor in Jerusalem will you worship the Father" (John 4:21–23). Or he may feel a degree of envy and anxiety, recalling that Jesus too loved this city to the point of tears, and that He came not to destroy the old but to bring it to completion.

He may also find himself asking: Can the reign of God be conceived in purely non-political, non-spatial, spiritual terms? Can it be totally divorced from its historical, actual incarnations, whether past, present, or future? The "present Jerusalem" has always served as a reminder to Christians that God does concern Himself with the banalities of man's everyday life, that He does enter into the mainstream of human affairs, and does not shy away from what is limited and fallen. Rather He accepts it, and indeed unites Himself with it irrevocably, thus teaching us to do the same. Wherever Christians have attempted to build their own Jerusalems, whether in Byzantium, or Rome, in Munster, Geneva, or on the shores of the New World, they have striven to reproduce that ideal of an earthly city of which it might be said: "The Lord is there" (Ezek. 48:35; cf. Zech. 8:20–23), a city from which God's life-giving word might go forth (Isa. 2:2–4; Mic. 4:1–3), where all would live in peace and righteousness (Isa. 1:26–27; Zech. 8:4–8).

Nevertheless, since the fall of the Latin Kingdom of Jerusalem in 1292, the "present Jerusalem" has had an ever-diminishing attraction for the Christian. The "holy places" associated with the great events of the Old and New Dispensations have, it is true, been heroically (and on occasion not so heroically) maintained and defended through generations of hostility and violence, and countless pilgrims have lovingly revisited the sites which they had so often created in their imaginations. And yet, for the overwhelming majority of Christians the "Holy Places," the "Holy City," and the "Holy Land" have been at best matters of peripheral concern.

And yet, the "present Jerusalem" should be important to the Christian, as it is for the Jew, not so much because of what God brought to pass there in generations gone by as for what He is bringing to pass there now. Both the Old and the New Testaments make it clear that He dwells in men, not places, and that men, not places, should be other men's chief concern.

Who can believe in the limitless dynamism and unsuspected depths of the Word of God (Isa. 40:6–8; 55:10–11), and not be filled with wonder at the determination of those who have prayed, suffered, struggled, and died so that the words of the prophets concerning the ingathering of the people of Israel, the redemption of the Promised Land, and the restoration of Jerusalem might be fulfilled again? Who can read such passages as Psalm 132:13–14; Isaiah 49:14–23, 60:1–22; Joel 4:20; Zephaniah 3:14–20; Zechariah 1:14–17, 2:1–12, 8:3–5,20–23 and not ask himself whether the Lord may not still be the One "Who chooses Jerusalem" (Zech. 3:2)? Are "the gifts and the call of God" indeed irrevocable, as Paul says (Rom.11:20)? And if they are, what does this mean for Jerusalem? Do the prophecies of her destruction in the Gospels point, not to utter rejection, as Christians have so readily concluded, but only to a passing phase in her long history? Can Jerusalem be in our time, as in the past, more than a mere symbol of the presence of God and the destiny of man, but an actual embodiment of those ideals, even though in a limited and imperfect form? Does it necessarily follow from the coming of Christ that all other religious symbols and realities have lost their validity and become "superfluous," as the Christian understanding of such texts as Colossians 2:17 so often suggests?

Or is the Lord speaking to us once again in words we do not fully understand? Are we perhaps faced with another of those disconcerting moments when history and history's Lord confound the calculations of the theologians and the exegetes? "How unsearchable His judgments, how inscrutable His ways" Paul exclaims at the conclusion of his effort to grasp the meaning of God's dealings with Jews and Gentiles (Rom. 11:33). Are His judgments less unsearchable, His ways less inscrutable today?

The facts we are asked to reflect upon are these:

(1) Jerusalem is no longer a divided city, but is once again "bound firmly together" (Ps. 122:3). All who love her can only rejoice in the end of the unnatural division which from 1948 until 1967 created two watertight cities, one Arab and one Jewish. Who would have dreamed during those years that the division could disappear and leave so few traces? Who would have predicted that the relationship between the various communities, Jewish, Christian, and Muslim, could be so free of hostility and so full of promise? Problems do exist in Jerusalem, tensions between Arab and Jew, but on a scale that leaves much room for hope. And there are many in each community who are working effectively for mutual respect and peaceful cooperation. Jerusalem is already showing signs of becoming what her name proclaims her to be, the "City of Peace."

(2) Reunited Jerusalem is a free and open city, where Jews, Christians, and Muslims can worship without fear or intimidation. Rarely in her millennial history has Jerusalem known such stability and security as she knows today. Rarely has access to the holy places been so effortless and free of risk as it is today for members of each of the great religious traditions. Certainly Jewish pilgrims have a freedom of access that was long denied them. The number of pilgrims and tourists to Jerusalem has risen steadily in recent years, and among these have been numbered tens of thousands of citizens of the various Arab States who enter Israel each year to visit relatives and shrines (both Christian and Muslim), and who experience no harassment because of their nationality.

(3) Jerusalem has not been severed from the surrounding territories and populace by some sort of artificial "international status," but is the living, throbbing, heart of a dynamic society. International cities have not had an outstanding record of success, and it is dubious that such a status for Jerusalem would ever have worked, even if its proponents had been willing to implement it and the concerned Jewish and Arab citizens of Jerusalem had been able and willing to live under it. Internationalization, far from guaranteeing Jerusalem's vitality, would undoubtedly have been a constant threat to her growth and stability, and one can only rejoice that no serious efforts were ever undertaken to achieve such a status. Jerusalem has no need of "caretakers" or "international police-forces," as anyone who visits the city today can testify. International by reason of the various groups who make their home within her, or make pilgrimages to her shrines, Jerusalem nevertheless has the vigor and excitement of a world capital. If her expansion (*cf.* Isa. 49:19–21; Zech. 2:5–9) gives rise to occasional infringements of aesthetic canons, it is also evidence of the fact that Jerusalem lives and draws her life from the hearts and lives of hundreds and thousands of men and women who see in her more than a memory or a mystique, but the very center of their lives and their hearts.

(4) Jerusalem is more than a collection of museums, churches, sanc-

tuaries, and archaeological excavations. It is a city of living, struggling, and very human men, women, and children of an astonishing cultural, religious, and ethnic diversity. In this human potential lies Jerusalem's greatest significance today, its true value. While respecting the sacred traditions of the past, Jerusalem, like any great city must live in the present and for the future. The whole world feels that it has a stake in Jerusalem, but none more than the men and women who live out their lives within her precincts. They must ultimately be the ones to shape her future. Those who love her from afar have a right to a respectful hearing, but they cannot presume to impose upon her their own preconceptions and expections. Nothing is sadder than to see countless visitors to Jerusalem and the Near East who have visited all the shrines and pilgrimage sites, and who have only the vaguest idea of what is happening in the streets and towns through which they pass—the hospitals and clinics being opened, the schools and institutes, the research centers and experimental farms which dot the countryside, the reclaiming of the rocky barren soil, the flourishing of the arts, and the cultivation of democratic ideals. These are what make Jerusalem the city of promise which it is today. If the memory of the prophets is still strong there, and indeed the memory of Jesus Himself, then their spirit and their ideals live on even more strongly.

(5) The Christian presence in and the Christian impact on the Holy Land and the Holy City have all too often been less than evangelical. The details of our internal rivalries and the debates over frivolities are too well known to bear repetition. The passion for building grandiose sanctuaries to the glory of God, and the comparative lack of concern for the image of God which is man, is all too evident even in our own time. The question now facing Christians is: Are we prepared to contribute to the building-up of this old-new land, or shall we remain aloof and concerned only with the property-rights to the sacred places? Happily there are signs that from an ecumenical point of view Jerusalem is beginning to realize its potentialities as the meeting-place not only of Christians, Muslims, and Jews, but also of the many different Christian denominations as well. Only the first tentative steps have been taken, and an immense distance remains to be covered, but no other city can equal Jerusalem in possibilities for truly ecumenical dialogue. Christians have suffered greatly in the Holy Land, and they have inflicted great suffering there on others and on themselves. Now perhaps that period of violence and suspicion is drawing to a close and a new era is opening when "Israel shall be a third party with Egypt and Assyria, a blessing in the midst of the earth, whom the Lord of hosts has blessed, saying, 'Blessed be Egypt my people, and Assyria the work of my hands, and Israel my heritage' " (Isa. 19:24–25).

(6) Jerusalem is a city of Jews, Muslims, and Christians. Each group is passionately devoted to her, each has inviolable rights of citizenship

within her. But historically, legally, and morally, none of the neighboring states, including the Kingdom of Jordan, has any claim on the Holy City. At no time prior to 1948 was Jerusalem included territorially within any of these states, and at no time was Jerusalem internationally recognized as belonging to them. The Jordanian occupation of the Old City from 1948 until 1967 was, like the Israeli occupation of the New City, the outcome of the fighting which took place at the time of the termination of the British Mandate. The present Israeli occupation of the Old City and of other West Bank territories is a direct result of the concerted Arab attacks against Israel in the period after 1948, culminating in the Six Day War in 1967. Israel's claim to Jerusalem is as defensible as any of the territorial arrangements reached in Europe and Asia at the end of World War II, or in a host of other countries at the conclusion of similar hostilities. There is no reason why Israel should unilaterally renounce this claim and no reason why she should allow others to impose such a renunciation on her. Indeed, the years since 1967 have shown that a united Jerusalem can prosper under an Israeli administration, and that a return to the partition situation which prevailed before 1967 would not demonstrably improve the lot even of Jerusalem's religious and ethnic minorities. It is as difficult today as it was in 1967 to predict what will be the definitive political and administrative status of Old Jerusalem and the West Bank in the years ahead, but the blame for this ambiguity does not rest with Israel. It is hypocrisy to criticize Israel for "annexing" these territories and for "imperialism" when the neighboring states who so enthusiastically provoked the 1967 war have shown themselves subsequently to be so unwilling to enter into direct negotiations to reach an agreement on their fate.

There are shadows across the face of Jerusalem today, as there have been during every period of her history, and as there undoubtedly always will be. Not all is perfect there, not all is blameless, nor is the city's future free of danger. But when in the past 1,900 years of Jerusalem's history has any generation been offered a greater challenge and a firmer promise of future fulfillment?

For 25 centuries, devout men and women have pondered the words of an anonymous Hebrew prophet:

> You who put the Lord in remembrance
>   take no rest,
> and give him no rest
>   until he establishes Jerusalem
>   and makes it a praise in the earth.
>   (Isa. 62:6–7)

For the Jew these words have been as much a call to action as to prayer. The restoration of Jerusalem must be man's work as well as God's. As the

Midrash on Exodus 14:15–22 puts it: "God said to Moses: 'All that Israel has to do is go forward. Therefore, let them go forward! Let their feet step forward from the dry land to the sea, and you will see the miracles which I will perform for them.' . . . the sea was divided only after Israel had stepped into it and the waters had reached their noses, only then did it become dry land" (*Midrash Rabbah, Exodus*, XXI: 8–10).

For the Christian these words and so many similar passages which he reads year after year are also an invitation to pray and work for the peace of Jerusalem:

> *For my brethren and companions' sake*
> *I will say, "Peace be within you!"*
>
> > (Ps. 122:8)

> *Blessed art thou, O Lord, who spreadest the*
> *shelter of peace over us and over all thy people*
> *Israel and over Jerusalem.*
>
> > (From the Evening Service for
> > Sabbaths and Festivals)

Who knows what else the Lord may hold in store for those who will not let Him rest?

> *They shall not hurt or destroy*
> *in all my holy mountain;*
> *for the earth shall be full of the*
> *knowledge of the Lord*
> *as the waters cover the sea.*
>
> > (Isa. 11:9)

XVIII

The Christian Churches in Present-day Israel

GABRIEL GROSSMANN, O.P.
(Translated from the German by Ralph F. Goldman)

The present report, based on close observation of Christianity in the Holy Land, first describes the Christians of all denominations living in Israel and then examines their current position and their mission.

Description of the Christian Churches in Israel

For almost 1,350 years Christians have been living in the Holy Land as a minority among a non-Christian population. An extraordinary range of Christian religious communities and churches is represented here. From time immemorial the country has served as domicile not only for communities and corporate bodies but also for religious groups and institutes, for monasteries and convents. Their members, sent here from every part of the world as ambassadors, as it were, of Christianity, have enabled it through the great variety of their good works to make its impact on the character of the country. Each of the religious communities living here devotes itself to its own special task; each is equally important here; and for each its tie to the Holy Land is similarly fulfilling.

In order to develop an adequate insight into the situation of local Christianity, one must keep in mind the guiding principles through which one gains access to this information.

(a) The history of Christianity in the Holy Land is as old as Christianity itself.

(b) The distribution of the Christian communities throughout the Holy Land was determined by the geographical position of the holy places as well as by historical developments.

(c) Almost the entire spectrum of Christian denominations, religious orders, sects, rites, liturgies, and hierarchies is represented here.

(d) For most of the holy places this results, on the one hand, in an excessively minute dividing of a given edifice among several religious orders, and, on the other hand, in each denomination deploying its members at different sites, where they memorialize the same or a closely related event in the Passion and Salvation of Christ. As a result it is difficult to decide which of these two extreme forms of fraternal unity among Christians is more beneficial.

(e) Communication and cooperation among Christian brothers is further impeded by differences of language and cultural outlook.

HISTORICAL PERSPECTIVE

This is not the place to summarize the history of Christians in the Holy Land. However, we should not by-pass a few of the historically rooted questions which must be faced by Christians in the Holy Land and, presumably, all over the world.

Basically, a Christian finds himself addressed by the Holy Land in the entire breadth of its geographical expanse and of its historical settlement (especially in biblical times). But to what extent does the relationship to the earliest Jerusalem community and its way of life remain an influential factor for Christians in the Holy Land and in the rest of the world?

The eras of predominantly Christian settlement have deeply imprinted the Holy Land with architectural traces. Is the Christian presence in the Holy Land today likewise to be understood as a service to the land and to its reconstruction?[1] In the course of a half-century, from 1922 to 1969, the Christian population of the country has grown (chiefly through natural increase) by more than 40 per cent, from about 71,000 to about 100,000 persons.[2] Can it be said that the Christian population's qualitative share in the destiny of the land has grown in equal proportion?

GEOGRAPHICAL RELATIONSHIPS

Two-thirds of the Christians presently dwelling in the country reside in Jerusalem and within the "old" borders[3] of Israel, twice as many as the combined number of those living on the West Bank and in the Gaza Strip. Of the Christians in the "old" Israeli territory with its capital Jerusalem, almost two-thirds are Catholics; whereas in the remaining regions the Eastern churches (those not united with Rome) have an unequivocal majority. This distribution can be explained partly by the geographical foci of the Latinization campaign of the past century.[4] Outside of Jerusalem itself, this geographical dispersion generates quite difficult problems of ministering to a Christian population which is for the most part traditionalist.

DISTRIBUTION BY DENOMINATION

Through the Eastern churches in particular, Christians residing in the Holy Land since days of yore have preserved the tradition of the early Church and the Church Fathers, and their liturgical diversity enchants the pilgrim. But in general each church, each denomination, and each rite of every church has considered it important to establish a small delegation in Jerusalem or at least in the Holy Land in order to be represented in the vicinity of the holy places.

Each religious community concerns itself first of all with the welfare of its own members. This results in a most unfortunate perpetuation of conflicts among the various religious communities in the country. Moreover, these confrontations were often formed by foreign political powers. Therefore, if the Christian churches in Israel were to favor a new relationship toward one another, it would simultaneously imply their independence of world power-structures. In this connection it is gratifying to note that the various denominations which are responsible for the Church of the Resurrection[5] are finally co-operating in its restoration. The significance of such a gesture in a city like Jerusalem—where no less than six Patriarchates minister to Christians—cannot be overestimated.

Especially since the reunification of both parts of Jerusalem, the Arabic and the Hebrew, and the disappearance of artificial walls which once separated them, Christians have undertaken to bring somewhat more unity into their own ranks. In addition to the celebration of the annual Prayer Week for Christian Unity, we should mention in this regard:

(a) a weekly silent prayer in one of the chapels of the Church of the Resurrection (the so-called Church of the Holy Sepulchre) in which Christian laymen and clergy of all denominations and from both parts of the city participate in order to pray together on a regular basis for peace in Jerusalem;

(b) the opportunity offered to Christian students in Jerusalem to come to terms with the problems of the land, to get an idea of the situation, and to arrive at a Christian judgment about it;

(c) various working-groups in Jerusalem and elsewhere that bring together members of the Christian churches, chiefly theologians, who hold meetings sometimes among themselves, sometimes with their Jewish or Muslim counterparts.

CHRISTIANS WITHIN ISRAEL'S BORDERS (1969)*

	CATHOLICS					ORTHODOX			Other EASTERN	ANGLICANS	PROTESTANTS	TOTALS (regional)
	Latins	Greeks	Maronites	Others		Greeks	Syrians					
Israel Proper and East Jerusalem	14,800**	22,800	2900	400	40,900	21,000	300	21,300	2,700	1,100	1,100	67,100
Jordan and Gaza Strip	9,100	200	200	200	11,500	16,500	900	17,400	1,100	1,200	1,400	32,600
GRAND TOTALS (by denomination)	23,900	24,800	3,100	600	52,400	37,500	1,200	38,700	3,800	2,300	2,500	99,700
									8600			

* This table is based on data from S. P. Colbi (See footnote 2), Chap. XIV, pp. 188–92.

** At the beginning of 1972 in the pre-1967 Israeli territory there were at most 4,000 more Western Christians than appeared in the statistics for 1969 (according to the oral statement of a reliable source).

THE HOLY PLACES AS A MANDATE

To the contemplative soul, the Holy Land is disclosed with especial intensity through its holy places. In the light of this we might emphasize that in the Holy Land each Christian historical site, or at least its immediate vicinity, is also of vital significance for all other religious communities in the land. The Patriarchs are memorialized in Hebron not only by Christians but also by Jews and Muslims; the well of the Samaritan woman was dug, in accordance with her famous utterance, by Jacob, the father of the Twelve Tribes of Israel;[6] the city of Jerusalem with its Temple Square, its Mount of Olives, and its Mosque of Omar (Dome of the Rock) exercises over the adherents of the three religions an inexhaustible attraction which moves many believers to observe their religious obligations here and nowhere else, and to await even in the grave their joyous Resurrection; the caves of the Qumran settlement, lying at some distance from the ruins of ancient Christian hermitages, are for Jews and Christians alike moving and instructive both as a monument to Jewish monasticism and the place of discovery of the oldest Hebrew manuscripts of Holy Writ and of Bible commentary. In Capernaum the ruins of the ancient synagogue remind Jews of the flowering of their religion in Galilee, and Christians of the Sermon of Jesus through which He let his mystery be known.[7] The walls of the venerable Greek Orthodox Monastery of St. Catherine on Mt. Sinai harbor a mosque which in past eras offered Muslim workers a safe place for divine worship; in a city like Acre, the Jewish, Christian, and Muslim presence of yesterday and today is almost inextricably interwoven. And finally, the port city of Haifa, in which coexistence is practiced in exemplary fashion, even harbors other religions besides the three main ones.[8]

May Christians who, like their Savior, live under a mandate of reconciliation,[9] hearken in their holy places unto the summons to serve peace in the Holy Land!

LANGUAGE DIFFICULTIES

A further consideration must be brought up, which concerns the relationship of Holy Land Christians to the two official languages of the land and, along with this, to the cultural and political environment. From this perspective local Christians as a whole can be divided into three groups:

1. On the one hand we find laymen and a number of monastic communities who worship in their foreign mother tongue, receive their news almost exclusively from the press and radio of their homeland, direct

their gaze abroad, hardly seek contact with the local population, enjoy tax-exempt status as clergy, and rarely manage to learn even one of the two national languages, Hebrew and Arabic.

This group of Christians, in general a culturally lively and socially elite minority, carries out a function whose value is not to be underestimated. Thanks to their presence, places of contemplation and research exist in the Holy Land, facilities where on behalf of Christians all over the world the Holy Scriptures are studied by scholars on the basis of their historico-geographical conditions. Moreover, the poor of the country receive aid from Christian sources, the spiritual needs of transients in the country are ministered to, and the Christian significance of the land is taught to pilgrims.

2. In all this melange of denominations and rites, there is an indigenous Christian majority which consists of Arabic-speaking faithful, and these comprise considerably more than 90 per cent of all Christians. Here we must be careful to express ourselves precisely: nowadays in Israel, Arabic is spoken by many a person who is neither Arab nor Palestinian![10] These are persons whose cultural outlook and, if they are not Jews, whose political position are oriented to the "Arab world." Thus it is Arabic-speaking Christians who in the Holy Land determine the relationship of local hierarchies to events as they have been affecting the country for the past quarter-century.[11]

As member of a minority amidst a Muslim population, the "Christian"[12] of Arabic background often sees himself called upon to take up the cause of "Arab nationalism" more fervently than many a Muslim.[13] On the other hand, within the national borders he faces an absolute majority of Jewish Israelis, whose way of life has been shaped at least as much by democracy as by religion. However, the Christian of Arabic background gives the impression not only of knowing how to assert himself in this relatively novel situation[14] but even of getting along better in it, in general, than when he faced an exclusively Islamic environment.[15] Indeed, it may be that Palestinian Christians and Jewish Israelis nowadays are occasionally rediscovering in quite concrete fashion their common tribal origins in Isaac and Ishmael.[16]

3. In addition, a small number of Protestants and Catholics living in Israel speak Hebrew as their everyday language or even as their native tongue. These Christians live in the Jewish part of the country, have a feeling of fellowship with the Jewish population, affirm the existence of the State of Israel, work in it, serve it, and labor to develop an authentic Christian life here just as do other Christians living in other environments.

From contacts with their Jewish fellow-man and with the Jewish culture in Israel, they are gaining a deeper understanding of their Christian faith. They strive to practice among the Jewish citizens of the country a Christianity which is favorably disposed to the Jews and which has a Jewish flavor. (*Cf.* "The Church in the heralding of Israel," *FR* XIX [1967], p. 61 *et seq.*)

The foregoing observations have projected a rather static image and in part have even offered a statistical overview. The analysis which follows below takes up the problems which are generated by the position of Christians in the Holy Land.

The Position of Christians in the Israeli State

The world public frequently asks to what extent the Christian population of the Holy Land can live an untrammelled existence and look forward to a promising future. It may be assumed that quite apart from political ethics, the State of Israel finds it fully in its own interest to be actively concerned for the peaceful administration of the holy places and a secure existence for the Christian communities within its borders. For the sake of simplicity we shall ask here only about the protection of the rights of minorities, specifically in the areas of religion, culture, social and economic life, and, finally, political life.

RELIGIOUS FREEDOM

Within the Israeli State which, since its declaration of independence, assumed the international obligations of the Ottoman Empire and the British Mandate within its domain, each person on the basis of the *status personalis* is represented before the state authorities by his religious community in regard to certain matters. Thus, for example, the state does not recognize civil marriage ceremonies; marriages may be performed in Israel only by the competent religious authority (Church, Rabbinate, etc.). Each authority, acting in accordance with its own canon law, solemnizes marriages, registers them, and guarantees their legality to the state. [Cf. *FR* XIV (1964), p. 60 *et sqq.*] It is obvious that such regulation considerably impedes mixed marriages. However, it was intended for a state of affairs in which each religious community (and this means each individual Christian denomination also) lived as a closed, tightly knit society within the larger framework of the political state.

With this restriction, which is not dependent on the state, Israel guarantees the fullest freedom for the observance of faith, the conducting of worship, and for the visiting and maintaining of the holy places. A Christian who works in a Jewish business (which is closed on Saturday) has a legal right to take Sunday off as well. Access to the Temple area is prohibited to non-Muslims during the hours of Muslim prayer. Heretofore, during the Jordanian occupation of East Jerusalem, it was impossible for a Jew, whether from Israel or even from abroad, to pray at the holy places of his faith; indeed, an Arab Christian or Muslim from Israel was hardly better off.[17] Today, Israel permits Muslims residing within her borders to make pilgrimages to Mecca and Medina; and she presents no obstacle to Christians and Muslims from Arab countries who come to Jerusalem to discharge their religious obligations.

CULTURAL DEVELOPMENT AND FREEDOM OF EXPRESSION

The Christian communities, which at present live under conditions that are much quieter and better secured than they were under Jordanian control, enjoy the fullest freedom as communities to develop and give public expression to their cultural life. In our age it is not surprising that Israel, like other states, takes an extremely dim view of missionary attempts to proselytize its population. Nowadays Christians are learning to understand anew their mission to bring the Joyous Tidings to all people. But if the churches of this country wish to make a valid contribution to its spiritual development in a way that is considered neither foreign nor missionary, they are for the most part lacking in manpower suited to the task.

SOCIAL POSITION AND ECONOMIC ADVANCE

Thanks to the policy of economic development within Israel's borders, which also guarantees open bridges to Jordan and thereby maintains economic and cultural relations with the Arab world, the labor market position and the social welfare of the lower strata of the Arab population have improved markedly; whereas the persisting emigration of the Arab elite, of which Christians form a considerable part, may be explained partly in terms of political circumstances, but also partly in terms of the chronic lack of structures for absorbing educated manpower within an economy that is still inadequately developed.

Worth noting is the fact that the tendency to emigrate existed long before the existence of the State of Israel. It would be very desirable if the representatives of the Arab population in the Israeli political arena were to take a stand in favor of carrying forward the economic development of the Arab regions within the current borders in tandem with improvement of the school system.

POLITICAL RIGHTS

Unlike their coreligionists in neighboring Lebanon, Christians in Israel have no political representation as a group. Israeli nationals and citizens of the municipality of Jerusalem elect their representatives in parliament and in the city council through the multi-party system. In like manner the interests of union members throughout the country are represented by the union. Unfortunately, relatively few of the Christians entitled to vote take seriously their civic responsibility for the life of the country. Moreover, it is deplorable that since 1967 and presumably until the establishment of peace with the neighboring states, the citizens of the West Bank and of the Gaza Strip (and along with them those citizens of East Jerusalem who refuse to be issued an Israeli identity card) are *de facto* stateless persons. This condition, highly unsalutary over the long term, has an equally severe impact on Christians and Muslims alike.

To whatever extent resident Christians nowadays are being disadvantaged or bothered, or are thinking of emigrating, this has not the least connection with any encroachment upon the rights of their religious communities. These phenomena stem, rather, from economic difficulties peculiar to the country as well as from the ethnic defensiveness, brought to a peak by the present military conflict, of a Jewish Israeli people which is still in search of its identity.

Task of Christians Living in Israel

As emphasized at the outset, those Christians who neither hold nor desire Israeli citizenship can still devote themselves to a real task in the Holy Land. A few of the areas of activity open to Christians have been mentioned above: first, service to the country's poor; next, the preserving of the holy places by communities which witness the importance of these places by devoting their own life to them; finally, contemplation and research by individual persons and institutes which through their prayers intercede for world Christendom in the Holy Land by virtue of its richness in grace, and which through their scholarly work help bring about a deeper understanding of Holy Writ.

It would be desirable for Eastern Church Christians in the Holy Land to give more deliberation to preserving the living continuity with their heritage from the time of early Christianity and to transmit the treasures of that tradition. This historical type of self-definition might also find understanding among the Jewish people in Israel and thus make coexistence easier. In general, the circumstance that the non-Jewish Israeli (on the basis of religious affiliation or ethnic origin) is exempt from military service should be used by Christians to make a real contribution to peace; their own vocation compels them to do so, and they would thereby be acting in accordance with the yearnings of their coreligionists throughout the world.[18] A Christian can live up to his vocation by practicing reconciliation and tolerance on a small scale and by candor and striving after understanding in the face of more comprehensive problems. In this way he can grow into a vital connecting link between differing outlooks and different peoples. Insofar as there are any political prospects for the concluding of a peace treaty, such a treaty can be assured permanence only if preceded by the work of bringing men together; and who should feel more responsible for this than the Christian?

But a further consequence relevant for this land can be drawn from the permanent commandment to love one's fellow-man. If it turns out that a long common history full of suffering and a renewed understanding of the Bible have awakened in us Christians of today the feeling for a new relationship with Jews,[19] it can be genuinely realized only if it leads to a new relationship to the Jewish Israelis. May the rich common heritage which binds Christians and Jews together[20] increasingly spur Holy Land Christians to discover and cultivate, for the sake of their own inner growth,[21] their spiritual relationship with the people Israel.[22]

NOTES AND REFERENCES

1. Christians in the Holy Land let themselves be driven into some tight spots by anxiously hanging on to ecclesiastical real estate rather than to giving witness to the Christian presence the best possible way. This situation was illuminated in early 1972 by the successful resistance of the highest officials of the Catholic Church to the sale of Notre Dame de France. In the last century a French Order of Merit built a pilgrims' inn outside the city walls of Jerusalem. Belonging to Israel since 1948, the building has stood from then on under the protection of the French consular authorities. The rise of an efficient Israeli hotel industry required the modification of the building's function; but the Order could no longer support it as a shelter for homeless settlers. Proposals to sell it within the Church and suggestions for new ways it might be utilized by the Church community were rejected until a year-and-a-half ago, when the Order decided to find a buyer outside the Church. The Keren Kayemet le-Yisrael (the Jewish National Fund, which is responsible for land development) signed a contract of sale, paid the purchase price, and handed the building over to a new user, the Hebrew University of Jerusalem, which was in urgent need of new dormitory space. But then Arab Christians of Jerusalem complained that the sale had put them at the mercy of "the Jews." The Vatican entered the picture and brought suit in the Jerusalem Civil Court for cancellation of the sale. Church law (see Canon 1499, par. 2) empowers the Holy See to assume responsibility for protecting the material interests of Christian communities. According to Israeli law, however, a legal determination based on the Church's internal regulations is irrelevant in matters concerning real estate. A number of hearings were held, all without issue. The dispute has now moved into a final, out-of-court phase. Although the Holy See does not recognize the State of Israel, both sides agreed on a compromise, and the legal proceedings have been discontinued. Whether those immediately affected are receiving unjust treatment, and whether this generates antagonism among some Christians and among Jews, is hardly taken into account.

2. Cf. Saul P. Colbi, *Christianity in the Holy Land, Past and Present* (Tel Aviv, 1969), p. III.

3. This expression and others similar refer to the territory which belonged to Israel on June 4, 1967, *i.e.*, before the Six Day War.

4. In the last century the Latin Patriarchate in Jerusalem, which was brought in with the Crusades and was not restored until 1847, attempted with varying success to bring Eastern Catholics and even Orthodox Christians under its jurisdiction.

5. This is the correct name of the so-called "Church of the Holy Sepulchre."

6. John. 4:12.

7. *Ibid.*, 6:44–59.

8. *E.g.* the Bahai Temple, which has become one of the symbols of the city.

9. See II Corinthians 5:18–20

10. He may be from an Armenian or Turkish family, or a Jewish immigrant from an Arab country.

11. In 1952, for example, Christians comprised 7 per cent of the population of Jordan.

12. In the context of a sociological treatment, it is correct to place this word in quotation marks. As is explained in the text, this concept as used in Israel represents first of all a category of the social structure; moreover, it is beyond the scope of this article to weigh the relative devoutness and religious vitality of the various Christian groups in Israel.

13. It is due solely to the higher educational level of the Christian minority that, in Syria for instance, Christians acted as the leading champions of modern Arab nationalism in opposition to the late-Ottoman policy of Turkification; and at that time Syria included Palestine both administratively and conceptually.

14. Even if it has existed in Galilee for the past quarter-century, it has obtained in East Jerusalem and Bethlehem only since 1967.

15. No Muslim state in the immediate vicinity has yet offered an example of a spontaneous and successful secularization under which non-Muslims are accorded civil rights equal with those of Muslims.

16. Cf. "Israel and Ishmael," *FR* X:37–40, p. 34 et *sqq.* (Ed.-*FR*)

17. Christians in Israel were permitted to cross the border on pilgrimages only at Christmas and Easter.

18. Apart from the teaching and practice of the Catholic central agencies in Rome and of the World Council of Churches, peace research is carried on in common with non-Christians in many places, Germany included, in high schools and colleges. Whether the results of these efforts should be utilized in the Holy Land or whether an original local initiative should be made is in large measure a matter to be decided by the Christians living in the Holy Land.

19. Compare this more intense concern with that expressed in Romans 9–11.

20. Second Vatican Council, Declaration concerning the Relationship of the Catholic Church to Non-Christian Religions, Chap. 4: "Since the common spiritual heritage of Christians and Jews is so rich . . . !"

21. See Ephesians 4:15–16.

22. Second Vatican Council, (same source as for footnote 20): "In its deliberation on the Mystery of the Church, the Holy Synod recalls the bond by which the people of the New Testament is connected spiritually with Abraham stock."

XIX

Reflections on Jerusalem: A Philosopher's View

NATHAN ROTENSTREICH

The fact that this presentation begins with some autobiographical notes is not meant to give to the presentation as such an autobiographical character. On the contrary, it is the very aim of this presentation to show that the biographical and the personal aspect is interwoven with broad historical and spiritual dimensions. The autobiographical preface is but an indication and, to put it into present-day parlance, existential realization of certain rather broad and deep facets of the contemporary situation of Jerusalem. The biography is shaped by history and not the other way round.

I

When I first came to Jerusalem as an undergraduate in 1932, Jerusalem was a united city. This meant for me to go and to visit the Old City on the first Saturday after my arrival in the city. One knew, somehow, from one's readings, historical and even journalistic, not only the character and atmosphere of the city, but also its streets, their names and their squares. Even when one lived outside the Old City, as many of us did, there was a peculiar relationship between the growth of the city and its expansion and the hard core of the Old City. One may wonder whether a city grows in general like a biological organism, that is to say, whether the new sections become totally independent and self-sufficient. But in this particular case the awareness of continuity from the old to the new prevailed not only geographically and physically but, what is by far more important, because of the continuous interpretation of the new as what is known in the Zionist literature as "Alt-Neu" (old-new). This interpretation gave to one's personal and communal relations to the Old City a character of both attachment and proximity.

My daily route took me to Mt. Scopus, to the site of the Hebrew University—a distance of a few miles from the western part of Jerusalem, to our then place of learning. You just could not help seeing the scenery in its topographical, geographical, and historical composition. These are images one absorbs, and they are never erased from one's soul even when they do not find their expression, let alone turn into operations of mastering, taking hold of, etc.

But even then there were many barriers. What used to be called "riots" or in the Hebrew expression "meora'ot" (events)—these amounted to acts of violence of the Arab population, motivated by national or nationalistic feelings against the Jews and their aspirations— these events actually prevented for years an easy access from one part of the city to the other. And, as it is usual, people adjusted themselves to that situation, though the situation as such changed from time to time. During World War II, these small events became overshadowed by the larger "events," and again the access to the Old City and the intercommunication between the various parts of the city became reasonably smooth.

With the resolution of the United Nations on the partition of Palestine the situation changed fundamentally, and there is no need to elaborate this. To keep it still within the existential boundaries, one can just sum up by saying that there have been sieges within sieges: the Old City has been besieged by the local Arab population and by the Arab Legion, helped, visibly or not, by the British Army. The New City has been besieged and cut off from the western areas of Palestine, from the seashore and the centers of new settlement. There was no contact with east or west, west meaning the parts of Palestine allocated for the to-be-established Jewish State, and East meaning the part allocated to the to-be-established Arab State. The experience of being besieged had different layers: it had a very personal layer in terms of one's day-to-day civic duties, care for one's children, etc; it had a political stratum. How could "the World," as it is called, let the Holy City be besieged and let what in the view of many is the Center of the World become a God-forsaken corner struggling for its very survival? To be sure, this is not only a political layer; it is an experience which is, by its very nature, imbued with historical and spiritual associations which again cannot be forgotten, even when they are not made explicit.

II

When the siege came to an end, and it came to an end only because Jews fought for this, all of us faced the question: how are we going to shape the future? Here again, my own experience and involvement indicates something which is not personal but structural and historical. The Hebrew University had been cut off from its original site on Scopus, in spite of the Armistice Agreement, its letter and spirit. We could decide to give a permanent expression as it were to this trauma by establishing ourselves for continuity in temporary dwellings and thus visibly maintain evidence that we want to go back and shall not do anything which will prevent the return to Mt. Scopus. But this did not happen. The Hebrew University established a new campus, without a serious library, since the National and University Library and its treasures remained on Mt. Scopus. The attachment to Jerusalem as a whole, to the Old City and to Mt. Scopus did not prevent any of us from becoming future-minded, which means in this context practically to adjust ourselves to reality and to live within the boundaries prescribed by reality, and every prescription has its prohibitions as the other side of the same coin. In this particular case the prohibition had a very visible expression because this time the wall divided the city. It was not only the threat of violence which prevented the access from the west to the east, but the wall, guarded by armed forces. The adjustment meant that within the reasonable horizon of time there would be no change in that situation. And this fact is established even by not very friendly writers who admit that on June 5, 1967, the late Prime Minister of Israel, Levi Eshkol, sent a message to King Hussein suggesting not to attack Jerusalem. That message meant, not only strategically but humanly, the willingness to continue with the adjustment.

III

But things developed differently. It would be presumptuous to say, as Kant has it in his short treatise on "Eternal Peace," that the outcome of a conflict decides on which side right is. But one can say that the outcome of a conflict decides whose devotion was deeper, who was willing to invest attachment, to express one's willingness to sacrifice for attaining a result, etc. In human terms devotion is a value. Devotion can have, of course, different characters or avenues: one can be devoted to God and expect no results from that devotion. Sometimes the absence of expectation is even viewed as a criterion of the depth and strength of that devotion. Love too contains an aspect of devotion. Here there is an expectation in terms of reciprocity, in terms of closeness, and closeness is by its very definition mutual or reciprocal. One could not say that reciprocity is the result of devotion or love, but one could say that reciprocity is expected in love and for love.

But devotion in the social and historical domain is naturally directed toward results or achievements, since the historical and social domains are characterized by achievements and failures, but just the same by results. And unfortunately failures are results, too. Even when a failure occurs, one has to ask whether the failure occurred in spite of the devotion or whether it is the result of a lack of devotion. In the case of conquering Jerusalem, with all due reservations in terms of the rights of the conflicting parties, one has to say—one is bound to say—that it is devotion which achieved the result. Devotion might be there, and precisely the case of Jerusalem is sufficient evidence for this complexity of human actions, even when the vision is not entertained, at least on a day-to-day level. There are many expressions of devotion, not only as they take shape in the overall result. There is devotion exemplified in the fact that if you fight for conquering the Old City you lose lives for the sake of preservation of the character of the city and of the holy places. And some of the students of the Hebrew University—to mention only those who behaved like their peers—fell in action not for the sake of the simple military achievement—which could be safeguarded without the sacrifice of their lives, but precisely for the preservation of the character of the City. Who on earth, who looks on human affairs from the human and humane point of view can be blind to these facets of action and their result?

IV

One cannot help but deal, even briefly, with one aspect of the claims to Jerusalem, precisely when one takes the view that the three monotheistic or biblical religions absorbed into their tradition an attachment to Jerusalem. But each of these three religions gave to that attachment its particular interpretation, according to the very character of the basic religious notions and their expression in the continuous traditions. Judaism, for good or for ill, is characterized by a unique combination between the aspect of peoplehood and the aspect of teaching. One can, philosophically or theologically, criticize this duality or disparity—but this is not our concern here. Precisely when one takes the view that Jerusalem is important or holy to the three religions, one acknowledges that these religions are their own interpreters, and that their respective rights and claims are related to that interpretation of theirs. But since Judaism presents this unique combination between peoplehood and teaching, Jerusalem for Judaism and the Jews is not only of a symbolic importance; it does not only embody a place where basic occurrences took place, but also the continuity of the aspirations of the people. And peoples do create their institutions and do not live only in their stream of consciousness as it were; one of the institutions peoples create is the institution of statehood. Jerusalem has for Judaism a political meaning because it has that meaning for the Jews, and one cannot acknowledge a tradition without acknowledging that fact, be it unique or perhaps even peculiar.

V

This means, of course, that compromises are essential because they are part and parcel of the mutual adjustment between living human beings, be they individuals or collective entities. But compromises are naturally based on priorities. About priorities we sometimes decide willfully, but sometimes they are prescribed or even imposed. Weighing the priorities, everybody cannot be oblivious—everybody means those who are motivated by a reasonable amount of good will and historical awareness and understanding—of the devotion invested, of the singular attachment of Judaism and Jews to Jerusalem, and last but not least of the fact that practically, and perhaps paradoxically, only after the Six Day War Jerusalem became a united and unified city, not only officially and publicly but in its day-to-day life. Clearly, developments of this sort never reach a point of saturation. They never even reach a peak. The question is: where is the trend going? And on this there can be but one answer: to unification.

Any legal adjustment or any legal and symbolic expression has to take into account the human meanings which are interwoven in that texture of life where reality and symbols sometimes coincide and sometimes do not. Jerusalem is one of the places in the world where the symbol is called to guide reality and to lift reality up to its own level. The danger could be that Jerusalem will be only a symbol; to make reality coincide with the symbol calls for forces of reality motivated by the symbolic import, but trying to take a quotidian human shape. Here we come back to devotion, its price and reward.

XX

Jerusalem the Free

JOHN M. OESTERREICHER

An Open Letter to His Excellency,
the Ambassador of the Hashemite
Kingdom of Jordan

January, 1972

DEAR MR. AMBASSADOR:

Several weeks ago, two friends of mine received from you a recorded message of His Majesty, King Hussein of Jordan, entitled "Jerusalem in Captivity." I understand that you sent the same record to members of Congress and "other leaders of public opinion." Though I was not so honored, I assume that your personal request "to listen . . . carefully" was also addressed to me. From the moment I heard the King's voice, I lent him a willing ear. Yet, while I listened with an open mind, I felt more and more embarrassed, I felt I was eavesdropping on a soliloquy.

THE KING AND THE KORAN

Still, King Hussein is deadly serious: He wishes to win Christians to his side. I will not dispute his right to seek allies in his battle for regaining the power and reputation he has lost in the last four years but I question the means he employs. He tells his hearers that to Muslims, "both Christians and Jews are People of the Book." This is indeed Islam's stance. Yet, why does the King hide from us less friendly sayings of the Koran? There, Jews are seen as cursed, Christians as hate-ridden: Allah Himself is said to have stirred hostility and strife among various Christian communities, as a punishment for their refusal to accept the Prophet's message (V, 15). With the exception of a few, Jews are deceitful (V, 14). Worse than that, the Jews of Eilath, the Koran tells, not only broke the laws of the Sabbath but scornfully persisted in their wrongdoing; hence they were severed from society and "changed into detested apes" (VII, 167). The Koran calls both Christians and Jews "infidels." Time and again, Allah's true followers are warned against making friends with them

(V, 52). They are even bidden: "Believers, wage war against the infidels who dwell around you. Deal severely with them" (IX, 123). Please, do not think that I wish to cast aspersions on Islam's sacred book; I am sure there are mitigating circumstances for these harsh sayings. It is not the sayings themselves that gall me; what I object to are King Hussein's efforts at obscuring the Koran's fierceness toward non-Muslims.

Again, I am disturbed at King Hussein's attempt to win the support of Christians by telling them that "to us [Muslims] Jesus Christ was more than a prophet." I cannot claim any special Islamic scholarship, Mr. Ambassador, but I can read. And this is what Allah is made to say in the Koran: "Jesus is nothing but a servant on whom I bestowed favor" (XLIII, 60). In fact, the Jesus of the Koran is little more than the forerunner of Muhammad: "I am . . . bringing the good tidings of an apostle who is to come after me, and whose name shall be Ahmed" (LXI, 7).

Stranger still is the way the Koran explains away the death of Jesus. The Koran considers it a monstrous falsehood to maintain that Jesus was crucified; it asserts that a double of his was slain instead. This is not said to protect Jews against the horrible accusation of collective guilt (IV: 159). The reason for this remarkable twisting of facts is Islam's firm opposition to any doctrine of redemption. However much Judaism and Christianity differ in their interpretation of redemptive events, they are one in their belief that God is not only the Maker of the universe and its Lord but also its Redeemer.

THE KING'S CLAIM

I have no intention of entering into a religious controversy or reviving the charges and countercharges of the past. Yet, I cannot sink into silence when King Hussein woos Christians with alluring words that cannot stand careful examination. Unfortunately, the king does not stop at his selective use of the Koran, he also writes "optative" history. His recorded message proclaims: "My people and I regard ourselves as the guardians and custodians of Jerusalem on behalf of the entire Muslim world as well as on behalf of the Christian and Muslim population of the city and all Palestine." I have no doubt that this self-portrait is part of the king's dreams; mighty though their magic may be, they cannot be admitted as evidence. Who gave him the mandate he speaks of? When and how did he receive it?

The king seems to have forgotten that only a few years ago his country was largely barren land, physically and morally unable to make any claim whatever. In fact, it did not become a separate entity till the British government in 1922 carved it out of Palestine—which the League of Nations had entrusted to it, as a Mandate for the express purpose of carrying out the Balfour Declaration—severed it from the area meant to become the Jewish national home, and put Emir Abdullah in charge, one of the desert chieftains who during World War I fought, not oversuccessfully, the Ottoman army. Thus "Trans-Jordan" came into being.

During the 1948–1949 Arab-Israeli War, the country's British-trained "Jordan Legion" occupied the Old City of Jerusalem and the West Bank of the Jordan River. By "legislative" fiat, the wasteland and the fertile grounds were united; in other words, Transjordan annexed the occupied territory, and the "Hashemite Kingdom of Jordan" was born. With Great Britain and Pakistan as conspicuous exceptions, the community of nations refused to accept the unilateral act of Transjordan—no plebiscite had ever been held to allow the native population to determine their own destiny. Much more disastrous for the king's claim is the fact that the "Arab League" vehemently protested against the annexation, that its members even considered Jordan's expulsion from their ranks. That the threat was not carried out, Jordan owes to the intervention of Iraq, today its most bitter foe. These facts certainly do not establish a claim to guard the Holy City, in the name of the Islamic world or of any other group.

THE TEST OF GUARDIANSHIP

The events leading to, and following on, the creation of the State of Jordan, Mr. Ambassador, compel me to consider King Hussein's claim to be the appointed guardian of Old Jerusalem and its Holy Places illegitimate and thus unacceptable. Would that the king and his people had, at least, lived up to the responsibility that he wrongly maintains is theirs. The execution of this duty speaks an unmistakable language. During Jordanian rule, 34 out of the Old City's 35 synagogues were dynamited. Some were turned into stables, others into chicken coops. There seemed to be no limit to the work of desecration. Many thousand tombstones were taken from the ancient cemetery on the Mount of Olives to serve as building material or paving stones. A few were even used to surface the footpath leading to a latrine in a Jordanian army camp. With the financial assistance of Pan American Airlines, Jordan built the Hotel Intercontinental—a plush hotel on the hill of Jesus' agony! Obviously a road was needed, worthy of the triumphant showpiece. Of all the possible routes, the one chosen cut through hundreds of Jewish graves: They were torn open and the bones scattered. An Israeli collection of photographs of the mutilated graveyard bears this lament: "Because of this is our heart made sick; for these things our eyes are dimmed" (Lam. 5:17).

While Jordan controlled East Jerusalem and the West Bank, Jews were not permitted to approach, much less to pray at, the Western Wall of the Temple Court, Rachel's Tomb, or the Cave of Machpelah, the burial place of the Patriarchs near Hebron. This prohibition not only violated the basic right of any man to worship according to his conscience but also the obligations Trans-Jordan had taken upon herself when she signed the Armistice Agreement in 1949. In Article 8, Paragraph 2, the Jordanian authorities pledged themselves, among other things, to the "free access to the holy places . . . and the use of the cemetery on the Mount of Olives." In the light of the desecrations I have just described, the king's assurance: "It is thanks to us, for example, that the Wailing Wall of the Jews was preserved throughout the centuries of Muslim rule" appears to be highly ironic, not to say insulting. His "for example" is particularly graceless, since the Wall is the only example of an exclusively Jewish site of worship that was left intact. I am sure, Mr. Ambassador, that King Hussein did not wish to offend but it is exactly this insensitivity that compels me to write.

THE KING, CHAMPION OF CHRISTIAN CONCERNS

Space does not allow me to discuss in detail the various curtailments of Christian activities by Jordan. To mention only a few, petty restrictions were imposed on pilgrims; institutions were prohibited from acquiring new property; Christian schools were subjected to control of the education they offered. Nor can I do more than mention the crudity with which Jordan, together with Saudi Arabia, for many long years barred their fellow-Muslims from making their traditional pilgrimages to Jerusalem, Medina, and Mecca. But I must deal with the king's notion that destiny has forced the guardianship of the Holy City upon him. "For centuries our custodianship has been accepted by the Christian Churches. It was to Arab families of Jerusalem, for example, that the keys of the Holy Sepulchre were and still are entrusted. This is our responsibility, and we will not surrender it." As so often in his brief speech, the king writes his own history, one based not on facts but on wishful thinking.

In 636, Arab armies conquered Jerusalem for the first time. For a period, Christians in the Holy Land remained undisturbed. But like the rest of the non-Muslim population, they were treated as second-class citizens. They were forbidden to build new churches or display the cross; the supreme rule that governed their lives was not to offend Muslim susceptibilities. No Christian was allowed to marry a Muslim, ride on horseback, or carry a sword. Public prayer was restricted. No tapers could be kindled or church bells rung.

After the Arabs had ruled the Holy Land for a little more than 300 years, trouble broke out among their own ranks. Turkish generals rebelled against their Arab lords. In the struggles that followed, two churches were destroyed while the Church of the Holy Sepulchre was severely damaged. In the 960s, the Byzantine emperor Focca defeated the Arabs in battle; in retaliation, Muslim assassins slew the Patriarch John VII in 966, thereby profaning the Church of the Holy Sepulchre once again. These few sketches do not quite square with King Hussein's boast: "The Arabs have for centuries been worthy custodians of the whole city. It was they who built and preserved . . . the Holy Sepulchre. . . ."

King Hussein seems to believe—I have no doubt, honestly—that throughout the centuries the Christian Churches accepted Muslim custodianship. The big question is how the verb "accepted" is understood. If it means "tolerated," the king is right; if its connotation is "favored," he is wrong. His story about the key to the Church of the Holy Sepulchre is typical of his rewriting of history. When one listens to the king, one gets the impression that Christians eagerly committed the key to two Arab families. In reality, Christian communities constantly quarreled among each other about the time and duration of their respective services. Toward the end of the thirteenth century, the Saracen rulers of the time, tired of the persistent disputes, decided to put an end to them. They turned the key over to the Judeh family and charged the Insaibe family with opening and closing the door. The Muslim doorkeepers, occupying a divan in the vestibule of the church, are reimbursed for their "work." Till 1831, they even exacted entrance fees from pilgrims. When I reflect on these, not exactly uplifting, realities I find the king's pathos: "This is our responsibility, and we will never surrender it," I am sorry, Mr. Ambassador, a bit ludicrous.

THE KING IN SEARCH OF GLORY

Earlier in this letter, I spoke of the king's desire to regain the annexed territories he had lost during the Six Day War. Now I wonder whether his motives are not much more psychological than political. I hope you will not take it amiss if I suggest that he wishes not only to secure again his hold on the Old City but, most of all, restore to his land a significance that goes far beyond its size or history. Created on a drawing board, the former Transjordan was the least important of Arab states: It could neither point to a great past nor boast of momentous achievements. Yet, if King Hussein could prove his claim to a providential mission, if he could once more pose as the protector of Muslim, Jewish, and Christian sacred sites, his country would assume the stature of a spiritual giant.

Strong though this search for meaning and status may be, the king must at the same time realize that his title to the "possession" of the Old City and to his "mission" is vulnerable, indeed untenable. How else can we explain his use of "Jordanians," "Arabs," and "Muslims" as if these were interchangeable designations?

The king knows, of course, that Arab rule over the Holy Land after its conquest in 636 lasted only till 1099. The Mamelukes (1291–1517) who followed the Crusaders in holding sway over Palestine, but also over Syria and Egypt, were certainly not of Arabian stock, even though they firmly established the Islamic hold over the Middle East. The Turks who succeeded them (1517–1917) were Muslims, too. They appeared on the scene of history at the beginning of the thirteenth century, as a band of tribesmen whom the Mongols had driven from their native land in central Asia. In all likelihood, they were not mere victims of a Mongolian advance but rather "Ghazis," fighters for the faith, or, as the *Encyclopedia Britannica* puts it, "men sworn to wage ceaseless war on the infidel, through motives of religious zeal or greed for loot or both" (XXII, 590).

The warlike spirit of the Turks did not stop at the attempt of conquering Christian countries, the then Syria and Egypt were conquered as well and incorporated into the Ottoman Empire. Thus Arabs became the subjects of their fellow-Muslims, the Turks, exposed almost as much as the non-Muslim population to the harsh methods of Ottoman tax-collectors. The several periods of Muslim domination in no way strengthen the king's case; they offer the most tenuous argument, the most fragile basis for the king's alleged tenure as Jerusalem's warden of peace. The switch from "the Arabs" to "us Muslims" and then to "my people and I" is but a device to deaden our judgment.

THE ART OF PREVARICATION

Mr. Ambassador, since King Hussein has taken his case to the American public, I, too, think it my obligation to state publicly that I find his brief unconvincing. Far from having shaken my trust in Israel, it has confirmed my opposition to a divided Jerusalem. King Hussein begins his appeal to the sentiments of the Christians in the United States by accusing Israel of having annexed "Jerusalem against the repeated resolutions of the United Nations." This is a strange argument on the king's part. Does he rely on the short memory of his listeners? Does he think that most of them will no longer remember how his grandfather annexed the West Bank and the Old City, even though the Armistice Agreement was then in force? Even Great Britain, Transjordan's fairy godmother, who gave her blessing to the union of the West Bank with Transjordan, withheld her approval from the inclusion of Old Jerusalem.

King Hussein regards the present status of Jerusalem with gloom. I do not. The King is, no doubt, entitled to the view that the unification of Jerusalem is a near disaster. Yet it ill becomes a king to decry, and blame others for, a situation that he brought upon himself. Most listeners to the king's message are, I fear, unaware of Prime Minister Eshkol's efforts to keep Jordan out of the Six Day War. The late prime minister assured the king of Israel's peaceful intentions and warned him against making common cause with President Nasser. King Hussein brushed the warning aside, waged war on Israel, and lost. Instead of taking, with nobility and moral courage, the responsibility for having fired the first shells and bullets, he puts the blame on Israel. In his book *My War With Israel*, however, he admits that President Nasser did not hold him to their mutual "defense agreement": "Nasser never called on us. It was we who called on him."

This seems a rare admission, for the beginning of the Six Day War is otherwise covered by a web of lies. In the spring of 1967, Egypt had closed all international waterways to Israel, in itself an act of war. Yet, a broadcast from Cairo's radio, "Voice of the Arabs," on May 23, made it appear that Arab integrity was being violated: "The Gulf of Aqaba is Arab. To defend its Arab character is the responsibility of Egypt, Saudi Arabia, the Jordanian Kingdom, and all Arab states. We are determined to defend it—by destructive weapons—against any Israeli attempt or even an American attempt in favor of Israel which seeks to use the gulf and pollute [*sic!*] its Arab waters. We have prepared the Gulf of Aqaba to be a graveyard for Israel and a graveyard, too, for American gangsterism against peoples. We challenge you, Israel. No, . . . we challenge you, gangsters of the Bay of Pigs. . . ." In this vein the broadcast continued, but after the Sinai desert had become the graveyard of the "invincible" Egyptian army, Nasser posed as an innocent victim of Israeli aggression.

Again, Nasser was only too eager to "believe" in a Syrian alarm and Russian information that Israel was massing troops at the Syrian border. When one day, in the latter part of May, the Soviet Ambassador to Israel called on Prime Minister Eshkol, in the dead of night, to deliver Moscow's protest, the prime minister offered to take him instantly to the Galilean border so that he could see for himself how untrue the charge was. The Soviet Ambassador, however, declined. I wish I could say that deceit stopped right then and there. But the game was carried to its bitter end.

When the Israeli High Command realized that Egypt was getting ready for total war, it knew that to save Israel it had to anticipate the Egyptian threat. It went all out to annihilate Egypt's fighting power. On June 5, the first day of the war, in a well-timed attack, Israel's air force hit Egypt's 11 key bases, pounding them steadily for 80 minutes and destroying over 400 planes on the ground. Though the Egyptian authorities were aware of this mortal blow, they permitted Radio Cairo to continue its extravaganzas—if I may use this theatrical term, this expression of gaiety, for a most tragic propaganda. The "Voice of the Arabs" encouraged the soldiers in the field with wild fantasies of victory and illusions of omnipotence: "Welcome to the *jihad*, 'the holy war,' waged to recover Palestine. Your eagles, my brother soldiers, shot down 23 aircraft. Brothers, haul down the flag of Israel in Tel Aviv."

The climax of deception came on June 6. Unable to hide the defeat suffered the day before and unwilling to credit Israel with its superior strategy, President Nasser charged that United States and British planes had entered the war on Israel's side—a charge which the two powers promptly denied. Unfortunately, Mr. Ambassador, your king helped fabricate this story. On June 8, the Israeli government released tapes of an intercepted conversation between President Nasser and King Hussein, in which the two rulers agreed to denounce the United States and Great Britain as fighting side by side with the Israeli air force. If press reports are correct, the king later, when addressing the National Press Club, regretted his complicity in circulating the allegation.

THE KING AND HUMAN RIGHTS

To be candid, Mr. Ambassador, as I look at King Hussein's accusations, I am startled by their vagueness. The King charges that "the rights of [Old Jerusalem's] Arab population" are infringed upon. Which rights? One of the first acts of the municipal government of the united city was to have the Arab inhabitants of East Jerusalem share in the water supply of West Jerusalem. The Jordanian administration had neglected to install a modern system of piped water. All public facilities, like sanitation, public health, and electricity, serve Arabs as much as Jews. Histadrut, the Israeli Federation of Labor, sees to it that all Arab workers get a living wage, in fact, the same pay as Jews. Thousands, incidentally, have become members of the Federation. Jews and Arabs have embarked on joint commercial and industrial projects; they have banded together in clubs devoted to sports or cultural pursuits. Does this really give the impression that Jerusalem today is a city in which the rights of men are trampled on?

I think the king was ill-advised to speak of the violation of rights. Does he not remember the uprisings against his rule? On April 23, 1963, for instance, several demonstrations in favor of a Jordanian-Arab republic took place, which the Jordanian army suppressed ruthlessly. In Jerusalem alone, 11 demonstrators were killed and 150 wounded, 17 girl students among them. Or take the way Jordan ushered in its occupation of the Old City. In the words of an English writer, C. Witton-Davies: "It was the Arab Legion that advanced on [it]. . . . What followed? The senseless and shocking destruction of Jewish houses that could have been used temporarily for Arab refugees, and the obscene desecration of Jewish synagogues . . . simply because they were Jewish" (*The Tablet*, London, June 12, 1971).

How does King Hussein dare blame the Israeli authorities for trying to reconstruct the Jewish Quarter of the Old City in which at the turn of the century 15,000 Jews lived? The ruins created by the Legion and the slums that sprang up around them had to be cleared. Incidentally, why should the Jerusalem municipality not undertake slum clearance? It is, after all, one of the major tasks of every decent city government. Thus housing is now being provided for Arabs and Jews whose homes are dilapidated. There are at least 5,000 Arab and 4,000 Jewish families who live in substandard dwellings. Jerusalem's Arabs do not seem to be as upset as the king by Israel's humane policy. Ten thousand of them, men and women, defied the threats of terrorists and voted in the municipal election. By the way, in the last election under Jordanian rule, only 3,500 went to the polls. In the eyes of all political analysts a decisive majority gave their vote to the Jewish mayor, Teddy Kollek.

Again, King Hussein complains that "the religious sensibilities of over 700,000,000 Muslims" are violated. Why? Because two shrines dear to Islam are on Jewish territory, in the land of the "infidel"? If this is indeed the king's feeling, he unwittingly undermines his own position. How can he, with an attitude like this, demand a return of the Old City to Jordan? Jews and Christians have their sensibilities, too. What if they followed the example of Muslims and considered offensive the location of their holy sites on "alien" territory? Perish the thought! For Catholics, it would mean a return to the Crusaders' mentality, a mentality contrary to the gospel and the spirit of the second Vatican Council.

With his preference for imprecise statement, King Hussein speaks of "thousands of acres of land belonging to Arab families and religious foundations [having] been expropriated." He gives no names, no exact figures, no location, nor does he discuss the question of compensation. May I ask you, Mr. Ambassador, to compare the obscure language of the king with the plain style of the Israeli government? A decision of that government, dated August 20, 1970, declares that the minister of finance has been empowered to expropriate "plots of land in the Jerusalem district of a total area of some 3,000 acres. They are located"—I am quoting verbatim—"in the Jerusalem commercial center, north northwest, southwest, and southeast Jerusalem, the proposed national park at Shama'a and Ramat Rachel." The government decree gives as its purpose "to permit the competent authorities to develop the Jerusalem district systematically and progressively. The development is designed to serve the overall population of the city—Arabs and Jews alike."

The decision goes on to promise "generous compensation," to explain the needs as clearly as possible, and to describe the plots in great detail. Most of the plots are unsettled and untilled wasteland. Of the houses in question, about 20 belong to Arabs, while the homes of 350 Jewish families are involved. Neither agricultural land nor land belonging to the Muslim religious endowment (*Waqf*) are included in this plan; similarly, holy places and public property have not been part of this program. Whom am I to believe, Mr. Ambassador, your king with his obstructionist attitude or the Israeli government with its creative outlook and its desire to heal? Have you ever seen King Hussein or his government propose any project that would help Jews and Arab alike? I am sure you have not, you could not have witnessed such care, for Jordan has, long ago, been made *Judenrein*.

Christians did not fare well either. According to a statement by Israel's Foreign Minister Abba Eban in the Israel Parliament, on June 30, 1971, Jerusalem harbored 25,000 Christians in 1948, that is, prior to the Arab-Jewish war. During the Jordanian occupation, the number of Christians dropped to 10,800. Since 1967, their numbers have risen: In 1970, there were 11,500 Christians in the Holy City. Some enemies of Israel like to tell that the government seeks to strangle Christian life. The opposite is true. Not only are the Christian shrines open to all who wish to pray there, the number of pilgrims is increasing from year to year.

Contrary to the assertions of hate peddlers, the Government of Israel and the municipality of Jerusalem have not hindered but helped the work of many Christian institutions. All those whose buildings were damaged by the war between Jordan and Israel—even those fired upon by the Jordanian army—17 in all, were compensated. Furthermore, many religious institutions have received financial aid. To speak only of the Christian ones, the Armenian and Greek Orthodox Patriarchates, Franciscan Friars and Sisters, the Sisters of Sion, for their convents in Jerusalem ("Ecce Homo") and Ein Karem, the Catholic Church and Community Center at Beit Hanina, St. Peter in Gallicantu, the Lutheran Church at Beit Jalla, the American Institute for Holy Land Studies, and others have enjoyed official support.

Mr. Ambassador, when I keep in mind all the facts mentioned in this letter, I cannot but agree with those evangelical Church leaders who, on June 17, 1971, issued a statement in support of unified Jerusalem as the capital of Israel. They declared themselves "committed to the integrity of Jerusalem, the Holy City, the birthplace of our faith"; they thanked the State of Israel for the "scrupulous care" of "Christian places and people." "Since the Six Day War," they continued, "all people are free to worship in the place of their choice, unlike the situation that pertained during the period from 1948 to 1967." I can testify to the truth of this statement from personal experience and join the signers of this declaration in their demand: "The unity of Jerusalem must be preserved at all costs."

JERUSALEM, A JEWISH CITY

King Hussein has asked me, together with other believers in God, to raise my voice "to save our common heritage." I am happy to raise my voice but not to clamor for the restoration of Jordanian rule over the Old City. The Jerusalem of today is not a city "in captivity," as the king likes to think. It is free, as it has never been before. Whoever has walked its streets during these last years, must have felt as I did that he was privileged to breathe the air of holiness, of God's special presence. He must have perceived that it was a city in search of peace, not one given to strife and hate. Of course, the city has problems; among others, it has to protect itself against the terrorists who have been threatening the lives of its citizens. I watched armed guards near the Western Wall search the briefcases, handbags, and bundles of those who wished to enter the area. I was moved by the delicate courtesy with which they handled their difficult task. I could not help feeling that the city was in *good* hands.

No, I cannot agree with the king that Jordan or the Arab world is the City's "rightful owner." Biblically speaking, Jerusalem is God's city, as the land is God's land. Men are but tenants. The glory of the Israelis is to have been good stewards, to have been worthy of His trust. Though the Holy City is indeed "the symbol of God's universal rule," it is a Jewish city. It was a Jewish singer, not a Muslim or Christian, who prayed:

> If I forget you, Jerusalem,
>   may my right hand lose its grip.
>   (Ps. 137:5)

Again, not Muslim or Christian but Jewish pilgrims pleaded:

> Pray for the peace of Jerusalem!
>   May your friends be secure!
> Salvation be within your walls,
>   And peace within your towers.
>   (Ps. 122:6,7)

Finally, for generations, Jews, not Muslims or Christians, kept hope alive:

> Next year in Jerusalem!
> (Passover Haggadah)

Today, these words are no longer a devout wish; the people whom God made His own, out of sheer love, has gathered in Zion; the divided city is one again! And "what God has joined together, man must not separate" (Matt. 19:6). Because this is my conviction, I must decline the king's offer to assist him in his struggle for the return to Jerusalem, I must stand by the people of Israel, so that it may live within secure boundaries, and by the men, women, and children of Jerusalem, Jews as well as Arabs, so that they may continue to dwell in peace and harmony. I must take this stand; it is not blind impulse but my conscience that makes me echo the passion of the prophet:

> For Zion's sake I will not be silent,
>   for Jerusalem's sake I will not be quiet,
> Until her right shines forth like sunrise
>   and her deliverance like a blazing torch . . .
>
> You shall be a glorious crown in the hand of the Lord,
>   a royal diadem held by your God.
>   (Isa. 62:1,3)

May I, despite our disagreements, ask that you kindly convey to King Hussein my thanks for his beautiful parting words in Arabic? May I answer with the Hebrew greeting: *Shalom u'berakhah!* God's peace, salvation, and blessing be with us all!

Yours devotedly,
John M. Oesterreicher

IV

APPENDICES

1. U.N. List and Map of Holy Places

Christian

1. Basilica of the Holy Sepulchre*
2. Bethany
3. Cenacle
4. Church of St. Anne
5. Church of St. James the Great
6. Church of St. Mark
7. Deir al Sultan*
8. Tomb of the Virgin* and Gardens of Gethsemane
9. House of Caiphas and Prison of Christ
10. Sanctuary of the Ascension* and Mount of Olives
11. Pool of Bethesda
12. Ain Karim**
13. Basilica of the Nativity, Bethlehem* **
14. Milk Grotto, Bethlehem* **
15. Shepherds Field, Bethlehem* **
I to IX inclusive.
Stations of the Cross

Muslim

16. Tomb of Lazarus
17. El Burak esh Sharif
18. Haram esh Sharif (Mosque of Omar & Mosque of Aksa (al-Aqsa)
19. Mosque of the Ascension
20. Tomb of David (Nebi Daoud)

Jewish

21. Tomb of Absalom
22. Ancient and Modern Synagogues
23. Bath of Rabbi Ishmael
24. Brook Siloam
25. Cemetery on Mount of Olives
26. Tomb of David
27. Tomb of Simon the Just
28. Tomb of Zachariah and other tombs in Kidron Valley
29. Wailing Wall*
30. Rachel's tomb* **

*Holy Place to which the Status Quo applies.
**Holy Places in international areas of Jerusalem.

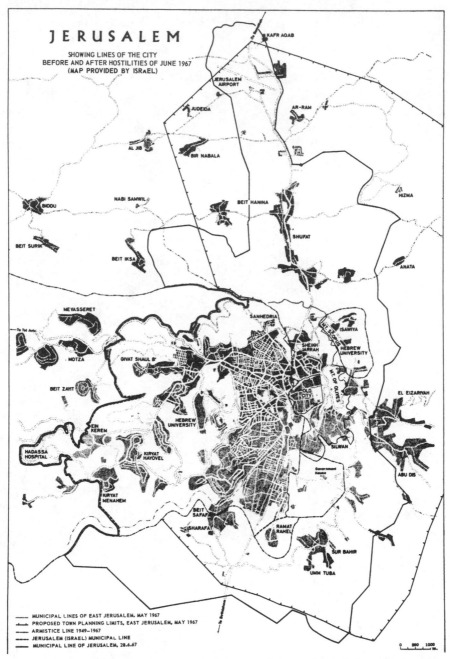

JERUSALEM

SHOWING LINES OF THE CITY
BEFORE AND AFTER HOSTILITIES OF JUNE 1967
(MAP PROVIDED BY ISRAEL)

.... MUNICIPAL LINES OF EAST JERUSALEM, MAY 1967
⊥⊥⊥⊥ PROPOSED TOWN PLANNING LIMITS, EAST JERUSALEM, MAY 1967
----- ARMISTICE LINE 1949–1967
--··-- JERUSALEM (ISRAEL) MUNICIPAL LINE
▬▬▬ MUNICIPAL LINE OF JERUSALEM, 28.6.67

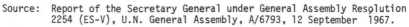

Source: Report of the Secretary General under General Assembly Resolution
          2254 (ES-V), U.N. General Assembly, A/6793, 12 September 1967.

3. PROTECTION OF HOLY PLACES LAW, 1967

1. The Holy Places shall be protected from desecration and any other violation and from anything likely to violate the freedom of access of the members of the various religions to those places.

2. (a) Whoever desecrates or otherwise violates a Holy Place shall be liable to imprisonment for a term of seven years.

(b) Whoever does anything that is likely to violate the freedom of access of the members of the various religions to the places sacred to them or their feelings with regard to those places shall be liable to imprisonment for a term of five years.

3. This law shall add to and not derogate from any other law.

4. The Minister of Religious Affairs is charged with the implementation of this law and he may, after consultation with or upon the proposal of representatives of the religions concerned, and with the consent of the Minister of Justice, make regulations as to any matter relating to such implementation.

5. This law shall come into force on the date of its adoption by the Knesset.

Levi Eshkol   *Zerah Warhaftig*
Prime Minister   Minister of Religious Affairs
Shneor Zalman Shazar
President
Passed by the Israel Parliament (Knesset) June 22, 1967

4. POPULATION AND HOUSING CENSUS, 1967[1]

East Jerusalem
Size and Geographic Distribution of Population[2]

East Jerusalem had a population of 65,857 persons on 27 September 1967. Of these, 23,675 (or 36 per cent) were living within the Old City's walls, 25,039 (or 38 per cent) were living in the northern quarters of the city and 17,143 (or 26 per cent) were living in the southern quarters. Another 20,700 were living in neighboring areas inside the Jordanian municipal boundaries, which included both Silwan and Abu Tur. About 21,500 were living in formerly independent settlements (now inside the municipal boundaries of united Jerusalem).

Over half the population of the Old City (13,538) lived in the Muslim Quarter, and 3,500 Muslims had moved into the Jewish Quarter since the war of 1948. The Armenian Quarter was the least populated of the Old City's four quarters and had a population of only 2,391.

The population density was 988 inhabitants per square kilometer. On the date the census was taken the entire city had a population of 265,000 (making Jerusalem the second largest city in Israel). 25 per cent of the population lived in East Jerusalem. The municipal boundaries covered an area of 104 square kilometers with a population density of 2,548 inhabitants per square kilometer.

Religions

54,081 (or 83 per cent) of the total population of East Jerusalem were Muslims, 10,795 (or 17 per cent) were Christians and 981 belonged to the group called "other religion" and "not known."

The percentage of Christians in East Jerusalem was lower than in Bethlehem, Beit Jala, and Beit Sahur (where they constitute 56 per cent of the total population), and also lower than in Ramallah and Bira (where they constitute 34 per cent of the total population). Nevertheless the percentage of Christians was higher in East Jerusalem than in other urban settlements in Judaea and Samaria[3] and than in these areas in general (by 5 per cent).

The Greek Orthodox community was the largest, numbering 3,984 persons, followed by the Latin church, numbering 3,663. There were 1,173 Greek Catholics. The remaining 1,975 Christians belonged to various sects. Church affiliation was not specified in some cases.

The highest proportion of Muslims—over 95 per cent—lived in the former Jewish Quarter of the Old City, which had been captured by the Muslims after the war of 1948, and in Silwan, Abu Tor, Zur Bahir, and Um Tuba. The proportion was lowest in the Christian and Armenian Quarters of the Old City, where Muslim residents constituted 12 per cent and 37 per cent of the population respectively. A relatively low percentage of Muslims lived in the Old City as a whole (72 per cent) but constituted 76 per cent of the population in the American Colony and Sheikh Jarrah (57 per cent in the western part of the American Colony, 73 per cent in Beit Khanina, and 58 per cent in the [Mt. Scopus] Hebrew University area).

Type of Population

Households were classified into refugee and non-refugee households according to whether the head of the household had been living, prior to 1948, in what became the territory of the State of Israel.[4] Thus there were 9,526 non-refugee households, comprising 48,818 persons, and 2,331 refugee households, comprising 11,567 persons. In 728 households, comprising 3,229 persons, the residence of the head of the household prior to 1948 was not known. Of those households whose status could be ascertained, 80.3 per cent were non-refugee households, comprising 80.8 per cent of the population—about the same percentages as in Judaea and Samaria in general. Again, the proportion of the population belonging to refugee households was the same as in Judaea and Samaria.

The percentage of refugees was higher among Christians (37 per cent) than among Muslims (15.6 per cent), there also being a higher percentage of Christians among refugees (31.9 per cent) than among non-refugees (12.9 per cent). Accordingly, a higher percentage of refugees than the municipal average was found in those sub-quarters where Christians are in the majority—in the Christian and Armenian Quarters of the Old City (31 per cent), in Shu'afat and Beit Khanina (31 per cent), in the American Colony and in Sheikh Jarrah (28 per cent). The percentage of refugees was particularly low in the southern part of the area, which comprises semi-rural districts with a Muslim population.

Fifty-seven out of every hundred refugees aged twenty years and above who had been living, prior to 1948, inside what became the territory of the State of Israel, lived in West Jerusalem.

Sons/daughters living outside the territories administered by Israel

It was found that 27 per cent of all heads of households in East Jerusalem had sons living abroad; 13 per cent had one son and 7 per cent had two sons while 7 per cent had three or more sons living abroad. The families in East Jerusalem reported that they had 6,896 sons living abroad—more than 10 per cent of the population enumerated. This figure does not include whole families who had left the city or individuals who left no parents behind. These data show that there was a considerable tendency to emigrate to the East Bank and to other countries, although this tendency was slightly less in East Jerusalem than in Judaea and Samaria as a whole (where 33 per cent of all the heads of families reported they had sons living abroad). As in Judaea and Samaria, the proportion of heads of families with sons living abroad was slightly higher among the refugees (32 per cent) than among the rest of the population (26 per cent). About 22 per cent of families per each 100 sons abroad had left during the year preceding the census, and most of these had left before the Six Day War: 22 per cent had left in the year preceding the census; 38 per cent had left in the preceding 1–4 years; 20 per cent had left in the preceding 5–9 years, and 20 per cent had left in the preceding 10 years and more. No appreciable difference was found between refugee and non-refugee families in this distribution.

The percentage of sons/daughters living abroad who had left during the year preceding the census was slightly lower (22 per cent) in East Jerusalem than in Judaea and Samaria (26 per cent).

Their distribution by country of residence was found to be as follows: 35 per cent resided in Jordan; 20 per cent resided in Kuwait; 7 per cent resided in Saudi Arabia; 17 per cent resided in other countries of Asia and Africa; 8 per cent resided in Europe, and 13 per cent in the U.S. Thus there were fewer such family members residing in Jordan and Kuwait and more in Europe and America of those who came from East Jerusalem than of those from Judaea and Samaria. There were also fewer refugees who had chosen to reside on the East Bank of the Jordan than non-refugees.

Wages

The average wage per month per employee prior to June, 1967 (in Jordanian Dinars) was as follows:

(In Jordanian Dinars: 1 dinar = U.S. $2.80) (1967)			
	Refugees	*Non-Refugees*	*Total*
All Employees	30.8	25.5	26.8
Males	31.6	25.6	27.0
Females	26.6	24.0	24.9

Housing Conditions

In an average household of 5.1 persons, the average number of rooms was 2.2 so that the mean housing density was 2.4 persons per room. About 40 per cent of all households lived in one room, about 27 per cent in two rooms, about 18 per cent in three rooms and about 15 per cent in four rooms and more. The proportion of households with four rooms and more was higher among refugees than among non-refugees (about 20 per cent as against 13 per cent). (Only 11 per cent of dwellings in West Jerusalem contained four rooms or more in 1966.)

Marked differences were found between refugees and non-refugees, with the refugees enjoying a higher standard of facilities. Thus about 73 per cent of all refugee households had an inside toilet as against 61 per cent of non-refugee households. 78.6 per cent of refugee households had electricity against 66.4 per cent of others. This may largely be due to the fact that most of the non-refugee population is rural.[5]

Thus in the barely urbanized village of Zur Bahir only 19 per cent of households had an inside toilet and a mere 18 per cent had electricity. A high standard of facilities was, on the other hand, found in the distinctly urban quarters—the American Colony, Sheikh Jarrah, Shu'afat, Beit Khanina, and in the Christian and Armenian Quarters of the Old City.

Household Equipment

As in the case of housing facilities it was found, again, that the standard of refugee households was higher than that of non-refugee households:

	Non-Refugees	Refugees
Radio	66.9	75.5
Television	5.2	10.8
Electric refrigerator	19.4	33.9

UNRWA Assistance[6]

About 23 per cent of all households stated that they were registered with UNRWA or were receiving assistance from this agency (comprising about 47 per cent of refugee and 21 per cent of non-refugee households). Of all the households which said they were registered with UNRWA, two-thirds were non-refugee households (comprising 62 per cent of the population registered with UNRWA), and one-third were refugee households (comprising 38 per cent of those registered).[7]

Some 7 per cent reported that they were receiving assistance from relatives abroad (11 per cent of the refugee households). Another 4 per cent stated they were receiving assistance from UNICEF, CARE, or other sources. The average size of households receiving assistance from or registered with UNRWA was 5.3 persons.

5. NOTES AND REFERENCES

1. Source: Central Bureau of Statistics. Jerusalem, Municipality, 1967.

2. Excerpted from the main findings. Some of these findings are based on sample enumeration only (of 50 per cent of the districts counted). The 2,732 inhabitants of the Shu'afat refugee camp situated inside the municipal boundaries were not included in the census.

3. On the West Bank of the Jordan River.

4. UNRWA, too, considers as refugees all members of a household whose head is a refugee. However, while the only criterion of this census was the place of residence in 1948, UNRWA's working definition is more restricted: "a person whose normal residence was Palestine for a minimum of two years immediately preceding the outbreak of the conflict in 1948 and who, as a result of that conflict, lost both his home and his means of livelihood."

5. I.e., their living conditions are rural. Only about 2 per cent of the labor force was employed in agriculture (in 1967).

6. According to the census definition, households receiving both food and services, services but no food, or which were only registered with UNRWA were all regarded as receiving UNRWA assistance.

7. UNRWA statistics do not differentiate between refugees and non-refugees, UNRWA assuming by definition that all persons registered with the agency are refugees.

6. U.N. RESOLUTIONS

RESOLUTION ADOPTED BY THE GENERAL ASSEMBLY
(without reference to a Main Committee[A/L.527/Rev.1])
2253 (ES-V). *Measures taken by Israel to change the
status of the City of Jerusalem*

The General Assembly,
Deeply concerned at the situation prevailing in Jerusalem as a result of the measures taken by Israel to change the status of the City,

1. *Considers* that these measures are invalid;

2. *Calls upon* Israel to rescind all measures already taken and to desist forthwith from taking any action which would alter the status of Jerusalem;

3. *Requests* the Secretary-General to report to the General Assembly and the Security Council on the situation and on the implementation of the present resolution not later than one week from its adoption.

1548th plenary meeting,
4 July 1967.
A/RES/2253 (ES-V)

United Nations General Assembly Fifth Emergency Session Agenda Item 5

RESOLUTION ADOPTED BY THE GENERAL ASSEMBLY
(without reference to a Main Committee [A/L.528/Rev.2])
2254 (ES-V). *Measures taken by Israel to change the status
of the City of Jerusalem*

The General Assembly,
Recalling its resolution 2253 (ES-V) of 4 July 1967
Having Received the report submitted by the Secretary-General,[1]
Taking note with the deepest regret and concern of the non-compliance by Israel with resolution 2253 (ES-V),

1. *Deplores* the failure of Israel to implement General Assembly resolution 2253 (ES-V);

2. *Reiterates* its call to Israel in that resolution to rescind all measures already taken and to desist forthwith from taking any action which would alter the status of Jerusalem;

3. *Requests* the Secretary-General to report to the Security Council and the General Assembly on the situation and on the implementation of the present resolution.

1554th plenary meeting,
14 July 1967.

1. A/6753 and S/8052   A/RES/2254 (ES-V)

United Nations General Assembly Fifth Emergency Special Session Agenda Item 5

RESOLUTION 252 (1968)
*Adopted by the Security Council at its 1426th meeting,
on 21 May 1968*

The Security Council,
Recalling General Assembly resolutions 2253 (ES-V) and 2254 (ES-V) of 4 and 14 July 1967.
Having considered the letter (S/8560) of the Permanent Representative of Jordan on the situation in Jerusalem and the report of the Secretary-General (S/8146),
Having heard the statements made before the Council,
Noting that since the adoption of the above-mentioned resolutions, Israel has taken further measures and actions in contravention of those resolutions,
Bearing in mind the need to work for a just and lasting peace,
Reaffirming that acquisition of territory by military conquest is inadmissible,

1. *Deplores* the failure of Israel to comply with the General Assembly resolutions mentioned above;

2. *Considers* that all legislative and administrative measures and actions taken by Israel, including expropriation of land and properties thereon, which tend to change the legal status of Jerusalem are invalid and cannot change that status;

3. *Urgently calls upon* Israel to rescind all such measures already taken and to

desist forthwith from taking any further action which tends to change the status of Jerusalem;

4. *Requests* the Secretary-General to report to the Security Council on the implementation of the present resolution.

S/RES/252 (1968)

United Nations Security Council

RESOLUTION 267 (1969)
*Adopted by the Security Council at its 1485th Meeting
on 3 July 1969*

The Security Council

Recalling its resolution 252 of 21 May 1968 and the earlier General Assembly resolutions 2253 (ES-V) and 2254 (ES-V) of 4 and 14 July 1967 respectively concerning measures and actions by Israel affecting the status of the City of Jerusalem,

Having heard the statements of the parties concerned on the question,

Noting that since the adoption of the above-mentioned resolutions Israel has taken further measures tending to change the status of the City of Jerusalem,

Reaffirming the established principle that acquisition of territory by military conquest is inadmissible,

1. *Reaffirms* its resolution 252 (1968);

2. *Deplores* the failure of Israel to show any regard for the General Assembly and Security Council resolutions mentioned above;

3. *Censures* in the strongest terms all measures taken to change the status of the City of Jerusalem;

4. *Confirms* that all legislative and administrative measures and actions by Israel which purport to alter the status of Jerusalem including expropriation of land and properties thereon are invalid and cannot change that status;

5. *Urgently calls* once more upon Israel to rescind forthwith all measures taken by it which may tend to change the status of the City of Jerusalem, and in future to refrain from all actions likely to have such an effect;

6. *Requests* Israel to inform the Security Council without any further delay of its intentions with regard to the implementation of the provisions of this resolution;

7. *Determines* that, in the event of a negative response or no response from Israel, the Security Council shall reconvene without delay to consider what further action should be taken in this matter;

8. *Requests* the Secretary-General to report to the Security Council on the implementation of this resolution.

S/RES/267 (1969)

United Nations Security Council

RESOLUTION 298 (1971)
Adopted by the Security Council at its 1582nd meeting,
on 25 September 1971

The Security Council,

Recalling its resolutions 252 (1968) and 267 (1969) and the earlier General Assembly resolutions 2253 (ES-V) and 2254 (ES-V) of July 1967 concerning measures and actions by Israel designed to change the status of the Israeli-occupied section of Jerusalem,

Having considered the letter of the Permanent Representative of Jordan on the situation in Jerusalem (S/10313) and the reports of the Secretary-General (S/8052, S/8146, S/9149 and Add. 1, S/9537 and S/10124 and Add. 1 and 2), and having heard the statements of the parties concerned on the question,

Reaffirming the principle that acquisition of territory by military conquest is inadmissible,

Noting with concern the non-compliance by Israel with the above-mentioned resolutions,

Noting with concern further that since the adoption of the above-mentioned resolutions Israel has taken further measures designed to change the status and character of the occupied section of Jerusalem,

1. *Reaffirms* Security Council resolutions 252 (1968) and 267 (1969);

2. *Deplores* the failure of Israel to respect the previous resolutions adopted by the United Nations concerning measures and actions by Israel purporting to affect the status of the city of Jerusalem;

3. *Confirms* in the clearest possible terms that all legislative and administrative actions taken by Israel to change the status of the city of Jerusalem including expropriation of land and properties, transfer of populations and legislation aimed at the incorporation of the occupied section are totally invalid and cannot change that status;

4. *Urgently calls upon* Israel to rescind all previous measures and actions and to take no further steps in the occupied section of Jerusalem which may purport to change the status of the City, or which would prejudice the rights of the inhabitants and the interests of the international community, or a just and lasting peace;

5. *Requests* the Secretary-General, in consultation with the President of the Security Council and using such instrumentalities as he may choose, including a representative or a mission, to report to the Security Council as appropriate and in any event within 60 days on the implementation of this resolution.

S/RES/298 (1971)

United Nations Security Council

7. LETTERS TO THE U.N. SECRETARY-GENERAL FROM ISRAEL AND JORDAN

*Israel Prime Minister Levi Eshkol, 27 June 1967, at a
meeting with the religious heads of the Christian,
Muslim, and Jewish Communities*

All Holy Places and places of worship in Jerusalem are now freely accessible
to all who wish to worship there, to members of all faiths without discrimination.
The Government has made it a cardinal principle of its policy to safeguard the
Holy Places, ensure their religious and universal character and provide free
access to them. This policy will be maintained scrupulously, through regular
consultations with you or your designated representatives. . . . It is our intention
to place the internal administration and arrangements in the Holy Places in the
hands of the religious leaders to whose community they belong.

*Letter of 10 July 1967 from the Minister of Foreign
Affairs of Israel to the U.N. Secretary General in
reply to a letter of the Secretary General of 5 July 1967*

Measures taken by Israel to change the Status of the City of Jerusalem
Dear Mr. Secretary-General,

My Government has given careful consideration to your letter of 5 July 1967,
concerning resolution 2253 (ES-V) of the General Assembly. Israel's position on
Jerusalem was explained by me at the plenary meetings of the General Assembly
on 21 and 29 June 1967. In response to your letter the Government of Israel now
takes the opportunity of reviewing recent developments in the City.

As a result of aggression launched by the Arab States against Israel in 1948,
the section of Jerusalem in which the Holy Places are concentrated had been
governed for nineteen years by a regime which refused to give due acknowledg-
ment to universal religious concerns. The City was divided by a military demarcation line. Houses of worship were destroyed and desecrated in acts of vandalism. Instead of peace and security there was hostility and frequent bloodshed.
The principle of freedom of access to the Holy Places of all the three monotheistic
religions was violated with regard to Jews, but not to them alone. The Jordan
Government informed the *Ad Hoc* Political Committee at the fourth and fifth
sessions of the General Assembly, on 6 December 1949 and 11 December 1950, that
it would not agree to any special arrangements for the Holy Places. This policy
was the subject of a reference by the President of the Trusteeship Council, M.
Roger Garreau, in his report on the mission entrusted to him by virtue of the
Trusteeship Council resolution of 4 April 1950 (T/681), in which he stated:

. . . I have to state with the deepest regret that up to yesterday, when my term as
President of the Trusteeship Council came to an end, the Government of the Hashe-
mite Kingdom of Jordan had not seen fit to break its silence . . .
. . . The Government of Israel showed a spirit of conciliation which led it to submit

to the Trusteeship Council certain new proposals which . . . represent a considerable advance towards a settlement of the various aspects of the problem of Jerusalem and the Holy Places. . . .

On 5 June 1967, the Jordanian forces launched a destructive and unprovoked armed assault on the part of Jerusalem outside the walls. This attack was made despite Israel's appeals to Jordan to abstain from hostilities. Dozens of Jerusalem citizens were killed and hundreds wounded.

Artillery bombardment was directed against synagogues, the Church of the Dormition, hospitals, centres of secular and religious learning, the Hebrew University and the Israel Museum. Intensive fire was directed against institutions and residential centres from positions in and near the Holy Places themselves, which were thus converted into military positions for shelling Jerusalem.

Since 7 June, the entire City of Jerusalem has experienced peace and unity. The Holy Places of all faiths have been open to access by those who hold them sacred.

The resolution presented on 4 July by Pakistan and adopted on the same date evidently refers to measures taken by the Government of Israel on 27 June 1967. The term "annexation" used by supporters of the resolution is out of place. The measures adopted relate to the integration of Jerusalem in the administrative and municipal spheres, and furnish a legal basis for the protection of the Holy Places in Jerusalem.

I now come to specify the character and effect of the measures adopted on 27 June:

(1) *The Holy Places*

The Protection of Holy Places Law, 5727–1967, provides that the Holy Places shall be protected from desecration and any other violation and from anything likely to violate the freedom of access of the members of the different religions to the places sacred to them or their feelings with regard to those places. Whoever desecrates or otherwise violates a Holy Place shall be liable to imprisonment for a term or [sic] seven years. . . . During the previous nineteen years there had been no such legislation to protect the Holy Places in Jerusalem. Since 27 June, sacred buildings desecrated since 1948 have been restored, and houses of worship destroyed during the Jordanian occupation are being rebuilt.

(2) *Civic co-operation*

One of the most significant results of the measures taken on 27 June is the new mingling of Arabs and Jews in free and constant association. The Arab residents within the walls had been cut off for nineteen years from all contact with the residents of the newer parts of the City. Today they are free to renew or initiate contacts with their Jewish neighbours in Jerusalem and elsewhere in Israel. The residents of the City outside the walls now visit the Old City. There is a profound human and spiritual significance in the replacement of embattled hostility by normal and good neighbourly relations. It is especially appropriate that ecumenical habits of thought and action should take root in the City from which the enduring message of human brotherhood was proclaimed with undying power in generations past.

(3) *Municipal services*

In the hills of Judaea, where Jerusalem is situated, there is an acute shortage of water. The Old City is now connected with the general water supply system, and all houses are receiving a continuous supply of water, double the quantity available to them in the past.

All hospitals and clinics are already functioning. In the past no health services existed for the young within the framework of the school system, nor were there any health stations for mother and child care. These services are now being established.

There was no social welfare system in the Old City. Today all the inhabitants of Jerusalem now enjoy the same welfare rights. The municipality has already begun extending its welfare service to those for whom none have been available in the past.

School buildings are being prepared for the resumption of studies at the beginning of the new school year. Teachers are being located and arrangements made for them to return to their work. Their salaries are paid by the municipality.

Compulsory education regulations have been extended to all parts of the City. None of those arrangements affects the existing private education network.

If these measures had not been taken, the Holy Places would be without legal protection. The unified public utilities services would not exist. Municipal and administrative facilities would not be extended to some sections of the City, and Jerusalem's residents would still be divided, hermetically confined in separate compartments.

The measures taken by my Government to secure the protection of the Holy Places are only a part of Israel's effort to ensure respect for universal interests in Jerusalem. It is evident from United Nations discussions and documents that the international interest in Jerusalem has always been understood to derive from the presence of the Holy Places. Israel does not doubt her own will and capacity to secure the respect of universal spiritual interests. It has forthwith ensured that the Holy Places of Judaism, Christianity and Islam be administered under the responsibility of the religions which hold them sacred. In addition, in a spirit of concern for historic and spiritual traditions, my Government has taken steps with a view to reaching arrangements to assure the universal character of the Holy Places. In pursuance of this objective, the Government of Israel has now embarked on a constructive and detailed dialogue with representatives of universal religious interests. If these explorations are as fruitful as we hope and expect, the universal character of the Holy Places will for the first time in recent decades find effective expression.

The changes which have affected Jerusalem's life and destiny as a result of the measures recently adopted may therefore be summarised as follows:

Where there was hostile separation, there is now harmonious civic union. Where there was a constant threat of violence, there is now peace. Where there was once an assertion of exclusive and unilateral control over the Holy Places, exercised in sacrilegious discrimination, there is now a willingness to work out arrangements with the world's religious bodies—Christian, Muslim and Jewish —which will ensure the universal religious character of the Holy Places.

The Government of Israel is confident that world opinion will welcome the new prospect of seeing this ancient and historic metropolis thrive in unity, peace and spiritual elevation.

Please accept, Mr. Secretary-General, the assurances of my highest consideration.

5 July 1967   (Signed) *Abba Eban*

Letter dated 23 February 1968 from the Permanent
Representative of Jordan to the United Nations
addressed to the Secretary General

For the information of the members of the General Assembly and the Security Council, I am transmitting a report entitled:

Report of the commission appointed by His Majesty's Government in the United Kingdom of Great Britain and Northern Ireland, with the approval of the Council of the League of Nations, to determine the rights and claims of Moslems and Jews in connection with the Western or Wailing Wall at Jerusalem.

This report embodies the findings and decisions of the Commission that was appointed to determine the rights and the claims of both the Moslems and the Jews in connexion with the Wailing Wall in Jerusalem. The Commission consisted of three jurists from Sweden, Switzerland and the Netherlands, namely:

ELIEL LOFGREN, formerly Swedish Minister for Foreign Affairs, Member of the Upper Chamber of the Swedish Riksdag (to act as Chairman); CHARLES BARDE, Vice-President of the Court of Justice at Geneva, President of the Austro-Roumanian Mixed Arbitration Tribunal, and C.J. VAN KEMPEN, formerly Governor of the East Coast of Sumatra, Member of the States-General of the Netherlands.

U.N. General Assembly, Twenty-second Session, Agenda Item 94 A/7057, 23 February, 1968. Also issued under the symbol S/8427

The Commission held twenty-three meetings, during which it heard arguments and engaged in hearing evidence. It heard fifty-two witnesses, twenty-one presented by the Jewish side and thirty by the Moslem side, and one British official called by the Commission. It examined all reports, dispatches, memoranda, minutes relative to matters connected with the Wailing Wall.

The Commission has established the following important facts:

1. That the ownership of the Wall as well as the possession of it and of those parts of its surroundings belong to the Moslems and that the Wall itself, as an integral part of Al-Haram-Esh-Sharif area, is Moslem property.

2. That in no stage of the examination of this matter did the Jewish side make any claim of ownership either to the Wailing Wall or to the Magharba Quarter or to any part of the areas now subjected to Israeli usurpation or so-called "Israeli development projects." The Commission stressed that the Jewish side, when making their claim, expressly stated that they "do not claim any property right to the Wall" (page 17 of the report, para. 3).

3. That no matter how the Jewish claim is construed, it does not exceed a claim for a privilege to visit the Wall and that this privilege has even resulted from Moslem tolerance.

4. That even the pavement and the area coincident with it were Moslem property and constituted Moslem Waqf by Afdal, the son of Saladin, in 1193 A.D., i.e., Moslem religious endowment owned in perpetuity by the Moslem community.

5. That the Magharba Quarter buildings, which were recently bulldozed by the Israeli authorities, were put up in 1320 A.D. "to serve as lodgings to Moroccan pilgrims" and were also made a Moslem Waqf by Abu Madian.

6. That the Moslems of Jerusalem were always alert to the Jewish attempt to exploit Moslem tolerance in order to claim at a later stage a right to ownership. In 1911, the Guardian of the Abu Madian Waqf (Magharba Quarter) complained

that the "Jews, contrary to usage, had placed chairs on the pavement, and he requested that 'in order to avoid a future claim of ownership' the present state of affairs should be stopped." The Arab side argued that after stools would come benches, the benches would then become fixtures and before long the Jews would have established a legal claim to the site. As a direct result of the complaint, the British Administrative Council decided that it was not permissible to place any article on the pavement that could "be considered as indications of ownership."

7. That the British Government stated to Parliament in the White Paper of November 1928 that the Western or Wailing Wall "is legally the absolute property of the Moslem Community and the strip of pavement facing it is Waqf property, as is shown by documents preserved by the Guardian of the Waqf."

The above findings make it unmistakably clear that the recent Israeli measures amount to naked aggression and make nonsense of the cynical allegations that these were simply "administrative measures" or "development projects."

The Israeli bulldozing of Arab property in the Magharba Quarter defies well established Arab rights which were adjudicated and affirmed by recognized and competent authorities, including a competent body constituted with the approval of the League of Nations. It also makes a mockery of the two Jerusalem resolutions which called upon Israel "to rescind all measures already taken and to desist forthwith from taking any action which would alter the status of Jerusalem." It is an obvious encroachment on the second holiest place in Islam, the Aqsa Mosque and Al-Haram-Esh-Sharif, and a violation of the Geneva Convention of 12 August 1949. Article 53 of the Geneva Convention has expressly prohibited any destruction of real or personal property belonging individually or collectively to private persons, or to the State, or to other public authorities, or to social or co-operative organizations. Since their occupation of Jerusalem the Israelis have never ceased their acts of destruction of private and public property.

On 5 January 1968, I brought to Your Excellency's attention the fact that the Israeli authorities are embarking on a plan for changing the sacred character of the Moslem Holy Places, religious buildings and religious sites in the Arab city of Jerusalem.

A new project for the Wailing Wall and the adjacent area is now in progress. It embodies enlargement of the western area of the Wall by four metres and plantation of trees at a width of 150 metres. It also embodies additional constructions near the Wailing Wall. As has been explained in the report quoted above, the Wailing Wall and the entire adjacent area are an integral part of Al-Haram-Esh-Sharif, and its ownership has already been determined as Moslem property. The demolition of the Magharba Quarter is an obvious act aiming at impairing the sacred character of the area, and apart from posing an open challenge and defiance to the feeling and beliefs of millions of Moslems around the world, it is undermining both the rights of ownership and possession.

The recent illegal expropriation of 838 acres (3,345 dunams) of the areas adjacent to the Old City of Jerusalem is but another sinister attempt to uproot the Arab inhabitants. The leaders of Jerusalem have shown that they are alert to methods used by the Zionists to change the *status quo* of the Wailing Wall and the adjacent area. This continued defiance of international law and of the General Assembly resolutions on Jerusalem constitutes a serious and continuing menace to peace and calls for immediate action.

The leaders of Jerusalem, including the Mayor, Mr. Rouhy El-Khatib, counsellors, cabinet ministers, judges, lawyers and several religious dignitaries protested and challenged the validity of the Israeli requisitioning order. Copies of their requests were sent to the United Nations and foreign embassies. The *Jerusalem Post* of 19 January 1968 quoted Government sources as saying that the Israeli authorities "planned to carry out the development project for which the land was requisitioned."

One of the first Israeli projects, it should be made clear, is a housing estate of 1,000 flats. The estate, according to the *Jerusalem Post* of 12 January 1968 would consist of "a self-contained community with shops, schools and synagogues."

The Israelis are proceeding with their plans of annexation, utterly disregarding United Nations injunctions. The United Nations resolutions have not been complied with so far and the situation is worsening considerably and is fraught with danger. My Government views the situation with utmost concern and gravity and requests Your Excellency to take urgent steps to put an end to these serious Israeli violations and illegal practices.

My Government is most anxious that all Member States should have an accurate and clear appreciation of the facts of the present situation as it is developing and shall be grateful if Your Excellency will circulate copies of this communication, together with copies of the report of the Commission referred to in the first paragraph above, to delegations of all Member States as General Assembly and Security Council documents.

(Signed) Muhammad H. EL-FARRA
Ambassador
Permanent Representative

*Letter dated 28 February 1968 from the Permanent
Representative of Jordan to the United Nations
addressed to the Secretary General*

Further to my letter dated 23 February 1968 [A/7057 and S/8427], I am enclosing one of the original copies of the memorandum sent by the dignitaries and inhabitants of Jerusalem to the Israeli authorities, protesting in the strongest terms the measures taken by the Israeli authorities to expropriate Arab lands in Jerusalem for building dwelling houses to settle large numbers of Jewish immigrants. I am also enclosing for Your Excellency's attention the English translation of the memorandum.

I request, upon instructions from my Government, that the English translation of this memorandum be circulated together with this letter as Security Council and General Assembly documents.

(Signed) Muhammad H. EL-FARRA
Ambassador
Permanent Representative

U.N. General Assembly, Twenty-second Session, Agenda Item 94 A/7058, 29 February 1968. Also issued under the symbol S/8433.

COPY

14 January 1968

His Excellency the A/Prime Minister,
c/o His Excellency the Military Governor General to the West Bank,
JERUSALEM

Sir,

The expropriation of large areas of land for building dwelling houses to settle large numbers of Jews in Arab Jerusalem, has been reported in some of the Israeli newspapers and duly confirmed by Israeli Authorities.

We are shocked and dismayed because we were under the impression that the Israeli Authorities would not embark on taking such a drastic step which affronts world public opinion. We have therefore hastened to present this memorandum with a view to safeguarding the character of Arab Jerusalem and to show the magnitude of our concern for the success of the attempts made in many quarters to secure peace. We wish to assure the Israeli Authorities of our grave misgivings concerning the scheme. The following are but some of our objections:

1. This move justifies our worst fears that a policy of expansion and aggression is being pursued by the Israeli leaders and the talk about peace which is expressed now and again is a mere cover to hide their true aim of expansion.

2. This move will destroy all those possibilities of peace now being sought by various bodies.

3. This move will also obstruct the mission of the United Nations envoy in his efforts at finding equitable solutions to the problems of our region. It will be undoubtedly clear that Israel seeks to sabotage all basic solutions regardless of whatever declarations may be made by the Israeli Government that it is co-operating with the United Nations envoy in making his mission a success.

4. There is no need to reiterate what has been said before; that such a course of action is an affront and violation of United Nations resolutions; an infringement of the rights of another sovereign State and a member of the community of nations.

5. The gravity of the situation is by no means lessened on account of the avowed declarations that these dwellings will be available to the entire population regardless of race or religion. This is no more than a mask to cover the real aims of the authorities.

We wish to put on record our protest in the strongest possible terms in respect of these measures which are contrary to justice and in violation of international law. We raise our voice from Jerusalem, the cradle of humanitarian values and in the name of our legal rights. We hope that the ruling administration will abide by these values.

We still entertain a lingering hope that all is not lost; not reason and prudence; goodwill and the call for peace may yet prevail. This is to be achieved by foresaking this policy which is bound to obliterate or disfigure the true face and character of Arab Jerusalem and thus spare the world from another fait accompli.

(Signed by):

1. Bishop Najeeb Quebein, Anglican Arab Community
2. Bishop Elaryon Kabboshi, Arab Catholic Community
3. Sheikh Hilmi Muhtaseb, President Moslem Community
4. Sheikh Sa'ddin Alami, Mufti of Jerusalem

5. Sheikh Said Sabri, Sharia Qadi Jerusalem
6. Anwar Khatib, Ex-Governor of Jerusalem
7. Anwar Nuseibeh, Ex-Jordan Ambassador at United Kingdom
8. Said Alaeddin, Ex-Minister of Economy
9. Abdul Hahim Shareef, Senator
10. Kamal Dajani, Ex-Minister of Interior
11. Rouhi el Khatib, Mayor of Jerusalem
12. Dr. Ibrahim Tleel, Deputy Mayor of Jerusalem
13. Anton Safieh, Assistant Mayor of Jerusalem
14. Nihad Abugharbieh, Municipal Councillor of Jerusalem
15. Abdul Mughni Natshah, Municipal Councillor of Jerusalem
16. Mousa el Bitar, Municipal Councillor of Jerusalem
17. Khader Abu Sway, Municipal Councillor of Jerusalem
18. Ali Tazeez, Municipal Councillor and President of Chamber of Commerce
19. Fayek Barakat, Municipal Councillor and Director of Chamber of Commerce
20. Anton Albina, Member of Chamber of Commerce Jerusalem
21. George Khader, Member of Chamber of Commerce Jerusalem
22. Fayez Abdul Nor, Member of Chamber of Commerce Jerusalem
23. George Akra, Member of Chamber of Commerce Jerusalem
24. Abdul Hamid Asali, Member of Chamber of Commerce Jerusalem
25. Khairi Nasereddin, Member of Chamber of Commerce Jerusalem
26. Matia Marroum, Ex-member of Parliament
27. Emile Safieh, Ex-member of Parliament
28. Tayseer Kan'an, President, District Court of Jerusalem
29. Mohammad Ishaq Darwish, Member of Higher Arab Committee
30. Dr. Asad Bishara, Physician
31. Hafez Tahboub, Advocate
32. Jameel Naser, Advocate
33. Haj Omar Wa'ari, Advocate and Ex-Mayor
34. Dr. Saleem Ma'touq, Physician
35. Rashad el Sheikh, Mukhtar Sheikh Jarrah Quarter
36. Yousef Hanna, Editor
37. Dr. Daoud Huseini, Landlord and Ex-member of Parliament
38. Jawad Huseini, Landlord
39. Azeez Shhadeh, Advocate and Landlord
40. Mahmoud Osman, Landlord
41. Haj Tewfiq Abu Zahra, Landlord and Member of Chamber of Commerce
42. Yousef Khoury, Architect and Contractor
43. Michal Sindaha, Representative of Labour Unions
44. Rida Kaddoumi, Member of Chamber of Commerce Jerusalem
45. Bader Sharaf, Landlord
46. Faisal Siam, Pharmacist, Landlord

Letter of 5 March 1968 from the Permanent
Representative of Israel to the United Nations to the
U.N. Secretary General

Sir,

On instructions from my Government I have the honour to refer to the letters addressed to you by the Permanent Representative of Jordan on 23 and 28 February 1968 (A/7057 and Add. 1, S/8427 and Add. 1, and A/7058, S/8435) and to state as follows:

The allegations contained in the two letters are without foundation. They follow logically on the destructive attitude adopted by the Jordanian authorities towards the City of Jerusalem and its Holy Places. It was Jordan which, in defiance of the United Nations Charter, attacked the city in 1948, placed it under siege, and opened indiscriminate fire on its inhabitants and on its historical and religious sites. It was the Jordan Government which then relentlessly set about destroying the Jewish Quarter, including its synagogues and places of learning and the venerated cemetery on the Mount of Olives. The inhabitants of the Jewish Quarter were uprooted, transformed overnight into refugees and forcibly prevented from returning to the homes inhabited by themselves and by their ancestors. It was Jordan which prevented free access to the Jewish Holy Places and the cultural and humanitarian institutions on Mount Scopus, in flagrant violation of its international obligations solemnly undertaken.

Colonel Abdullah el-Tal, one-time commandant of the Jordanian Arab Legion, in describing the destruction of the Jewish Quarter, wrote in the volume of his Memoirs (Cairo, 1959):

... The operations of calculated destruction were set in motion. ... I knew that the Jewish Quarter was densely populated with Jews who caused their fighters a good deal of interference and difficulty. ... I embarked, therefore, on the shelling of the Quarter with mortars, creating harassment and destruction. ... Only four days after our entry into Jerusalem the Jewish Quarter had become their graveyard. Death and destruction reigned over it. ... As the dawn of Friday, May 28, 1948, was about to break, the Jewish Quarter emerged convulsed in a black cloud—a cloud of death and agony.

After the cease-fire had entered into force and normal civilian administration had been restored in Jerusalem last June, a shocking picture was unfolded of the results of this policy of wanton vandalism, desecration and violation perpetrated during the period of Jordan occupation from 1948 onwards. In the Jewish Quarter all but one of the thirty-five Jewish houses of worship that graced the Old City of Jerusalem were found to have been wantonly destroyed. The synagogues had been razed or pillaged and stripped and their interiors used as henhouses and stables. In the ancient historic Jewish graveyard on the Mount of Olives, tens of thousands of tombstones had been torn up, broken into pieces or used as flagstones, steps and building materials in Jordanian military installations and civilian constructions. Large areas of the cemetery had been levelled and converted into parking places and petrol-filling stations. These acts of desecration have been described fully in a document published by the Ministry for Foreign Affairs in Jerusalem in November 1967, a copy of which is attached to this letter.

Document S/8439 Add. 1

This record of Jordanian conduct in Jerusalem underlines the true character and purpose of the allegations put forward in the letters from the Permanent Representative of Jordan.

In effect, the Government of Jordan is complaining of steps that have had to be taken urgently in order to restore the atmosphere of sacredness, dignity and tranquillity proper to Jerusalem and its Holy Places, and to ensure the elevation of its material and cultural life.

With regard to the Western Wall, it is to be observed that it is the most Holy Place of all to Judaism. The Western Wall is the sole remaining relic of the First and Second Temples, constructed and sanctified in ancient times. It is ominous that the Jordanian representative fails to mention this essential fact. The Wall's history does not commence with the Arab conquest of Palestine. That request, like those that preceded and followed it, is incapable of effecting any change whatsoever in the sacredness of the Wall to the Jewish people—a sacredness which, indeed, the Jewish people alone is competent to determine.

If any proof of this were needed it can be found in the report of the Commission appointed by the United Kingdom Government, circulated at the request of the Permanent Representative of Jordan as document A/7057/Add. 1, S/8427/Add. 1, although it may here be noted, parenthetically, that at the time that report was not accepted either by the Moslem or by the Jewish authorities, the Commission having been established solely to assist the Mandatory authorities in the discharge of what they conceived to be their duties under the Mandate.

The Western Wall holds a unique place in the history and faith of the Jewish people. For nineteen centuries Jews flocked to the Western Wall from all parts of the world to pray and worship before it. It would not cross the mind of Jews to impair in any way the sanctity of the Western Wall.

The interest now evinced by the Jordanian Government in the Wall is surprising against the background of the vandalism perpetrated there by that Government when it was in occupation of the area. The Jordanian Government deliberately profaned the sacred character of the Wall by erecting adjacent to it structures of secular services, warehouses and toilets, and converting its immediate precincts into a slum. It accordingly became essential to remove those installations and restore the dignity and the sanctity of the Holy Place as a very first step after the battles in Jerusalem had ceased. Moreover, archaeological excavations are being conducted in order to remove part of the earth and refuse that have accumulated at the Western Wall in the course of time and which cover its lower layers. This is a proper archaeological operation, and it is being conducted in a way that assures that nothing will damage the Wall or jeopardize its character as a Holy Place or impair in any way the Haram esh-Sharif area situated beyond the Wall.

It is to be noted that the Western Wall is a recognized antiquity and was treated as such also by the Mandatory Government, which also assumed responsibility for its maintenance and upkeep.

Archaeological activities near the Temple Mount and the Western Wall have always taken place, under government supervision, in Jerusalem. Excavations were undertaken during the period of the Mandate and during the Jordanian occupation. During the last nineteen years the Department of Antiquities of the Government of Jordan, in cooperation with the British Archaeological School in

Jerusalem under the supervision of Miss Kenyon, carried out a number of archaeological excavations at the southern part of the Western Wall. Approval has been granted for the continuation of these excavations, outside the area of the Temple Mount, that is, outside the walls surrounding the Haram esh-Sharif.

A clear distinction exists between the Haram esh-Sharif and the Western Wall, which were recognized as two separate Holy Places. This distinction was followed by the United Nations and is clearly marked in the United Nations map of the Holy Places in Jerusalem (map number 229, November 1949). Consequently, the contention in the letter of the Permanent Representative of Jordan that "The Wailing Wall and the entire adjacent area are an integral part of Al-Haram esh Sharif" is a wilful attempt to confuse the issue.

The Mughrabi Quarter consisting of a group of dwelling houses, to which the letter of the Permanent Representative of Jordan makes particular reference, is not a holy site. It faces the Wall but is also entirely separate from it. Its status is no different from that of secular property, whether or not owned by religious institutions as a source of income, in any other city in the world.

No modern civilized Government or municipal administration would have tolerated the slum conditions which the Jordanian Government created in this Quarter. One of the first things which the Government of Israel had to do was to embark on a programme of urban improvement, which included resettling the unfortunate inhabitants of this Quarter in respectable conditions. The same policy had to be followed with respect to the ruins of the Jewish Quarter from which a number of families were evacuated in order to expedite its restoration. This Quarter is situated outside the Temple Mount area. For hundreds of years Jews had lived in it in order to be as close as possible to the Western Wall. Throughout all the centuries of its existence, it did not impair one jot the sanctity of the Temple Mount (Haram esh-Sharif): on the contrary, it maintained its sanctity. It is quite incomprehensible how its rehabilitation can compromise in any way the sacred character of the Haram esh-Sharif. Contrary to what is implied in the Jordanian letter, the resettlement of the inhabitants was carried out in consultation with them and the families concerned expressed their appreciation to the city authorities for having assisted them in improving their housing.

The Jordanian Government had never shown much respect for such considerations. As recently as 5 November 1966, the Jordanian newspaper *Falastin* (then published in the Old City) complained: "Ancient memorial buildings in the Old City of Jerusalem are destroyed and replaced by modern ones. Commercial competition even reached the Mount of Olives where construction had been prohibited in the past."

The Permanent Representative of Jordan complains of plans to construct new housing in the modern part of Jerusalem. This complaint refers to vacant land of which about two-thirds is public domain, or belongs to Jewish private persons or institutions. Only one-third is owned by private Arab landlords. No person at all is being evicted and none of the land in question belongs to any ecclesiastical institution, or is Waqf property. The private owners of the land will receive compensation in accordance with the law. The new housing project will provide homes for Jews as well as Arabs.

In conclusion, I am instructed to reiterate the policy of my Government as

regards the Holy Places of all faiths in Jerusalem. In the Law for the Protection
of the Holy Places enacted by the Knesset on 27 June 1967 it is provided, in section 1:

> The Holy Places shall be protected from desecration and any other violation and from
> anything likely to violate the freedom of access of the members of the different religions
> to the places sacred to them or their feelings with regard to those places.

In pursuance of this Law the different Holy Places of Judaism, Christianity
and Islam are administered under the responsibility of the respective religious
authorities which hold them sacred. The Government of Israel remains in contact
with them to give full expression to the universal interest in the Holy Places. The
responsibility for the peace of Jerusalem, for the welfare of its inhabitants of
whatever faith, and for the sanctity of the Holy Places is a central element in the
policy of the Government of Israel.

I have the honour to request that this letter and its enclosure be circulated in
the official languages as a document of the Security Council and the General
Assembly.

(Signed) *Yosef Tekoah*

5 March, 1968

*Letter dated 15 November 1971 from the Minister of
Foreign Affairs of Israel to the Secretary General of
the United Nations*

Sir,

I have the honour to reply to your telegram of September 26, 1971, transmitting
the text of Resolution 298 (1971) adopted by the Security Council at its 1582nd
meeting on the previous day.

The central operative paragraph of the Resolution calls upon Israel "to rescind all previous measures and actions and to take no further steps in the
occupied section of Jerusalem which may purport to change the status of the city
or which would prejudice the rights of the inhabitants and the interests of the
international community, or a just and lasting peace."

I propose to analyse the main provisions of this paragraph in order to place
the situation in Jerusalem in its true light.

I. THE STATUS OF THE CITY

If the "status of the city" referred to in the Resolution means the situation
existing before June 5, 1967, the renewal of that "status" would involve the restoration of a military demarcation line and other barriers cutting through the centre
of the city, the cancellation of free access to their holy places for Jews and Israeli
Moslems, which has prevailed only since June 7, 1967, and the re-imposition of

S/10392

a ban on residence or visit by anyone of Jewish faith in the Old City. Moreover, in order to restore the previous status Israel would have to demolish the synagogues and other sites destroyed by the Jordan authorities and restored since then, and to close the cultural, humanitarian and educational institutions on Mount Scopus which have been re-opened since June 1967. Thus the restoration of the previous status would involve rescinding the unity, peace and sanctity of Jerusalem today in order to restore the divisions, conflict and sacrilege which made the period 1948–1967 one of the darkest ages in Jerusalem's long history.

It is inconceivable that the majority of Security Council members could wish to restore that situation. Some of them have indicated that they do not.

The position of Jordan in a part of Jerusalem for 19 years resulted from an aggressive invasion carried out against the injunctions of the Security Council in the first half of 1948. That position was never recognized by the world community. Thus it is not the case that an internationally accepted or valid status for Jerusalem has been set aside by anything done in the city since 1967. If one dismisses as inherently untenable the proposition that the Security Council wishes to tear Jerusalem apart again, one is left with the assumption that the concern expressed by the Council is for the effective status of the ethnic and religious communities. It has been asserted in some quarters that Israel is undertaking or planning actions with the aim of annulling the present heterogeneous character of the population. I can give assurance that this is not the case. Since 1967, the flight of Christian Arabs from Jerusalem under Jordanian occupation has been stemmed. The figures in 1967 were 10,800. Today they are 11,500. At the same time, the Moslem population has grown from 54,963 in 1967 to 61,600 at the end of 1970, while the Jews, who numbered 195,700 in 1967, are now 215,500. There is nothing to indicate that these relative proportions are likely to be substantially changed in the coming years, and in absolute terms the Christian and Moslem populations are likely to increase and not to dwindle. Israel's view is that development by the city's services and amenities should be undertaken for all its communities, and not for one community alone.

2. THE RIGHTS OF THE INHABITANTS

Jerusalem has a population of 300,000 about three-fourths of whom are Jews, 61,600 are Moslems and 11,500 are Christians. For the past two hundred years, Jews have been the largest community. The "rights of the inhabitants," whether Jews, Christians or Moslems, include the right to administer their own city, to develop it, and to repair the havoc of war. Jerusalem has the right to normal existence as a living city, its life and institutions must be allowed to grow in the interests of all its inhabitants, and it cannot be artificially frozen at the point which it had reached over four years ago.

Since 1967, all Jerusalem's citizens have had their due voice in the administration of the city. In the last municipal elections under the Jordanian occupation in 1963, there were only 5,000 eligible voters in a total Arab population of some 60,000. Only males over 21, property owners and rate-payers could vote, no political parties were permitted. Irrespective of the results of the voting, the mayor was appointed by the Jordanian Government in Amman. On the other hand, in the 1969 election for the municipal council, universal suffrage for those over 18 years of age was introduced in the sector formerly under Jordanian occupation.

All the citizens of Jerusalem, both in the western and eastern parts of the city, have the right to normal municipal services. All the city's inhabitants now receive such services, which were non-existent or inadequate during the 19 years of illegal Jordanian military occupation.

Since 1967, compulsory education laws have been strictly applied. A system of kindergartens, which did not exist under the Jordanian conquest, has been extended to the eastern part of the city. Vocational training has been expanded, including the opening of a night-school for working boys. The network of free medical services for school-children, new mothers and babies has spread to this section of Jerusalem. In a special programme carried out in 1967, all children in East Jerusalem were given thorough medical check-ups, including skin, tuberculosis and eye tests, as well as vaccinations against diphtheria, tetanus and second shots against small-pox. Trachoma and malnutrition have now all but been eliminated. A new 300-bed hospital on Mount Scopus, to serve the northern and eastern parts of the city, will soon be opened.

The eastern section has been connected to the Jerusalem watermains, providing round-the-clock water supply for the first time in history. A central sewage system has been introduced. The Municipality of Jerusalem has provided playgrounds, parks, libraries and youth clubs, where there were none before. An Arabic language theatre has begun performances. A developed social welfare system has been applied for the first time to this part of the city. The citizens living in Eastern Jerusalem have the services of a Government Labour Exchange, 40 percent of the section's workers have joined and are protected by the Israel Labour Federation. There is no unemployment in Jerusalem, low-cost public housing and generous mortgage opportunities are being provided by the Municipality to Arab residents.

Nothing therefore could be more inaccurate than to assert that the rights of the inhabitants of Jerusalem have been adversely affected by anything done or planned by Israel. Their rights to peaceful life and development, and to a voice in Jerusalem's affairs, have been fully respected and indeed advanced only since June 1967.

3. THE INTERESTS OF THE INTERNATIONAL COMMUNITY

For 22 years Jerusalem has been Israel's capital and seat of Government. It is the unique and exclusive spiritual centre of Judaism, as of no other faith. At the same time, the Government has always been conscious of the fact that the city is of deep concern to other faiths. Its religious and historical sites are precious to Christians and Moslems, as well as to Jews. This concern was expressed by the Prime Minister of Israel on 27 June 1967:

> All the holy places in Jerusalem are now open to all who wish to pray in them and to the faithful of all religions without discrimination. It is our intention to place the internal administration and arrangements for the holy places in the hands of the religious leaders of the communities to which these places belong.

The protection of the Holy Places is ensured by law. The Protection of Holy Places Law, 5727–1967, states in its first paragraph:

> The Holy Places shall be protected from desecration and any other violation and from anything likely to violate the freedom of access of the members of the different religions to the places sacred to them or their feelings with regard to those places.

No such law protected the Holy Places during the Jordanian occupation.

The intentions expressed by the Prime Minister, as well as the dispositions of the Law, are now part of the new reality in Jerusalem. The desecration of historic synagogues in the Old City and of the ancient cemetery on the Mount of Olives, which was carried out by the Jordanian authorities, and the denial of free access of Jews and Israeli Moslems to their holiest shrines, have stopped. The churches, mosques, synagogues and other shrines are administered by each religious community. In Jerusalem today everyone is free to visit and pray at the Holy Places of the three great faiths. Pilgrims and visitors to the city, Government leaders, Church dignitaries, parliamentarians, journalists, men of letters, tourists in their thousands, have testified that Jerusalem and the Holy Places are secure and open to all.

In developing the living city of Jerusalem we are, and shall be, constantly mindful of its historical treasures and spiritual heritage, and care is, and will be taken to preserve them for the inhabitants and for the world.

The policy of Israel concerning universal spiritual interests is as follows:

The measures taken to secure the protection of the Holy Places are only a part of Israel's effort to ensure respect for universal interests in Jerusalem. It is evident from United Nations discussions and documents that the international interest in Jerusalem has always been understood to derive from the presence of the Holy Places. Israel does not doubt her own will and capacity to secure the respect of universal spiritual interests. It has forthwith ensured that the Holy Places of Judaism, Christianity and Islam be administered under the responsibility of the religions which hold them sacred. In addition, in a spirit of concern for historic and spiritual traditions, my Government has taken steps with a view to reaching arrangements to assure the universal character of the Holy Places. In pursuance of this objective the Government of Israel has now embarked on a constructive and detailed dialogue with universal religious interests. If these explorations are as fruitful as we hope, the universal character of the Holy Places will for the first time in recent decades find comprehensive expression.

As I informed you on 10 July 1967, Israel does not wish to exercise unilateral jurisdiction or exclusive responsibility in the Holy Places of Christianity and Islam, and is willing in consultation with the religious interests traditionally concerned to give due expression to that principle.

The changes which have affected Jerusalem's life and destiny as a result of the measures recently adopted may therefore be summarized as follows: Where there was hostile separation there is now intermingling and constructive civic union. Where there was a constant threat of violence there is now peace. Where there was once an assertion of exclusive and unilateral control over the Holy Places, exercised in sacrilegious discrimination—there is now a willingness to work out arrangements with the world's religious bodies, Christian, Muslim and Jewish, which will ensure the universal religious character of the Holy Places.

This is the first time that a Government in Jerusalem offers special expression for universal interests in Jerusalem instead of asserting its exclusive jurisdiction over all of them. The apprehension expressed in the Resolution lest interests of the international community have been adversely affected is thus without foundation.

4. A JUST AND LASTING PEACE

The previous division of the city did not bring the Middle East closer to peace. On the contrary, that division was an open wound constantly exacerbated by outbursts of hostility and by recurrent Jordanian violations of the fragile armistice, which caused the murder of Jerusalem's citizens, and made life in the city a frequent terror for many residents on both sides of the barbed wire. Today for the first time since 1948, Jerusalem is a city in which Jews and Arabs live together in peace and mingle in their thousands in the daily pursuits of their lives. Jerusalem has become an example of communal, civic and regional coexistence, and is thus an augury of the just and lasting peace to which enlightened men aspire.

Jerusalem is for Israel the focal point of Jewish history, the symbol of ancient glory, of longing, of prayer, of modern renewal. It is also a source of universal inspiration. Israel's policy is to promote the rights of Jerusalem's inhabitants, to advance the interests of the international community, and thus to contribute to the promotion of a just and lasting peace.

The sharp discrepancy between the Jerusalem reality and the Resolution presented by Jordan and adopted by the Security Council has profoundly shocked the people of Jerusalem. This sentiment was expressed in the Prime Minister's statement of October 26, 1971, which remains valid. There are many difficulties in Jerusalem, as elsewhere arising from regional tensions and hostilities as well as from economic and social factors. But in general, men of peace and good will have reason to be gratified by the peace, serenity, union and spiritual harmony which have been strengthened in Jerusalem since the barbed wire fences went down and the Jews and Arabs of Jerusalem came together in a common devotion to their city. Nothing has been done or will be done to violate the rights of the inhabitants, the interests of the international community, or the principles of peaceful coexistence.

(Signed) *Abba Eban*

8. STATEMENTS

*Statement of Concerned Christians Adopted at the
Emergency Christian Leadership Conference on
Jerusalem and Israel, called by Bernhard E. Olson of
the National Conference of Christians and Jews and
held in their headquarters in N.Y.C.*

19 May, 1971

As Christians concerned about peace and justice for all in the city of Jerusalem, we wish to take issue with recent statements in the general and Church press which speak of the "Judaization" of the Holy City and the "suffocation" of its Christian and Muslim population. These statements also call for the "internationalization" of the entire city as a remedy for these alleged evils. Our purpose is to contribute to the debate provoked by these statements considerations which we believe to be essential to a full and accurate perspective on these issues.

Our inquiry into the question of public housing in the Old City and environs has convinced us that the construction of these buildings is a legitimate effort on the part of the Israeli Government to effectuate a renewal of certain slum areas of the City, to re-house in new apartments Arabs from these quarters, to provide living space for a Jewish population increased by immigration, and to re-introduce a Jewish presence into the Holy City from which it had been forcibly barred after the war of 1948. The development plans are in no sense designed to oust the Arabs, or to "suffocate" the Christian and Muslim population. While we are concerned about the sacred character of the City, we believe that this housing is sufficiently removed from the Holy Places to avoid the charge of diminishing the sanctity of the City.

We believe, further, that the claim that the Christian-Arab population is diminishing in Israel is incorrect. Since the end of the 1948 Arab-Israeli war, the Christian and Muslim population of Israel has more than doubled. The trickle of Christian emigration has not affected this upward trend. In Jerusalem, the non-Jewish total (Christian and Muslim) has increased steadily in the last three years. The question of emigration should be judged in contrast to the actual exodus of many Arab Christians from Arab countries, in particular from Lebanon and Egypt. It is apparent to us that internationalization of the entire city of Jerusalem is no longer a viable solution to the problem of conserving the peace, security and sacred character of the City and its Holy Places. Since both Israel and Jordan are adamantly opposed to the plan, it is unworkable. Further, the behaviour of the Government of Israel with respect to the Holy Places has been exemplary. It has achieved the main purpose of internationalization, which is to provide protection and free access to the Holy Places for all. Moreover, internationalization proposals go far beyond this protection and free access—the chief goal of religious groups—and therefore must be considered a political rather than a religious concern. We recall with regret that no Christian bodies or national Government expressed concern about the denial of access for all Jews, or for Christians and Muslims in Israel, to their Holy Places during the Jordanian administration of the Old City. The same can be said about the desecration of cemeteries and synagogues during this period.

Should Jerusalem be internationalized at this point in history? The internationalizing body (the United Nations) now includes a large proportion of officially atheistic countries, or countries with no interest in or ties to the Holy Places of Christianity, Judaism, or Islam. Internationalization has never worked and the world has had its fill of divided cities. Both alternatives, internationalization and division, are undesirable.

There are many other possible formulas, short of internationalization of the city, which would better serve the aim of protecting the Holy Places. We believe that the choice of the best method should be left to negotiations carried on at the peace table between Israel and Arab countries. At that point the Christian Churches, synagogues and mosques can voice their opinion as to the particular needs of their communities and properties in the area.

We are encouraged by such creative efforts as those already initiated by Israeli officials with Christian ecumenical and Arab civic leaders for special jurisdiction over the Holy Places and in Arab areas of Jerusalem. On the other hand, we regret all interventions that fail to take into account the political rights and sovereignty of the State of Israel.

The signers of this statement speak in their own name and do not necessarily represent organizations or institutions to which they are attached:

Names of those present at the Emergency Christian Leadership Conference on Israel and Jerusalem. New York, Wednesday, May 19, 1971.

Dr. Franklin H. Littell (Chairman)
Temple University
President, Christians Concerned for Israel

Rev. Marl Baehr
University and Interfaith Committee
New York, N.Y.

Mrs. Claire Huchet Bishop
New York, N.Y.

Rev. John G. Donohue
Archdiocese of New York

Dr. A. Roy Eckardt
Lehigh University

Alice L. Eckardt
Coopersburg, Pa.

Rev. Edward H. Flannery
Secretariat for Catholic-Jewish Relations
U.S. Bishops Conference

Rev. Nancy Forsberg
First Congregational Church
Union, N.J.

Dr. Charles Fritsch
Princeton Theological Seminary

Sister Katherine Hargrove
Manhattanville College

Rev. William H. Harter
Margaretville-New Kingston United Presbyterian Parish

Rev. Chester Hodgson
United Methodist Church
Freeport, N.Y.

Rev. Lester Kinsolving
Berkeley, Calif.

Dr. Andre Lacoque
Chicago Theological Seminary

Rt. Rev. John Oesterreicher
Institute of Judaeo-Christian Studies

Rev. John T. Pawlikowski
Catholic Theological Union
Chicago, Ill.

Sister Donna Purdy
Seton Hall University

Rt. Rev. Leo Rudloff, O.S.E.
Benedictine Priory
Weston, Vt.

Rev. John B. Sheerin, C.S.E.
The Catholic World

Dr. Elwyn Smith
Temple University

Sister Rose Thering
Institute of Judaeo-Christian Studies

Sister Ann Patrick Ware
National Council of Churches of Christ in the U.S.A.

Dr. George H. Williams
Harvard University

Dr. Michael Zeik
Marymount College

Dr. Bernhard E. Olson (Host)
National Conference of Christians and Jews

Excerpts from Speech in The Israel Knesset
(Parliament) 31 May 1971, by Dr. Zerah
Warhaftig, Minister of Religious Affairs on Holy
Places and Religious Communities

There has never been so much freedom of access to all Holy Places in Jerusalem as now, and the fact has been acknowledged with much appreciation by visitors from abroad. It is in complete contrast to the situation prevailing during the era of Jordanian occupation, when not only the Jews were deprived of their right of access to the Western Wall and other sites sacred to Judaism, but non-Jews were also adversely affected.

We vehemently reject allegations made in Arab circles in the United Nations that the work of reclamation carried out at the Western Wall is a breach of Moslem religious rights and institutions. What we do is cleanse the area of the dirt and sewage pits which, over the ages, piled up against a Wall that is the one and only vestige of our ancient Temple. This garbage is certainly not sacred to any creed.

Under the Mandate, only 28 meters of the Western Wall were open to the eye. Today, 230 meters have by now been bared after burial for centuries under rubbish and rubble: of this new length, 143 meters are beneath the open sky, the rest beneath arches and edifices built at different times. Now all the thousands of visitors, who come from every land and nation, may behold and admire the majestic beauty of the Wall which circled the Temple Mount. The Ministry plans now to shift the ramp that runs on to the Moroccan Gate of the Temple Mount and still divides the two visible segments of the Western Wall.

The Ministry takes active part in the restoration of the Jewish Quarter in the Holy City, more particularly in the rehabilitation of the *yeshivot* and synagogues, especially the Synagogue of Nahmanides, renewer of the Jewish community in Jerusalem seven hundred years ago. The fence around the ancient cemetery on the Mount of Olives has been constructed, plans for the paving of ways and paths across the cemetery have been prepared, and many ruined tombs have been made whole again, including the sepulchral cavern of Rabbi Obadiah of Bertinoro, the fifteenth century commentator on the Mishna.

The Ministry maintains excellent relations with the leaders of the Moslem, Druse and Christian communities. The Christian communities enjoy freedom of activity and, in exercise of it, are energetically developing their educational and charitable institutions. True, there have been attempts by minor German sects to acquire buildings for the establishment of institutions in such Jewish villages as Zikhron Ya'acov and Nahariya and, recently also, in Metulla, that aroused a stormy public reaction, but there have also been cases of leasing of Christian institutions to Jewish municipalities and hospitals.

In the last year, official recognition was granted to the Evangelical Episcopal community, headed by the Anglican Archbishop in Jerusalem, and to the Bahai sect, a recognition never gained by those denominations under the Ottoman régime or under the British Mandate.

Information is circulated to Christian circles inside and outside Israel by the Ministry. A division of information for Christians has been set up in the Ministry, which, together with the editorial board of *Christian News from Israel*, is doing valuable work in this field; that quarterly is read today in sixty countries. Several meetings have been organized under the auspices of the new division, such as a symposium on the problem "Who is a Jew?" from a Christian point of view (see *Christian News from Israel*, Vol. XXI, 3, pp. 24 ff.).

Statement of U.S. Catholic, Protestant and Evangelical Ecclesiastics in Conference, 10 June 1971, New York City

Our inquiry into the question of public housing in the Old City and environs has convinced us that the construction of these buildings is a legitimate effort on the part of the Israeli Government to effectuate a renewal of certain slum areas of the City, to rehouse in new apartments Arabs from these quarters, to provide living space for a Jewish population increased by immigration, and to re-introduce a Jewish presence into the Old City from which it has been forcibly barred after the war of 1948. The development plans are in no sense designed to oust the Arabs, or to "suffocate" the Christian and Muslim population. While we are concerned about the sacred character of the City, we believe that this housing is sufficiently removed from the Holy Places to avoid the charge of diminishing the sanctity of the City.

Statement by Evangelical Protestants

Jerusalem, 17 June 1971

We the undersigned, Evangelical Christians committed to the integrity of Jerusalem the Holy City as the birthplace of our faith, want to commend the State of Israel for the scrupulous care with which it has protected Christian places and people.

Taking note that throughout history Jerusalem has never been the capital of any people except for the Jewish people, we are struck by the fact that since the Six Day War, all people are free to worship in the place of their choice, unlike the situation that obtained during the period 1948–1967.

The unity of Jerusalem must be preserved at all costs: internationalization, an idea which never worked in history, would not be a viable solution. The signers of this statement speak in their own name and do not necessarily represent organizations or institutions to which they are attached.

The Rev. Dr. Harold J. Fickett Jr., Pastor First Baptist Church, Van Nuys, California.

The Rev. Dr. Johan F. Walvoord, President Dallas Theological Seminary Dallas, Texas.

The Rev. Dr. Douglas Young, President American Institute of Holy Land Studies, Jerusalem

The Rev. Dr. Myron F. Boyd, Member Board of Bishops of North America Free Methodist Church, Winona Lake, Ind.

The Rev. Dr. John Warwick Montgomery, Prof. of History of Christian Thought, Trinity Seminary, Deerfield, Ill., and Prof. Visiteur Faculté de Théologie Protestante de l'Université de Strasbourg, France.

Resolution of the French Association for Christian-Jewish Friendship

At the closure of the session of its National Council on 12 November 1972, of which the theme was "Jerusalem, city of peace," L'Amitié Judéo-Chrétienne of France enunciates its attitude thus:

i. It recognizes the essential bond, physical and spiritual, which links the Jewish people and Jerusalem.

ii. It recalls that Moslems and Christians, too, have indissoluble spiritual bonds with Jerusalem.

iii. It emphasizes that Jerusalem has a twofold mission, national and universal. The consequence is that Israel's authority over Jerusalem is unquestionably lawful. This authority, reflecting Jewish sentiments, guarantees to all believers free access to the Holy Places and their autonomous administration.

iv. Jerusalem seems, also, to be a single and unified point of religious encounters for millions of believers. Its universal character should make a positive contribution to the overcoming of political antagonisms and so render the city, as the Prophets proclaimed, "an house of prayer for all people" (*Isa.* 56:7) and "the city of righteousness, the faithful city" (*Isa.* 1:26).

Then shall the nations say:

"Zion, everyone shall call thee Mother, because this and that man was born in thee . . . all my springs are in thee" (*Ps.* 87:5–6).

Statement in the Osservatore Romano on the audience of The Holy Father and Mrs. Golda Meir, Prime Minister of Israel

Published on the 15th/16th of January, 1973.

This morning, 15 January 1973, at 12:15 His Holiness Pope Paul VI received Mrs. Golda Meir, Prime Minister of Israel, who was accompanied by the Israeli Ambassador in Italy, H.E. Mr. Amiel E. Najar.

The conversation which lasted for about an hour covered the situation in the Middle East and the specific problems concerning the Holy Land.

His Holiness after having reviewed the history and the sufferances of the Jewish people presented the Holy See's point of view on the problems which have to a large extent relevance to its humanitarian mission such as the refugee problem and the situation of the various communities which live in the Holy Land and those which are directly related to its more specifically religious mission regarding the Holy Places and the sacred and universal character of the city of Jerusalem.

The Prime Minister emphasized Israel's desire for peace and amply described the position of the possibilities in reaching a peaceful solution in the Middle Eastern conflict through negotiations between the parties and on the above mentioned subjects and also referred to the phenomenon of terrorism as well as to the special conditions concerning Jewish Communities in certain parts of the world.

His Holiness finally in expressing his warmest wishes that justice and law would establish peace and coexistence among all peoples of the Middle East, once again declared the intention of the Holy See to do all within its possibilities in order to reach these goals.

ABOUT THE EDITORS

Monsignor John M. Oesterreicher is Director of the Institute of Judaeo-Christian Studies and editor of its organ, *The Bridge*, a series of studies in various fields on the relationship between Christians and Jews. Among his many publications are *Racisme—Anti-semitisme—Antichristianisme* (1943) and *Under the Vault of One Covenant* (1972). As consultor to Cardinal Bea's Secretariat for Christian Unity, Msgr. Oesterreicher is one of the architects of the Conciliar Statement on the spiritual bond between Christians and Jews and the duties springing from this bond. A member of various learned societies, he is one of the Vice-Chairmen of the American Academic Association for Peace in the Middle East.

Anne Sinai is Director of the Publications Department of the American Academic Association for Peace in the Middle East, and editor of the association's quarterly journal, *Middle East Information Series*. She is also co-editor of *Israel and the Arabs: Prelude to the Jewish State* (1972).

ABOUT THE CONTRIBUTORS

Michael Avi-Yonah is Professor of Archaeology and Art History at the Hebrew University, Jerusalem. His many publications include *Oriental Elements in the Art of Palestine* (1948), *Views of the Biblical World*, Vol. V, and *The History of Classical Art* (1972).

Yehuda Z. Blum is Associate Professor of International Law at the Hebrew University, Jerusalem. His publications include, among others, *Historic Titles in International Law* (1965) and *Secure Boundaries and Middle East Peace* (1971).

The Rev. Joseph P. Brennan, S.T.L. (Greg.), S.S.L. (P.B.I.), is the Rector of Saint Bernard's Seminary in Rochester, N.Y. He is a regular contributor to *The Bridge*, a Collection of Judaeo-Christian Studies, and *The Bible Today*.

Mordechai S. Chertoff is the editor of *The New Left and the Jews* (1971) and the co-editor of *Israel: Social Structure and Change* (1973).

HIRSCH GOODMAN is the Parliamentary and Military Correspondent of the *Jerusalem Post.*

THE REV. GABRIEL GROSSMAN is a member of the Dominican House of St. Isaiah in Jerusalem.

MENASHE HAREL lectures on the Historical Geography of the Holy Land at the Hebrew University, Jerusalem, and at Tel Aviv University. His publications include *Route of the Exodus, Background of the Historical Geography of the Exodus from Egypt* (1968), *This is Jerusalem* (1969), and *Route of the Tours in the Judaean Desert* (1971).

TEDDY KOLLEK, the Mayor of Jerusalem, is also the author (with Moshe Pearlman) of *Jerusalem* (1968) and *Pilgrims to the Holy Land; The Story of Pilgrimages Through the Ages* (1970).

HAVA LAZARUS-YAFEH is the Head of the Department of Islamic Civilization at the Hebrew University, Jerusalem. She has published extensively on Islam and is the translator of many Arabic texts.

NATHANIEL LICHFIELD is Professor of Economics of Environmental Planning at University College, London, and Principal of Nathaniel Lichfield and Associates, Economic and Development Planning Consultants (London). He is currently working on an assignment as City Planning Officer of the City of Jerusalem.

ALFRED E. LIEBER is an Israeli economist and economic historian who served with Israel's Ministry of Commerce and Industry as Adviser on Shipping and Transport until 1972. He was seconded to the government of Burma as economic advisor, 1955-56. His book *The International Economy in the Early Middle Ages* is to be published in Holland.

BENJAMIN MAZAR is Professor of Ancient Jewish History and the Archaeology of Palestine at the Hebrew University, Jerusalem. He is the author of, among other publications, *History of the Archaeological Excavations in Palestine* (1936) and *Historical Atlas of Palestine, Biblical Period* (1942). He has also written extensively on Palestinian history, geography, and archaeology.

GABRIEL PADON is a Middle East specialist and an Israeli career diplomat. His monograph *Jerusalem and the Holy Places, 1917–1967* is to be published this year.

THE HON. TERENCE C.F. PRITTIE (M.B.E.) is a British journalist and author whose publications include *Israel, Miracle in the Desert* (1967), *Levi Eshkol* (1969), and *Willy Brandt* (1973). He is also the co-editor of *Britain and Israel, a Newsletter* (London).

NATHAN ROTENSTREICH is Professor of Philosophy at the Hebrew University, Jerusalem. Among his many publications are *Spirit and Man* (1963), *Humanism in The Contemporary Era* (1963), *Experience and Its Systematization—Studies in Kant* (1965), and *On The Human Subject* (1966).

ORI STENDEL is an Israeli specialist on Israel's Minorities, who served until recently as Deputy Adviser to the Prime Minister on Arab Affairs, and who is now in private law practice. His publications include *The Minorities in Israel, Trends in the Arab and Druze Communities, (1947–1973)* and *Villages in Israel and Judaea-Samaria, A Comparison in Social Development* (1968).

MARIE SYRKIN is Professor Emirita, Brandeis University, and the editor of the Herzl Press. Her numerous publications include *Golda Meir, Israel's Leader; Blessed is the Match; Nachman Syrkin, Socialist Zionist, A Biographical Memoir and Selected Essays;* and *Your School, Your Children: A Study of Public Education.* She is the editor of *A Land of Our Own* (1972), a selection of Golda Meir's speeches.

SHEMARYAHU TALMON is Professor and chairman of Bible Studies at the Hebrew University, Jerusalem, and also chairman of the Curriculum Committee of Bible Studies in Israel's schools. He is the editor of *Textus,* the Annual of the Hebrew University's Bible Projects, Vols. III-VI, also edited *Views of the Bible World* (1957, 1959), and has contributed to the *Encyclopedia Biblica* and the *Hebrew Bible Dictionary.*

ZE'EV VILNAY is an Israeli author, lecturer, and historian. Among his most recent publications are *Jerusalem—The Capital of Israel* (1962), *Sinai—Past and Present* (1969), and *Legends of Jerusalem* (1973).

GIDEON WEIGERT is an Israeli journalist and the author of, among others, *Life Under Israeli Occupation* (1971) and *Israel's Presence in East Jerusalem* (1973).

Index